Be Always Converting, Be Always Converted

OBOOKIAH,

a Native of Owhyhee.

BE ALWAYS CONVERTING, BE ALWAYS CONVERTED

An American Poetics

ROB WILSON

Harvard University Press

Cambridge, Massachusetts, and London, England   2009

Frontispiece: The engraving of Henry Obookiah by Asher Durand et al. is from 1818 copperplate in the collection of the Cornwall Historical Society, Cornwall, Connecticut, used in the 1818 and 1819 editions of *Memoirs of Henry Obookiah*.

Library of Congress Cataloging-in-Publication Data

Wilson, Rob, 1947–
    Be always converting, be always converted : an American poetics / Rob Wilson.
        p.   cm.
    Includes bibliographical references and index.
    ISBN 978-0-674-03343-6
    1. Conversion—Christianity—Biography.   2. Christian converts—Biography.
    3. United States—Religion.   I. Title.
    BV4930.W55 2009
    248.2'4—dc22   2008045345

To: *Rose Hawthorne Lathrop, who became Mother Mary Alphonsa (1851–1926); Sam Cooke (1931–1964), who went from gospel to soul and beyond; and Father Michael J. McGivney (1852–1890), who went from his birthplace on Railroad Hill in Waterbury and set out on the roads to Beatitude . . . "A Change Gonna Come"*

In like manner, we see literature best from the midst of wild nature, or from the din of affairs, or from a high religion.

—*Ralph Waldo Emerson, "Circles"*

Contents

Be Always Converting, Be Always Converted

Henry, Torn from the Stomach

As in dwelleth in the light. And we have raised up a
young Hawaiian unto the light, in Torringford by the
bleak. Drafted him weeping into Yale College,
orphaned from his warring blood. And we have raised
up a nation of color into the same light.

Of contracts, from the President (my uncle, the poet) on
down to the darkest slaves of his kin (his mother, the
warrior). My name is Edwin Dwight, as in chosen to
the light.

My name is Edwin Dwight, as in white.

His name is Henry Obookiah, as in torn from the king's
stomach into lava.

Henry came and he saw dog-eyed on the stoops of New
Haven. Orphaned, he came into language with the
sweetness of a nativity heart, washing into tenderness
of waves, *praying without ceasing* as he sang in the
Torringford snows.

A heart so big the snows melted into light.

All the ships of history had cooperated to bring him to
that stoop. The little English he knew was the hook
into eternity. To hang Honolulu into New Haven and
hand down the family of the saved.

Henry was the sweetest child of the light, sweeter than
the mango stolen from a tea closet. The bifurcations
were not mine to contest. And we conquered his people into the light, within a matter of twenty years.

You who stand on the other side of history. You who
stand outside the covenant in your lost country your
unhavened country. But we took Henry in and we
buried him into the light of the Dwight family.

—Rob Wilson, from *Automat: Unsettling Anglo-Global
American Poetics along Asia/Pacific Lines of Flight*

Introduction: Conversions against Empire

"And afterward we were born again, and many times . . ."

Inā e maka ke kanaka, e ola hou anei 'o ia?
'O nā lā a pau o ku'u au,
E kali no au no ka loli 'ana a'e.

[If a man die shall he live again? / All the days of my appointed
time will I wait, / Till my change come.]

> —Queen Lili'uokalani, "A Chant" (hymn from
> *The Plymouth Collection,* Honolulu, 1884)

As I was walking around today I noticed many tall steeples
and big churches and stained glass windows. Let me tell you
once again: God's not necessarily found in there. You can't get
converted in no steeple or stained glass window. Well, Jesus is
mighty to save, if He's in your heart, He'll convert you.

> —Bob Dylan, onstage rap, Buffalo, New York concert, 1983

"Religion," 2006 Nobel-prize winner in literature Orhan Pamuk once
told the Associated Press, "was considered to be something for the poor
and the provincial," an *archaic force* that could only impede or shatter
the relentless march to secular modernity and prosperity that his native
country of Turkey, with its long-standing Ottoman Empire ties, ethnic
fragmentation, religious divides, and East/West antagonisms as well as
its "borderland" civilizational crossings, had labored long to overcome.[1]
Yet, Arif Dirlik, my scholarly comrade in transnational cultural studies,
has long reminded me by his life and work in Chinese Marxism and postcolonial studies that Turkey was not only a nodal point on the Silk Road
to the empire of China but was also a homeland for Saint Paul. Turkey
was thus linked to the "road to Damascus" that has long served as global
prototype for the proselytizing morphology of rebirth, a form that (to
echo Wallace Stevens conjuring the Bible-drenched wilderness in Ten-
nessee) "took dominion everywhere." In these United States of America,

such a claim for the "archaic irrelevance" of religious conviction could never be made about its population, high and low, global or local, folk or archaic, pop-culturalist or elite. Truckers, farmers, black nationalists, tattoo artists, boxers, confessional poets, baseball stars, supreme court justices, presidents, dharma bums, and economic hit men are all too driven by the tropes and dreams, energies, stories, codes, and sedimented figurations of the American religious imagination. Writers as diverse as Flannery O'Connor, Jack Kerouac, Blind Willie McTell, Mary McCarthy, Albert Saijo, Dana Naone Hall, Brother Antoninus, and James Baldwin have long acknowledged this allure of raw religiosity from Greenwich Village to San Francisco, Azusa Street, and the Big Island of Hawai'i to the back roads of the Delta and the deep South.[2]

Conversion is not so much in the air or (more strictly speaking) confined inside the churches, synagogues, temples, ashrams, and mosques as it is circulating in the cradles and graves of this contemporary America. Everywhere we look, we witness its ratification from songs on country or blues radio stations to tactics of twelve-step recovery programs via self-surrender to "God as we understood him," in yoga quests and faith-based diets, to over-amped seekers for epiphanies, such as Madonna (who has gone from small-town Michigan Catholic to cross-stomping "material-girl" paganhood to Kabbalah quester in a matter of decades). Conversion becomes materialized around the white church steeple and the town green in far-flung towns like Kona, Hawai'i (Henry 'Ōpūkaha'ia's birthplace), or is given more freewheeling shapes in the religious pluralism of that left-coast "visionary state," California, where as Eric Davis phrases it, "conversion [feels] too much like consumerism."[3]

In recent decades across the corridors of the White House, the "born again" experience of Southern Baptist evangelical persuasion has pulled American presidents in opposing directions. It has motivated the left-leaning populism and liberal internationalism of Jimmy Carter, as it has fueled the fundamentalist binaries, ideological fixities, and unilateral globalism of George W. Bush.[4] A profane U.S. popular culture example of this pull of polarities is illustrated in the final HBO television episode of *The Sopranos*. Fastidious "wise guy" Paulie (Tony Sirico) confesses to his boss Tony Soprano (James Gandolfini) he once had a vision of the Blessed Mother at the strip club they work out of, giving him second thoughts about his life of racketeering and violence. "One time, at the Bing . . . I saw the Virgin Mary," said Paulie. Mocking this "profane illumination" amid the lucre, sin, and slime of New Jersey streets, Tony taunts back, "Why didn't you say anything? Fuckin strippers, we coulda had a shrine, sold holy water in gallon jugs [. . .] coulda made millions."

The next scene shifts to a medium shot of a stray cat gazing up from the sidewalk, as if admiring Paulie's newfound aura of spirituality (a stray animal being perhaps the only plausible witness of such a lapsed-Catholic conversion into tenderness, life change, and possibly death).

The American colonies, initially founded on a transatlantic quest to secure freedom of religious worship, evolved with revolutionary fervor during the latter Republican era and the American Renaissance into a far-flung and ever-pluralizing polity as "one nation under God." The consequent Protestant proliferation of faith states, belief systems, extreme forms of inward commitment, and more radicalized modes of elective affinity provided the conversion experience an abiding power to prop up myriad "great awakenings" and inform spirit-drenched subjects speaking in tongues of prophecy, castigation, beatitude-quest, therapeutic transformation, social aversion, or outright redemption. This long-standing valorization of what Ralph Waldo Emerson called spiritual "influx" created an ethos of possibility, over-belief, and life-risk in which "conversion" and/or "counter-conversion" (as shall be elaborated here, echoing at its core the *theo-poetics* of Emerson and the pragmatic semiotics of conversion as posited by William James in *Varieties of Religious Experience*) saturated the territory of American consciousness and democratic subject-formation. The burden of this study comprises my attempt to unpack and retrace the trajectory of conversion as a form of self-making and pluralized commitment to modes, mores, and vocations to beatitude. This trajectory of souls on the road to beatitude, as Jack Kerouac might put it, crosses and loops over oceans, rivers, and continents, from the first Native Hawaiian convert to New England congregationalism, to the born-again Pentecostalism of major poet-songwriter Bob Dylan. Buckminster Fuller articulated this semiotic dynamism as a leap that converts blockage into renewal and repetition into newness: "I seem to be a verb," he boasted by embodying this will to build and transform world anew.[5]

This books aims to show through its intensive focus on an eclectic (yet carefully chosen) range of postcolonial converts, from Henry 'Ōpūkaha'ia (the first Native Hawaiian convert), to Bob Dylan (Jeremiac troper of the American polity), the Tongan novelist Epeli Hau'ofa's counterformation into a transracial ecumene he calls "Oceania," and Ai (Afro-American-Japanese poet and maker of frontier violence and racial masks), that the "born-again experience" can open up a language of possibility, metamorphosis, transregional migration, cultural unsettling, and geopolitical becoming that is much more unstable, open-ended, and world-shattering—as an event of social transformation and self-reinscription—than any doctrinaire account of religious conviction, semiotic certainty, colonized subjection, or ideological fixity would suggest. Such a conversion experience may undeniably reflect and refract the by-now-global Protestant and American-pragmatic orientation, opening the self toward forces of newness, change, risk, and the life-altering powers of *poesis*. However, it will be urged here that this conversion experience is not so much about "salvation" or finality of belief as such as it is about "experimentation," life change, and a "crossing over" on the road toward an enhanced life worthy of obligation.[6] Conversion of the sort that experimenting subjects such as Sara Miles experienced are never to be taken lightly, for example. Even arriving late (in her case at forty-six as a secular intellectual) or in routine circumstances (such as in a communion service at St. Gregory's Episcopal Church in San Francisco), the experience can produce a permanent and socially transformative effect and life change: Miles introduced food distribution services mitigating the welfare-dismantling policies of her time.[7]

Conversions in a Land of "Influx"

Conversion along these experimental lines of subjective plurality will stand here, in *Be Always Converting, Be Always Converted* for this radically enabling process of self-making and the transformative reaches of *poesis* (active meaning-making, recreating, reimagining of self and life-world through a poetics of belief) in these U.S. American transnational contexts that go on spreading across the millennium, eras, genres, and oceans. For this *charismatic moment of influx* that is the conversion experience still signifies a life-altering moment of "before/after" and enacts the revolutionary possibility that the everyday self of drifting confusion, ideological bewilderment, or suspended commitment can be made anew, suddenly or by long-forged conviction, and urges that the very world of secular materiality and everyday thrownness of the self can be changed, *at once and for the better*. "The purpose is to convert," as Jack Kerouac wrote of his writings during the long composition period from *On the Road* to *Dharma Bums*, as he worked on a life of Buddha called *Wake Up* and thought of calling his Beat road novel *Souls on the Road*, a mandate to rebirth in keeping with the myriad forms of "beatitude" proposed herein.[8]

In quest for radical transformation and inner attachment to what Charles Taylor calls that "place of fullness" that can orient us toward experiencing "the presence of God, or the voice of nature, or the force that flows through everything," contemporary Americans commonly switch faiths at least once in their lives.[9] Taylor's *A Secular Age* backs up the against-the-grain conviction that religiosity and spiritual hunger for "new and unprecedented itineraries" of conversion pervade secular modernity, particularly so in the American novum of pluralized freedom and its openness to mobility and change across the "thickets and trackless wastes" we live in.[10] As Luis Lugo, director of the Pew Forum on Religion and Public Life, summarized a survey of these increasingly pluralized belief patterns and sense of denominational "churning," Americans "not only change jobs, change where they live, and change spouses, but they change religions too."[11] Breaking from or through the immanent order of scientific secularism, "so many influential converts in the last two centuries have been writers and artists," as Taylor notes, often charged with finding a new language or extreme style to express this quest for something beyond "the self-contained system of everyday explanation."[12] Conversion, as William James recognized on the threshold of American modernity, is becoming less the exception than some kind of experiential, subject-forming norm rife with pragmatic variety and expressive possibility.

For radically inclined modernists like W. E. B. Du Bois, conversion came to mean a turn away from subjective faith-leaps of American pragmatism or the "Black Christ" of forbearance toward stronger forms of international commitment and global activism emergent across Russia, Asia, and Africa. Others more aesthetically driven, like Gerard Manley Hopkins, had forged an altered language of "inscape" to break with the sordid ugliness of the urban industrial order that was taking global dominion in England.[13] For Emerson, articulating the dynamics of self-trust and the creative kinetics of "newness" in such trauma-haunted essays as "Circles" and "Experience," America had emerged as a land of perpetual Pentecost and tropological efficacy, in effect made into a resource of empowerment, self-renewing singularity, capitalist disruption, and relentless change. "I am ready to die out of nature," Emerson wrote, affirming himself as a John the Baptist of sublime possibility opened up to American conversion, "and be born again into this new yet unapproachable America I have found in the West."[14] Each essay started from or returned toward this core affirmation of self-empowerment and rebirth. Yet this conviction of reclaimed beatitude, becoming the voice for the Holy Spirit inflooding the self, was subject to radical discontinuity and counter-conversion into fits of faith-lack, opacity, and emptiness: "Strange this succession of humors that pass through this human spirit. Sometimes I am the organ of the Holy Ghost and sometimes of a vixen petulance."[15]

Yet *to be born, and born again many times,* became Emerson's aim—transitioning from blockage into semiotic empowerment—in essays, from "Circles" to "Fate" to "Power," as shall be touched on here and in the conversion-semiotics of Chapter 3. By no means strictly Christologi-cal in his rebirth patterns, from the "Divinity School Address" onward Emerson nourished this notion of American literary emergence as a complex relay of energies drawn from world literature and world religion, conversionary forces of "vast-flowing vigor" drawn from Hafiz and Zoroaster to Mencius and Buddha. He did so even as his ephoebe Thoreau felt the "pure waters" of Walden Pond were linked not just to ice-exchanges with India but to regenerative patterns tied to what Wai Chee Dimock calls "deep time" in the Bhagavad Gita and to an array of world epics and "Bibles of the world" that figures like Bronson Alcott kept miming as life-influence.[16]

This conversion assumed a baptism not of water nor of flesh, not of Bib-lical absorption nor of churchly reckoning per se, but one of spiritual in-flux (being "born again" can also mean, as Terry Eagleton notes of the Greek verb *anothen* in John 3:3, being "born from above" by the spirit)[17] come from experiencing, on original terms, that "unbounded substance" we cannot rightly find a name, place, sanction, or limit for: "Fortune, Min-erva, Muse, Holy Ghost—these are quaint names, too narrow to cover this unbounded substance."[18] Situated beyond the trauma of history or limits of culture or regionality, a small New England town like Concord could become a world-space of transregional linkage this baptism-by-nature opened up to the self-quest for sublimity in any "puny democratic ego" (as Alexis de Tocqueville mocked them) adequate to the task of this vocation to immensity.[19] Even when God-drenched with radiant sublimity, this American-vernacular voice of the Holy Spirit was apt not to speak the po-lite Latin of the "Veni Creator Spiritus" vespers hymn Pope John Paul II recommended as Muse in his "Letter to Artists" of 1999, but more likely to sound like the literalized voice of this Mississippi Pentecostal speaking across a sawdust assembly in 1909, "Pentecost! Pentecost! Last message! Get under the blood! No time to lose!"[20] In the epigraph to this intro-duction, Dylan activates an unchurched force of Holy Ghost-becoming, expressed in a voice of "pentecostal absolutizing" his poetry very often ironized, rasped, or overcame in lesser modes of Beat humility.[21]

"Behold all things are become new, a new heaven and a new earth is here in the Americas" is a mandate of redemptive possibility that gets now and again registered, as lyric-prophetic outcry, by a myriad range of sub-jects at the Pauline extreme of Judeo-Christian monotheistic utterance. This study is by no means limited to this core mode; indeed, Polynesian "counter-conversions" (as shall be discussed later in Hawai'i- and Pacific-based chapters) would nowadays run quite the other way toward a re-sacralization of a polytheistic earth and ocean as in Epeli Hau'ofa, Joseph

Puna Balaz, Dana Naone Hall, Haunani Kay Trask, Albert Wendt, Patricia Grace, and other postcolonial Pacific writers and cultural activists.[22] Still, at the core of this study abides the radically charismatic claim for "rebirth" as emplotted in the life of Saul-becoming-Saint Paul in Damascus or in the on-the-road life of Robert Zimmerman becoming retroped and masked as "Bob Dylan" in the coffee houses of Minneapolis and Greenwich Village. Dylan later troped his poetic persona into Jesus's chosen poetic son of sorts on such albums as *Saved* and (to throw some caustic oil into the fundamentalist waters of forgiveness, "so the wrong ones can't find it") *Infidels, Empire Burlesque,* and that most Jeremaic of albums wherein covenant nation and erotic muse are entangled into a Precious Angel of global transformation *Slow Train Coming.*[23] Dylan's "trickster-like" honoring of Yeshua over Yahweh, affirming son-masks and modes of grace-influx over father mores following the law, abides in the vernacular American traditions of theo-poetics and fits the revolutionary-becoming of the 1960s that Dylan *never fully abandons.*[24] With its emphasis on mercy, justice, feeding the poor, resisting Empire, and welcoming the downfallen and socially abandoned, as Eagleton notes, "the kingdom of heaven turns out to be a surprisingly material affair."[25]

Metanoia: Turns and Returns

Conversion, in the more Catholic sense elaborated through two centuries of catechesis, remains close to the Greek verb *metanoia,* meaning a grace-drenched change of mind and thought turning the subject away from wrong living and sinfulness toward a pursuit of godliness and the vocation to beatitude that William James (stressing the consequences of lived belief) called, in various modern contexts, "saintliness." Conversion is most commonly translated into English as the verb "repent," as in the mandate from John the Baptist (Mark 1:15), "The time is fulfilled, and the kingdom of God is at hand: repent ye, and believe the gospel." Such a conversion "turn" implies a three-stage pattern of turning around, from sinfulness (conversion), as a conviction of wrongdoing and wrong living (repentance), toward regenerating acts of sacrifice and transformation (penance). Suggesting the immersion of "conversion" as such in the language process of speaking, inscripting, and rewriting the self, *metanoia* also entails the rhetorical process of recalling a statement, or of strengthening or weakening a prior declaration via self-correction. It has become a technical term of rhetoric, similar to what is called in Latin *correctio.*

Conversion-as-metanoia rewrites the self into a new set of terms that go beyond conformity, anxiety, smallness, boredom, and limitation as

Robert Barron finely shows.[26] Susan Harding elaborates this rhetoric of faith as a *three-stage* "born-again" experience of evangelical turning, along Pauline lines, whereby "the inner speech of convicted sinners is transformed as they are alienated from their previous voices (the old self, natural man); cast into a limbo (lost, in need of, searching), that is to say somehow in a liminal state, a state of confusion and speechlessness; and begin to hear a new voice (an inaudible voice, the Holy Spirit)."[27] There is a change of mind and, no less so, a shift of *language* due to the transformation of repentance to "go beyond" *(meta)* the worldly "mind" *(nous)* of everyday lostness. Conversion, in this sense, *turns over* prior narratives of self and world and gives the subject a changed set of convictions, an altered direction, and another language of active choice, empowerment, and becoming. The process resonates with the diction and syntax of "newness." We commonly need, even daily, such a conviction of world over-turning that goes beyond the attitude and life stance we now have.

Conversion centers on an unstable process of recoding the self with a new meaning and narrative shape. Indeed, the question of belief and semiotic conviction that the conversion experience raises—with the implication of some kind of a habitual change in life-practices and cultural codes—still cuts to the heart of literary experience even in our days of postcolonial flux and global-capitalist liquefaction of all things sacred and profane. Conversion represents a *turning* of any selfhood into emplotted sign and whole narrative: a metaphor becoming metamorphosis even in these secular times of seeming biblical abandon. Converting to conversion, called to convert, this born-again process of re-symbolization can, by a process of mimetic contagion, convert other lives into similar signs and stories of "new world" becoming. As Michael Ragussis summarizes the ideology of conversion dispersed in genres from modern British fiction to sermons of evangelical discourse across the Enlightenment, "the conversion of the Other (heathen, infidel, or Jew) is the surest sign of the conversion of the self, so that the true convert proves himself by becoming a proselytizer."[28]

Metamorphose Yourselves!

Conversion, as radically American *influx,* speaks as this activating power of anti-imperial newness. For conversion—even in our own bleak times of post-9/11 global postmodernity and stasis—time and again centers the terms and trajectory of its subject-formation around what Paul Gilroy has called (troping upon life-transformations of Jimi Hendrix from a paratrooper formed in the Pacific Rim city of Seattle via his reconfiguration into "apostle of love" in San Francisco, Greenwich Village, and London) an "axis" of libidinal possibility. "Toward that end, we should always remember that Hendrix was a soldier and think of him as an ex-paratrooper who became a hippie in an act of profound and complete treason that would make him an enemy of power to this day," as Gilroy urges of this vocation to intervene via rock poetry into state polity, as when Hendrix deformed the Star Spangled banner anthem at Woodstock in 1969 into sonic emendation.[29] Such a conversion (and there were many at that time in California) enacts a crucial *turn* from blockage and social entrapment ("fate") into empowerment, influx, creativity, and spirit-knowing and embodies that crisscrossing process of metamorphosis and alter-becoming that can impart an altered language for the self.

In this move toward expressing creatural conversion via new selfhood, Jimi Hendrix was, and still is, ahead of our own left-leaning melancholia and grimace, adding cosmic spatiality and redemptive torquing to Dylan's quasi-medievalist warning song, castigating the market-idolizing nation and its will to global plunder, as if we live in some kind of neo-Roman Empire in which the spirit is lost cause. In the song Hendrix carried to cosmic levels via his electric-guitar spatialization of temporal terror and pause, Dylan warned in "All Along the Watchtower," from the album *John Wesley Hardin* (1968): "Businessmen, they drink my wine, plowmen dig my earth / None of them along the line, know what any of it is worth."[30] *That*, to say the least, remains our global plight in this covenanted nation that will not listen to any contemporary Jeremiah, from Billy Graham, Pope-and-president-blasting Sinead O'Connor ("you've got people like George Bush bringing Christianity into disrepute"), or Dave Chappell to Dylan (more on this latter-day figure of poetic prophesy throughout this book) or a history-haunted poet of redemptive violence like Ai.[31]

Given the deadening affect of our own cultural-politics (a "left-leaning melancholia" not even the Irish lyricism of a Van Morrison could exorcize) coming to reign after what Hendrix embodied as "apostle of love" and cross-racial confederation in 1968 singing against the U.S. security-state apparatus, global warfare, and the stalemated identity-politics of terror, stealth, and racial abjection, we need another mode of doing things, *making things happen,* to act beyond the stasis of cynical reason or the relentless hermeneutics of suspicion.[32] Kindred in spirit to the tactics of this study, Paul Gilroy's approach to undoing *Postcolonial Melancholia* urges the world toward a different, joyously creative, and activist-driven "worlding" of space, self, life-world, planet, and time from given subject formations of neo-liberal globalization. Gilroy's post-ethnic manifesto of sorts is based around the Wellek Library Lectures in Critical Theory at the

University of California at Irvine, May 2002, a site where many of these identity-codes are fabricated and disseminated, if not reified, within a matter of months, not to mention decades of professional circulation in the shadow of theoretical giants like Jacques Derrida, J. Hillis Miller, Julia Kristeva, Homi Bhabha, and a cast of thousands.[33]

The power of "rebirth" can and often does get translated into a U.S. Empire–subverting power of "metamorphosis" and forces that are unsettling, countervailing, or dangerous to state convictions and conformist pieties. Troping upon love's new-made body as a political force for renewal in contexts of global politics and what he termed "Dionysian Christianity" in *Love's Body,* Norman O. Brown gets to the root of these transgressive meanings to "rebirth" and the conversion experience as a call to social-becoming, in his radical retranslation of Greek text into a decolonizing American English (from Romans 12:2), which he affixes as epigraph to the mandates of his last book, *Apocalypse and/or Metamorphosis:* "And be not conformed to this world [*be nonconformists*]; but be ye transformed [*metamorphose yourselves*] by the renewing of your mind." Such a call to life-change sounds closer to the Walden Pond "rebirth" vocation of Henry David Thoreau than to any fundamentalist conformation as in, say, Jerry Falwell, whose conviction of "speaking [as] believing" could lead to dogmatic denunciations as when he blamed feminists, queers, and agnostic leftists for the fall of the Twin Towers.[34] A 1960s-haunted will to self-transformation and social change leads Brown to invoke Emersonian mandates of poetic vision and tropological excess he affirmed as the will to express *conversion-as-life-becoming,* "We cannot live without imagination; adorning and exaggerating life; lavishing of itself in change."[35] Rebirth, being "born again" or "born from above" as variously experienced, came to be seen as a performative act of troping and projecting forward more than a propositional reckoning.

The times were rife with possibility, the landscape charged with immanent immensity, as a poetry-troping boxer who could "punch like a butterfly and sting like a bee" named Cassius Marcellus Clay Jr. could remake himself in 1964, through counter-conversion, into Black Muslim faith and redemptive power (still living on yet) and antiwar activist named Muhammad Ali. Ali, a man of God in a time of high-capitalist secularism, has proved a model and inspiration to many, from Dylan and Little Stevie Wonder to home-run king Barry Bonds.[36] Deeply committed to the Qur'an, Ali later converted from the Nation of Islam to the more mainstream form of Sunni Islam in 1975, as explained in his autobiography, *The Soul of a Butterfly: Reflections on Life's Journey* (2004). Speaking of such strange, earth-shattering conversions, we might all the more so invoke the Malcolm X turn (at least twice) from street pimpdom to more modal forms of Islamic conviction, Black Muslim counternationhood, and global redemption in *The Autobiography of Malcolm X,* which recalls the remaking of James Little into X and then into prophetic castigation. Admitting that "bending my knees to pray—that *act*—well, that took me a week," the new-made minister (under the tutelage of Elijah Muhammad) writes of his new name, "The Muslim's 'X' symbolized the true African family name that he never could know." "For me," Malcolm X continues in the book he wrote with Alex Haley, "my 'X' replaced the white slave-master name of 'Little' which some blue-eyed devil named Little had imposed upon my paternal forebears."

This semiotic reinscription into Muslim selfhood had radical consequences: "The receipt of my 'X' meant that forever after in the nation of Islam, I would be known as Malcolm X." He goes on to speak his black version of an American jeremiad, this time directed back against its Puritan myth-makers like John Winthrop or Cotton Mather: "We [American blacks] didn't land on Plymouth Rock, my brothers and sisters—Plymouth Rock landed on *us!*"[37] Later, in the Holy City of Mecca or while praying on Mount Arafat, Malcolm X would embrace nation-obliterating modes of religious belonging by which "blue-eyed blondes to black-skinned Africans" felt a spirit of transracial unity, as if "the 'white' attitude was removed from their minds by the religion of Islam."[38] In later contexts of urban multiculturalism, while pondering his struggle to express black identity in sites of conflicted racial plurality, such as Honolulu and Jakarta, the change-driven Barack Obama writes that "Malcolm X's autobiography seemed to offer something different" in its "repeated acts of self-creation" promising "a new and uncompromising order, martial in its discipline, forged through sheer force of will," which Obama admired as a "blunt poetry" of hopefulness calling out for change.[39]

Nowadays, the choice of a Muslim dietary regime or modes of New Age fasting can still imply the break—reflecting the intimate and committed choices of this "born-again" conversion—with more worldly idioms and taken-for-granted cultural mores that are wearing down and dividing the self into littleness, ill health, depression, and demoralization.[40] The divided subject, through some influx of vision-faith, can become freed up to the meaning-making powers of newness and "self-creation," a largeness of vision, altered regimes of selfhood, no longer just subjected (as such an over-determined subject) to the letter of the law, compulsions of desire, polity, class, or the reign of Empire, all of which the transcendentalizing Emerson cast under the spell of social powerlessness he mocked as *mere* "Fate." "We rightly say of ourselves," affirms Emerson in radically

Protestant terms of self-empowerment and American life-becoming, "we were born, and *afterward we were born again, and many times*" [emphasis mine].[41] As the life of Malcolm X or Bob Dylan shows, the born-again mimetic of conversion would itself be born again, in multiplying contact scenes of global or New World encounter with varieties of spiritual "influx," into a form of counter-conversion and imperial dissent. Accounts of American religiosity as fundamentalist conviction and a reflection of the global drive to Empire (as materialized world-containment), demoralized by the right-leaning religiosity of George W. Bush, or Charles Colson in post-Watergate narratives of repentance like *Born Again* (1976), or sheer "boomeritis," say, tell far from the whole story of this "born-again" becoming as process of self-inscription and committed inwardness. The struggle over the meanings and forms of conversion is far from over.[42] John Lennon, torn between occult beliefs, a non-proselytizing Buddhism, and more surprisingly the born-again Christianity of televangelists like Oral Roberts he was drawn to across the 1970s, settled upon a mask of postmodern irony he was comfortable with—identifying himself in the end as a "born again pagan"—and he wrote "Serve Yourself" as a rejoinder to Christological mandates in Dylan's "Gotta Serve Somebody."[43]

If critical theory at the university level seems trapped in post-deconstructive wariness and perspectival struggles between worldliness and unbelief in anything immaterial, trans-secular, or (worse yet) sacred, magical, or occult, as Eric Lott has discussed as so many modes of radical "disappearance," we might all the better turn (beyond Emerson, Bush, or Colson) to invoke the dialectics of radicalized faith as outlined in Alain Badiou in *Saint Paul: The Foundation of a Universalism*. Badiou shows that the subject-formation of the *conversion-as-event* is one in which "every subject is initiated on the basis of a charisma [grace over law]": a Saint Paul for whom charismatic subjects of de-reified newness can affirm redemptive "events" materialized outside the law of Hebraic particularity, Greek logos, or the rules and norms of Roman empire.[44] Badiou invokes this power of "conversion" in his hegemony-shattering figuration of Saint Paul speaking Christ-language against the norms of Roman Empire, which he theorizes as well, post-9/11, to shatter the banality of American neo-liberalism.

In some respects, the mimetic contagion of Paul's example of a subject-inaugurating conversion from Jew to Christ-drenched militant on the road to Damascus led Martin Luther, in pondering the world-shattering dynamics of justification-through-grace as outlined in the Epistle to Romans, to experience his born-again plot of before/after. Here, deadness of letters becomes newness of spirit and creative power with huge consequences in the Reformation. As John W. O'Malley outlines the imperative traditions of "Prophecy and Reform" that a Jeremaic poet like Dylan would work in, he shows how Martin Luther had experienced through the Pauline Gospels "a dramatically reorienting insight, a eureka-experience, a conversion that led to a sharp and irreversible break with his past," so that the German Protestant reformer could proclaim (in his own extreme terms of sacred exaltation and worldly denunciation), "Here I felt altogether born again and had entered paradise itself through open gates."[45]

Why Conversion?

Why would anyone in these secular times of Biblical abandon and marke-tized reason want to invoke "conversion" or even "counter-conversion" in and across the waters, landscapes, and languages of redemption from New England and Hawai'i, Tonga, Arizona, and the American Pacific? Why, in this attempt to challenge the cultural-political modes of the contemporary and/or modern U.S. Empire, would one want to call conversion a "post-colonial tactic" of the utmost urgency and worldly importance? Why talk about God-quests at the shopping mall, 24/7 online, or while musing over the Chez Panisse California cuisine at the oh-so-Berkeley dinner table? Why try to wrest this conversion apparatus or "morphology of rebirth" from the right-wing hegemony where (some would say in the United States) it more properly belongs? Admittedly, unless one is working for the fundamentalist U.S. right for whom "God" is without guilt, shame, or doubt most commonly spelled "G-O-P," this would not be considered a useful subject to reflect upon or, worse yet, advocate.

Given our times of hybridity, liquefying neoliberalism, and postmodern lightness being explained to children and idiots everywhere from the inter-net to the shopping mall, this move across borders in cultural criticism "goes against cultural policy," as Dylan put it on the liner notes to *World Gone Wrong,* and bumps up against the reigning discourse of postcolonial fixity (filled with menace, dread, and shame) wherein the possibility of change, willed choice, joy, or good news seems frozen in stalemate, as if "conversion" for the American self as such belonged only to the Bush 2 war-regime. That is to say that conversion belongs to those war forces of neo-Roman Empire that Allen Ginsberg had memorably castigated in *Howl* as the false God of "Moloch," as he invoked a "spectral nation," and what Griel Marcus evokes as an "invisible republic" of the spirit from Amos and William Lloyd Garrison to Philip Roth and Bob Dylan et al.

In this study, I stand aligned to this American geopolitical becoming of democratic possibility, mongrel community, and multilingual newness whose shape and time is yet to come.[46] For me, following in the wake of Josephine Miles, Henry Nash Smith, Richard Poirier, Masao Miyoshi, Jack Kerouac, and Harold Bloom, the tropes of Yahweh and Yeshua hover over our "American sublime" poetics, making it by many twists and turns what I would call a *theo-poetics* from Anne Bradstreet and William Cullen Bryant to Emily Dickinson, Bob Kaufman, and Allen Ginsberg down to Fanny Howe, Gary Snyder, Teresia Teiawa, Faye Kicknosway, and worse.[47] Not to be undone or humiliated by a literary canon with the Emerson-Whitman nexus of redemptive possibility at its core, Dylan has often mocked (as does Bloom) the more neoliberal/postcolonial "cultural politics" of PC conformity, perpetual in-betweenness, therapeutic comforts, New Age polytheism, and faux-transformation, as, for example, on an album of Old School reruns conjured up from white gospel and black blues called *World Gone Wrong*. And we need to recall the subjective mandate keenly formulated by Max Weber as the core ethos of post-Puritan American conversion, that "the Calvinist, as it is sometimes put, himself creates his own salvation, or, as would be more correct, the conviction of it."[48] And "though the man cannot return in his mother's womb and be born with new amounts of vivacity," as Emerson warns his doubtful Nicodemus of a reader in "Power," he can follow the path of self-trust into election and enhanced life-force: "You must elect your work; you shall take what your brain can and drop all the rest. Only so, can that amount of vital force [or Holy Spirit] accumulate which can make the step from knowing to doing."[49]

Conversions against Empire

In this post-9/11 America taking global dominion from France to the Pacific Rim, as portrayed in the satirical novel *Empire 2.0: A Modest Proposal for a United States of the West by Xavier de C****, ex-radical Régis Debray narrates how what he calls an *"agenda Dei"* of conversion-to-Empire has infiltrated the neoliberal politics of the United States of America, absorbing "ex-superpower Europe" and Rim-booming Asia into its expanding global hegemony, even as (he worries), "In places like Dallas, the Bible seems to be the only book of wisdom in circulation."[50] Raising grim parallels to the Roman Empire and Greek domination to challenge this doctrinaire agenda of globalization-as-Americanization, Debray cautions (through the wry voice of the ex-French subject Xavier de C***, defending this new world order), "Cosmopolis America must be reinvented" (23). Still, this émigré-convert now and again urges submission to this new *United States of the West*, "with a capital that can be moved [from Washington] to Honolulu or to Athens, or Ankara for that matter" (55). If this politics seems tied to a failure of imagination to go beyond Empire or to invent a cosmopolis wherein difference can be respected and dissent allowed, we need to open up the mimetic faculty of conversion and alterity to forces other than this plot of "conversion to empire" and its postcolonial multitudes presumes.

Empire, for Debray, merely expands the scope and contact zones of the U.S. conversion project to install its "agenda Dei" as global redeemer.[51] But we do still live, as Juliana Spahr shows in the catastrophic post-9/11 eco-poetics of her long poem *this connection of everyone with lungs*, inside a "deep unsortable history" that entangles local-indigenous Pacific sites (like her beloved Hawai'i) into the long durations of U.S. national and global power, transnational commerce, altered worlds of ecology, techno-simulation, and war: "How can we be true to one another with histories of place so deep, / so layered we can't begin to sort through it here in the middle of / the Pacific with its own deep unsortable history."[52] A focus on the poetics and politics of conversion in all its situated complexity can help us to hear such emergences and language differences as the terms and tropes of counterformation and social struggle being articulated from the Pacific to New England, Latin America, Asia, or the New Europe.

Still, looking back into the periodic waves of the Great Awakening animating this U.S. geo-culture with various forces and forms of conversion from the Western Massachusetts forests of grace in Jonathan Edwards to the Cane Ridge Revival of 1801 down to the Azusa Street healing rains, speaking in tongues, and across the conversion-laden islands of Hawai'i and Tonga, it can be hard to tell a "Mississippi operator" from a "Great Healer," belief-states from confidence-games of prophecy or imperial burlesque, to this day still, as Melville warned in that blasted allegory of American religiosity, *Confidence Man*.[53] As if the doomed ship Pequod were not warning enough against securing a manifest destiny in the Pacific, Melville stocked his midwestern ship *Fidèle* with confidence men, water healers, Jeremy diddlers, prowling Jesuits, Indian-haters, minstrels, money counterfeiters, charity-bilkers, land frauds, and worse.[54]

No less subject to truth-masks, self-myths, and the will to tropological mimicry, as I shall later elaborate, Bob Dylan's born-again experience cannot just be tied to one Christological event (though there was this in 1978), for example, as the process of poetic and spiritual renewal he traces in the "Oh Mercy" chapter of his autobiography, *Chronicles*, gets multiplied across the post-*Saved* 1980s to hearing an old jazz crooner tap into spirit-voice in San Francisco, relearning a triadic guitar pattern of melodic innovation from Lonnie Johnson, crossing a performative abyss one devil-ridden night in Locarno, Switzerland, when techniques failed him, or, most of all (as if predicting his turn to becoming a DJ on XM radio in 2006), hearing a disk jockey named Brown Sugar fill the Delta night-air with half-forgotten rhythm and blues on WWOZ in New Orleans.[55] "In a weird sense, I felt like I was starting over," Dylan noted, summarizing these turns of metamorphosis to overcome "some godforsaken hole" of blockage and emptiness and to renew the recurring poetic-religious sense that he "[was] beginning to live [his] life again."[56]

Beatitude Quests

Conversion to beatitude abides at the core of the all-but-forgotten Californian poet William Everson, from Sacramento and Fresno, who undergoes a full-frontal conversion at a Roman Catholic mass and becomes "Brother Antoninus" of the Dominican orders called to social service in Oakland; and then, not all that much later (amid the crazed sexual political energies of the 1960s in post-Beat San Francisco and coastal Santa Cruz he recounts in the final, hippie-influenced chapters of *Archetype West* and in myriad poems of sacramental eroticism via the anima), undergoes a trope-drenched process of "counter-converting" (a framework of psycho-social subjectivity I will invoke via the theo-poetic plurality of William James in *The Varieties of Religious Experience* in Chapter 3 of this study) into a ludic pagan hippie of sorts on the Pacific edge. William Everson refashions his priestly self from "residual years" of Catholicism into a quasi-Jungian quester for anima-like soul mates drawn to erotic sacramentalism in his A-frame cabin and printing press abode in the Pacific coastal town of Swanton.

This "vocation of [becoming] the Poet" and will to transform his postwar life via prophetic *poesis,* as Everson portrayed this process in the three-term pedagogy of his "Santa Cruz Meditations," had been his dream from the socialist-anarchist days of his youth, through conscientious objection, to the Kenneth Rexroth- and Jack Kerouac-led urban scenes of "beat Beatitude" in San Francisco and its environs from the Pacific Northwest to Big Sur; he wanted to work not at the core of the U.S. Empire, but inside its peripheral abodes, where the humble might be exalted and the mighty cast down and mocked. This psychosocial landscape of redemption through a beatitude-quest was tied together by the railroad lines and monasteries that ran through the agricultural multicultural towns of Watsonville to Santa Cruz and Mission Dolores and sacred retreats in Marin

County, not to mention Santa Barbara to the south, where Kerouac had encountered his Franciscan hobo of the Jesus prayer and beaten-down tenderness on a train to nowhere in *Dharma Bums*. Everson embodies what his kindred spirit Allen Ginsberg had termed in *Howl* the "spectral nation!" of a counter-imperial subjectivity and countercultural alternatives. The death-and-war gods of Moloch and money gods of Mammon had to be defeated by conversion as a queered or mongrelized alternative, meaning for such Beat poets the forging of a counter-poetics drenched in a secularized beatitude. One famous night of California extremity at UC Davis, Brother Antoninus—with a flair for the dramatic gesture of selfhood— threw off his Dominican brotherhood cloaks and donned the buffalo skins of a prophetic beatnik, as he left the black-clad priesthood of the Roman Catholic Church for the bead-laden robes and semiotic powers of poetry and prophecy, an embrace of *semiotic becoming* as a vocation to poetry, self-making, and community build-up along the Big Sur.

One could also look back to (and move forward toward) another amazing Northern California poet, namely, Sister Mary Norbert Korte, who went from life in her vocation as a Catholic nun to becoming a "beat nun"/beat poet at the Berkeley Poetry Reading of 1965 and a vigilantly committed ecological activist and all-around compassionate human being. This is a poet of integrity and redemptive wilderness conviction, seeing the sacred in the humble and the sublime, like some post-Sierra Club John Muir walking anonymously across the streets and fields in fog-drenched Mendecino County.[57] William Everson has passed on from view, and Brother Antoninus is just for post-Beat poet scholars like myself a poetic specter or "dharma bum" to invoke in our prayers and poems petitioning his coastal legacies, but Mary still lives on and writes in Arcata, California, in Mendocino County, embodying the quest for "beat beatitude" still.[58] All this is serious matter, not something to mock, or to conjure up from oblivion like some forgotten tomes or tombs. As John Henry Newman remarked on his long-meditated conversion from Anglicanism to Catholicism, as elaborated in *Apologia pro Vita Sua,* conversion was not a thing one could propound "between the soup and fish" at a dinner party.[59] We are talking about life-choices still and the possibility of redemption for self and other, life and planet, cross-pollinations of belief and influence, from New England to the coasts and shores of the mighty Pacific or ashrams and zendos of Asia, and back again. Conversion, in such terms, means the possibility of change and, as social project, the transformation from U.S. Empire into a postcolonial republic and zone of eco-planetary becoming from Swanton to Hilo and Taipei.

This book, *Be Always Converting, Be Always Converted,* is *not* about William Everson as such nor about his masks as Brother Antoninus (that is an interesting West Coast story to be sure); nor about the ecological post-Beat poet Mary Norbert Korte, who may never get in the poetry pages of the *New Yorker* nor, for that matter, in a leftist journal like *The Nation,* where she might be at home. But this study reflects upon, urges, and elaborates over the larger process of *conversion* itself and would enter into the innermost semiotic power that gets opened up for the democratic self as a process of world-becoming and life transformation. For to speak in such huge, shattering terms, this is what the "turning" moment of commitment via conversion entails. Still, in its looseness of sources and mobility of belief, "the American Religion," as Harold Bloom has outlined its core tenets and will to self-freedom, may be closer to the "gnosticism" this against-the-grain literary critic of theo-poetic vision associates with the Gospel of Thomas rediscovered among the Nag Hammadi texts and used as New Age text: a set of apothegms that seem "creedless, Orphic, enthusiastic, proto-gnostic, post-Christian."[60] The belief abiding at the core of this literalization of Christianity moves toward an achieved identification, however overreaching in the self, with "the emergence of Jesus-as-God pragmatically created."[61]

Conversion to such a free-standing Jesus, via some "gnostic knowing" of the "heaven" awaiting inside the self, might feel more like adopting a meditating guru than submitting to the savior crucified by Empire as that "Man who came and died a criminal's death" for you, as Dylan avowed in the visionary divides of *Slow Train Coming* in the post-oil-crisis malaise of 1973.[62] The Judeo-Christian muse in Dylan's conversion poem, heavily Americanized, is quite *agonistic* in its virtually civilizational divides of faith and unbelief: "You were telling him about Buddha, you were telling him about Mohammed in the same breath / You never mentioned one time the Man who came and died a criminal's death." But this *death-by-crucifixion,* it should be recalled with Dylan and Terry Eagleton, was a manifestation of the Roman Empire's power to humiliate, wound, terrorize, criminalize, and destroy all such forces of otherness that attempted to oppose or challenge its reign, including the enigmatic Yeshua of Nazareth, so-called King of the Jews, who tried to disavow such worldly power or claims to a rival emperium apart from the kingdoms of life-beatitude. Perhaps Dylan would agree with the post-Beatitudes policy of the antiwar veteran and visionary-affirmations-of-peace activist Doug Zachary, as he takes part in Maxine Hong Kingston's pro-peace writing *sangha* in

Northern California: "The Bodhisattva Jesus is my secretary of state, the Beatitudes my national security doctrine."[63]

Democracy, liberty, and *opportunity*—those shibboleths of American populism coming down from the Popular Front into mass-mediated forms of translation, influx, and adaptation—if anything mean the very freedom to shape and choose the wildest version of conversion possible.[64] With this on-the-road version of the quest for the godhead, as Harold Bloom frames this *gnosis* of wandering and theo-poetic self-invention, "rebirth involves joining Thomas as a sharer in the solitude of Jesus, or being a passerby with Jesus," the self reborn into semiotic power and exalted plenitude like Walt Whitman before a blade of grass in "Song of Myself" or like Jack Kerouac finding visions of beatitude by a stream in Watsonville or by the dirty railroad tracks in San Jose in *Dharma Bums*.[65] This Jesus is by now tenderly Americanized, in multiple ways: "he is multi-everything."[66] Democratizing the spread of beatitude into the multitudes in crowds and on the road, this Jesus embodies, in radical form of sonship found in Kerouac or Albert Saijo, a "sublime introjection of Yahweh," hardly any solace to conversion tactics from the Torah or Qur'an, which this "daemonic counter-Sublime of hyperbole" would repudiate, challenge, or overcome.[67]

The world we are living in, seemingly given over to wars in the Middle East, nuclear umbrellas in East Asia, mediated banality, and the globalization of the life-world everywhere under market mandates, is indeed a "world gone wrong," meaning by this a *worlding* of global banality and stalemated possibility. If this is the global democracy that Bush 2 stands for, then we need to get a new constitution and forge the semiotics of a different life. For the God-relying Dylan, never one to be pushed around by conformist codes, conversion entails commitment, with no middle ground of compromise or secular drifting: "You either got faith or you got unbelief, there ain't no neutral ground" is how he put this binary in the high-holy grounds of *Slow Train Coming* during the oil crisis in 1978, invoking the complex muse figure of a *covenant-woman-as-covenant-nation* trope that courses throughout his poetics of metamorphosis, from "Angelina" and "Sad-Eyed Lady of the Lowlands" to the "praying from the mother" on the quasi-Catholic hermeticism of *Modern Times*. A country tied to Mammon regimes or given over to Global Empire aspirations cannot easily hear the antagonistic dimensions of what Dylan still stands for, not so much as the Jeremiah per se as the poet-king David with tambourine, harp, Bible, and gambler's moustache leading us back into promised land of democratic possibility and post-Beat redemption.[68]

"Be Always Converting, Be Always Converted"

To summarize the shape of what this book surveys: the six chapters and auto-reflective epilogue would link the on-the-road becoming force of Dylan's trajectory across American highways and byways to the oceanic crossing of the first Native Hawaiian convert to American Christianity and the rebirth morphology of self-becoming, namely, Henry ʻŌpūkahaʻia. The mighty orphan "Henry Obookiah," as renamed in New England "praying families" around Yale College and points west, emerges in a line of flight across the Pacific like that lucid orphan figure in Bob Dylan's "Thunder on the Mountain" who recruits an army of tough sons of bitches from the orphanages just after he says his religious vows at St. Herman's church in Alaska.[69] And although "Henry, torn from the stomach" (this organizing trope/figure of the first Hawaiian convert and transpacific migrant will be explained in the first third of this study) may be dead and buried, and although his body has been brought back from the stony earth of Cornwall, Connecticut, to his tropical native homeland on the Big Island of Hawaiʻi, where the King Kamehameha I regime of ruling chiefs had taken over the modernizing nation, this *death* of the Hawaiian spirit is not a taken-for-granted fact.

In effect, what I am doing is conjuring up Henry ʻŌpūkahaʻia's born-again life and writings as a spirit of possibility from long-forgotten tombs in New England and Hawaiʻi, as if to unblock the present and to remake the terms of a U.S. covenant as something *subject to poesis* and change, as self and nation can be renewed in quest for grace at all points, with nothing certain. What I am aiming to do is to unlock the process of American subject-formation as a conversion process, which I will elaborate on as a feat of "becoming semiotic" in Chapter 3 as well as in other parts of this book. In some sense, I am bringing it all back home from waters of the Pacific to the cold scrappy state of Connecticut, where I was born and reborn, and that many times over, as I will also explain in the Epilogue.

Christian mimicry of the converted subject and will to proselytize others across the domains of U.S. Empire into confessions-and-professions of conversion had animated the Hawaiian "heathen" life of Henry ʻŌpūkahaʻia, whether being converted in the hills of New England or when later sent out to convert in the optative waters of the colonial American Pacific, as I will elaborate in Chapters 1 and 2. In these opening chapters, I will push toward the postcolonial openness "counter-conversion" begins to take on more fully in Epeli Hauʻofa's ecumenical "Oceania" in Chapter 4. At other times in this study, especially in Chapter 3, I will invoke the "counter-conversion" syntax of William James. I mean by this turn a pragmatic semiotics of rebirth tied to the influx of empowerment in figures such as Emerson, "born and born again" many times under that sign of newness, semiotic mobility, and god-drenched unrest. Such poets and converts often begin seeking power and states of enhanced selfhood ("beatitude") via writing. In Chapter 5, the masks of regenerative violence in Ai's poetry, whereby Florence Anthony Ogawa refigures herself into historical masks of aggression and rebirth and converts lyric subjectivity into multiplicity, will be linked to regenerative figurations of frontier violence and racial subjection the poet cannot dissociate from "sin," "guilt," and the "killing floor" that shadows Afro-American history and her conversion-poetics with trauma.

Later, in Chapter 6, exploring the lyric chase of a belief-drenched poetics, I will elaborate the born-again, relentlessly dismantled poetic life of Bob Dylan as a post-Beat version of this semiotic becoming and will to profess conversion as Judeo-Christian poet and Jeremiah of U.S. Empire. The Epilogue will reflect back upon lines of force and flight in my own life that lead to affirmations of minority-becoming and social alteration through literature and its dramas of conversion and life-amplification. What I would track here, ultimately, in these versions of a trans-American poetics pushing toward states of oceanic becoming and land crossing, is what Nathaniel Mackey has called (in the experimental poetry of Edward Kamau Brathwaite, undoing "golfcurses" in the Caribbean), "an X-ing of the self, the self not as noun but as verb," a counter-conversion forged against Empire not as given by inherited belief, but as language-made, dissonant, wry.[70] These social dramas of regeneration are all around us, from Dock Boggs and Blind Willie McTell to the nostalgias for Anglo-global British Empire in T. S. Eliot ("Men have left GOD not for other gods, they say, but for / no god [though they worship] Money, and Power.").[71] No partisan of any counter-converting Invisible Republic of the spirit, the trans-Atlanticist Eliot waxes nostalgic for logocentric domination by the Word and, more broadly, for an Anglican England of "imperial expansion" and Anglo-global hegemony when the British had dominated the world by exporting "intellectual enlightenment / And everything, including capital / And several versions of the Word of God."[72] In a faith-drenched poem like "The Rock," Eliot connects the recovery of this enlightened world to building an Anglican church in his émigré British homeland, so that religion can be installed as world-center. In this study in conversions and life-transformations forged "against Empire," this is *not* what I would aim to mean by opening up the dynamics— or *poesis*—at the heart of postcolonial conversion.[73]

Given the stress on the *semiotics of conversion as choice,* altered language, and a reflection of social becoming and self-fashioning, conversion-by-force (meaning a coercive tactic of global war and social domination) is also *not* at the core of my discussion here, though conversions have in the past and are still talking place under conditions of force and struggles for religious hegemony and control (our so-called holy war) in a given era or social context.[74] These would be the kind of compulsory transformations of belief and narrative, as elaborated by Masao Miyoshi in his discussion of the modern Japanese novel, through which "individual writers underwent ritual conversions *(tenko)* as they abandoned their critical opposition and adapted themselves to the imperial programs."[75] The absorption into the globalization project of U.S. Empire is not so unidirectional, fabricated, dire nor complete in its modes of evangelization and world redemption from the West down to the East.[76] In cosmopolitical terms, the United Nations Declaration of Human Rights defines religious conversion as a human right, founded in a right to choose, including the right to adopt or change such beliefs without being subject to coercion, abuse, or penal sanction: "Everyone has the right of freedom of thought, conscience and religion; this right includes freedom to change religion or belief" (Article 18) or to adopt atheistic views as well.[77] As exemplified here, conversion and counter-conversion assumes this utter malleability of tropes, codes, and languages of conviction, transformation, willing, and belief. Conversion enacts, at its core, the very making of human freedom and becoming along a line of transformation, world alteration, and flight.

Writing in contexts of global terror, death-glamorizing video games, and militarized misunderstanding as daily "news," I would side with the lines from Bob Dylan's "The Wicked Messenger," from a cryptic ballad of evangelical Americana on *John Wesley Harding* (1968): "And he was told but these words / Which opened up his heart / 'If ye cannot bring good news, then don't bring any'."[78] All the more so, these latter-day acts of self-invention and "good news" can go the other route toward a counter-conversion moving from sacred to profane, as in Sam Cooke's post-gospel music in the 1979s, say. Conversion of sorts also occurs in the restorations of the sacred in Czeslaw Milosz's visions of California across the 1980s; or in Robert Hass's more ascetic quest to achieve a quasi-Buddhist "emptiness" and release from male love-grief in the temple hills above Pusan, Korea, on the booming Pacific Rim.[79] At a counter-cultural extremity of conversion, we might consider this on-the-road avowal from William Burroughs, writing across border-lines of community, Cold War nationhood, and faith to another global form of God-quest, "close as the vein in our neck": "My religious conversion now complete. I am neither a Moslem nor a Christian, but I owe a great debt to Islam and could never have made my connection with God ANY-WHERE BUT HERE," Burroughs affirms in a letter to Ginsberg from Tangiers in 1957. "And I realize how much of Islam I have absorbed by osmosis. . . . I have never even glimpsed peace of mind before I learn the real meaning of 'It is As Allah Wills.' . . . And remember 'God is as close to you as the vein in your neck.' "[80] Conversion, that is to say, haunted even a cyborg-like subject of paranoid narratives as the author of *Naked Lunch*.

But at the outset, I will begin this study by considering (in some textual and historical detail) the wondrous life of Henry 'Ōpūkaha'ia, the first Native Hawaiian subject who, orphaned from place and polity and freed up to modern newness by Pacific ocean-crossings to New England, turned his life around and found self-renewal through the Hawaiian mimesis of rebirth.

Beat Beatitude Still . . .

As I drive or walk along the Pacific coastal town of La Selva Beach down to the sprawling multicultural city of Watsonville, California, with its long-standing ties to the Americas of Baja California and to Asia Pacific crossings from China, Japan, the Philippines, and Hawai'i, I would imbibe (as *spirit of place*) the huge farmlands and ocean vistas as well as (even more important) the "Beat beatitude" of the humble people who go on working inside (and often against) the modalities of the U.S. Anglo-global Empire. Nearby is the unassuming Saint Patrick's Church, the Iglesia de San Patricio, on Main Street, funded in its brick-by-brick rebuilding after the Loma Prieta earthquake of 1989 by Bill Graham and Winterland Incorporate, as if all the rock concert tickets I had bought in the years 1967–1976 could do some lasting good. For Watsonville, "sweet Watsonville," is a place only the "dharma bum" wisdom and beatific post-Catholicism of Jack Kerouac from Lowell, Massachusetts, and parts unknown could presciently see and love for what it was and is: a place and people (what some Gary Snyder disciples have called our "Pacific Rim communitas") born of the rivers and the spirit of visionary community of love, outreach, co-existence, and mutual forgiveness as path to Eternity as creatural and close.[81]

Beat beatitude is still rising up on these streets and in the hearts of this hard-working and pious, if beaten-down, community: that remains my underlying claim. That force abides as ground of immanence from "the filthy Passaic" of William Carlos Williams in New Jersey to the fishing coves of Bamboo Ridge on Oʻahu island on which I have lived and (now resettled in coastal California) would forge this anti-imperial poetics of reborn-becoming as empowering, resacralizing, wondrous, and tied into the Over-Soul. Conversion now and again affirms that self and world can be *made new* by the incoming force of what I can only call (still, as I did in the days of my youth) the Holy Spirit, for which I can and will give praise.

CHAPTER ONE

The Poetics and Politics of
Henry 'Ōpūkaha'ia's Conversion

"The Hawaiians hence felt that their gods had returned
[overseas from Tahiti, or the primordial place called 'Kahiki']
in the Bible. The size of the type used in the printing caused
them to think that their gods had come in that shape [of printed
words, *palapala*]."

> —Mary Kawena Pukui, as recorded in Martha Beckwith,
> *Hawaiian Mythology*

Courage and skill
navigated life to Kealakekua Bay
long before this sun
rose on the
Empire.

> —William S. Chillingworth, "Requiem"

"What our Saviour mean," said he, "when he say, 'In my father's
house are many mansion—I go prepare a place for you.' What he
mean, *'I go prepare a place?'* "

> —Henry 'Ōpūkaha'ia to Edwin Dwight,
> *Memoirs of Henry Obookiah*[1]

"God took to himself..."

In the village of Cornwall in the northwestern corner of Connecticut,
nestled in scrappy Litchfield County where many of the conversions during the Second Great Awakening to New Light Theology had taken
place, there is a grass-encrusted gravestone carved over a quadrangular
tomb of rocks, "worn and weathered by a thousand New England
storms." The flatbed inscription reads:

IN
Memory of
HENRY OBOOKIAH
a native of
Owhyhee.
His arrival in this country gave rise
to the Foreign mission school,
of which he was a worthy member.
He was once an Idolator, and was
designed for a Pagan Priest; but by
the grace of God and by the prayers
and instructions of pious friends,
he became a Christian.
He was eminent for piety
and missionary Zeal. When almost prepared
to return to his native Isle to preach the
Gospel, God took to himself. In his last
sickness, he wept and prayed for Owhyhee,
but was submissive. He died without fear
with a heavenly smile on his
countenance and glory in his soul.
Feb. 17, 1818;
aged 26

Ministering in Hawai'i after the islands had acquired U.S. statehood, Reverend Edith H. Wolfe urged readers—through her learned introduction and notes to a re-edition of the *Memoirs of Henry Obookiah,* compiled for the Woman's Board of Missions for the Pacific Islands in 1967 and reprinted in 1990—"Take a long look at that gravestone: it is the hinge on which the door of the history of modern Hawai'i swung."[2] Linking a global diaspora of cultures and oceans, this grave of Henry 'Ōpūkaha'ia becomes an uncanny door through which New England mores and methods had first entered into shaping the Hawaiian soul. Modern Hawaiians were transformed by his conversion: Henry Obookiah's regenerative life endures as icon and sign of a "reborn" beginning for a promised land on earth and across the oceans.

Given this Native Hawaiian's studious life and pious death as recorded in the *Memoirs of Henry Obookiah,* which were first compiled into narrative by Edwin Welles Dwight in 1818, just a few months after Obookiah's burial in that gravesite in Cornwall, Henry 'Ōpūkaha'ia (c. 1792–1818) has become *the* exemplary agent of Hawaiian globalization and Christian conversion under the American missionary dispensation in Asia-Pacific. As I have suggested, his born-again life galvanized the American foreign missionary cause of conversion and acculturation that would diasporize New England culture to the Pacific shores of Hawai'i in 1820, connecting these oceanic islands with a distant Boston "mainland" and its post-Puritan mores. As the learned nineteenth-century Hawaiian historian Samuel Kamakau summarized 'Ōpūkaha'ia's conversion and its enduring modern Hawaiian impact (while writing on the custom-shattering reign of King Kamehameha's heir, King Liholiho, in a Hawaiian newspaper in 1868), "A young Hawaiian named Henry Opu-kaha-ia had gone to live in New England in the United States and had been welcomed freely and educated there. He believed that Christianity would benefit his people, who were still under the influence of false gods. He traveled about to the cities in the eastern states urging the sending of preachers to preach the word of God to his people."[3]

Kamakau, a major Hawaiian journalist and scholar of history, having converted from American Congregationalism to Roman Catholicism because he felt closer to the latter denomination's modes of image-worship, ritual, prayer, hymn, and iconic veneration, wrote with piety, respect, and conviction of his more austere Hawaiian Protestant precursor. More given to modes of ritual and iconophilia, Kamakau even claimed (writing for a Hawaiian newspaper in 1859), to ratify his deep-felt counter-conversion from Native Hawaiian polytheism to Protestantism and then to the Catholic faith, that Roman Catholicism had first "come with the Spanish ships [that arrived in Hawai'i before Captain Cook] and that [thus] the Christian and pagan forms of worship were mixed together" in Hawaiian priestly forms, such as the practice of pointing the right hand to heaven; praying with the congregation in unison; sprinkling holy water; decorating images with flowers, ferns, and vines; and even "the erecting of images outside the *luakini* [a type of Hawaiian stone altar] and other *heiaus* [altars to the gods] in order to give an appearance inspiring fear and awe." For Kamakau, "the Roman Catholic form of worship [best] resembles the ancient Hawaiian and also that [faith] of the Jews."[4]

Global in transpacific vision and local-hybrid in his mix of ancient roots and routed modern aims, the first native convert 'Ōpūkaha'ia becomes for the converted Kamakau (himself deeply aligned to Hawaiian cultural-political preservation and national sovereignty) the precursor and paradigm of the modern Hawaiian subject. As will be detailed here, Henry was at once converted to Christianity, and more broadly, he became acculturated to the mobility and creative influx of peoples, ideas, cultural frames, belief systems, codes, mores, and stories in this post-contact episteme. As such, 'Ōpūkaha'ia initiated and mobilized in the Pacific the life-altering process of modern identity-representation that I will call "becoming semiotic."[5] In his brief, pithy life, full of uncanny *manna/mana* flows of spirit-power and the haunted significance of imitating the faith-forms of an altered Deity, Henry embodies the going and coming of Native Hawaiian culture across the Pacific islands, moving to and from New England much as inhabitants of the modern postcolonial world now do in this era of globalization termed neoliberal empire.

The spelling of Henry's native place as "Owhyhee" in his *Memoirs* (as on his tombstone in Cornwall) still uses the quaintly onto-poetic English of Captain Cook's expeditions to mimic the place-name. This representation of Hawaiian words would soon shift into standardized orthography that Henry Obookiah himself had started to transcribe in his compilations of Hawaiian grammar, spelling lists, and vocabulary recorded in his New England journals. The American missionaries would more fully implement this romanization of language later. We know that Henry's initial standardizations of the Hawaiian language had been compiled with help from Yale's Professor of Sacred Literature and Divinity, Eleazar Fitch, and that these were to be shaped into standard modern forms by Samuel Ruggles of the pioneer mission.[6] This modernizing process of native-language transcription, which Henry's written works had started to Romanize, initiated the translational process of turning what was an oral language and archive of orature, by no means exclusively, into the Gospel of the missionary conversion apparatus. In effect, Henry was activating a process of self-fashioning via this new *mana*-laden technology of *writing*, which allowed him to imitate (via abstract representation and mimicry) and make contact with (via touch and physical embodiment) the sacred forms and energy flows of Christian alterity.

This ministerial retraining process—by long ancestry, Henry was already serving in training as a priest (*kahuna,* that enchanted word) on the Big Island—took place via "the prayers and instructions of pious friends" taught under the direction of Edwin Dwight who was himself a descendant of the famous theologian of regeneration through grace, Jonathan Edwards, and was the learned nephew of Yale president and author Timothy Dwight. The Dwights of Connecticut were an elite writing and converting family, to be sure, devoted to pedagogy and very much well-situated at the core of the post-Puritan elite. Oddly enough, the racial seme of "white" is all but spectrally buried in this well-known Yale-family name (D-white), as "book" comes to be embedded in Henry's last name, as it becomes romanized (Obookiah) in English, suggesting their uncanny coproduction into some kind of *white book.* Be that as it poetically may,

Edwin Dwight was the ministerial editor from Yale College who led Henry's way into the world of published English. Dwight's posthumous publication of the *Memoirs of Henry Obookiah* began the translational process of shaping, cutting, drawing meaning from, and narrating Henry's reborn life into national and global influence, as if speaking as and for the name of Henry Obookiah who (as we saw) spelled his name 'Ōpūkaha'ia and became an originator of the Hawaiian alphabet and student of English, Greek, and Hebrew.

Henry's truncated life had "bridged the idol worship of the Pacific with the Christianity of the Atlantic," to quote the cover blurb of the 1990 edition of the *Memoirs* printed by the Women's Board of Missions for the Pacific Islands. In effect, Henry not only had learned to spell "cap" and "pig," those domestic words for clothing and food he would encounter in New Haven; but he had begun to learn the precepts of the Westminster Catechism and to take them, translated, interiorized, lived out, affirmed, into his own native heart by mimicry of the other's *mana*-laden sayings and priestly forms. "I spell four syllables now, and I say what is the chief end of man," he told Dwight in a letter (his first in English) written from Torringford in 1810 in a broken but serviceable pidgin English (*Memoirs*, 19). Henry seeks to vocalize in these new terms the "chief end" for what he must have recognized as chiefly a life of sacred *mana*. Certainly it was a life well suited for Henry, as a priestly offspring, whose orphaned flight from his homeland of "aloha" could be healed by this newfound family and newfound faith.

Growing up under modernizing power shifts and becoming-nation mandates of King Kamehameha I in his homeland on the Big Island of Hawai'i, Henry 'Ōpūkaha'ia had already served several years in training to become a native priest (kahuna) under his uncle, Pahua, a celebrated priest of Lono-worship at Hikiau Heiau at Kealakekua Bay. Indeed, this was the *mana*-laden site where Lono-miming figure of Enlightenment science Captain James Cook was slain by Hawaiians, to the world's horror, in 1779. Such training into the mimetic habitus of the priestly caste for the Hawaiian harvest-god, Lono, had all taken place for this youth before Henry left on a sealing ship bound across oceans of capitalist commerce and missionary outreach for the ports of the Pacific Northwest, Macau and Canton in China, and back to eastern America on the Atlantic.

Modern Pacific Crossings

This Pacific crossing is no middle-passage journey of abjection and enslavement for the modern and adventurous Henry 'Ōpūkaha'ia, but his life is an outreaching one of adventure, risk, study, language amplification, and self-transformation. After he suddenly chose to leave Kona as a common sailor at sixteen, Henry's life turns around in such globally affiliative ways of what Paul Gilroy calls *outer-national* and transcultural becoming: border-crossing transformations and adventures into world-space mingling providence, caste, homeland nostalgia, Hawaiian aloha, *mana*, and political fate.[7] Henry's life had been turned around by this mutual mimicry of codes, as he lived to become converted (or, in part at least, *counter-converted from beliefs and practices of Hawaiian nativism*) into modern subject-formation and training to serve as a modernizing native priest converting his polytheistic people to these new codes of faith, rebirth, and worship.

Subject and agent of the conversion mimetic with a superb talent for *mimicry* that years before Darwin had noted as an endemic "native" attribute on the Pacific beaches at Tierra Del Fuego, Henry enacted for the modern Hawaiian subject the mimetic process of becoming a trained missionary for the American Board for the Commission of Foreign Ministers (ABCFM). He had been raised up to educate, serve as othering-model for, and convert the Hawaiian people as vanguard subject of American modernity, a worldly sailor-student becoming teacher and minister if not senator back at home (if he had lived on). *"Ke ala iki a kahuna,"* as Mary Kawena Pukui cautions in her evocation of a traditional Hawaiian proverb, meaning "[it is] a narrow trail on which priests [kahuna] walk," a priestly way toward *mana* empowerment filled not just with prayers, chants, orations, and rituals, but also with restraints, codes, and life-or-death restrictions upon their imitator.[8] Dangerously full of uncanny power and political risk, Henry's path toward this mimetic vocation, moving from native to Christian modes of praying to become another kind of "priest," was not an easy one.[9] Even to this day, as I shall later discuss, Henry's vocation can be taken as a sign of Hawaiian colonization better left forgotten or ignored in contexts of the struggle for sovereignty and American decolonization.

Caught between rival belief systems, gods coming and going from the animistic polytheism of 400,000 gods to the *mana* of Judeo-Christian monotheism, Henry's path from priesthood to priesthood is filled with diasporic tensions, elective lines of flight and dissension, expressing vocational and national contradictions from his "rough birth" in Kau to his pious death in Cornwall, as shall be elaborated. The tombstone story of darkness and light, before and after, splitting Henry's life in two—"He was once an Idolator, and was designed for a Pagan Priest . . . [But he] became a Christian"—does not get at this bicultural complexity, this figure of aloha, *mana,* and uncanny translation that he stands for. Henry was torn from the Pacific and Hawai'i and cast into the "promised land" at New Haven and torn from America into modes of transcultural belonging in which the Hawaiian language and modes live on in him as well, as we shall see in this chapter and the next. Mutual miscomprehension could also lead to moments of self-altering curiosity. Dwight, while "pleasantly" conversing with and teaching Henry how to read and write in English, also politely and, in different contexts, made "inquiries concerning some of the habits and practices of his own country"—that is, Hawaiian cultural practices concerning how the people of Hawai'i dressed, walked, prayed, carried water, and so on (*Memoirs,* 15).

In the Wake of *Thaddeus*

After Henry's death, conversion across the Hawaiian archipelago was by no means instant, unidirectional, or complete. This was true even with the coming of the Sandwich Islands Mission company lock, stock, and barrel (not to mention with the mimetic technologies of the sacred book and printing press and publication of the Bible in Hawaiian in 1839). The Christian missionaries on the good ship *Thaddeus* had arrived at the Hawaiian Islands after a five-month and 18,000-mile journey from Boston in March 1820. In waves of native conversion lasting from Queen Ka'ahumanu's and Kalanimoku's royal examples of Christian conversion by ruling ali'i wahine at Kawaihao Church in 1825 until the belated "great awakenings" of commoners in Hilo and Waimea in the 1840s, a severe brand of American Calvinist piety came to supplant and supplement the dissolving kapu-system of nativist belief. Hawaiian terms like "pono" and "ea" began to resonate with Christian and governmental meanings like "righteousness" and "sovereignty" as the kingdom took on international status as a recognized nation with a distinctive literature and language.[10] Christian mimicry took place letter by letter, sermon by sermon, even as this new code of restraints and empowerments contended against secular forces, rival religions, commodity-desires, and modern mores streaming in from England, China, Russia, France, and (increasingly) the United States.

These modern mores and commercial influences were commonly carried across the Pacific by adventurous, bawdy seafaring "men who hung up their conscience on Cape Horn when they sailed to take up residence in the islands," as described by Gavin Daws, who urges such a case for modern hybridity and the path to democratization.[11] The Pacific Ocean was long crisscrossed with Native Pacific peoples and languages, not to mention customs, goods, signs, and ships since contact with Captain Cook, if not earlier through stray Spanish vessels, as King David Kaulākaua liked to affirm while collecting and writing Hawaiian myth, song, and legends during the era of his re-nativizing reign, as did Samuel Kamakau in his newspaper writings. Hawaiian sailors were so broadly dispersed across the modernizing Pacific waters that, by the 1840s (before Melville had landed in his Marquesan "Eden" far away from Nantucket), "kanaka" (the Native Hawaiian generic word for man) had already become a generic pidgin signifier for *any native of the South Seas* and was used this way in colloquial English across the Pacific Ocean from ports in Australia to coastal towns and missions in California *(Oxford English Dictionary).*[12]

For years after his death, no matter how uneven the hold of this Christianity across the eight islands of Hawai'i Nei, Henry 'Ōpūkaha'ia's life story in the *Memoir* proved emblematic of the born-again potential for Hawaiian modernity, as it circulated from Connecticut to Burma and Canton and fed back to Honolulu and Hilo. It "could reduce entire classes [of natives] at the mission schools to tears no matter how many times it was told," Daws claimed of this conversion memoir (*Shoal,* 98), reading the story years later, after American statehood seemed a settled fact and the struggle for Hawaiian sovereignty a thing of the past. It was a time in the "Aloha" state of Hawai'i, the fiftieth state to join the union, when, as Joseph Puna Balaz urges in his pidgin-voice drama on the struggle to reclaim Hawaiian sovereignty, "Hawaiian politics, you about as brown as Snow White," as "Uncle Kaulana [Who] Gives One Speech" says on the difficulty to articulate Hawaiiness within U.S. state forms and racial policies that all but dispossess natives of voice, being, rationality, and place.[13]

Following trips to California and Oregon, the New York journalist Charles Nordhoff visited Hawai'i (as a travelogue-writing "tourist") in 1873 and considered the "modernization" of the islands—on the American-Christian model—all but a *fait accompli.* Looking around at the numerous schools, white-frame houses, racial mix, public safety, and native churches of Honolulu, Nordhoff boasted, "Patiently, and somewhat rigorously, no doubt, they [American missionaries] sought from the beginning to make New England men and women of these Hawaiians; and what is wonderful is that, to a large extent they have succeeded."[14] That said, as travel agent for an emerging U.S. Pacific Rim vision that would absorb this tourist Pacific by tying periphery to center as the "contado" of San Francisco, Nordhoff concedes in his touristscape of *Northern California, Oregon, and the Sandwich Islands* that "the Hawaiian is no more a perfect Christian than the New Yorker or Massachusetts man" and remains very much tied to "traces of old customs and superstitions" (24). But as a customary rule, this Native Hawaiian who has been subjected to modern change across contact zones of the British Victorian global ecumene still evinces a "strong feeling of nationality" that would thus render him "very strongly opposed to annexation" by the American government or any other foreign power, Nordhoff accurately urges (96).

If the path to Hawaiian modernity had been all but secured, Nordhoff recognizes (as did Mark Twain, writing at the time in the pro-annexationist interests of California sugar more than cruise-ship tourism, which he would soon embrace in the faux-sublimity of *Innocents Abroad*) that Native Hawaiian sovereignty was about to be challenged by global powers from Europe, Asia, and the Americas in the coming decades.[15] This was due not to any native incapacity but to the geopolitics of imperialism intersecting, clashing, and redistributing capital, military might, and power across the Pacific. Nordhoff's assumption of nineteenth-century Hawai'i as an *already Americanized* space of exotic ex-primitive fascination and romance—Hawai'i on route to becoming a proto-New England of the Pacific, as it is for travel writer Paul Theroux in *Happy Isles of Oceania*—no longer comes as much of a surprise. We now commonly assume, when speaking of Hawai'i as an American state since 1959, the multicultural forces and mass jet-age tourism validate the "golden man" fantasy (as the narrative telos in James Michener's *Hawaii*) that had been installed across the American Pacific. In such terms, a writer like Henry 'Ōpūkaha'ia might serve as a precursor to the pidginized poetics of Bamboo Ridge multiculturalism or just some kind of a background voice, speaking as a sublated Hawaiian, for the Anglo-centric anthologies of the Pacific literary canon maker, A. Grove Day.[16]

Still, as anthropologist Marshall Sahlins records, post-contact Hawaiians remained tied to the impact of *British* culture from the time of Captain Vancouver's last peace-making visit with Kamehameha I in 1794 until around 1825, a bond of national affiliation rendered uncanny/ *unhomely* to the English with the slaying and symbolic circulation of Captain Cook's body as a Lono figuration, not to mention his "apotheosis" as white god of British myth.[17] Sahlins quotes the summary made by the major American historian of early-modern Hawai'i, Ralph Kuykendall, who writes, "Great Britain held the highest place in the thought of Hawaiians about foreign countries; they considered themselves under the protection of that nation and frequently referred to themselves as *kanaka no Beritane* (men of Britain)."[18] By the close of the War of 1812, American clipper ships went on "whitening" the Pacific with those swarming "energies of the capitalists" in a globe-encircling quest from New England for adventure, whales, converted souls, and profit. As Owen Chase writes, after his shipwrecked survival near the Marquesas and Tahiti, which served as source-text for the Pequod's whaling misadventures in *Moby-Dick,* "At the conclusion of peace, those energies burst out afresh; and our sails almost whiten the distant confines of the Pacific."[19]

Unhomely 'Ōpūkaha'ia

The twists of Hawaiian national history are such that this offshore body of 'Ōpūkaha'ia has by now returned to Hawai'i not as "barbarian" or "heathen" *other* (as he was for the first generation of Yale scholars) but as an *unhomely* force of "Christian"/"civilized" modernity (as he has now become for contemporary anticolonial visions of indigeneity and *kanaka maoli* authenticity). The life work of Henry 'Ōpūkaha'ia now disturbs, in effect, the making of any fixed racial/national identity or postcolonial conversion code.[20] Decolonization in the contemporary Pacific has come to stand for an ongoing process of nativist "unfaithing," meaning a long delayed anti-Western critique that goes hand in hand with a process of affirming the *re-nativization* and re-goding of beliefs, language, and modes of belonging.[21] As Anne Hatori contends in a counter-converting poem called "Ladrónés" ("Thieves"), written in 1999 in response to Ferdinand Magellan's abject naming of Chamoru Islands as the *Islas de los ladrones* in 1521, the Euro-American feat of making Pacific islanders over into "religious converts" often meant reforming native subjects (as in her native Guam, one of the sites where Christianity first came to remake the Pacific) who have become "Over-modernized"/"Over-theologized"/"Over-Americanized" [and]// "Under-Chamoricized."[22] As such, this process of colonial overidentification needs to be de-sublimated and *reversed* via a process of "counter-conversion" to reaffirm native beliefs, rites, signifiers, habits, and signs.[23] Dana Takagi captures this will to sovereignty and native rehabilitation in the Pacific by the struggle of Hawaiian nationalists resurfacing in the 1990s, whose motto can be summarized, "Forget postcolonialism—Hawai'i is still colonized [by the United States]."[24]

These are global/local times of injustice, critique, and multiscaled reframing of national polities and cultural practices, rife with clashing articulations of indigeneity, attitude, and belief.[25] In July of 1991, the United Church of Christ at its 18th General Synod began a process of apology and redress toward Native Hawaiians on behalf of the Congregational Church by admitting "historical complicity in the overthrow of the

Hawaiian monarchy."[26] Would these same churches apologize for the forces of "rebirth" they had helped to evangelize in converting subjects like 'Ōpūkaha'ia and Kamakau? Could the United States acknowledge the long duration of its own will to Empire in the Pacific? President Bill Clinton's signing of the Apology Bill in 1993 at least acknowledged the United States' role in the loss of Hawaiian independence in 1893 and helped to win broader support for the Native Hawaiian sovereignty movement.[27] The Apology Bill did apologize, as if seeking historical forgiveness, without returning any land or performing any legal or distributive redress.

Given these colonial contexts, our reading habits and grammars of reception for mixed-cultural works like the *Memoirs of Henry Obookiah* can become prefabricated and rigid, in need of some unsettling and risk. We cannot approach this white-missionary project of "evangelization" (spreading the Gospel around the Asia/Pacific reaches of the globe)[28] without hearing—as James Clifford has written of Maurice Leenhardt's ethnological project in New Caledonia—those terms, forces, genres, and forms that are "culturally destructive, [bespeaking] a spiritual aggression inseparable from colonial domination."[29] We can still hear this *lethal* enthusiasm to convert the pre-Americanized native in the colonial voice of Hiram Bingham as he made landfall along the Kona coast of Hawai'i in 1820: "Animated with the novel and changeful scene, we longed to spring on shore, to shake hands with the people, and commence our work by telling them of the great salvation of Jesus Christ."[30] We fear for salvation-targeted natives as when Bingham begins to speak of "the *heiaus* [temples] of idolatrous worship" as so many "fortification[s] of Satan's kingdom" and "heathen abomination." The New England minister soon seeks to vilify, burn, and (with the help of converted Hawaiian rulers like Kamehameha III) *demolish* them. Conversion to Christianity went hand and glove, in this one-way dispensation, with conversion to American laws, contracts, rules of order, and forms of civilian modernity.[31] This is why the poet-activist Haunani Kay Trask can mock, in her call for Hawaiian sovereignty in 1993, modes of "niceness" or the sharing of "aloha spirit" that would still seek to cover up abject submission and accede to colonized political defeat.

Wary of racializing rhetoric and its binary codes, we are not Hiram Bingham or his missionary heirs inside Empire.[32] But the histories we tell or literatures and ethnographies we shape, however experimental or demonumentalized we make them across the decolonizing Pacific, cannot escape those "Manichean dichotomies created and reproduced by colonialism," whether then (as written in the colonial past) or now (writing in our postcolonial moment of Empire).[33] Raciology, as Paul Gilroy shows in *Against Race,* haunts the way we can think about, signify, or activate, even in an ethno-centered or indigenous way, the modern vocabulary of place, identity, nation, and culture.[34] If his *Memoirs* come down to us in such hazes of "colonial hagiography" or enchantments of nativist myth, 'Ōpūkaha'ia's life-history need not just remain a pious, banal, defeated legend of a colonized identity.[35]

Transplanted from the organic community into which he was born, Henry crossed two oceans and settled in Connecticut. Further, through his world-shattering conversion in 1815, he moved beyond ties to place and nation toward overcoming the "ridiculous and/or traumatic scandal" of becoming a hybrid modern Hawaiian who yet believed in agape and Christ as the grounds of writing "an *alternative* community" situating the self beyond the identity of blood, nationhood, and place.[36] Agent and maker of his history and new community of believers, Henry 'Ōpūkaha'ia is by no means one of those impoverished, abjected, and degenerating Hawaiian natives ("idolaters converted into *nominal* Christians") who, by 1840, in the hysterical tropes of Melville's *Typee,* had already been "civilized into draught-horses; and evangelized into beasts of burden" in downtown Honolulu.[37]

Mired in fatal-contact historiography and white-American contempt for the global south, Melville's portrait of King Kamehameha III as civilized native is demeaning to the point of tropical abomination. "His 'gracious majesty' is a fat, lazy, negro-looking blockhead, with as little character as power. He has lost the noble traits of the barbarian, without acquiring the redeeming graces of a civilized being," Melville opines (258). The *mana* (chiefly power) and *koko* (blood) lauded in the Hawaiian monarch evoke Melville's white horror and cosmopolitical ridicule: "The 'blood royal' is an extremely thick, depraved fluid; formed principally of raw fish, bad brandy, and European sweetmeats, and is charged with a variety of eruptive humors, which are enveloped in sundry blotches and pimples upon the august face of 'majesty itself,' and the 'princes and princesses of the blood royal'!" (258). Melville's portrayal of such *converted Hawaiians* is off the mark for understanding modernizing subjects of globality like 'Ōpūkaha'ia: as makers of literary history, we need to rescue Henry not just from reductive native activists but also from the wildly racializing tropes of such writers as Melville, Theroux, Michener, and Jack London.

Any stance affirming native conversion as a feat of semiotic agency and outer-national becoming, as I am proposing here, calls out for an against-the-grain postcolonial reexamination of what we mean by identity making and the will to change. We can situate the *Memoirs of Obookiah, a native of Owyhee and a member of the Foreign Mission School who died at Cornwall, Conn., February 17, 1818, aged 26 years* (New Haven: Office of the Religious Intelligencer, 1818)[38] within a dialogical, multiple, uneven, yet empathetic poetics/politics that recognizes (like Gauri Viswanathan writing on evangelical conflicts of Anglican-Hindu religiosity across colonial India) the "dual characterization of conversion as assimilation and dissent."[39] History, literature, and scholarship in the Pacific face a seemingly perpetualized "postcolonial" moment of multisited decolonization and counterconversion, when modern frameworks are coming undone and the Pacific gods go on returning and erupting as spectral force.[40] But conversion is seldom a one-way street toward fixing a stable, predetermined meaning, for self or others, in these contact zones of metamorphosis. Most readings of *The Memoirs of Henry Obookiah* barely move beyond textual paraphrase, historical example, or doctrinal application as coded into larger forms of pro-missionary or American national history.[41] The life and career of 'Ōpūkaha'ia proves more interesting, as literary trope and rhetoric, when pondered as a narrative of conversion filled with divergent meanings and unsettling claims upon the present.[42]

The *Memoirs* went through twelve editions and a print run of over fifty thousand copies: these have had such an impact on the transatlantic culture of New England that it is invariably "mentioned by missionaries in their letters of application to the ABCFM" (Zwiep, 14–15). As Gavan Daws has noted in his summary of the impact of 'Ōpūkaha'ia's short life, as described in the *Memoirs,* on the American missionary project to "Go Ye Forth into the World" and convert, " 'Ōpūkaha'ia was an exemplary convert. He took delight in praying, publicly and privately, and wherever he went he exhorted people in the name of God. He kept a model Christian journal, translated the Book of Genesis into Hawaiian, and began to work on a Hawaiian grammar, dictionary, and spelling book" (*Shoal,* 61). His accession to linguistic power and textuality proved exemplary here, as I have suggested, and Hawai'i (from the reign of Kamehameha I to Kamehameha III onward) became one of the most literate nations in the Pacific. Although missionaries are often credited with rendering Hawaiian into a written language, 'Ōpūkaha'ia was actually the originator or at least the key co-agent of this modernizing process. Linguists now recognize the importance of his impact on the transcription and standardization of the Hawaiian language (see *Voices,* 85–97). And "some of 'Ōpūkaha'ia's grammar is reflected in that of [Samuel] Ruggles," who began studying Hawaiian language and culture with Henry at the Foreign Mission School (*Voices*, 256).

The U.S. liberal historian Thurston Twigg-Smith (publisher of the influential *Honolulu Advertiser* and anti-sovereignty activist until his retirement in 1993) recalls with pride of possession (as grandson to Lorrin A. Thurston, one of the post-missionary agents of the "Hawaiian Revolution" that deposed Queen Lili'uokalani in 1893) how his great-great grandfather, Asa Thurston, member of the first mission to Hawai'i, was motivated to relocate to the Pacific by first reading these same *Memoirs:* "Driven by the inspiration of Hawaiian scholar Henry Obookiah, he [Asa, having graduated from Yale in 1816 and later its Divinity School to become a minister] wound up in Hawai'i in 1820 where his son, Asa G., was born in 1827" (to become founding president of the Missions Children's Society, which would later send missionaries to the South Seas. At another extreme of historical affiliation are those Hawaiian scholars and native historians such as Samuel Kamakau and David Malo. Their writings express ties to the modern enlightenment project, national learning, history writing, comparative cultural studies, and the Christian habitus of 'Ōpūkaha'ia even as they retell the power of Hawaiian customs and march of history according to a darkness/light binary conceptual schema of redemption this Yale-influenced student had helped, as Hawaiian self-image, to instill.

Rebirth Semiotics

Even the "before-and-after" story of Christian conversion that proved crucial to the "missionary discourse" across the post-contact Pacific can remain divided. It is too other-directed and thus, in the words of Oceania anthropologist Nicholas Thomas, "never encompassed indigenous consciousness or indigenous understandings of colonial change," due to forces of cultural discrepancy and hermeneutic incomprehension.[43] Saul does not just become a Pacific Paul reborn on the lava coasts of Kona, as I shall discuss later in Chapter Four on the Pacific counterconversion to Pacific gods in the writings and cultural work of Epeli Hau'ofa. For if "conversion is a subversion of secular power," worldly in textual and social impact, we can approach the conversion story of Henry Obookiah as a complex plot of subject-formation expressing incorporative drives of the American missionary project but also voicing the disidentification, cross-cultural tension, and displacement dynamics that were driving him to leave, mourn, and yet plan to return to his faction-torn Hawai'i.[44]

The "mutability" of native character and alien cultures that evangelical discourse depends upon proves pivotal to generating the narrative of conversion, as it effects the Pacific subject's born-again translation of signs and scriptural codes into realized meaning.[45] In an era of theological reshuffling, when academies in New England, such as Mount Holyoke, were being founded "on the principles of our missionary operations" in Asia and the Pacific that aimed to awaken, as Mary Lyon had encouraged her college students, "large desires for the conversion of the world," Henry 'Ōpūkaha'ia remained a haunting example that the work of conversion could occur.[46] Conversion is seldom a one-way street of fixity, damage, and death. Conversion needs to be understood as a signifying process of self-representative agency and risk, not just as a prefabricated event of native downfall and symbolic abdication, colonization effected (as Ann Douglas puts it), whereby "do-gooders, [who] in their ignorance and scorn of indigenous culture, were corrupting, not converting the natives."

Becoming semiotic in the mode of Calvinist self-interpretation means reading any life (via the Gospel) for signs of sinfulness and grace. In this language of the Protestant ethnic, called to labor for and to seek grace, 'Ōpūkaha'ia becomes the first Hawaiian caught up in shaping, translating, and circulating "the mimetic capital" of Christian self-representation and narrative "turn" of conversion. Henry activated this vocation and initiated a project brought to large-scale impact with the coming of the printing press and other technologies of dissemination to Hawai'i.[47] 'Ōpūkaha'ia's interest in learning the core beliefs, behavior patterns, and language habits (such as journal keeping or the more mysterious feat of "praying with ceasing") nurtured by Bible reading/translating and sermonizing had inspired the founding of the Foreign Mission School, and he aided his school masters there to make "the first concentrated efforts to study the language."[48] Theology-drenched Americans from New England brought this language-work to fruition, by promoting and circulating it via the first Ramage flatbed printing press they lugged 18,000 miles around Cape Horn to Hawai'i with the aim of preaching, teaching, and printing.[49] In the Pauline terms of Alain Badiou, conversion initiates for 'Ōpūkaha'ia the semiotic process of "becoming subjective," as a singular Christian subject searching for signs of grace, charismatic possession, backsliding, and/or rebirth into newness: "Every subject is initiated on the basis of charisma; every subject is charismatic."[50] Conversion texts turn on this trope of subjective performance, the turn toward a call to be "born again," "born from above," reborn as a self.

We can begin to read Henry 'Ōpūkaha'ia's text not as writings by a denativized and colonized subject, but as world agent—as well as a bicultural and multilingual writer—expressing a challenging, wry, and outer-national fate. Torn from the stomach of his Native Hawaiian culture and cast into New England schools and settlements, Henry's charismatic terms of subjective transformation and alter-becoming cross and link the contemporary U.S. transpacific to a decolonizing Hawai'i never fully incorporated or understood—never (I would hazard to say) fully converted (or translated) into one neoliberal frontier U.S. subject.[51] Settled into a process of language learning and cultural acquisition in New England, Henry soon turns, in his letters, conversations, and journals, to questions of what it means *to be living with and as a Christian.* "What shall I do to be saved?" Henry asks himself in a letter written while he was living and studying with the steward of Andover's Theological Institute in 1810. "I know that God is able to take away blind eyes and wicked heart, we must be born again and have a new spirit before we die," he answers himself along Pauline lines, voicing the "born-again" plot and charismatic images and passages that will shape his inner life and motivate his scholarly studies to become a minister (*Memoirs,* 25) among his own people. He soon travels to Tyngsborough "to see a boy who came from Hawai'i," and after he talks to him *(in Hawaiian)* about the invisible God of Genesis who made the world, the youth responds in kind, as would Kamakau, Malo, and others later, "O how foolish we are to worship wood and stone gods; we give them hogs, and cocoa nuts, and banana, but they cannot eat" (*Memoirs,* 28). Readers learned from Henry's narration that his priestly (kahuna) uncle, Pahua, had demanded a pig from Captain Brintnall as "a hog for his god" (Lono), in exchange for Henry's release so that he could become a common sailor on Brintnall's New Haven ship (*Memoirs,* 7).

The coming of Christian monotheism and Anglo-American modernity as well as Chinese contacts and exchanges had a disruptive effect, to be sure, even when native beliefs lingered on, went underground, or were transformed into more subliminal or subterranean mores and affects. In *'O'lelo No'eau: Hawaiian Proverbs and Poetical Sayings,* Mary Kawena Pukui records a telling proverb that is still used to this day by Christian Hawaiians to express their mounting superiority over the "little" gods of old Hawai'i: *Ke akua li'li'i'ole I ka lani me ke honua* ("Little God who did not create heaven and earth"; 180, proverb number 1671). At least by 1810, Henry reveals that the principles of de-nativization and rejection of the "little gods" of his birthplace were already organizing the Hawaiian self-image of religious practices. For converting also meant counter-converting from such prior beliefs and cultural practices of native language, and this was seldom total or complete.

Noted "to be diligent in his literary studies" (*Memoirs*, 69), Henry learned English and (later) studied Hebrew and Latin to grasp, translate, and interiorize the life-altering meaning of the Bible. Dwight lauded how Obookiah had "translated into his native tongue the whole of the Book of Genesis" (*Memoirs*, 78), a line-by-line process he facilitated ("of his own accord, without a regular instructor") by studying and translating from the Hebrew: "He had a peculiar relish for the Hebrew language, and from its resemblance to his own [Hawaiian], acquired it with great facility; and found it much less difficult to translate the Hebrew than the English into his native tongue" (*Memoirs*, 78). However, baffled and brought up short at times by some biblical passages, we can see how Henry was caught up in the difficult cross-textual process of *translation*, which in a kind of "de-canonizing" move into voicing foreignness "brings out all that is idiomatical, all that is customary, all that is quotidian, all that is nonsacred, all that is prosaic in the original."[52] The text so pidginized, at least momentarily, can become "de-canonized" and estranged of its sacred aura, rendered worldly, disjunctive, opaque, or mundane.

When Henry encounters a scriptural passage such as "in my father's house are many mansions" (John 14:2), he does not recognize the trope of mansions, nor can he grasp the prosaic phrase "goes to prepare a place" at the table (see epigraph to this chapter). At such times, translation falters word by word before linguistic gaps, foreignness, and cultural differences. But translation ('Ōpūkaha'ia became the first Hawaiian-English expert at this) also mediates cross-cultural gaps, haltingly—as in a world-estranging process of "linguistic mimicry" and innovative "pidginization."[53] Henry crosses the divide between text and meaning, context and event, world and subject in a way that distorts "our cosmological conversations with Hawaiians."[54] David Samwell, surgeon's mate on Captain Cook's last voyage to Hawai'i, noted the difficulty of eliciting even the simplest information from Native Hawaiians, never mind grasping their complex cosmology of Kū/Lono worship at Kealakekua Bay: "It must be remembered, that there is not much dependence to be placed upon these Constructions that we put upon [Hawaiian] Signs and Words which we understand but little of, and at best can only give a probable guess at their meaning."[55] When mimicry falters, mutual miscomprehension became a way of living with (and as) cultural otherness, for both Dwight and 'Ōpūkaha'ia.

The priestly 'Ōpūkaha'ia's "great inquisitiveness" (*Memoirs*, 33) and "inquisitive mind," as Dwight recounts many times, challenges what 'Ōpūkaha'ia reads and hears as naturalized signs, what hidden or assumed meanings he searches for, and what spellings and meanings of words he chooses to interrogate. At the same time, Henry "quoted passages [from Scriptures] appropriate to almost every subject of conversation" (*Memoirs,* 32) and carried (another minister noted) his Pocket Testament everywhere to keep busy, to remain "diligent in his literary studies," and to redeem the time (*Memoirs,* 69). Another minister at Andover seminary noted (miming Henry's ungrammatical eagerness in pidgin English) that "When he heard a word which he did not understand or could not speak, it was his constant habit to ask me, 'How you *spell?* How you *spell?*' And when I told him he never forgot" (*Memoirs,* 26). Speaking of Henry's studious work habits, a head minister from the American Board of Commissioners for Foreign Missions (ABCFM) concluded: " 'I have rarely if ever,' says Mr. Perkins [of Amherst], 'seen a person who seemed to set so high a value on time as Obookiah' " (*Memoirs,* 69). This is high Puritan praise for the disciplinary ethos of a transplanted Pacific islander, working with "praying famil[ies]" (*Memoirs,* 16) across a New England region where the "Waterbury watch" was driving citizens to standardize its working days and praying moments to a modern regime, as Timothy Dwight noted in his *Travels in New England and New York* (1821–1822). Called to a new life, 'Ōpūkaha'ia was not so much a protesting as a prophetic ethnic, figuring the future as a call to shape one's own vocation.[56]

Laboring to Convert

Reverend Titus Coan, who proved instrumental to the conversion of thousands of souls during worship services around Hilo in Hawai'i's "Great Revival" from 1839 to 1842, took a dim, dismissive, and (like Bingham) abjecting view of Native Hawaiians as sailors or potential workers.[57] These "indolent and unskillful natives," Coan wrote in his *Life in Hawaii: An Autobiographical Sketch of Missionary Life and Labors (1835–1881),* "knew nothing of the motto, 'Time is money.' So long as they were supplied with fish and poi, all was well."[58] Taro fields abounded across the island, as did aquaculture sites, and Hawaiian husbandry is praised by visiting explorers from Britain, Russia, and France. But colonial fetishes of native sloth are repeated with demonic relish in the missionary journals of Cochran Forbes in 1832, for example ("Indeed idleness appears to be *the great curse* of this people. . . . There is no publick clock in the town. And they will not work any more than just support from day to day which they can do in about 2 hours out of 24" [29–30]; and similar maledictions of race run through the missionary history of Sheldon Dibble published in 1843, as when it is claimed that the Hawaiian "is only thinking of some roots in the wilderness that may be good for food" rather than the aesthetic beauty of nature).[59]

Still, Titus Coan labored to convert natives to his mode of born-again Christianity and adopt, as cultural habitus, his own modern Calvinist regime of "Time is money." It was not an instant or automatic process. Relentlessly calibrating his calling to work in conversion at his church in Lahaina ("Yesterday was our communion when 138 souls were for the first time admitted to the Lord's table"), Reverend Cochran Forbes must lament (before he flees back, semi-impoverished, to his native Pennsylvania in 1847 and is released from ABCFM service) the sheer impossibility of the Hawaiian conversion task: "O heathenism! What hast thou done! Completely sapped the whole man! Hardly can Christianity elevate them from their dreadful heathenish torpor."[60] Henry's own scholarly, sailing, and farming labors had given the lie to such racialized views of "heathen" Hawaiian sloth or their unredemptive squandering of time and nature. But ministering in backsliding contexts, Forbes remains unconvinced of "conversion" for these ethnics.

This memoir of Henry Obookiah and its quoted relation, anecdotes, journal entries, and letters "will doubtless be interesting" as material "to all the readers of these memoirs," Dwight urges in the beginning of his collated text, because it can be "considered as the production of a heathen youth" (Memoirs, 3). "His own ideas and, in general, his own language will be preserved," Dwight claims (Memoirs, 3), meaning Henry's English with some Hawaiian scattered in it. Ever the self-effacing mentor and friend (he often effaces his own name into "an early friend"), Dwight aims to ensure the authenticity of native/convert voice, even when he searches for signs of abiding grace and the morphology (narrative sequence) of "true conversion." Henry is first quoted by Dwight on page one, describing the native war in which Henry lost his parents: "When Obookiah was at the age of ten or twelve, both his parents were slain before his eyes, 'in a war,' to use his own language, 'made after the old king [Chief Kalaniopu'u] died, to see who should be the greatest among them'" (Memoirs, 1). Much of the quest for signs of conversion is conveyed through handwritten letters and the journal written in Henry's own voice, who was by then writing a fluent, even elegant if Bible-drenched English.

This "interesting scene" of native savagery was recorded in Henry's ostensive words by Joseph Harvey and relayed, again, in Dwight's editing of the memoirs: it conveys the native eyewitness to native savagery, the slaying of parents right before a Hawaiian child who was then taken to live with the man who had slaughtered them, as ethical violations mount. The child Henry also sees his own infant brother slaughtered on his back and his aunt throw herself to her own death to escape his father's rival warriors (*Memoirs,* 5): " 'At the death of my parents,' he says, 'I was with them; I saw them killed with a bayonet—and with them my little brother, not more than two or three months old. So that I was left alone without father or mother in this wilderness world' " (*Memoirs,* 5). Isn't this native abjection of the native, but told in proto-Christian terms already, the native world recoded as a "wilderness world" for a pilgrim? Rescued, physically saved, Henry's life, even in his native land, shows signs of regeneration bespeaking the goodness and "designs" of God, "the hand of Providence" working in Pacific history already (*Memoirs,* 4). He is always "mercifully saved [even by rival natives] for purposes which will appear in the subsequent history" to become a born-again Christian convert (*Memoirs,* 5). Noting that Henry showed "deep solicitude for the conversion and salvation of others," Dwight compares Henry's letters and journal in the same context to the writings of "devoted Brainerd" (*Memoirs,* 58), meaning Reverend David Brainerd, a white American whose autobiography of his work with Native Americans had influenced many young people to serve the missionary cause (*Memoirs,* note 105). Henry, in some respects, had been *prefigured* to some New Englanders as just another Praying Indian. But his conversion went further than cultural expectation or fabricated code.

Global Missions, Pacific Natives

In a life-shaping event we can interrogate, this "minister's nephew (the minister of that place)," although apprenticed to become a Lono-worshipping kahuna at the site of Captain Cook's death at the hands of Hawaiians, Kealakekua Bay (*Memoirs,* 6), left Hawai'i for good, bound for the world of transpacific otherness and cross-cultural creativity along a line of outer-national flight. Seafaring Hawaiians were already working offshore on seal-hunting crews, as later on sandalwood and whaling ship crews.[61] Expert swimmers and wave riders, as Richard Henry Dana conveyed, Hawaiians had worked on ships back and forth to China and the Pacific Northwest, for which Hawai'i served as wintering port since the days of Captain Cook. Hawaiian sailors spread and communicated across the commercial-era Asia-Pacific, as can be seen from the cosmopolitan and broken-English-speaking kanaka who comes back from Australia and negotiates Tommo's release from native captivity in the lurid Marquesas of *Typee*.[62]

Writing the maritime history of a coastal state that for two hundred years had made the Bible its topo-spiritual guide and "the sea the material sustenance of Massachusetts," Samuel Eliot Morison recounts the first round-trip voyage from Boston to Canton by the *Columbia* in 1787–1790, which opened the Northwest Pacific fur market and enabled "the merchant adventurers of Boston to tap the vast reservoir of wealth in China." This first ship to China from the mainland United States rather spectacularly had contained a Hawaiian sailor on board. "A rumor ran through the narrow streets," Morison writes of globalizing postrevolutionary Boston, "that a native of 'Owhyhee'—a Sandwich Islander—was on board; and before a day was out, curious Boston was gratified with the sight of him, marching after Captain Gray to call on Governor Hancock. Clad in a feather cloak of golden suns set in flaming scarlet, that came halfway down his brown legs; crested with a gorgeous feather helmet shaped like a Greek warrior's, this young Hawaiian moved up State Street like a living flame."[63]

Hawai'i's ties to transpacific trade with China and Russia were so strong that by the time the American missionaries first landed in 1820, they found one of the chiefs, Kalanimoku, "decently clad" in "black silk vest, yellow Nankeen pants, shoes, and white cotton house, plaid cravat, and fur hat," while some of the female rulers at Kawaihae had over their heads "a huge Chinese umbrella" to go with "the nodding *kahilis* or plumed rods of the nobility."[64] Henry tells how his own ship, the *Triumph,* moved from Oregon to Macau, where, after securing permission from the British, it sailed into Canton harbor, and "we sold all our seal-skins and loaded our ship with other sort of goods, such as tea, cinnamon, nankeens [cloth], and silk," before returning to its homeport of New Haven in America (*Memoirs,* 9).

Over one hundred commercial ships had already called on the ports of Hawai'i between 1786 and 1820 by the time the fateful American sealing ship *Triumph* that would take Henry away to New England took anchor at Kealakekua Bay. This was the meaning-laden site of global infamy and cultural disruption where Captain James Cook had been slain in battle with Hawaiians in 1779. Before launching a missionary outpost to Hawai'i, the ABCFM had established strong ties to Asia-Pacific as a region of the group's primary evangelical concern, having sent missions to Burma in 1812, to Ceylon in 1816, and to India, Ceylon, and Palestine in 1819.[65] Such large-scale contexts of global-local interaction between East and West, Atlantic and Pacific, and outside and inside cultural frames were among the forces driving the priestly heir, Henry, to seek his conversion work in New England toward an extranational missionary project and homeland return that his death by typhoid fever would seemingly cut short in the winter of 1818.

British, Chinese, American, and Pacific Islander cultural influences had clashed and mixed in the mercantile Pacific, as Melville showed through the transnational crew of "mariners, renegades, and castaways" working the Pequod and, here and elsewhere in transoceanic sites, putting (as C. L. R. James saw) the Protestant work ethic to divergent postcolonial uses.[66] Such global-local contexts multiply interconnections between Asia-Pacific-influenced New England and New England-drenched Hawai'i over the "Americanizing" course of nineteenth-century Hawai'i.[67] Tied to the missionary project in Hawai'i, as we have seen through the Dwight family affiliations to the first Hawaiian convert, Yale College had long-standing ties to Asia, as its major benefactor and symbolic namesake, Elihu Yale, recycled his imperial fortune through the export of Madras textiles as an erratic administrator serving twenty-eight years in the British colony of India.[68] Yale's capital and cultural capital, in these intertwined pedagogies of theology and literature, were tied to successes in Asia and the Pacific, particularly India and Hawai'i.

Creating Reborn Selfhood along a Line of Flight

Leaving his native birthplace by fate or a fluke, Henry 'Ōpūkaha'ia was willing to risk forces of social ostracism, shame, solitude, deculturation, and death by the cold Atlantic or getting lost in the rains and markets of Canton. He left his birthplace along a line of flight from the Hawaiian polity and proved willing to break with his priestly uncle (who strongly opposed his leaving, as did his tear-filled grandmother, wondering why Henry would want to "go with people whom [you] know not" [Memoirs, 7]). Activating an ocean-crossing diaspora that, in effect, severed genealogy and geography from any prior "ontologization of place," Henry would seek "some other country" (Memoirs, 6) where an orphan from the troubled and globalizing Kona coast might better, or alternatively, build himself up and belong.[69] When Henry revisits "his early friend" from New Haven, Edwin Dwight, and says, "I want to see you great while: you don't know how you seem to me: you seem like father, mother, brother, all" (Memoirs, 76), the Hawaiian values of 'ohana and adoption (hanai) by an extended family have been given an uncanny transpacific resonance, as if Dwight can help dismiss the burden of native loss.

It is important to remember that Henry 'Ōpūkaha'ia, although he became the first known Hawaiian convert to Christianity in 1815, never legally became an American citizen; he never lost his desire to return to work as a minister in his homeland; and he never, more to the point of cross-cultural poetics, abolished his use of the Hawaiian language and customs. Indeed he spread, dialogized, formalized, and returned them to his homeland of Hawaiʻi. Even in his English-language "relation" of his life story ("history of his past life written by himself several years before his death" [3]) told to Joseph Harvey, Henry uses a Hawaiian word (*Memoirs*, 2–3) as he tells how his little brother was "pierced through with a Pahoa, a spear, while being carried on his back.[70] At such points, we need to unravel the text's garb of colonial conformity, its "unspectacular and nonmomentous" quality as writing to understand the difference Henry makes to Hawaiian literature and history, as read under a renewed understanding of cross-cultural claims.[71]

At the Heathen School in Wintry Connecticut

With Edwin Dwight, a recent graduate of the Divinity School of Yale College, now placed as first headmaster in charge of "Owhyhee boys at the Heathen School," the Foreign Mission School was founded in 1816 with the express purpose of training an array of Asian-Pacific sojourners and Native American peoples as so many "young men of many races to act as Christian missionaries among their own people." As Henry wrote in a letter to Amherst in 1817, "Our school is going on very regularly, and the scholars are making some progress in their studies. One of the members is become new born in Christ since he has been here, and I trust there is no small degree of happiness. He is now rejoicing in the hope of the glory of God" (*Memoirs*, 84). Conversion to becoming "new born in Christ," in the Hawaiian expression for it, meant achieving "ola hou" *(new life, again life)*.[72] If conversion and rebirth into this "new life" at the Foreign Mission School was not the direct aim of the curriculum, and the linguistic study and secular subjects like geography and geometry were quite important, still, it was an implicit effect in the scholarly project of preparing natives for work as missionaries to their own peoples. The mission of the foreign school aimed to make missionaries of the foreign students, converting natives eventually into missionaries serving their own people.

In the ten years of its existence, the school educated some one hundred students, including forty-three American Indians, twenty Hawaiians, thirteen white Americans, and the rest "mainly other natives of the Pacific, including two Chinese" as Sydney Mitchell writes in his history of Cornwall (quoted by Schutz in *Voices*, 87). The six-month Hawaiian missionary voyage from Boston in 1819 aboard the brig *Thaddeus* and related expeditions would soon prove the efficacy of the pedagogical project in cross-cultural translation and modern disciplines, even if the passage of time rendered it out of date or installed in the wrong place. (The Foreign Mission School was precipitously closed in 1826, as was well known, due to the scandal of two interracial marriages, which the rural townspeople could not tolerate [Schutz, 94] as threat of cross-cultural mongrelization.) Learning from New England modes, the periphery of Hawaiʻi was fast becoming the missionary center of inculcation, with schools founded at Lahainaluna on Maui in 1831 and the more white-affiliated Punahou on ʻOahu in 1841.

The Foreign Mission School in Cornwall, Connecticut (relocated in 1817 from nearby Morris, where it had started in 1816) which Henry Obookiah had attended for close to two years until his death (he was mostly taught while boarding and working in live-in "praying family" [Memoirs, 17] residencies in New Haven, Torrington, Goshen, Cornwall, Amherst, Andover, and Bradford, across which spread what Henry called "Gospel land" [Memoirs, 37]) was also called by the more abjecting term "Heathen School." Early and late, Henry became widely known through his Memoirs (and later representations of his impact on the missionary project in works by Hawaiian scholars and missionary memoirs and those closer to white mythology, such as James Michener's epic novel and movie Hawaii) as the "heathen" of color from the southern tropics who had proved convertible, learned the language, and mimicked the manners of the Yale Divinity School scholars, becoming de-nativized to a point yet capable of distinguished higher education, moral individualization, and modern nation-building all administered under the sign and subject-formation of Christian enlightenment. "[Through Obookiah] many have become interested for the benighted heathen, and satisfied that the conversion of them to Christianity is practicable" (Memoirs, 72) is how Reverend Nathan Perkins, a fundraising agent of the ABCFM, phrased Henry's textually crucial role as inspiring Hawaiian convert in a letter to Edwin Dwight written shortly after Henry's death.

As a reading of the Memoirs, in its geopolitical contexts shows, Henry acted the part of Christian convert and missionary to his own Hawaiian people in an exemplary (or representative) way, yet it was also full of mimetic contagion toward otherness (not to mention the conversion and missionary work of others) as well as of moments of estrangement, menace, and bafflement, keeping mixed-cultural ties to his own people and place as he came into the English language and New England manners of an educated pious gentleman. Henry's Hawaiian words on his deathbed, which Dwight records as "the parting salutation of his native language, 'Alloah o e.'—My love be with you" (Memoirs, 91), still haunt the text of his *Memoirs* at its closure and show that 'Ōpūkaha'ia's native language and customary ties to his people and transpacific bonds to place had never left but had stayed utmost (or subliminal) in his mind even as he turned this "aloha" practice into love of God, Hawaiian people in diaspora, and future-transforming dynamics of conversion.

Still, the language of Henry's Connecticut gravestone tells the narrative of this enlightenment plot, as does the conversion narrative of the *Memoirs,* which over-codes the past-breaking shape of Henry's story as the self-made subject who converted (turned away) from "idolater" to "Christian' life-call and a path towards modernity. As Dwight summarized the plot of *Memoirs,* Henry's life represented a successful journey from self-tormented sinfulness to the bliss and certainty of grace that gave signs of "decisive proof of true conversion" (*Memoirs,* 30). Later in the text, Dwight speaks of several conversations between Henry and diverse New England hearers "destitute of grace," which "made impressions which have terminated in an apparent conversion of the soul to God" (81). In other words, the converted Henry from the tropic sun, "this native of the South" (*Memoirs,* 101), by now had the power and drive to convert others to service, inwardness, and grace. The convert indeed was called to this practice of "becoming always converted."[73]

With mental gifts for reading and expressive talents for speaking, memorizing, and acting, Henry proved a master mimic in New Haven, as Dwight records, noting Henry's mimicry of American manners and speech gestures after he had cried out (in pidgin English) *"Who dis?"* "Obookiah noticed with uncommon acuteness and interest every singularity in the speech and manners of those around him; and in the midst of his own awkwardness, to the surprise of all, he suddenly began to show himself dexterous as a mimic" (*Memoirs,* 15–16). More broadly imitating the Protestant-ethnic habitus of pious labor, everyday efficiency, and studious self-reflection in keeping his own written journal, the native subject from the southern tropics and "Islands of the South" (*Memoirs,* 95) is reborn by 1815 into the expansive Pauline community of the Congregationalist ecumene, becoming in nine studious years a worthy New Englander "eminent for piety and missionary Zeal" yet remaining (as we still ponder) a "native of Owhyhee."

Henry's diaspora as an orphan was motivated in response to shifting geopolitics, as the local became in tangled in the global and Hawaiian cultural forces in the making of a modern nation under the sway of the Kamehameha lineage. 'Ōpūkaha'ia's parents and younger brother had been killed (before his eyes) in a war between Kamehameha I and Namakeha during the battle of Kaipaloa in 1797, when Henry was ten (*Memoirs,* notes, p. 99). One has to wonder whether the severe treatment of Henry's family, heirs to a priestly lineage at the Hikiau Heiau at Napo'opo'o on the shores of Kealakekua Bay, did not have something to do with mounting rivalry and "long-standing opposition between the king and the Lono priests of Kealakekua," which had been aggravated by Cook's visit (spectacularized by the Lono priests) during the destabilized reign of Chief Kalaniopu'u and led to the demotion of the Lono priests by Kamehameha, whose *mana* of political power was affiliated with the worship of Kū.[74] For Dwight, Henry's "departure from his native country" was part of an individual quest for "the happiness which the death of his parents had taken from him, and which nothing now to be found in his own country could supply" (*Memoirs,* 3). Christian family and friends would fill this need for an imagined genealogical community, one of consent not descent, spirit not blood. Captain Brintnall became a first surrogate father: "his kindness much delighted my heart, as if I was his own son, and he was my own father" (*Memoirs,* 6). This practice of adoption was common in Hawai'i.[75] Henry's uncle was going to become a surrogate father, as was the man who had slain his parents. Born again, and that several times, to phrase this in Emersonian terms of modern self-formation and cultural mobility, Henry would have many alternative fathers and brothers and would seek to create a different, more transnational community and cultural framework than the one into which he was born.

The coming of Captain Cook had radically impacted the native nation of Hawai'i as culture and polity. Reverend L. Desha, compiling a Hawaiian-language biography of *Kamehameha and His Warrior Kekuhaup'io* in the 1920s, recounts Kamehameha's battle at Kaipalaoa with the people of Namakea, which led to the latter's defeat and sacrifice to the war god Kū: "[Namakeha] was pursued and taken before Kamehameha as a captive and was offered as a sacrifice to Kuka'ilimoku, Kamehameha's war god. . . . This was also the battle in which the parents of 'Ōpūkaha'ia were killed as told in the story of Henry 'Ōpūkaha'ia [i.e., the *Memoirs*]."[76] This bloody battle of 1796 was Kamehameha's last on the Big Island; rival rulers on Oahu and Kauai capitulated, and as Desha writes, "thus he ["the moi Kamehameha"] became the supreme ruler of the entire archipelago" (*Kamehameha,* 451) and governed commoners and elite alike with justice and concern for the good of the land. His parents murdered and to the dismay of his priestly uncle, who took him under his mentorship, Henry broke with Hawai'i, but *still spoke and prayed in the Hawaiian language every chance he could* (as ultimately on

his deathbed) and showed care to speak to and nurture his fellow Hawaiians as they crossed his path, as through letter writing across New England. He kept this "aloha spirit" alive even in a wintry place.

Explaining the modern "kapu" taking sway against pre-enlightenment
beliefs and practices, Reverend Desha heaps scorn on dark practices of
the "kahuna" priests and their ancient Hawaiian practices (in other
words, Henry's specific caste): "This is about the belief of those ancient
people of our land when, sometimes, the old *kahuna* used the deadly poison *(apu koheoheo)*, black-magic prayers *pule ('umi)*, and power of
sending prayers *(pule ho'ounauna)*. These were the other actions performed by some of our race in those times which were not wondered at
by our ancestors" (*Kamehameha*, 325). Desha (who worked from 1884
to 1889 as a minister at the Naupo'opo'o Church, where Henry is now
buried) relativizes this indictment of Hawaiian practices, comparing
them to witch-burning mores of Puritan ancestors, and goes on to praise
Henry's break with idolatrous practices and his conversion to the modern. "The ancestors of the British race did likewise," Desha writes, "and
also the Christian worshippers of the American race [nation]. Some young
women were burnt because of the beliefs of some Americans in those
by-gone years. These actions were known in the land in which Henry
'Ōpūkaha'ia shed his tears for his beloved race [and their heathen prac-
tices], those tears which became the hand which knocked on the heart of
religious Americans" (*Kamehameha*, 324).

This local event of warfare was proof to missionary writers such as
Hiram Bingham and even the Kamehameha-ratifying history of Stephen
Desha, who recounts how "at the rebellion of Namakeha 'Ōpūkaha'ia's
parents were wickedly slain" by the forces of Kamehameha (*Kamehameha*, 401), that Henry *needed to break away*. Such modes of violence and bloody sacrifice are indicted as sins and power abuses, even as
they led to the building of a culture and nation (annexed by then as a
territory to America) that Desha admires. These post-contact modes of
violent vengeance cannot be separated from the larger global entanglement of Hawai'i into the political project of nation-making that Kamehameha I had been involved in (with the advantage of Western arms,
supplies, and ships) since the coming of Captains Cook and Vancouver
had alerted this multicentric Polynesian kingdom to the geopolitics of
imperial rivalry and the nexus of commercial contention from Hilo to
Canton.

By 1852, the ABCFM would famously declare that the Hawaiian Congregational Church was firmly established and could stand on its own for

funding and governance, even as the American missionary enterprise (already fluent in Polynesian languages and customs) had expanded its frontier to the Pacific Basin with Anglo and Hawaiian missionaries settled at Kusai and Ponape in the eastern Carolines as well as church stations in Tonga, Samoa, and Sumatra. And later generations of missionary offspring, as the proverb goes, came to do good and did very well for themselves indeed.[77] Mormons, Catholics, Pentecostals, Shin Buddhists, New Age yogis, Zen meditators, Muktananda, and Beat refugees from the mainland (like Albert Saijo) all would multiply their claims on the conversion of such modern Hawaiian subjects as Henry.

Racial Figurations

Through his conversion and death, Henry no longer bore the stigmatized "countenance" of racial darkness; instead, his convivial countenance counted Henry among the saved and the spectral, with a heavenly smile of conversion and assimilated belonging in the cold New England ground. Henry's life and death as reborn subject expressed the cross-racial if disembodied certainty of redemption and change. As Edwin Dwight writes of the earlier, savage-raised Henry in his *Memoirs of Henry Obookiah*, which was *the* book that proved crucial to motivating, funding, and framing the far-flung missionary enterprise to Hawai'i by the ABCFM in 1819, "When Obookiah was first discovered at New Haven, his appearance was unpromising. He was clothed in a rough sailor's suit, was of a clumsy form, and his countenance dull and heavy" (*Memoirs*, 13–14). In other words, Henry, at first appearance as secular sailor, bore the racialized "stigmata of otherness (name, skin color, religious practices" that marked the "insurmountability of cultural difference."[78] This marking for signs of darkness, dullness, and otherness Balibar connects to a categorical racism "at first sight."[79] Compassionate but white, Dwight cannot help but enact this *hate-at-first sight*. The first racial sighting was, in effect, a citing of time-honored Pacific stereotypes of savagery and inferiority that further human contact between teacher and student, friend and friend, and becoming brothers in the reborn spirit would finally overcome. Soon, the bodily stigmata of darkness and dullness had turned, vanished, and converted Henry into a creature of brightness and light, more "olive" then Negroid or Indian. The *us/them* binary of Euro-American raciology and saved/heathen was overcome in the before-and-after narrative of conversion, making them into us, in a transregional and cross-racial ecumene.

The break with savage ways was not that complete; indeed, the prodigious memory training to become a pagan priest under his uncle served Henry well in his subsequent language training and Bible study as well as his ability to learn and remember everything from abundant scriptural passages and maxims (like Paul's "let us *pray without ceasing*," as Henry recommended to a Greenfield friend in June 1817 [*Memoirs*, 83]) to the use of a farming tool like a scythe (*Memoirs*, 18) or the sober habitus of a minister. "Here [in farms around New Haven and Litchfield] I learned some sort of farming-business: cutting wood, pulling flax, mowing etc.— only to look at the other [once] and learn from them" (*Memoirs*, 18), Henry notes of his mimetic skills, a quality his elders and peers called "remarkable" (*Memoirs*, 18). Reverend Perkins wrote of Henry after his death that, as befits a priestly vocation in New England as well as back in Hawaiʻi for the priestly caste, "Prayer seemed to be his daily and nightly business" (*Memoirs*, 81). "Eminent for piety and missionary zeal," as the words say, Henry's Cornwall gravestone could have been written into scriptural typology and moral exemplum by Cotton Mather, though it probably was written by the no-less-eminent Reverend Dr. Lyman Beecher who preached to some didactic length at Henry's funeral along with Edwin Dwight who spoke more demurely at his Connecticut graveside. As mentioned above, only in 1993 were Henry's remains finally returned to Hawaiʻi to be reinterred in his native birthplace on the Big Island where some of his relatives still live and, for the most part, practice their humble Christian faith.

Later additions to the text by the American Tract Society's editions of the *Memoirs* in 1831 speak of "the sainted spirit of Henry" (*Memoirs*, 92) and add a poem that ratifies Henry's central role in the Hawaiian conversion project with the typology of canonization (*Memoirs*, 95):

> And thou, Obookiah! now sainted above,
>   Hast joy'd as the heralds their mission disclose,
> And the prayer has been heard, that the land thou didst love
>   Might blossom as Sharon, and bud as the rose.

As Edwin Dwight later comments, summing up the life of Henry Obookiah as a spiritual biography worthy of emulation and narrative circulation, "His form, which at sixteen [when he first arrived in New Haven in 1809] was awkward and unshapen, had become erect, graceful, and dignified. His countenance had lost every mark of dullness; and was, in an unusual degree, sprightly and intelligent. . . . His complexion was olive, differing equally from the blackness of the African and the redness of the Indian" (*Memoirs*, 76). As the lithograph prints of the five worthy Hawaiians around the Christian pedagogy and language training at Yale College made clear, these Hawaiians were made into gentleman on the white American model, and Henry was the brightest and worthiest of them all, the prototype of the native scholar: "His hair was black, worn short, and dressed after the manner of the Americans. . . . In his understanding, Obookiah excelled ordinary young men. His mind was not of a common cast" (*Memoirs*, 76).

The racial typology of this quasi-abolitionist framework (many of the missionaries came from homes on the underground railroad that gave slaves passage from the South to safety in the North)[80] became clear in a description of Henry proffered by Reverend Nathan Perkins of Amherst, a key agent of the ABCFM who had guided Henry on his sermon tour through New England to raise money for the foreign school ("The success of the solicitations was greatly promoted by the presence of Obookiah" [*Memoirs*, 68], Perkins knew) if only as a prelude to the missionary outreach to Hawai'i and across Asia.[81] As Perkins wrote, in a letter quoted by Dwight in the *Memoirs*, "Obookiah's visit to this part of the country was of essential service to the cause of Foreign Missions. It has silenced the weak but common objection against attempting to enlighten the heathen, that they are too ignorant to be taught" (*Memoirs*, 71). Perkins denaturalized this ignorance and racialized mode of categorizing native peoples (whom he calls "people of color") as a by-product of the degradation caused by the system of slavery and racial exploitation.

> This sentiment [of racial ignorance] has prevented much exertion. It had a wicked origin. We have first enslaved our fellowbeings, then degraded them by every menial service, deprived them of the means of mental development, and almost of human intercourse; and because, under this circumstances [sic], people of color are devoid of knowledge, we have hastened to the irrational conclusion that all of the heathen are a race of idiots. Adopting this conclusion, multitudes are utterly opposed to making any attempt to turn them from darkness to light (*Memoirs*, 71).

The conversion of Henry Obookiah, as well as his predilection to alter-imitation and his priestly drive for religious knowledge and language acquisition as tools of pragmatic-symbolic efficacy, had proved the enlightenment capacity of the native Pacific peoples, at least those from Hawai'i: "But the appearance of Obookiah has done much in this region [New England, especially the Connecticut River valley from New Haven to Amherst] to wipe off the disgrace thrown upon the heathen, and to remove the objection so often made. The proof he gave of talents as well as piety, carried conviction to many that the heathen had souls as well as we, and were as capable of being enlightened and christianized" (*Memoirs,* 71–72). The "benightened heathen" (*Memoirs,* 72) trapped in darkness, superstition, dullness, and backwardness, this very ignorance visible and stigmatized on Henry's skin and countenance, had proved a person "capable of being enlightened and christianized." Henry Obookiah was the fait accompli of conversion, as his tombstone narrative signified: "he became a christian" through the grace of God and his own piety, as much as through the mediation of language and decorum from teachers like Edwin Welles Dwight of Yale.

Henry had proved that so-called heathens from "the heath" of the tropical wilderness of Oceania are not representatives from "a race of idiots" but a field full of potential Christians, saved souls, grammarians, and future doctors. The object of the Foreign Mission School, established in 1816 under the auspices of ABCFM, made clear its goals of social uplift in a charter written under the leadership of Reverend Timothy Dwight,[82] president of Yale (whose household Henry had first stayed in after his arrival in New Haven and the instant care of Edwin Dwight, who so the famous missionary story goes found Henry weeping on the steps of Yale College): "The object of this school shall be the education of heathen youth in such a manner, as that with future professional studies, they may be qualified to become useful missionaries, schoolmasters, interpreters, physicians, or surgeons, among heathen nations, and to communicate such information in agriculture and the arts, as shall tend to Christianity and civilization" (quoted in notes to *Memoirs,* 97–98).

If Henry had been denaturalized of his own language and codes of animistic Hawaiian piety, he went on estranging his own prior training as pagan priest. As Henry wrote in a letter of 1812 from Amherst to a "dear Christian friend," "I hope the Lord will send the Gospel to the Heathen land where the words of the Savior never yet had been. Poor people worship the wood, and stone, and shark, and almost every thing their gods; the Bible is not there, and heaven and hell they do not know about it" (*Memoirs,* 27). Henry is referring to the gods and practices of his own Native Hawaiian peoples here, whom he portrays as heathen with idolatrous practices, such as shark-worship or consultation with owls and lizards as animistic sins, which Henry knew so well as a kahuna under the training of his priestly uncle at the Hikiau Heiau at Napo'opo'o on the shores of Kealakekua Bay on the Big Island.

To the amazement of his tutoring whites, Henry could mimic the gait, traits, and behavior of the gentleman at Yale to ludicrous effect and could enjoy such mimicry of his behavior to the point of bursting out in laughter (*Memoirs*, 16). Dwight records in the same passage that Henry could also imitate their mind-set, their set of beliefs and attitudes, which he soon adopted toward his own native peoples (*Memoirs*, 16):

> The same trait of character [dexterity as a mimic, ability to render behavior ludicrous via imitation and menacing repetition] was discoverable in the manner in which [Henry] was affected with respect to the idols of the heathen, upon the first instruction given him concerning the true God. He was at once very sensibly impressed with the *ludicrous* nature of idol worship. Smiling at the absurdity, he said, "Hawaii gods! they *wood, burn.* Me go home, put 'em in a fire, burn 'em up. They no see, no *hear,* no any *thing*"— then added, "*We make them—Our God,* (looking up,) *he* make *us.*" (*Memoirs*, 16)

Early nineteenth-century London Missionary Society accounts of missionary work in Polynesia and Asia made clear, through such reiterative abjection, that "idolatry was the hallmark of heathenism, and the destruction of idols conveniently marked conversion."[83] Hiram Bingham and Sheldon Dibble tell the history of the Sandwich Islands according to this binary schema of lightness and darkness but go beyond this narrative of modernization by racializing pagan subjects with a typological punishment in excess of caritas, closer to abject workings of the colonial stereotype and fetish repeating difference.[84] Even major scholars of Hawaiian customs history, such as Kamakau and Malo, would mimic Henry's idol-burning and stone-overthrowing gesture expressing for later generations or readers their turn to a textual God of theocratic totality.

By mimetic contagion and the symbolic reversal of power-flows whereby tactics of representing otherness and mimetic alterity can "share in or take power from the represented," Henry had also helped Edwin Dwight to laugh at or denaturalize some of his own taken-for-granted practices and cultural norms at a point where parody exposes and mocks construction as a mutual task.[85] Henry conveyed this power of mimicry to Dwight by imitating some of his speech habits and trying to teach him some Hawaiian cultural styles Dwight could not imitate or master, such as carrying water in gourdlike hands, even as Henry could not pronounce an "l" but turned it into an "r" (*Memoirs*, 14–15), "an important lesson taught as to the ease or difficulty with which things are done by us that are or are not natural to us, to which we have or have not, from early life, been accustomed." If this heathen "designed for a Pagan Priest" could be trained to become a Congregationalist minister and a missionary to his own people (called "lāhuikanaka" in the 'Ōpūkaha'ia monument erected to his memory in Napo'opo'o, where he practiced to become a Hawaiian priest), the instability of custom and relativity of belief, in global-local contact zones, also threatened Dwight and his fellow missionaries with mimetic contagion, with *becoming native*. So translated into polite or comical forms of mockery and menace, Dwight, like Henry, could also become subject to doubt and unbelief, daily anxiety mastered by over-coding, emplotting, arrangement, the temporary mastery of space and subjectivity that the *Memoirs* showed in its structuring of Obookiah's letters, diaries, and prior narratives into the shape of a converted ex-native life ("he became a Christian").

Comparative ethnology had to be learned on the fly, at times turning white missionaries in Connecticut into "proto-ethnographers" of native traits and savage modes.[86] Such makers of colonial knowledge, turning native subjects toward learning languages and cultural traits like reading, writing, and conversation, were also making native subjects over into willy-nilly voices of "pidgin anthropology."[87] This went along with the language training taught and was learned and dialogically exchanged at the Foreign Mission School, as later in contact zones of missionary outreach into Asia Pacific. "To learn a language," Stephen Greenblatt reminds us (in contexts of New World appropriation when native translators were often kidnapped to serve as Euro-American mediators of cultural, linguistic, and territorial possession), "may be a step toward mastery, but to *study* a language is to place oneself in a situation of dependency, to submit."[88] The missionaries were submitting to a self-altering process of "marvelous dispossession" by studying, learning, and writing Hawaiian—the first newspaper in Hawai'i, *Ka Lama Hawai'i* at Lahaina Luna School on Maui in 1834, was printed by and in Hawaiian.[89] Matters had come a long way from when Henry first declared, seeking a job in Kona, "Yet I know not what he [Captain Brintnall] says to me, for I could not speak the English language" (*Memoirs,* 6).

Crossing the Pacific to live with praying families in New England, Henry 'Ōpūkaha'ia, through his narrated conversion in the *Memoirs,* started Pacific island cultures down the lava road from Kona and Hilo to Damascus and Rome, as back to Suva and Oceania. He did not become a novelist or poet, just a journal-keeper, letter-writer, fundraiser, and *ad hoc* sermon-giver. Still, this priestly Hawaiian activated a process of "becoming semiotic," translating a dynamic of self-fashioning I will discuss more broadly as an American pragmatic ethos in the next two chapters. Torn from history and native culture, Henry 'Ōpūkaha'ia did not live on to explain where these mimetic technologies (like writing, reading, translating, representing, and sermonizing) he had acquired might lead his people. Nor could he know where these tools of modern alterity would take the "beloved community" of mainland Salvationists and diasporic Hawaiians into which he had been transplanted and reborn as a writing subject embodying his own version of a "pidgin anthropologist" to the New Englanders in their turn to the Pacific Ocean.

CHAPTER TWO

"Henry, Torn from the Stomach"

Translating Hawaiian Conversion and Rebirth into Dynamics of Outer-National Becoming

when they are converted to your gods
do you know who they are praying to
do you know who is praying
    —W. S. Merwin, "Conqueror"[1]

"In Latin, nobles were called *ingenui,* well-born, as if from *indigeniti,* indigenous, which was then shortened to *ingeniti,* inborn. Indigenous clearly meant the natives of a land [in Rome or Greece], and *dii indigetes* its native gods, which meant the noblemen of the heroic cities: for they were called gods, and the Earth was their mother, as we have seen."
    —Giambattista Vico, *New Science*[2]

"Be Always Converting..."

"Be always converting, be always converted"—that was what the Puritan minister Thomas Shepard urged the First Church of Cambridge, Massachusetts, at the end of his *Ten Virgins* sermon series, around 1640, as he reminded them—as John D. Barbour argues in his study of "deconversion" as the loss of faith and mounting eruption of narrative uncertainty—that "Puritan piety requires not simply conversion, but repeated reconversion" in an often punishing process of self-examination, uncertainty, trauma, dismantlement, public testimony, humbling, and loss.[3] *Be always converting, be always converted* serves as mandate of subject-formation, from the earliest forms of American expression down to the hyperliterary present, still, as I have been urging in this study. This drive to become "always converting" was the case even as this morphology of conversion spread across the Pacific to Hawai'i and later took root in a conversion-driven site like Korea, with a stress that needs to be placed (as urged in my introduction) more on the gerundive present-tense *(be always converting)* than on the past preterite conviction of "saved" in grim certainty *(be always converted)* as did occur, spookily at times in figures like Cotton Mather or Hiram Bingham, in the diasporic Puritan elect.

The "turn" toward the energies of rebirth implicit in the English-language verb *convert* implies as much this process of "turning from" old beliefs and forms of selfhood as it does the struggle of "turning toward" new ones. Conversion enacts a process of self-formation that will open up the subject to an ethos of change and to the regenerative influx of new knowledge and maybe even to the long-awaited beatitudes of grace. *No knowledge without conversion* is the implicit mandate driving this conversion plot, right from the world outset, from the Sermon on the Mount down to our own New Age era of plural calls, atheistic mores, and diverse agendas.

In the Augustinian conversion experience, long influential among New England Puritans and their American offspring, the core event of "conversion" (recalling the turn toward *metanoia* or "repentance" in the Greek) depends on the self's action of this "turning," in the root religious sense, at once a *turning* of the will *toward (ad)* as well as *with (con)* God. Kenneth Burke, elaborating the Latinate power of "vert-family" actions in his language-as-symbolic-action reading of Saint Augustine's *Confessions,* tracks the movement from "perversion" (false loves, pagan gods) toward "adversion" (rejected beliefs, inadequate philosophies) into "conversion." Burke invokes the predicament of the Old Testament prophet Jeremiah to capture this turning of the will not so much *toward* as *with* God's own turning of the subject (con/version) around toward him: " 'Turn thou me, and I shall be turned' (*converte me et convertar—Jeremiah* 31:18)."[4] "Since the work hinges about a conversion," Burke notes, "as might well be expected, the whole vert-series is particularly active (adverse, diverse, reverse, perverse, eversion, avert, revert, advert, animadvert, universe etc.)."[5]

Perhaps the Los Angeles folk-rock group the Byrds were tapping into this conversionary power of *turning/returning* when they took a folk song from Pete Seeger's album *The Bitter and the Sweet,* with lyrics from passages in Ecclesiastes (3:1–8), and set it to electronic mandolins and twelve-string guitars, in the drug-hazy days of 1965, when all such didactic "messages" seemed passé or lost in the jingle-jangle dawn of Dylanesque newness: "To everything, turn! turn!, turn! / There is a season, turn! turn! turn! / And a time to every purpose under heaven." But very often, as is the case with Saint Augustine's returning to haunt Dylan's dreams and ballads with saintly specters looming up against the midnight glass of our neo-Roman Empire, the past looms up ahead of modern selfhood and calls out for action *(repent/convert/become reborn).*[6]

This "turning" process of subliminal or willed transformation into a "twice-born" subject of beatitude ("saintliness") is the psychological action of change and renewal William James puts at the core of the "conversion experience," gradual or sudden, in *The Varieties of Religious Experience* (1902). Pluralizing conversion as a modern psychological option of uttermost inner importance, James noted the preoccupation with the rejected past of this old worldly self, "so that conversion is '*a process of struggling away from sin rather than a striving toward righteousness.*' "[7] Here, as elsewhere in his world-famous Edinburgh lectures on the morphology of conversion, James was drawing on the studies and data given to him by Stanford professor of education Edwin Diller Starbuck, whose *Psychology of Religion* (1899) was the first to propose the category of "counter-conversion" (as far as I can tell) to signify the crucial possibility (in James's words) of "the transition from orthodoxy to infidelity" that haunted nineteenth-century modernity and its mounting technologies of selfhood and change.[8] "Religion," James concluded, became "only one out of many ways of reaching unity [and enacting] the process of remedying inner incompleteness and reducing inner discord," via the private or inward experience of conversion, after "a period of storm and stress and inconsistency" lived through by the subject.[9]

Be always converting, be always converted at once signified the grounds of self-torment as well as a site of psychic renewal as this took place across Victorian England. Here, across diverse contexts of modernity in the secular age, "reconverting" Christian subjects moved toward, or away from, such modes of secularism and doubt to embrace belief (or the other way around).[10] Surrounded on one side by *deconversion* (the abandonment of a prior faith in false or inferior gods, as when Saint Augustine turns from the Manicheans or John Henry Newman turns from lukewarm mores of Anglicanism to Roman Catholicism during the Oxford Movement). On the other side of modernity, conversion was haunted as well by *counter-conversion* (meaning, the pluralist possibility of a secular inscription into nonreligious modes of meaning-making), since any conversion was far from a unilateral or done deed.[11] It commonly proved easier to be *always converting* than to be *always converted*, as even the tears of Saint Peter lastingly proved in his often cowardly or shamefaced failure before the calls of the tender and beaten-down Jesus. This instability proved so even in the most pious and earnest subjects—for example, the first Hawaiian Christian convert, to whom we once again turn.

"Designed for a Pagan Priest"

"Designed for a Pagan Priest" while growing up in his homeland of
Hawai'i, as the tombstone in the covered-bridge town of Cornwall, Connecticut, signifies his life story, Henry 'Ōpūkaha'ia (c. 1792–1818) arrived in the United States at New Haven in 1808. But living, studying,
fund-raising, and preaching across this God-drenched area of "praying
families" in New England, he had become a born-again Christian, in
training to become a minister, by 1815. His studious habits and life of
piety and warmth helped to generate the founding of the Foreign Mission
School in Cornwall, and, so the story of his New England Congregationalist acclaim went, after his death in 1818 (as the monument to his work
in Napo'opo'o, Hawai'i, signals), this first Hawaiian convert to Christianity had "inspired the first American Board Mission to Hawaii in 1820."
Torn from the mores of native life and transported across the Pacific into
modern modes of American worldliness, Henry's life-project embodies a
story of two cultures, languages, and countries, interacting in a far-flung
Hawaiian and New England global diaspora of outer-national becoming
that produced something wondrous, uneven, tormented, and new. Moving
from Hawai'i to New England, and from training to become a "kahuna"
to training to become a minister, we might say that Henry 'Ōpūkaha'ia
went from *becoming a priest to becoming a priest,* but the syntax and
specifics of this spirit-drenched vocation tell a larger story of divergent
cultures, one that helps to unpack what we mean by the mandate to "rebirth" in America.

Empowered by the troping language tactics of conversion and the
mimetic tactics of modernity, Henry's call to vocation represents a process
of subjective becoming, global interconnection, and transformation-via-
conversion that is not reducible to colonization and voice-abolishment,
nor to a process of assimilated Americanization. It would be better to see
this process of conversion as the "transmigration" of meanings across the
Pacific and as a translation to and from New England Christianity, across
regions and codes and across eras, thus enacting what contemporary
Mohawk poet James Thomas Stevens has deemed his transtribal " 'sui-
translations,' translations for the self," whereby familiar biblical passages
or native songs become strange and new when translated in between
Hawaiian and pidgin English.[12] With aloha, *mana,* stylistic cunning, and
talents for mimicry of others and for self-alteration, Henry fashioned
his life into a narrative of "rebirth" [see frontispiece photograph from
the Cornwall Library collection]. Bilingual and polycultural, Henry

'Ōpūkaha'ia helps us to see the possibility of life-becoming and alter-imitation in the by-now-global morphology of American conversion.

Making the English language translation of the Bible even more foreign than the Greek or Hebrew, Henry 'Ōpūkaha'ia puts transliteralizing questions to biblical texts in his pidgin English and native Hawaiian that open passages to translational gaps and Pacific earthly practices linking mansion to hut, kahuna to forces of migrancy and a change of place: "What our Saviour mean," said he, "when he say, 'In my father's house are many mansion—I go prepare a place for you.' What he mean, *I go prepare a place?*'" as Henry 'Ōpūkaha'ia challenges Edwin Dwight to explain his tasks as priest.[13] His question resonates with the pragmatism and bewilderment of a transpacific immigrant, a Hawaiian newcomer into the taken-for-granted genteel culture of New Haven. In Milton Murayama's local Hawaiian novels portraying three generations of Japanese immigrant workers on the sugar plantations of Maui—*All I Asking for Is My Body, Five Years on a Rock, Plantation Boy,* and *Dying in a Strange Land*—when the aging father of the Oyama family, Isao Oyama, prepares (in elegant Japanese calligraphy) for his own funeral service to be held at Pepelau Methodist Church in Lahaina, he chooses a telling scripture from the same John 14:1–7: "Let not your heart be troubled. I go and prepare a place for you." His wife, Sawa, the storyteller and all-binding heart of the family, shrewdly taunts her husband on his choice from the Bible (she herself had stayed a Shin Buddhist on the plantation and in California), "Ah, you're talking like an immigrant!"[14] Henry, too, had been talking (also in Hawaiian Creole English) like a concerned immigrant thinking of other immigrating Hawaiians who were about to enter Connecticut or the promised land for that matter still asking about the enigmatic Jesus: "What he mean, '*I go prepare a place*'?" Murayama, himself a diasporic writer from Hawai'i to New York City and San Francisco, would recognize the concern for immigrant others and the pragmatic literalism of Henry's (or his father's) query in the transpacific translation of this messianic parable. Maybe, as one Native American autobiographer (Charles Eastman) later put this, quoting a Sioux elder to the cross-cultural effect that, "Jesus was an Indian."[15]

Fleeing his broken family as an orphan to become a sailor on the ship *Triumph* coursing "on a sealing voyage [from New Haven and New York] to the Pacific Ocean and China" (*Memoirs,* 100), Henry first became a seafaring diasporic Hawaiian in 1809, sailing to New York via stops on the fur-gathering Pacific Northwest and in the textile and ceramic markets of China. The portrait of Henry Obookiah on the cover of his *Memoirs,* dressed in the suit and linen cravat of a Yale gentleman, circulating the globe as a pro-Christian text just ten years after he left his native country, soberly (if less spectacularly, in its own textual way) manifested Hawai'i's global-local and Atlantic-Pacific ties and cross-cultural circulations. In the nation of Hawai'i, Henry was ranked with "the common people," although his slain mother had been related to the family of the ruling chief. Like some transpacific Joseph, he escaped two exposures to violent death among his own people (*Memoirs,* 1, 4) and was rescued and transformed (so his biographers declared) at the hand of providence for the destiny of transnational conversion.

Used to the multilayered density of the Hawaiian religious language, prayer, ritual, and various forms of chant, Henry 'Ōpūkaha'ia had been in training to become a *kahuna* (usually translated into English as "priest") on the Big Island of Hawai'i, where the powerful Kamehameha lineage of Royal Chiefs held sway and first consolidated the islands into a modern nation-state after the coming of British ships to the Pacific islands. So this careful mimesis of sacred texts, rituals, codes, and scriptures filled with *manna/mana* was a fit calling. Henry's life embodied mimicry of religious habits by self and other. Conversion, in such bicultural contexts, activates dynamics of translation and cross-coding in a process of semiotic alteration and estrangement from givens of place and language that cannot be reduced to colonial silencing or native betrayal. Narrating conversion in different passages of his journals and memoir, Henry (to be sure) writes himself as a born-again subject who declares and preaches his way into the Christian community of enlightenment, universal singularity, and redemption that had spread across the globe since the evangelical times of Paul and the conversion of Constantine. Rebirth very much presumes a performative speech act. Such a conversion enacts terms of newness sharing (in the counter-worlding to Empire terms of Alain Badiou) *as event* in "the same universality of address, the same global wandering" that motivated Saint Paul to visit fearlessly, like some militant figure, the ends and edges of the Roman Empire as conversion sites.[16]

We can approach the power of 'Ōpūkaha'ia's *Memoirs* by reading its language of "rebirth through Christ" as haunted by forces of American incorporation, as well as by moves to express particular lines of Hawaiian resistance, flight, transformation, and critique. The *Memoirs* evince tactics expressing domination as well as challenge, its utterances refracting power in more than one context, at home and abroad. The text shows talents for mimicry and menace and evokes cross-cultural dialogue and mimetic fascination. "Parts of these [Hawaiian] prayers [Obookiah] often repeated to gratify the curiosity of his friends, after he came to this country. They regarded the weather, the general prosperity of the island, its defense from enemies, and especially the life and happiness of the king," as Dwight noted of Henry's priestly background and his rich Hawaiian training in prayer, exorcism, and ritual that aptly prepared and suited him (we could now see) in his vocation to become a Congregational minister called to spread the language of the Gospels (*Memoirs*, 3).[17] Before bolting on a ship for America, Henry had been in training at Hikiau shrine on Hawai'i, which belonged to the paramount chiefs of Hawai'i, and in particular where he resided with his uncle at Kakooa (now Napo'opo'o) "was dominated by the priests of Lono and their entourage."[18] After the Kū-affiliated chiefs of sacrifice and war got entangled with the Lono-worshipping fertility priests following the disturbed ritual dynamics of Captain Cook's visit, homage, and death, Henry's family was caught up in the drive to hegemony by Kalaniopu's fierce heir, Kamehameha I, and Henry's family was slain by opposing warriors.

The *Memoirs* represents, in effect, a "mo'olelo" (as it was called in its first translation into Hawaiian in 1867, meaning *story*) or "ho'omana'o" *(remembrance)* written by a subjected native born in the bloody aftermath of this unstable era. Moving between Hawai'i and the Atlantic cost of America more than between one island and another or to the Pacific coast or the Northwest as became commonly the case, 'Ōpūkaha'ia is at once fleeing from and toward these altering modes of subjection and domination. Another of the students in the Foreign Mission School, George Tamoree (Kaumuaalii) was son of the paramount chief of Kauai island, Kaumuaalii, who alone among the other island chiefs resisted (even soliciting the help of Russian forces in 1815) the attempt by the Hawai'i Island chief Kamehameha to unify the islands under his arms-backed rule. Although he had been early baptized, George was not a lasting convert and (reversing the rebirth mimesis) fought as a common sailor for the United States in the War of 1812: his return to Hawai'i was full of drunken, unruly behavior, so his father ceded all his lands to King Liloliho and left in 1824 nothing to his heir, who fought for but failed to recover the land.[19]

Mark Twain, who declared that any "plain unvarnished history that takes the romance out of the Hawaiian killing of Captain Cook's assassination" would judge this an act of "justifiable homicide," became sympathetic to Hawaiian subjects and was fascinated by another converting (and backsliding) Hawaiian, as he was by that "sensitive savage," Henry 'Ōpūkaha'ia.[20] "Obookia was converted and educated, and was to have returned to his native land with the first missionaries, had he lived," Twain wrote in 1866. "The other native youths made the voyage, and two of them did good service, but the third, Wm. Kanui, fell from grace afterward, for a time, and when the gold excitement broke out in California, he journeyed thither and went to mining, although he was fifty years old." William gained six thousand dollars, went bankrupt after the collapse of Page, Bacon, and Company, and as Twain ruefully concludes of this Protestant ethnic seeking, gaining, and losing a capitalist fortune, "the blighting hand of poverty was laid upon him in old age and he had to go back to preaching again."[21] The bank had cleaned him out of money but *not* of belief or soul: "One's heart bleeds for him," Twain admitted over William's obituary notice.

Read both as native memoir and as biographical tract, the *Memoirs* needs to be situated in dual relation to the entangled global/local polities and discrepant belief-schemes of America and Hawai'i. Shorn of father and mother, Henry longed to break from this factional Hawai'i at an early age, as he first recounted in *A Narrative of Five Youths from the Sandwich Islands,* that fund-raising pamphlet of as-told-to narratives or "relations" compiled by Reverend Joseph Harvey from Goshen in 1816 (Henry's part soon becoming a major source-text for the *Memoirs* of 1818). "While I was with my uncle, for some time I began to think about leaving that country [Hawai'i] to go to some other part of the world," Henry recalls. "I did not care where I shall go to. I thought to myself that I should get away, and go to some other country, probably I should find some comfort, more than to live there without father or mother" (*Memoirs,* 6). Thinking it was better to go the diasporic route outward across the Pacific than stay rooted in a place he had seen full of warfare, displacement, caste contempt, bloodshed, and rival blood claims to status and power, young Henry (who was either sixteen or twenty-one, depending on his birth date by American or Hawaiian sources [*Memoirs* notes, 99]) offered himself as a ship's hand to Captain Caleb Brintnall. Although he "could not speak the English language," Henry met an unnamed sailor on board the *Triumph* (it was not Thomas Hopu, "soon to be my fellow-traveler" [*Memoirs,* 6] whom he befriended) who could speak what we now call a nautical register Pacific Pidgin English and helped to secure from the captain Henry's passage to the Pacific Northwest, China, New York, and New England. Some 250 Pacific islanders sailed voluntarily or were "blackbirded" on such Euro-American ships across this era, and they worked like "double ghosts" on board, not fully recognized by their own people nor, in far-flung global diaspora from the Pacific Northwest and New England to China and Australia, by their new nations as legal subjects.[22]

This is to give an unusual postcolonial valence to conversion than is usually the case in such scenes of contact and white pedagogy. Admittedly, for generations of American Puritans evangelizing by Bible, dictionary, and gun "our Indian" subjects in the wilderness-errands of New England, "the project of conversion, like the project of war, [meant] eradication," as Mitchell Breitwieser has described this mournful practice in his study of Mary Rowlandson's much-discussed captivity narrative. Conversion was part of a large-scale and at times genocidal attempt to decompose the cultural integrity of any alternative system of customary godhead: to render them, by typological conversion and warfare, at best into mimetic copies, as "Praying Indians" in the wilderness enclaves of piety and terror that spread across New England.[23] In mimetic aspects, even Rowlandson's captivity with Indians in Massachusetts enacts her embrace of certain Indian-like states of becoming and her captivity narrative is written in passages of antitypological flight, what Breitwieser shrewdly calls "unprecedented and unsanctioned counter-conversions."[24]

Yet "the gods of the cannibals will be a cannibal," ex-minister of New England Unitarianism Ralph Waldo Emerson reminded modern Americans in the cross-cultural speculations of "Worship" in the industrial era, warning (around the time of the Civil War) that "the interior tribes of our Indians, and some of the Pacific islanders, flog their gods, when things take an unfavorable turn."[25] But for Emerson, one Euro-American figure of elected beatitude, as agent of self-relying energy and global empowerment (like Michelangelo in the Vatican or Charles Wilkes leading exploration of the American Pacific), was "worth all the cannibals in the Pacific."[26] In "Power," Emerson's comments on Irish and German immigrants were no less dismissive of racial disposition, seeing them as close to the guano they worked upon. The right-stuff of Christian interiority, rephrased as "self-reliance" on the godhead within, seemed at times an all-too-Anglo disposition in Emerson or Thoreau, in their calls to America as land of perpetual selfhood. Still, Henry went on searching for pious signs in his journals and sermons: he had learned to examine if not to flog—to expend and empower—himself in the guilt-ridden, melancholy, yet self-creating language of Christian subject-formation. His *Memoirs* endeared him to the theosophical culture of New England in its Asian-Pacific world outreach and entanglement of Indians and cannibals into the "be always converting" morphology of conversion.

Mark Twain's portrayal of Henry ʻŌpūkahaʻia in his Sacramento journalism of 1866 is richly sympathetic to the converted native as "The Hero of the Sunday School Books," even if marred by tropes of savagery and colonial abjection toward this "sensitive savage." Twain's report is sent back to Sacramento from Kealakekua Bay, loaded Big Island site where Cook was slaughtered and Henry's ancestors had worshipped the fertility god Lono:

> The high chief of this temple—the priest who presided over it and roasted the human sacrifices—was uncle to Obookia, and at one time that youth was an apprentice priest under him. Obookiah was a young native of fine mind, who, together with three other native boys, was taken to New England by the captain of a whale ship during the reign of Kamehameha I, and were the means of attracting the attention of the religious world to their country and putting it into their heads to send missionaries there. And this Obookia was the very same sensitive savage who sat down on the church steps and wept because his people did not have the Bible. That incident has been very elaborately painted in many a charming Sunday School book— aye, and told so plaintively and tenderly that I have cried over it in Sunday School myself, on general principles.[27]

Twain admits in other passages that Native Hawaiians might have been better off never to have learned of Christian guilt and sin, that whole missionary apparatus: "How sad it is to think of the multitudes [of Hawaiians] who have gone to their graves in this beautiful island and never knew there was a hell!"[28] But as he ponders the site of Lono worship and recalls savage rites, Twain summons admiration for Obookiah and mockery toward pre-modern ways, in a *before/after* narrative of conversion from "old" to "new" man: "This was the same Obookia—this was the very same old Obookia—so I reflected, and gazed upon the ruined temple with a new and absorbing interest. Here that gentle spirit worshiped; here he sought the better life, after his rude fashion; on this stone, perchance, he sat down with his sacred lasso, to wait for a chance to rope in some neighbor for the holy sacrifice; on this altar possibly, he broiled his venerable grandfather, and presented the rare offering before the high priest, who may have said, 'Well done, good and faithful servant.' It filled me with emotion."[29] Twain's "sensitive savage," altered into a New England priest, still seems to have native flesh dripping from his mouth, even as he learns altar rites of ecumenical sacrifice and biblical redemption.

"Torn from the Stomach" into Michener's Novel

Reflecting on the connections between the portrait of a converted homeland-returning Hawaiian youth, Keoki Kanakoa, in James A. Michener's outsized novel *Hawaii*,[30] and the real-life model, Henry 'Ōpūkaha'ia, in the praying families and Foreign Mission School of Connecticut, Larue W. Piercy retells this glorious story of American acculturation and care as the starting point for the missionary project. A transplanted resident from New York to Kailua-Kona and historian of Mokuaikaua Church, Piercy begins his Christian saga with "The Fateful Life of Henry Obookiah" as motivating origin for these "descendants of the Puritans [who would not] let Henry's precious goals [of converting his fellow Hawaiians] go unfulfilled."[31]

Piercy recounts how this orphaned Hawaiian youth (first Hawaiian convert to Christianity) had sailed away from warring factions of his savage life on the Kona coast in 1808 to become an exemplary student of Yale College mentors. Over the course of the next ten years (before his death by typhoid fever in Cornwall, Connecticut, in 1818), these various mentors (like the learned New England preachers Edwin Dwight and Lyman Beecher) taught him English, codes of American-genteel manners, the habitus of being a scholarly gentleman, and some Hebrew and Greek, as well as the world-transforming tactics and born-again methodology of salvation. Expert at mimicry of Western alterity and the mimesis of genteel forms, as Dwight noted with some amazement (like Darwin on his landfall with the natives at Tierra del Fuego in the 1830s), Henry learned this path to self-mastery well. Destined not to be sacrificed to forces of tribal rivalry on his home island of Hawaii but to become civilized in the scholarly training ground of New Haven, so the story of conversion into Anglo-American selfhood goes, "ʻŌpūkahaʻia became Henry Obookiah."[32] "Henry Obookiah was the name he became known by [in New England]," Piercy recounts, "but that was the English spelling of his Hawaiian name, which for some reason means 'ripped belly.' "

Does such a pagan-era Hawaiian surname like *Obookiah* lastingly denote (as it does for Piercy) that Henry's belly *(ʻōpū)* was actually ripped open *(kahaʻia)*, reflecting some inexpressibly savage practices of disfigurement where reason cannot enter? Or was the name of this pre-conversion Henry more likely a reflection of the long training of his priest-caste family genealogy from the Big Island region of Kau? That is, his Hawaiian family name signified a way of connecting to his people and place by such a pungent name-sign, *Opu-kaha-ia* (as the learned Hawaiian historian Samuel Kamakau spells it), for having cut open a rival warrior's belly? Like many of the literary-historical speculations in *Hawaii, Truth Stranger Than Fiction: The True Tales of Missionary Troubles and Triumphs Fictionized by Michener,* Larue Piercy's rendering of Henry's Hawaiian surname gets it half-right. His is a work of Americanizing narrative reflecting the canonical work of his idolized Michener, whose Cold War-era novel *Hawaii* might as well pass as teleological history as seen from some God's-eye "epic" viewpoint of American manifest destiny to redeem Asian and Pacific sites from Hawaiʻi to Burma and Japan. This Anglo-global translation of Henry Obookiah into English surname offers a compound of liberal history, ethnographic presumption, and white fantasy reflecting the normality of an Americanizing epic.

A Catachrestic Naming: "Henry, Torn from the Stomach"

"Henry, Torn from the Stomach" (the literal translation of Henry's name from the Hawaiian into English) will be invoked throughout this study as a catachrestic renaming that bespeaks, in material and tropological ways, how the youthful, brave, and pious Henry was torn from prior Hawaiian contexts of his upbringing on the Big Island, cast across the Pacific waters to contact zones in Canton and New Haven, thus becoming a world-diaspora figure of vanguard modernity, outernational quest, and hybrid rebirth. Torn from the stomach of his Hawaiian homeland upbringing, as it were, Henry can be seen to stand for and embody a kind of pidginized cross-cultural ethnography and translational learning resonant with risk, mutuality, transformation, and humility. As a figure of world rebirth, Henry Obookiah (as his mentors Romanized his name) stands for a representative yet fully remarkable story of how American newness enters the world and change happens linking far and near, New England and Oceania, past and present, as well as subject and world in a trajectory of alter-becoming. In the literary realm, Henry's writings impact and show up in Twain's Hawaiian travelogue journalism, and this reborn subject is later figured as a modern protagonist in the 956 pages of Michener's novel of multicultural fusion, serving as a prefigurative hero for the literatures of statehood. This far-fetched metaphor (which is the root meaning of "catachresis") suggests an "abuse" of the literal terms of ordinary-language naming, as George Puttenham called it in *The Arte of English Poesie*. Calling upon the return of "Henry, Torn from the Stomach" would be a way of rescuing Henry from two centuries of neoliberal misreading or abuse and/or postcolonial native disuse as sublated subject of Empire.[33] To be sure, Michener's history-trumping epic novel, *Hawaii,* actually compounds the life-experiences of *five* diasporic Hawaiian youths into the racy archetypal portrait of *one backsliding Hawaiian* drawn back into incestuous forms of pagan love and sin who nonetheless sets his native nation of Hawaii Nei on the path to conversion. Henry becomes a prefigurative trope or incarnated figure for what Michener calls the "golden men" of Hawaiian liberal statehood, multicultural post-orientalism, and the carrier of a prolonged process of assimilation-by-Americanization.[34]

In the cross-cultural and trans-historical contexts of modern converting, "Henry, Torn from the Stomach" serves as a far-fetched trope (retranslation) for this 'ōpū (stomach, bowels) kaha (cut, tear, operate) 'ia (past tense) Hawaiian man known (in American English) as Henry Obookiah, whose wayfaring life, scholarly regime, conviction of aloha, and profound conversion to Christianity, in 1815, began the long process of converting and counter-converting native subjects in Hawai'i and the American Pacific.[35] On his deathbed, 'Ōpūkaha'ia is famously said to have uttered "the parting salutation of his native language, 'Alloah o e.' My love be with you" (Memoirs, 91). In another twist on his family name, 'ōpu does not just mean "stomach" but can also connote "heart" or heart-felt conviction, as in the traditional Hawaiian proverb "E ōpu alii" (Have the heart of a chief). Obookiah, in the English translation, turns a stomach into a "book," an O-book where the Anglo name of God is written into the flesh and Hawaiian name of Henry. Obookiah thus typifies the fallen native soul destined to be converted to mores of these New England people of the book. My metaphor would chart a differing metamorphosis for Henry, one in which conversion embodies a trajectory of becoming to newness: the transformation of self-and-world via the mimesis of alterity.

Read as such in its topological "afterlife" as meaning, the diasporic life of Henry 'Ōpūkaha'ia/Obookiah can be understood as representative of transpacific forces, charismatic mixtures, and mongrel becoming: at once enacting and generating, as such, the self-refashioning process of semiotic becoming and "becoming semiotic" in the modernizing and, later, decolonizing contemporary Pacific. Although cognizant of larger geocolonial contexts and geopolitical imbalances, my own stress presumes an agency of the converted subject and the bilingual preservation of cultural ties to native values, modes, genealogies, and beliefs under uneven conditions of knowledge/power in colonial contact zones. We need to disentangle this still small indigenous voice from the history of U.S./Hawaiian codes and hegemony of Empire.[36]

James Michener's center-stage portrait of Keoki Kanakoa is partly based around materials from one of his key source-texts for the missionary-era part of his book, A Narrative of Five Youths from the Sandwich Islands (1816), which included 'Ōpūkaha'ia's life-relation in its composite narrative. In any event, then, the dual-cultural life of Henry 'Ōpūkaha'ia (Hawaiian subjecthood as reformed in his New England and transoceanic diaspora) activates the writing process and modern subject-formation I will theorize as "becoming semiotic" (via his journal, letters, sermons, and writings). This is a process of colonization-cum-modernization that opens

Hawaiian cultural identity making and subject-formation to various transpacific forces of outer-national, translational, mongrel, and geographical becoming. Conversion is not just conquest or liquidation but a *turn* toward semiotic difference and newness, linguistic torquing, historical becoming, in the arc of rebirth: "when they start to use your language / do they say what you say / who are they in your words," the Hawaiian-based poet W. S. Merwin writes in "Conquerors," as he opens (and questions via gaps and overlays of syntax) a cross-cultural *gap* between languages, beliefs, and mimetic practices (see epigraph to this chapter) as space for modern freedom and postcolonial alterity.

To theorize and historicize the potentiality of conversion, we can further conjure the meanings of the first Hawaiian convert to Christianity, Henry 'Ōpūkaha'ia, to speak from beyond the waters of the Pacific and burial in Connecticut, so as to contest by this spectral resurrection (as Norman O. Brown might call this return) the codes of some pregiven recognition of the Hawaiian Christian self as a colonized subject, as mere creature of American mimicry. In her notes to the 1968 and 1990 editions of the *Memoirs of Henry Obookiah*, the United Church of Christ's Reverend Edith Wolfe (with the added scholarly help of Margaret S. Ehlke) is more on the linguistic mark, as she looks into a Hawaiian subject she admires. " 'Henry' was the name given to the young man by the American sailors who could not pronounce his Hawaiian name," Wolfe writes, describing a common practice, as the supercargo of the *Triumph* did the same for Henry's fellow-traveling wayfaring sailor, Thomas Hopoo (Hopu).[37] Henry's first name, or the Hawaiian translation for his given first name, is *Hanale*, which also means (when not capitalized) "hunger" or "hungry."[38] The name Henry is often Romanized as "Heneri," as it was in the first Hawaiian translation of the *Memoirs* as *Ka Mo'olelo o Heneri 'Ōpūkaha'ia* done in 1867 by Reverend S. W. Papaula, minister of Kahikolu Church in Kealakekua, Hawai'i.[39]

More to the cross-cultural point, Reverend Wolfe notes that Henry's last or "Hawaiian name, 'Ōpūkaha'ia, was spelled phonetically by the New Englanders who taught the Hawaiian youth to read and to write" (*Memoirs*, 97). Wolfe goes on to unravel the mystery and to translate the metaphoric strands of myth, cultural assumption, and history embedded in the family name: "The Hawaiian name, 'Ōpūkaha'ia, literally means 'Stomach-slashed-open.' According to the learned Hawaiian historian, Charles W. Kenn, it commemorated 'an event in which a chief was disemboweled' " (*Memoirs*, 97). Again, 'Ōpūkaha'ia's family name meanders in this Hawaiian-into-English translation and swerves from language into history and trope, shifting Hawaiian denotations into Enlightenment connotations abjecting pre-missionary practices. Perhaps, mistranslation, or cross-cultural misrepresentation, is the best we can do: was a Hawaiian chief "disemboweled," at Henry's birth, in some act of bloody vengeance that (for those missionary-historians Larue Piercy et al.) those Hawaiian factions were wont to do?

Albert J. Schutz, a learned scholar of Hawaiian linguistics writing a history of Hawaiian language studies, starts from ʻŌpūkahaʻiaʻs English-translation practices (a formation he calls "The Cornwall Connection") as these come down to the re-nativizing present when Hawaiian language study flourishes. Schutz is more on the linguistic and historical mark. As Schutz explains, while studying the rudimentary grammar, spelling book and dictionary texts first compiled by ʻŌpūkahaʻia, which the New England missionaries for the ABCFM first used to begin their systematic conversion of Hawaiian from an oral to a written language following their arrival in 1820, "The name [ʻŌpūkahaʻia] literally means 'slit belly,' hence, 'cesarean.' ʻŌpūkahaʻia himself might have been born by cesarean, or perhaps his birth coincided with that of a high chief born by cesarean."[40]

Henry ʻŌpūkahaʻia, in other words, was *torn from the stomach* at birth, or his birth took place under the sign of a chief, mentor, family member, or priest whose birth was "torn from the stomach." It signifies a *rough birth* for Henry Obookiah, in any event, not only a tearing of this wisdom-hungry Hawaiian from native contexts but a difficult (but not impossible) translation from ungainly terms of Hawaiian into the globally dispersed sounds of American English language and rebirth codes of Christian beliefs. "Henry, Torn from the Stomach"[41] can serve as a contemporary metaphor (translating means *carrying across* some linguistic-cultural abyss) for the altered meanings, voluntary dynamics, and narrative burdens of "conversion," as I urged in the introduction. Translation converts conversion, as it were, back into a very materialized problem of language, culture, and history: his *mana* torn by signifiers and codes, Henry cannot be easily translated, nor can he be converted into glib, canonized, prefabricated language. ʻŌpūkahaʻia is not a dupe nor a de-nativized subject but an agent, voice, and maker of literature and history. American and Native Hawaiian forces collide in the scripted life of Henry ʻŌpūkahaʻia.

Westward toward Asia and the Pacific

Westward into oceanic spaces of Asia and the Pacific extended the global reaches and conversion-cum-translation aims of New England missionaries. Central to the space and modes of this project from its global inception, Hawai'i had become the crucial offshore site in the Pacific for latter-day American Puritans still reading their journey into the oceanic wilderness as a flight into redeemed settlements like "New Canaan" and "New Haven" not to mention "Providence" or new-English sites like Litchfield or Mattatuck (renamed Waterbury in the process of sublating Indian names into English place-names). The fine private school, Punahou Academy (where President Barack Obama was educated in multicultural Honolulu in the 1970s) was founded by and, in many respects, still stands for the dissemination of elite New England culture and theology, even if Hawaiian royalty from the Kamehameha kings to the last Hawaiian queen studied there from the outset. Later generations more commercially driven than these first and second generations of incoming New England missionaries kept moving to Hawai'i's shores to find or instill redemption, a second chance on life, or simply a better life than the one they left behind on the mainland of the United States, or back in Asia, Australia, Oceania, or the so-called Old World of Europe. Writing genres brought in by forces of American Christianity, if at times abjecting, also opened up alter-mimetic possibilities for self-fashioning, modernity, flight, and outer-national becoming. Later, in more overtly decolonizing contexts, the Pacific would come to signify the counter-conversion of "Oceania" by ex-Christian reformations and a postcolonial regional unity. The writing process opened up possibilities of malleability, empowerment, transculturation, and movements across borders, escape.[42] The Polynesian gods were hardly vanquished or removed from the native premises, as some of the missionary settlers had grimly hoped. Reversals and re-nativization of selfhood as much as redemption or mobility became an ever-present possibility for colonists as well as for indigenes, in those "racial and cultural borderlands of the Pacific" that clashing empires opened up across the nineteenth century.[43] The Hawaiian verb "hanauhou" ("life again") came to mean *born again, reborn,* or *baptized,* reflecting this new spirit.

As Victoria Nalani Kneubuhl dramatizes in a postcolonial Hawaiian play *The Conversion of Ka'ahumanu* (1988), the conversion of this post-contact Hawaiian, Queen Ka'ahaumanu, unleashed forces of social becoming and drives to social equality that had a transformative power for women and those of more marginalized standing in the Hawaiian community (like Henry the orphan), as Kneubuhl portrays through the voice of Pali, one of the "kaua" (outcasts) who were branded and marked as slaves. As Hannah Grimes, a mixed-race or "hapa" Hawaiian puts the defense of conversion to Ka'ahaumanu (whose conversion will bring about widespread shifts in Hawaiian beliefs toward embracing

American modes of Christianity), "There is a gentle kindness about Mrs. Bingham. And they [*mikanele*, or American missionaries] know how to read and write! To know the palapala is to know many things."[44] This power of *palapala*, a Hawaiian word for the *mana* of knowing how to read and write paper documents, unleashes that inaugural power of social becoming, the possibility of conversion, and self-transformation I will elaborate as "semiotic conversion," meaning conversion through and toward the power of language, mutability, and metamorphosis. As Kaʻahaumanu urges later into the Kneubuhl play, talking herself into re-birth and the breaking of the old kapu-system she had started, "The [Hawaiian] gods [and priests] ruled over us in ways I did not like. . . . I know if I take this [Christian] god, the people will follow" (68), which indeed they did en masse.

These postcolonial days in Hawaiʻi, Christianity seems all but a cover story for settler colonialism, haole domination, and the master-narrative of service to macroforces of sugar, real estate, Polynesian tourism, and U.S. statehood. "Civilizing the [Hawaiian] kanaka" became the express goal for these waves of modernizing Americans. As Jack London had lamented at the outset of the twentieth century and Hawaiian home rule overcome, "This being the fruit of seed of the Gospel, the fruit of the seed of the missionaries (the sons of the grandsons) was the possession of the islands themselves, of the land, the ports, the town-sites and the sugar plantations."[45] The incoming American missionaries came to do good, as the local joke in Honolulu goes, and they stayed and did quite well. Su-sanna Moore, an American novelist who grew up amid the racial hierar-chies and genteel comforts of poststatehood Hawaiʻi, invokes Jack London's tragic summary of Hawaiians' dispossession from their land and sovereign nation by white-settler colonialism, as in a trope of the "disappearing Indian" who leaves only remnants of spirit-power in the landscape and language. At the same time, she holds out for residual an-imistic beliefs in ocean spirit, lizard spirit, night rider, and fire goddess: what she calls "the myth of Hawaiʻi" reconfirmed by her settler entan-glement in local native-belief as a Magical Realist novelist. "I myself have seen it" is her recurring vow and title phrase, which she takes as echo from the Molokai storyteller of the night riders, Harriet Ne.[46] (Moore's title, "I myself have seen," echoes one of those colonial-era performatives of "ocular proof" that were used by British explorers in New Zealand, as late as 1832, to confirm that Maoris were terrific un-Christianized savages who still practiced modes of cannibalism.[47]) Conversion to cultural particularity, moving via counter-mimicry in an-timodern reverse to native beliefs, customs, and modes of community, became commonplace for generations of white and Asian settlers in modern Hawai'i.[48]

This is to urge, in postcolonial terms, that these language waves of errant Christian adaptation (from the outset) often have been translated via counter-mimesis—converted into body, place and community, and language—not merely into forces of social conservation and colonial abjection. These language waves of conversion and counter-conversion have no less often been translated into something mixed, errant, and pragmatic, as forces and forms bespeaking survival tactics amid the business culture, white mimicry, and machinery of U.S. geopolitics in the Pacific. "Any translation is also an act of betrayal," as Amitava Kumar warns in his nation-crossing portrayal of the contemporary Indian diaspora into global cities of England and America, "a sharing of intimacy with another tongue."[49] But if there is the risk of betrayal and native desertion, there is also a line of flight into freedom, errancy, and empowerment. Activating language in its potentiality as "afterlife," translation can tap into energies coming out of the future.

Translation extends the "afterlife" of Henry's quasi-literary and prayer-drenched language across cultural divides.[50] It helps prolong the semiotic potentiality of Henry 'Ōpūkaha'ia's Hawaiian/American vision, his foreign life and homeland name, reflecting the de-canonizing trajectory of his specific "mana."[51] "Mana is the name given in the Pacific to a kind of supernatural and impersonal power," Elias Canetti observed in *Crowds and Power*, "which can pass from one man to another" and which enhances the vitality and power of the survivor as a kind of incorporated *blessing.*[52] As Dennis Kawaharada explains the Native Hawaiian version of this belief as the basis for a kind of poly-spiritualized ecoscape linking place and self, "Mana [which can be embodied in individuals of specific talent and accomplishment] is the creative and procreative power of the Universe: it makes plants grow, fish and animals multiply, the human population increase; it makes human projects, such as building houses, canoes, lo'i (kalo ponds), or fishponds successful." "Mana" as the power of spirit-transmission and spirit-evocation itself was one of those Polynesian terms like "taboo" and "tattoo" appropriated into English when, in the wake of colonialism, "magic lexicons of subjugated peoples were absorbed into European vernaculars," as Simon During claims of sacred remnants in *Secular Magic.*[53] (Words like *moccasins* and *succotash,* along with techniques of forest warfare, had been earlier American Puritan borrowings from the Massachusetts Indians, not all of whom would be "White Indians.")[54]

Translating the Bible into Tinfish English

Translation can in these unstable ways begin to enact a process of counter-mimesis, transacting the flow of an altered spirit-mana and differentiated embodiment. Consider this earthy translation of the Twenty-Third Psalm by Kalani Akana into contemporary pidgin poetics, in a work of translation-downward from high English making for a vernacular survival tactic in Halawa Valley Jail, where many poor Hawaiians are incarcerated for drug use, disorderly conduct, petty theft, or worse. Deforming images of the King James source-text and Hebraic psalms, Akana carves out a minor tongue that makes the body of subjected Hawaiians glow with aura, self-respect, and altered vision, as his crisscrossed terms of materialized translation configure a reign of pastoral consecration the state cannot confiscate nor mass media demoralize with idle chatter:

> The Lord my kahuhipa
> I no need nobody else.
> He go, "Lay down ovah deah in da grass, brah, rest.
> Yeah, ovah deah by da stream." Cool;
> Whoah I feel some good.
> He lead me down da trails
> Cuz he like dat, pono, cuz he no like me fall
> Even tho I stay in Halawa valley maximum security,
> Brah,
> I no scared
> Cuz he stay watch my back
> His oʻo and his ihe, brah, make be brave lai dat.[55]

Whacking dictions from Hawaiian ("kahuhipa" is Hawaiian for shepherd, "pono" for righteousness, "oʻo" for lance), the King James Bible, black and local hip-hop ("he stay watch my back"), and street codes of dope slang ("cuz" and "brah"), the collage forms an innovative language of communal recognition, kinship, adoption, openness, courage, and support. As in the Afro-American chain-gang rap to Je-sus-a in Robert Duvall's film *The Apostle*, Akana enacts an *a-canonical* translation of High Christianity into mixtures of pidgin poetics, miming local motions of Pentecostal vision. Within the rock walls of a prison, in a time of global war, dirty air, defunct rhetoric and techno-worship, Akana offers, via poetic recoding, what Wallace Stevens called (in a late poem called "The Rock") a "figuration of blessedness"—the poem as a curing of the native ground coming out of the biblical text's afterlife into the profane present.[56]

Converted to a hip-hop mode of Christian logos, the postcolonial poet Kalani Akana is praying (as Merwin's poem "Conqueror" recognizes in its gap between colonizing language and native belief) to an array of different gods who co-exist intimately in this mongrel innovative tongue called Hawaiian Creole English. He performs the code-switching space of a counter-narrated survival, with Lord Jesus becoming a Pacific-language poet in the well-respected postmodern and postcolonial journal edited by Susan Schultz, called (as if mocking the imperial white grandeur of the whale Moby Dick) the *Tinfish* of Honolulu. A local poet named Kalani Akana, speaking for those Hawaiians imprisoned and colonized in their own homeland, feels the spark and aura of freedom, an accession into godhead, and becomes voice of a reborn self, "free both of other selves and of the created world"—to invoke the quasi-gnostic liberationism of American religiosity. Like a pidgin-speaking Emersonian endowing self with beatitudes of freedom and new-made language, though imprisoned in abject social conditions and the plight of postcolonization in Hawai'i, Akana becomes (as he translates himself into a shining force of influx) "in perfect solitude, the American spirit [who] learns again its absolute isolation as a spark of God floating in a sea of space."[57] "He wen make me one luau for me, cuz," Akana affirms of this beatitude-making Lordship, as the beaten-down yet exalted poem continues, "Right in front of my enemies; / He go give me gel for my hair—make me look sharp / Hook me up like that." Hooked into a nexus of freedom, power, and expressive religious embodiment that is post-biblical poetry, Akana blesses and is blessed with aura as much as hair gel, macho street jive, or luau vestments. The natives of the land, in Vico's sense of theology later become troping power (see the chapter epigraph), can become children of the land—become, at the very least, the pidgin-speaking ethnographers of their own situation and story of rebirth in the postmodern Pacific.

To Love and Risk Belief: *No Knowledge without Conversion*

To love and risk belief in communal empowerment and to enact the will to solitary charisma, all these are placed at risk in this huge global/local interface of customs and codes, via these mutating mores and mementos, converting contagions of language, more, and belief. Admiring the vernacular nativization and survival tactics of poetry in such diverse writers as Kalani Akana, Susana Moore, Bob Dylan, Denis Johnson, Ai, Epeli

Hau'ofa, Pamela Lu, Sesshu Foster, and Juliana Spahr, I want to activate forces of postcolonial translation as conversion into forms of "becoming semiotic" and the power of mana-contamination. Such translations can and will open up lines of creative flight and express experimental or "minor" challenge to state codes or what counts as American or as mimetic-real of globalization. The movements across ideological divides are unstable, reversible, and contagious. Ironizing mimetic contagions of doubt and belief in the Cold War era, Philip Roth's short story from 1959, "The Conversion of the Jews," portrays a rebellious Jewish youth, Ozzie Freedman, willing to jump from a synagogue roof to open up freedom (as freed-man) of religion and code for his New Jersey Jewish community of theological conformity: "And then he made them say they believed in Jesus Christ—first one at a time, then all together."[58]

As a writer of journals, autobiography, sermons, and letters, Henry 'Ōpūkaha'ia is by no means a postcolonial experimenter like Epeli Hau'ofa, the missionary offspring from Tonga and Papua New Guinea, who (as shall be discussed in Chapter 4) would later amid the postcolonial ferment of political independence launch textual forces of mockery, carnivalesque overthrow, and generic deformation to rewrite the Pacific conversion-and-development story. In raucous works, such as *Tales of the Tikongs* (1983), *Kisses in the Nederends* (1987), and the more visionary essay "Our Sea of Islands" (1993), Hau'ofa rewrites narratives of conversion and evangelical Christianity in order to put them to diasporic counterpurposes, populist subversion, and neonative usages in sites like Tonga and Fiji. This pan-Pacific portrayal of counter-conversion and critique of "over-influence" took place even as he turned away from the epistemic certainties of social science (anthropology) and developmental leadership to track the warping of global modernity by becoming a comic novelist and geopolitical re-imaginer of "Oceania." Hau'ofa underwent a conversion of writing genres, in effect, moving from social science to literature.

This reversion to storytelling modes of representation and polytheistic gods of the Pacific and postcolonial Oceania was occurring even as another Pacific novelist and cultural critic of visionary importance, Albert Wendt (born in Western Samoa in 1939, the same year as Hau'ofa), had begun to affirm tactics of re-nativization, neotraditional cultural rehabilitation, and a decolonizing mode of "tatauing the Pacific," which his earlier works of fiction, including *Sons for the Return Home* (1973) and *Pouliuli* (1977), had called into question and his later works re-envisioned across shifting geopolitical contexts, as in *Black Rainbow* (1992) and the Jerusalem-haunted Pacific diaspora in *Ola* (1991).[59] Contemporary Pacific writing is rife with paradoxes and surprising moves across cultural frames. As such, Hauʻofa's laughter-drenched and re-nativizing postcolonial Pacific becomes the site of unpredictable counter-conversions, motley lines of flight, mongrel becoming. But as in the innovative postcolonial works of Hauʻofa, this lava road from Kona would lead postcolonial Pacific peoples toward the post-Anglo-global creation of a "counter-conversion" and ways of writing alternative visions of identity and transpacific maps that lead somewhere else. This new "Oceania" emerges a very long way from the New Light Theology or white deconstructionism at Yale University, closer to the place-based ethnography and minority-language poetics Hauʻofa calls, half-mockingly in a debunking story called "The Glorious Pacific Way," the University of the Southern Paradise.[60]

Henry ʻŌpūkahaʻia's act of getting on board Captain Caleb Brintnall's *Triumph* (with its fortuitous ties to New Haven and Yale College) was by no means singular or simple, but his line-of-flight conversion to Christianity was, and it was a world-making *event* at that. Wisdom-hungry and torn-from-the-stomach, by crossing the far-flung Pacific to study, read, and write amid the learned families and guilt-ridden biblical pedagogy of Yale College and the Foreign Mission School, Henry ʻŌpūkahaʻia started down the lava road (as would Hauʻofa years later, *but in reverse*) from the Kona coast to Damascus. The shapes and tones of this early-modern process are recorded through his narrated conversion in the *Memoirs*. The Americanizing and de-nativizing dynamics of this first Hawaiian conversion need to be grasped, as does the contestatory potential of conversion as semiotic transformation in a full, life-changing sense.

The commonplace conviction that Christian missionaries stripped Hawaiians of their language, culture, land, agency, and soul is ruefully conveyed in the fatal-contact narrative of Paul Theroux's faux-local novel, *Hotel Honolulu* (2001), in which contemporary Hawaiians are depicted as "lost souls" working in hotel service jobs when not feeding on American welfare, junk food, and cultural kitsch. "They [i.e., the Hawaiians] had welcomed the missionaries—and they had swallowed them up. So blame the missionaries if you like—they had transformed the Hawaiians, taken everything away, even their memory. They could not remember a time when they were not Christians. Their history was the Bible, the language was Bible language, and even the ones who claimed to worship Pele the fire-goddess sounded as sanctimonious and tiresome as Bible-thumping Baptists."[61] For Native Hawaiians, Theroux forecloses such life-altering mimicry and nativism and leaves them locked in bastardized alternatives: they cannot believe in the Christian God, and they cannot go back to the gods of the native *mana*. Conversion, in this scenario, means cultural death: converts are those crazed speakers (so-called Jesus Freaks or Krishna Heads) you encounter in airports like Honolulu International or going the rounds of neighborhoods like Kahala trying to convert you to some end-time vision, cultic belief, or oddball donation or lost cause. Their language is seemingly dead on arrival, or circulates in a closed communion of grim fixity and all-too-didactic joy.

"Be Always Converting"

American conversion has often been narrated as routinized, banalized, and sad, signifying the mere turn toward some constitutionalized American godhead or global theocracy, as if conversion occurs just this side of a shopping mall site and results in ideological fixity and world closure.[62] To the contrary, however, I follow the pragmatic democrat, William James, in believing that states of intense faith can form the innermost basis of individuality and that exalted states of religious experience can bring change home and turn a hardware store owner's son named Robert Zimmerman, say, into a God-relying poet-prophet named Bob Dylan as we shall discuss in Chapter 6. At the various edges and contact zones of American empire, as across the vast surging waters of Oceania, conversion, and counter-conversion, remains a global/local story of semiotic interest and abiding historical importance in this era of Hawaiian sovereignty, Anglo-global hegemony, and Pacific decolonization. As the self-baptized preacher E. F. in the movie *The Apostle* (1997), to use a mainstream example, Robert Duvall portrays such Holy Ghost-eruption in songs of gospel-possession like "I'll Fly Away," in chain-gang raps to Je-sus-A, and in spectral radio sermons that can stop a white racist from bulldozing the tiny One Way to Heaven Holyness Church. Faith-states for this white fugitive from Texas justice would gather mixed races into a new community of the spirit, via the use of an AM radio studio and crazed Baptist sermons, spreading Holy Ghost power across the Louisiana Bayou and Texas.

Such a quest to achieve a glistening influx of spirit-force amid the abandoned reaches of American social space, to get back to the New England side of this diaspora, figures in the no less dim barroom settings of Frederick Exley, who finds a life-exalting force in watching the New York Giants on an anonymous Sunday afternoon in the Parrot Bar, as if communing at some hidden sacrament of American football: "But as one year had engulfed another, and still another, each bringing with it its myriad defeats, as I had come to find myself relying [that Emersonian turn of phrase for the influx of the godhead] on the Giants as a life-giving, an exalting force." Exley writes in *A Fan's Notes*, "I found myself unable to relax in the company of 'unbelievers,' in the company of those who did not take their football earnestly or who thought my team something less than the One God." In drunken flights near despair, loss, and death, the mere-fan Exley turns into priest of some Lost Testament, "like a holy man attempting to genuflect amidst a gang of drunken, babbling heretics," and the bar become a space of sacral transmutation more powerful than those quaint "old limestone churches" of upstate New York.[63]

The damaged souls searching some "Lost Testament" for signs of "rebirth" mount up to high-heaven along aging interstate highways, closed farms, scrapped technologies, cracked records, abandoned inner cities, or rural towns "buried half the year under leaden skies and heavy snows, and all the year under the weight of its large and intransigent ignorance."[64] These postindustrial days of the lost republic, that "Airline to Heaven," as Woody Guthrie called the conversion apparatus in his own latter-days of folk-prophetic *poesis* across the American 1950s, seems downsized, broken down, out of use. Amplifying the cultural forces of the Popular Front, Guthrie urges that messianic forms of transformation can still work miracles in the dust, come out of the global techno-future with wry Gospel messages, as Guthrie opined: "You can get away to heaven / On this aeroplane / Just bow your head and pray // Them's got ears, let them hear / Them's got eyes, let them see / Turn your eyes to the lord of the skies." The post-Beat author, heroized in Jack Kerouac's *Big Sur* as a dharma-bum force now transplanted and writing on the Puna edges of the Big Island of Hawai'i, Albert Saijo refuses to be slotted into any "PROCRUSTEAN" ethnic identity as Japanese American and calls himself (in the characteristic all-capitals and dashes of *OUTSPEAKS: A Rhapsody*), "A REBORN HUMAN."[65] By pot-smoking, cum-meditation, and backpacking, Saijo of the hipster beatitude quest is *born again* into a strong cosmopoetics of survival on the Pacific edge. Author of on-the-road haiku coauthored with Jack Kerouac and Lew Welch, Saijo has survived and outlived his Beat peers. In this latest reincarnation of creative selfhood, he is reborn beyond ethnicity, nationhood, or race into forms of ecological confederacy and ranting modes of post-Beat newness that are quite original, experimental, and important as modes of worlding Hawaiian space and time.

"Still Small Voice"

One site to help unravel the uncanny threads of this off-center history of American spirituality and mode of conversion morphology is with the poetics and politics of "Henry, Torn from the Stomach." If traditional

Hawaiian art and cultural poetics does not evacuate the precedent of the past nor evacuate the habit and hold of custom and native belief, but "reaches back—or Hawaiians would say *I mua* [goes forward], toward the things *in front of us*—with the goal of rediscovering or recreating something from the past," then maybe the conversion experience, language practices, and "becoming semiotic" of Henry 'Ōpūkaha'ia can suggest a path forward into the multilingual, innovative, and mongrel making of the contemporary Pacific known as sublime Oceania.[66]

We need to look back into the ocean-crossing life and link to the messianic energies of Henry 'Ōpūkaha'ia and his postcolonial heirs. Awakened to modern times and native transformations of polity, custom, and dress, Henry's life, as it spread across the Pacific Ocean from Hilo harbors to Canton commerce sites and into the praying families of New England, embodied Emerson's quest-affirming insight about transoceanic becoming in "Civilization" that "chiefly the seashore has been the point of departure, to knowledge, as to commerce."[67] Emerson's quasi-Hegelian insight into world-transforming powers of the oceanic system goes against his history-denying claim (earlier in the same essay) that, "The Indians of this country [of which Henry would be considered one, Hawaiians so-called since the journals of Captain Cook and the American mariner of those Pacific journeys, John Ledyard] have not learned the white man's work; and in Africa the negro of today is the negro of Herodotus."[68] Ledyard, another New Englander remaking his life in the Pacific, became a globe-trotting mariner; he was called (by his family) to become a Dartmouth-trained missionary to Indians, which he never did. Ledyard's journal as crew member of Captain Cook's third journey to the Pacific resulted in "the first travel account by an American to be published in the new nation" and the making of "a self-consciously American attitude" of democratic kinship, human kinship, and pragmatic mutuality toward Pacific native peoples.[69]

Henry's "change of shores and population," as he became sailor, student, and minister in New England, did not (*contra* Emerson) "clear his head of much nonsense of the wigwam," but rather linked his life-world into the decolonizing twists and translational frames of American modernity, writing selfhood, and Hawaiian nationhood. The *Memoirs of Henry Obookiah* stands for far-flung encounters with myriad forces of nonconforming transformation and the will to "metamorphose yourself." Long buried under white-colonial affiliations or taken for granted as an American-converted subject, Henry 'Ōpūkaha'ia remains an uncanny (if still underexamined) force of modernizing impact upon post-contact Hawaiian history. Henry's learned remains came back from his New England grave in the summer of 1993 for reburial in the Kahikolu

Church Cemetery in his native birthplace at Napoʻopoʻo Hawaii to haunt the commemoration ceremonies, which were protesting the overthrow of Queen Liliʻuokalani by American forces in 1893 with another story—speaking not of history as "done-to" Hawaiians but of their multilingual agency, polyvocal entanglement, and uneven complicity in the march of enlightenment history and conversion to Christianity and the cultural-political sway of American civilization.[70]

Haunani Kay Trask's outcry of decolonization, "I am not an American, we are not Christians" on stage at the large-scale January 1993 annexation protest at Iolani Palace,[71] although important as political rhetoric, cannot gainsay the still small voice, global impact, and complexly *outer-national* story of Henry ʻŌpūkahaʻia/Obookiah, which goes on speaking its alternative modes, aims, and claims (in English/Hawaiian) upon Hawaiʻi from beyond the grave. By "outer-national," Paul Gilroy denominates a cultural-political process that cuts across borders of nations and cultures in transnational and transcultural routes of oceanic becoming, crisscrossing, uprooting, and ongoing forces of modern transformation. "Retreating from the totalizing immodesty and ambition of the word 'global,' diaspora is an outer-national term," Gilroy urges, "which contributes to the analysis of intercultural and transcultural processes and forms. It identifies a relational network, characteristically produced by forces of dispersal [from a place of dwelling] and reluctant scattering [to a place of sojourn]"[72] "Outer-national" signifies the movements of the multitudes, not just the strategies of the elite transnational class.

The "still small voice" of Obookiah goes on being dispersed, as translated into global legacy, renewed, and rewritten via his untimely memoir from the destabilizing era of white-settler colonization. Boarding with Reverend Joseph Harvey in Goshen in 1814 while working on a grammar, spelling book, and dictionary of Hawaiian, Henry wrote this self-reflection on his inward quest for the conversion experience, which would be ratified by his public reception into the Torringford Church of Christ in April 1815: "I seeked for the Lord Jesus for a long time, but found him not. It was because I did not seek him in a right manner. But still I do think I have found him upon my knees [in prayer]. *The Lord was not in the wind, neither in the earthquake, nor in the fire, but in the still small voice*" (*Memoirs*, 36).

The body of Henry ʻŌpūkahaʻia has been removed from the cold Connecticut earth, was carried back over the Pacific, and lies buried in his beloved Hawaiian homeland. Liʻikapeka Lee had urged the transpacific drive in August of 1993 to return her ancestor Henry's remains to Hawaiʻi with the support of United Church of Christ leaders from Honolulu to

Connecticut: " 'We are just carrying out his wishes,' his modern relative said, pointing to the book about Henry 'Ōpūkaha'ia [Memoirs] that tells of his desire to return to Hawai'i and spread the Gospel."[73] The orphan's text has been linked to divergent genealogies and agendas, but it can be ignored no longer. Indeed, Henry 'Ōpūkaha'ia may be what the Lacanian cultural critic Slavoj Žižek calls one of those "disavowed ghosts" of recalcitrant materiality and writing semiotics that still haunt (even from offshore spaces) the decolonizing and, in effect, de-whitening multicultural Pacific and its imperial dispensations, thus exerting an *uncanny* impact on the accepted or abjected ingredients of the Native Hawaiian homeland. Such spectral poetics, rising up from such tombs and sites of cross-regional meaning, can help to undo and contest the taken-for-granted spaces, times, and subject-forms of globalization.[74]

And creating by these materialized powers of conversion and metamorphosis, then as now, can take place along lines of flight, courage, and risk on the roads leading into newness, beatitude, and life-change.

"This Morning I Am Born Again"

If Henry 'Ōpūkaha'ia had lived on into the Dust Bowl times of Woody Guthrie, as recuperated (or, better said, *translated* into the postcolonial present) by the plangent strains of Slaid Cleaves on his album *Broke Down,* Henry might very well have recognized the "second birth" figurations of the "promised land" he had been called to across New England and Hawai'i, in expansive terms captured in Woody's song lyric. "This Morning I Am Born Again" is a radiantly outer-national song, at once exalted and lowly (like a Sermon on the Mount for drifters and seekers) in its rejection of golden streets and mansions, linking beatitude ("I was born again") to life-powers from "the life of Jesus and old John Henry too," the mighty rail pounder, no longer looking for heaven in any "deathly distant land" or typed by the rhetorics of race, creed, or culture as destiny.[75]

> This morning I was born again and a light shines on my land
> I no longer look for heaven in your deathly distant land
> I do not want your pearly gates don't want your streets of gold
> This morning I was born again and a light shines on my soul . . .
>
> This I was born again, my past is dead and gone
> This great eternal moment is my great eternal dawn
> Each drop of blood within me, each breath of life I breathe
> Is united with these mountains and the mountains with the seas

I feel the sun upon me, its rays crawl through my skin
I breathe the life of Jesus and old John Henry in
I give myself, my heart, my soul to give some friend a hand
This morning I was born again, I am in the promised land

This morning I was born again and a light shines on my land
I no longer look for heaven in your deathly distant land
I do not want your pearly gates don't want your streets of gold
And I do not want your mansion for my heart is never cold.

CHAPTER THREE

"Be Always Converting, and Be Always Converted"

Conversion as Semiotic Becoming, and Metamorphosis into Beatitude

In whose mind's [Emerson's] all creation is duly respected
As parts of himself—just a little projected;
And who's willing to worship the stars and the sun,
A convert to—nothing but Emerson.

> —James Russell Lowell, *A Fable for Critics*, 1848

That is why the inner psyche is not analyzable as a thing but can only be understood and interpreted as a sign.

> —Voloshinov/Bakhtin, *Marxism and the Philosophy of Language*

"I [Tagata, the Flying-Fox] went back, Pepe. Back to the lava fields, and it has brought me up from hell again. Lava is the only true thing left. It cannot change. The rock from whom we came, and it is with us [Samoans] in the back of our souls. You get me?" he says. "It is there I found the self again." . . . *One laugh laughed loud will keep away sorrow and your father and the Romans and the L.M.S. and the modernaitu* [modern gods] *and the police and the Judge and bad breath.*

> —Albert Wendt, "Flying Fox in a Freedom Tree."[1]

Conversion as Encounter

In conversion, broadly speaking, one encounters a life-force of amplified being such as the New Haven ship coming into harbor for Henry 'Ōpūkaha'ia or his meeting the "praying families" of New England, or Dylan's seeking out the folk-mentorship of Woody Guthrie as reborn in a New Jersey sickbed, or Allen Ginsberg meeting Kerouac and Snyder on the Beat roads leading westward to San Francisco and writing *Howl*. The surrealist Beat poet Philip Lamantia was so shaken by his dark mystical "conversion" to Catholicism in 1955 during a near-death experience after having been bitten by a scorpion down in the "fellaheen" streets of Mexico City, that he began to abandon earlier poems he had written or published as so many "mortal sins" and mistaken forms of vulgar beatitude.[2] Conversion, as Lamantia embodied in these various theo-poetic encounters, means a *turning with and as some force of newness*. Conversion, activating myriad forms of metamorphosis, affirms, plugs into, and enacts various energies of becoming, eruptive ideas, recomposition, and a creativity (or *beatitude*) latent or now damaged in the self. "He [becomes] a new creature: old things are passed away; behold, all things are become new" reverberates the staggering present-tense claim for conversion, down through centuries of repetition, for the incoming-power of the inaugurating/reborn subject ("new creature") of early Christian modernity.[3] An unexpected version of such life-change and turn to *caritas* is New England Puritanism offspring Rose Hawthorne Lathrop's opening of (Saint Rose's) Free Home for Incurable Cancer on the Lower East Side, after her conversion to Roman Catholicism in 1891 (Rose and her novelist father had long loved the maternal beliefs and warm piety of Italy) and her founding of a Dominican order under her new name, Mother Mary Alphonsa.[4] As ex-gospel singer Sam Cooke had hauntingly affirmed, in the aftermath of being transformed by Dylan's lyric prophecies during the Civil Rights era and their march upon Washington when Martin Luther King, Jr., was demanding that American be reborn, "A Change Gonna Come."

Yet any "conversion experience" is by no means a fixed, grimly ideological, or unidirectional process of self-formation expressing a will to unchanging identity or belief. Rebirth records, more commonly, an unstable process of subjective-becoming and semiotic recoding that takes place between troubled poles of de-nativization, traumatic forms of symbolic death, and a turn to re-nativization. Conversion as such tracks a mobile trajectory between belief and prior rejection, birth, hollowing out, and the drive to affirm rebirth. Otherwise phrased, conversion activates some life-changing "encounter" with events and forces circulating through discourse and signs (language-circulating holy spirit) coming down from the colonial regime/ecumene to our own more postcolonial regime/secular ecumene of New Age multiplicity and neoliberal suspicion. As the Indian-caring minister Thomas Shepard had memorably urged his congregation at Cambridge, Massachusetts (with all the rhetorical "turns" and textual puns of a Cambridge University graduate),

Be always converting, and be always converted; turn us again, O Lord. . . .
Not that a Christian should be always pulling up foundations, and ever doubting: but to make sure [of regeneration], be always converting, more humble, more sensible of sin, more near to Christ Jesus.[5]

This born-again dynamic that comes down from post-Puritan times, to be "always converting, and always converted," places a radical burden on the self as site of renewal and world-change, what Emerson termed "unsettling," even as *conversion* became surrounded on one side by *deconversion* (rejection of prior beliefs) and on the other side by *counter-conversion* (turns to alternative beliefs and a plural range of calls), as we shall see in this chapter. Crucial to this dynamic of *turning-around* one's life are the powers of "becoming semiotic," as I have touched upon in the discussion of 'Ōpūkaha'ia's adaptation of Christian language and modes of writing his rebirth in New England despite the ties he maintained, in many ways, to the Hawaiian language and mores. *Always converted* (turning upon the past tense of *convert*) rather more narrowly means fixed, set upon in belief; *always converting* (turning upon the present tense of the same verb) means always experimenting, open to story, *subject to change* (what Kerouac called "souls on the road"), as I will further elaborate here.

Conversion in the poems and sermons of this American climate may stand for some kind of "unofficial religion" that has long pervaded American culture, from its theo-haunted polity to its quasi-pragmatic philosophy of belief and out into its popular culture, and may depend upon those forces that Harold Bloom regards as "more Emersonian than Christian" in its embrace of "self-relying," meaning by this turn an unhoused religion of desettlement that relies on the self's powers of spontaneity and desublimation to break conformist molds via "aversion."[6] As Emerson affirmed of this drive to convert a deadened life-world and routinized self into a force activating "newness," a transition into becoming different and reborn as spirit-man, "This one fact the world hates, that the soul *becomes.*" Conversion transitions the anxious self into an "in-streaming" power that works as experimental force and imparts a spirit-filled language the new agent can then further circulate. Early and late, Emerson troped this force as "self-reliance," generated daily across an abyss of blockage and diminishment, into *God-reliance.*[7] As the Concord bard of American difference summarized this power in his abolitionist jeremiad of 1854 in New York City, "self-reliance, that height and perfection of man, is reliance on God."[8] For African Muslims in the Americas, to the racial contrary, conversion to Islam was troubled by interdiction, forced deconversion, "pseudoconversions," and (very often) *reconversion* to faith in Allah.[9] Bloodhounds and barbed-wire fences on the Underground Railroad to New England and Canada, Frederick Douglass realized in Emerson's era, surrounded black conversion as a turn to freedom and amplified self-expression. Douglass, nonetheless, activated and embodied this change and has had an unceasing impact upon his nation and the world from his day until now.

Expressed in more Deleuzian terms based around later, multiple quests for freed-up powers and what he called the process of "becoming-productive" and life-world transformation, meaning by this turn a power of acting, composing, assembling, and thinking that can be increased by this fateful encounter with Outside force, where, as in Spinoza's para-Christian geo-materialism, "we 'approach' the point of conversion, the point of transmutation that will establish our dominion, that will make us worthy of action, of active joys."[10] Conversion, in this sense of energized self-becoming, becomes all the more amplified by the post-Christian frameworks of modernism (as in Nietzsche) and activates a mode of self-overcoming "sad passions" in reactive conservation, complacent being, stability, and social tyranny.[11] Intensified life-gladness gets affected via the gospel of amplified being and becomes active as a mode of recomposing a lyric self freed from death-values or drives, de-literalized, torn from decomposing forces, made new. Nietzsche, like Dylan who nonetheless Eucharistically affirmed on *Infidels* that he never could drink that blood and call it wine, remains *anti-priest*.[12]

In this body-soul assemblage outside the temple, conversion can take place in unexpected encounters on the road or across the ocean, as in Whitman with a live oak in New Orleans or Dylan lost to himself in Juarez or some Brownsville become Armageddon: "the soul is neither above nor inside [the body], it is 'with,' it is on the road, exposed to all contacts, encounters, in the company of those who follow the same way, 'feel with them, seize the vibration of their soul and their body as they pass,' the opposite of a morality of salvation, teaching the soul to live its life, not to save it."[13] The soul becomes linked to forces outside the closed or blocked self, and thus meets up with its new self on the road to Damascus (or it could be Kona or Golden Gate Park): change *(newness)* does happen. *Becoming,* in this radically strong Deleuzian sense of subjective de-territorialization, means that the conversion-event has materialized into a metamorphosis: "becoming means transcending the context of historical conditions out of which a phenomenon arises."[14] Defending this Deleuzian turn to enact a radical" encounter," Slavoj Žižek continues (in the vein of Alain Badiou on conversion as an Empire-shattering *event* by which newness enters the world), "This is what is missing in historicist anti-universalist multiculturalism: the explosion of the eternally new in/as the process of becoming."[15]

Although we do appear to be "mere walking bundles of habits," encoded with social convention to the core, still, as William James affirmed in contexts he deemed *habit*, "sudden conversions, however infrequent they may be, unquestionably do occur" and make self and world come alive with possibility and change.[16] For James, pluralism as he came to define it during the last three decades of his life would maximize latent forces of individualism and multiply faith-states of amplified possibility. Even within the alienating maelstrom of American modernity which increasingly required emergent therapies of self-help and self-suggestion to cope with everyday capitalist life, James investigated various modes of subjective belief and turns to over-belief, however strange or untoward, with deep empathy and psychological respect. He affirmed everywhere in the lectures that came to be called *Varieties of Religious Experience* that different subjects, ancient and modern, using different sets of belief and rules of action, could activate occult transactions with spirit-power and awaken burgeoning forces of energy enhancement his beloved mentor Ralph Waldo Emerson had validated as the influx from the self-relying Over-Soul. In his approach to the born-again experience, as variously elaborated in his classic text, *The Varieties of Religious Experience,* James sought "to call attention to what conversion enables one to do, not to what conversion does to one."[17] Conversion meant this possibility to activate life-change and renew belief, meaning here the power of chosen language differences and beliefs to *change* the world and, crucially, to make a difference in the self as pragmatic and healthy-minded agent.

Conversion as Turning

In terms of reworlding, shifted belonging, and semiotic change, becoming *converted* registers an altering mimetic process of self-formation. Conversion signifies this perpetual *turning,* as the trope of "verse" embedded in *con-vert* or the related Emersonian verb of *ad-vert* implies, not to mention the more authority-driven Catholic or Muslim verb *revert* for returning-believers; turning means that there has been some veering toward life-alteration via an encounter with significant spiritual force.[18] *Metanoia* as such enacts a process of death, penance, and rebirth, via some *turning back* to the godhead as an encounter with a life-transforming language (scriptural "good news"). Tracking what happened to Saul-becoming-Paul along "the anonymity of a road" to Damascus in the year 33 or 34 C.E., Badiou describes the model-setting "conversion" of Saint Paul that took place there as "a thunderbolt, a caesura . . . a conscription inaugurating a new subject" by the power of a singular "event" blasting the subject outside the hold of Church, state, ritual, dialectics, or Empire.[19] Yet, haunted by law and the unresurrected subjectivity of desire or dead literality and sinfulness, of stale signs, even this Pauline process of *justification-through-grace* ("that we should serve in newness of spirit, and not *in* the oldness of the letter" [Romans 7:6]) *turns* (as in a verse's forward-moving enjamb-ment) into unstable movements, the potentiality for *falling back* or *falling from* a state of sanctification or everyday beatitude. Conversion in effect converts believing subjects into elected agents of malleability and semiotic change. In various modes and world contexts, such transformed believers want to share the "good news," as Jesus did so early in the Gospel of Matthew as a baptizing call across the divisions of race, class, gender, caste, and nation, to *repent/convert*.

The plot of conversion can also see an eventual or sudden reversal, a *turning back* ("backsliding") full circle. This is what William James called the pragmatic and no less crucial or fateful turn toward some "counter-conversion"; that is to say, toward embracing modes of liberal modernity or other faiths. For many Roman Catholics, following upon the unsteadiness of Saint Peter more than the militant conviction of the newly converted Saint Paul, *conversion* can entail a daily event of for-giveness and self-renewal, the quest for grace taking place through the liturgy and sacramental interface with the Real Presence of the mass. As John R. May (elaborating upon 1 Corinthians 11:17–32) describes this everyday drama as one of the repenting and returning self before the mass, "Conversion, a fundamental change of heart, is the 'test' necessary for proper participation in the Eucharist."[20] The believing subject, poten-tially can in the end *turn away from, turn toward, turn around,* or *turn back* to earlier or displaced signs, adverting the innermost *instability* of any individual conversion. Examples here might range from Samuel Ka-makau and Rose Hawthorne to Sam Cooke and Bob Dylan. I might also invoke a Chinese-American photographer I have heard about from Min-nesota named Wing Young Hui whose mother made him pray to Buddha every Chinese New Year, whereas the hippie-era movie on Jesus Freaks and rock music, *Jesus Christ Superstar,* became for his work as artist a kind of "cultural touchstone."[21] That American Puritan of voracious New World energies, Cotton Mather, knew that conversion was less a specific event of *one* sanctifying change than "a recurring drama," and though the conviction of grace in states of self-vastation may have eluded him in his own life, his vocation to unrelenting work writing four hundred books of massive American typological hermeneutics was designed "to instigate pious conversions" in others.[22]

Another Puritan of public admission, Mary White Rowlandson, writing of her captivity by, and redemption from, the Algonquians in 1676, came close to adopting "unprecedented and unsanctioned counter-conversions," as Mitchell Breitwieser describes her wilderness stay, meaning a reversion to modes of "Indianity," as in her death-side mourning, her written "dediabolization" of Indian typology at times of other-identification, or just sheer physical reduction to states of raw vitality—for example, when she "eats hoof, bear, fetus fawn, and enjoys."[23] Unmoored from Puritan typology, these days conversion gets broadly applied as therapeutic tactic and as everyday news. Republican presidential candidate Mitt Romney's shifting ("flip-flopping") of attitudes of social concern to conservative voters in the 2008 election—gay marriage, abortion, embryonic stem-cell research—was explained as "[his] conversion" on CNN television news (June 15, 2007). The brilliantly conniving Hitchens brothers' shifts from right to left and back were narrated as "conversion experiences" by the British press tracking their political transformations from conservative upbringing to socialist affiliation and back again during the long-drawn war in Iraq.[24] Describing Richard Rorty's "turn" to postmodern philosophy, Roger Scruton wrote, "At a certain point, Rorty suffered a conversion experience, rebelling against analytical philosophy not, primarily, because of its finicky irrelevancies, but because of its entirely erroneous vision [of mimetic certitude as portrayed in Rorty's *Philosophy of the Mirror*]."[25]

Ernest Fenollosa, to cite an earlier transpacific example, whose immersion in Chinese and Japanese poetics transformed (via Ezra Pound) the very imagistic basis of modern American poetry, was himself the product of a large-scale counter-conversion into Asia-Pacific modalities of belief, as a monument erected in Japan in 1920 registers, its very terms of counter-belief drenched in New England Protestantism. As the monument records this morphology of becoming, "Professor Fenollosa was a great believer in the Buddhist religion. After long study he became a convert to it, and he received a baptism from the abbot Sakurai, Keitoku of Enjo-ji." In taking the Buddhist name Tei-Shin, Fenollosa became a precursor figure crossing into the transpacific "poetics of emptiness" for such writers as Gary Snyder, Philip Whalen, Armand Schwerner, and Leslie Scalapino.[26] More extranscendentalist than dharma bum, Fenollosa converted to Asian Buddhist differences of belief that made a huge difference in life practices and how he saw his own scholarly writing and the career he lived in Boston and Tokyo. Conversion is found not only in and across the Asia-Pacific but also gets delivered as morning news, still.

Born-Again Subjects: "Be Always Converting"

Unmoored from its root ties to penitence, conversion takes on a broader social meaning as convicted change. Stanley Cavell captured the mutability power of conversion and counter-conversion—"the turning implied in conversion"—in his unpacking of Emerson's call to his American readers toward modes of *nonconformity* in "Self-Reliance," wherein the Concord sage urges on the American-modern self that "Self-reliance is [conformity's] aversion." "Aversion is a striking word," Cavell affirms of this calling, "not to be taken lightly as description of his writing as such. It invokes the preacher's word once familiar to his life, that of conversion, and accordingly should raise the question whether the turning implied in conversion and aversion is to be understood as a turning away from the society that demands conformity more than as a turning toward it, as a gesture of confrontation."[27]

Earlier, in the Catholic doctrinal formulations given imagery and shape by Dante, even the exiled poet's post-Augustinian quest for confession and salvation in the *Divine Comedy* was no less haunted by simulacrums of inauthenticity and antagonism, unstable or false signs, what one learned Dante scholar calls the "conversion manqué."[28] "Conversion implies the destruction of a previous form [in the self] and the creation of a new form," as John Freccero urges, yet Dante follows Augustine's *Confessions* in his mode of interrogation seeking for authentic/inauthentic forms of this converted experience as registered in the (sinful, wavering, love-bewildered) self caught in states of in-betweenness. This is exactly where the *Divine Comedy* famously opens in mid-life confusion and just this side of purgatory and hell.[29] Grace was something Dante feared had *not* fully penetrated the courtly-love heart nor broken the strong will of his beloved poet-rival, Guido Calvalcanti, whose selfishness may have damned him to lesser states of charity and poetic beatitude, as portrayed in the Inferno section of the *Divine Comedy. Howl,* too, registers a purgatorial topology of this angel-headed turn from infernal to blissful states of Beat beatitude.

The contemporary Haitian poet Denize Lauture, working as a welder in New York City, cannot exorcise, in his cursing Creole French or anguished English, what Christianity had meant as reverse-crucifixion for his own native beliefs in the West Indies, spelling out their damnation and demonization, their near-liquidation, "Sou yon kwa maledikson":

> My mouth spits blood
> With each uttered word.
> I am from the guts of a land
> Whose soul has been crucified
> Head down
> Upon a horrendous cross.[30]

Abjection did not always mean rejection but uncanny counter-turning. The London Missionary Society had early recognized the instability for any converted Pacific Island native subject, in noting the regal shifts of Tahiti's Chief Pomare *toward,* and *away from,* and *back* into a converted Christian subject: "Pomare himself [as exemplary native subject modeling Christian behavior and British-affiliated power for his people] was the most prominent and flagrant example of Polynesian backslider, first professing belief, then sinning, then contrite."[31] Conversion could happen in the other direction in these contact zones, in the South Pacific example of counter-conversion to Pacific nativism, as portrayed in Lord Byron's anti-imperial British romance, *The Island* (1823), wherein a Scottish sailor and lone survivor from the *Mutiny* crew, Torquil, is reborn as a native Tahitian son after being erotically ministered to in the darkened crimson caves and native resources of a royal Toobanai daughter, Neuha, who saves him from death and recapture by white imperial forces.[32]

Born-again native subjects get caught between old and new, pagan and modern, unstable calls to conformity and unconformity. Unmoored from land, even the lone American Owen Chase feared being attacked by "dreaded cannibals" while shipwrecked in the Pacific, but Melville urged that the whaling crew of the Essex had nothing to fear because "for more than 20 years the English missionaries had been resident in Tahiti."[33] Pacific savages had been converted from such cannibalistic practices, so the white discourse of conversion went, even though in this case it was the white Quakers from maritime Nantucket (as in Poe's morbid *Narrative of Arthur Gordon Pym, of Nantucket* [1838], based on Benjamin Morell's *Narrative of Four Voyages to the South Seas and Pacific* [1832]) who had reverted to man-eating to survive. Thus, the civilian sailors of Enlightenment America could be *counter-converted* back into savages in the wild waters of the Pacific or wilderness terrains and descend, beyond good and evil, into Antarctic or antipodean disorientation. Conversion was seldom a fixed, one-way turn toward redemption.

Unstable Conversions, Hawaiians "Run off to America"

Conversion implies an unstable process, subject to pressures of socialization and subjective ratification (or *dissent*), especially given that "venture in exegesis" that is post-Puritan America, whereby (in the strong typological terms of "consensus" argued by Sacvan Bercovitch in *The Rites of Assent*), "the discovery of America is converted into a process of self-discovery, whereby America is simultaneously internalized, universalized (as a set of self-evident absolutes), and naturalized (as a diversity of representative social, creedal, racial, and ethnic selves)."[34] A Hawaiian chant from the whaling days of the 1840s captures the instability of modern cultural affiliations and threat of American conversion to the Native Hawaiian nation, in contexts of imperial rivalry, through metaphors of transpacific romance, as native sweethearts on shore can get lost to incoming white sailors from those global powers of Britain, France, and America: "Lawe o Maleka I ka hoa la; lilo!" (America takes your mate/partner/friend; [she is] gone!)[35]

The process of "becoming Americanized" is signified by a similar Hawaiian phrase, "Ua hoʻolilo ʻia I ʻAmelika," meaning "lost/gone to America."[36] The verb "lilo" is used to represent this world-altering process of being gone, possessed, run off, or turned into an American *(Americanized),* as if taken by a new love coming from across the huge Pacific. The Hawaiian verb for conversion, "loliʻana," uses the verb "loli," meaning to change, vary, alter, turn, and turn over, as in changing forms or clothes.[37] (Also, "huliʻana" is used to mean to turn, reverse, reform as in changing an opinion or manner of living.) Altering inner and outer forms, conversion implies a *change* of signs and fashions, beliefs, loves, habits; one can change churches, cultures, and nations in this subject-altering process of world transformation. As these Hawaiian proverbs suggest, however, conversion is also haunted by betrayal, loss, the stigma of broken covenants, and abandoned loves or discarded faiths.

Counter-conversion lurks on the uncanny horizon of indigenous conversion, as a recall of the abandoned culture or past way of life, as can be shown in the phenomena of current-day Hawaiians *turning back* to native modes, beliefs, and language and of the longing for forms of national and cultural-political sovereignty.[38] Counter-conversion could also mean the turn to plural beliefs of modern secularism, as discussed in the last chapter. The call to *becoming semiotic,* as in the turn to writing and sermonizing by the self-resignifying ʻŌpūkahaʻia, can also install an unstable process of *semiotic becoming,* that is, the future turn to altered signs, myths, and genres, as in the "re-nativization" turn from social science and anthropology to fiction and poetry, if not the de-Americanization taking place across contemporary Oceania, as we will examine in Chapter 4.

The prototype for the threat or admission of counter-conversion, mingling anxiety as reprobation and self-doubt, comes from the journals of no less than John Wesley, who wrote, upon his return from sermonizing in the U.S. state of Georgia, across a region where the born-again morphology of post-Methodist conversion was to take enormous and lasting American impact (consider the gospel music–drenched movie of charismatic community O *Brother, Where Art Thou?* [2001] or the gospel music of Sun Records in Memphis): "I, who went to America to convert others, was never myself converted to God."[39] Pope John Paul II recognized the far-reaching power of indigenous conversion in the New World, then and now, when he belatedly canonized Juan Diego Cuauhtlatoatzin, the first Indian saint of the Americas in Mexico City in 2002. The Virgin of Guadalupe is said to have spoken to the Aztec peasant in his native Nuahuatl on a hilltop in 1531, and his vision of a dark-skinned (or "mestizo"-faced, as the Pope said) Mary "helped catalyze the conversion of natives throughout the hemisphere to Christianity during the Spanish colonial period."[40] Indigenous conversion in the Americas, as we have seen in Pacific contexts, registers a complex feat of multilingual and transcultural adaptation, hardly a one-way "conversion" in any mathematical sense of equivalencies where one sign equals another.

Conversion is commonly translated into English as the verb "repent," as in the mandate from Mark 1:15, "The time is fulfilled, and the kingdom of God is at hand: repent ye, and believe the gospel." "Born-again" conversion implies a three-stage pattern of (1) turning over, turning around, from sinfulness to God *(conversion);* via (2) a conviction of wrong-doing and wrong-living *(repentance);* and (3) a life-changing turn toward generating acts of sacrifice *(penance)* and what post-Calvinists called everyday signs of "sanctification."[41] Suggesting the immersion of "conversion" as such in the language process of speaking and writing as one "saved," what Susan Harding calls the fundamentalist conviction that rebirth entails "speaking [as] believing," we could add that *metanoia* entails a rhetorical process of recalling a statement, of strengthening or weakening prior declarations or speech-acts via self-correction.[42] It has become a technical term of rhetoric, similar to what is called in Latin-based rhetoric *correctio,* the rewriting of a prior utterance. Conversion centers on a performative speech act enacting signs of newness.

Conversion-as-metanoia, then, rewrites the self into a new set of terms, corrects the prior language: the self becomes reborn, initially, via a process of semiotic transformation. There is some change of mind and language due to the transformation of repentance into a second, transcultural, birth. One of the suggestive passages in Pope Benedict XVI's *Jesus of Nazareth* ("has anything good ever come out of Nazareth . . . ?") stresses that the word *Gospel* itself, as saving message, implies "not just informative speech, but performative—not just the imparting of information, but action, efficacious power that enters the world to save and transform."[43] Conversion *performs* a changed self, in a performative speech-act charged with vigor, Holy Ghost power. In the words of Billy Bray, that "excellent little illiterate English evangelist" James was fond of invoking as example, "I can't help praising the Lord. As I go along the street, I lift up one foot, and it seems to say 'Glory'; and I lift up the other, and it seems to say 'Amen.' "[44]

All across "sweet" Watsonville, California, ski caps, motorcycle jackets, and t-shirts inscribed to "Morenita" ("dear brown Madonna") can be found on sale these days, a Guadalupe sign or image often made in Korea, Guam, or China. The canonization of the indigenous Saint Juan Diego by the Roman Catholic Church, five hundred years later in re-nativizing post-colonial times, was declared in contexts of rising global poverty, indigenous resurgence, and the power of charismatic forms of Protestant evangelism (and even Islam) booming across the Americas. Across the Pacific Rim, as site of proliferating conversion energies, New Age cults are rising up in stranger modes of East/West syncretism with their own eclectic neosacred configurations of conversion, community, ritual, erotic consummation, and belief-quest, as Kenzaburo Ōe depicts in his raucously transnationalized novel, *An Echo of Heaven*. In the Japanese religious cult described by Ōe as a Japanese New Age diaspora in Mexico, an aging guru named Little Father pours over Saint Augustine's *Confessions* in a Swedenborg Church in that fallen Rim city of San Francisco, searching for signs of his own "true conversion" amid New Age East/West syncretism, sexual lust, and an all-too-eroticized quest for faith across a global diaspora in which Zen, Blake, Yeats, and Our Lady of Guadalupe all intermingle as they do in Ōe himself.[45]

Conversion, in this "twice-born" sense I have been urging here, turns over prior narratives of self and world and gives the subject a changed set of convictions, an altered diction, a new language of rebirth encoding active choice, direction, and life-becoming. The whole "semiotic" process of self-performance resonates with what Charles Taylor calls (via a reading of James's religious individualism) the turn toward "committed inwardness" that activates the syntax and terms of this newness and self-alteration. In a move beyond "agnostic intellectual culture," then and now, Taylor finely zooms in on "James as describing the point of choice [in conversion], the flip-over point where one can go from belief to unbelief or the reverse" as well as the leap beyond "agnostic vetoes" or ambivalence toward "committed inwardness" taking place globally, far from the North Atlantic cultures where these forms had taken dominion.[46]

"In Paul's language, I live, yet not I, but Christ liveth in me" is how James described the "unselving" process of second-birth along Pauline lines.[47] But the instability of this conversion process, its flip-over *turn* from belief to unbelief or back again, is actually closer (in some sense) to a Saint Peter model than to the Saint Paul subject form—the former being the uneasy figure who denied Christ three times, whom Jesus had to ask three times whether he loved him, who then washed and renewed himself in tears of repentance and was forgiven. These two forms, one more *fixed* (like the fundamentalist born-again version of being "saved" as a state of being *converted*) and the other more paradoxically humbled and unstable form (like the Catholic version based around renewed everyday repentance and the need for perpetual "converting"), are kindred to what James memorably contrasted as the "sudden" versus the "gradual" formations of religious conversion.[48]

Conversion as Pragmatic Leap

Conversion entails a leap across some abyss of prior selfhood, and reflects a crisis of reversing, rotating, or traversing, from one (inferior) mode of life to another status of power and language. According to the plot of conversion as sketched out in the pluralistic, quasi-literary, and subject-ridden capaciousness of William James's *Varieties of Religious Experience,* the heterogeneity and flux in the modern liberal self are, suddenly or gradually, as if by some strategic positing of a life-altering "turning point," given wholeness, vital direction, and narrative shape through conversion.[49] The trope of "turning" animating the term *conversion* (amid all this Jamesian interior flux of psychology) suggests that there has been some altered change of language from one state of inscribed selfhood to another, as well as the conversion of powerlessness and self-division, into the shapes and telos of turned identity. Shepard's Jeremaic mandate, "Turn us again, O Lord," came to signify different modern outcomes.

This mutability of conversion, given the open domains and market spheres of a liberal society such as the United States, offers a way of overcoming the very incommensurability of given cultures and knowledge-frames. The fixity of given cultures-of-birth can be transformed, altered via the mediating processes of translation, conversion, transliteralization, and dialogue (as discussed in early-modern Hawai'i). Such horizons can remain open to the postcolonial American selfhood as a social horizon of modern becoming, nonconforming dissent, still, and what Norman O. Brown embraced as praxis of self-refiguring "metamorphosis."

Conversion registers the arc of unsteady movement toward this wholeness of becoming-new: from profane to sacred (as in the modes of Saint Paul and Saint Augustine); from cerebral to passionate (as in John Stuart Mill's reading of Wordsworth to feel again); from secular-dead to spiritual-alive, or sin abiding to grace abounding (Bunyan's allegorized pilgrim); from self-dividedness and weak willing to psychological wholeness (as in William James himself); from a self-stance of social irrelevance or reactive critique to one of symbolic efficacy and national engagement (as in Emerson, Thoreau, Melville, Orestes Brownson [who became a Catholic in 1844], and Whitman [who became a cosmos in "Song of Myself"]); from subjective isolation to semiotic community (as in Josiah Royce); or, later, from "asymbolia" and the absence of meaning to a "new narrative" that reinscribes the unconscious with forgiveness and semiotic plenitude (as in the psychoanalytical model of Julia Kristeva); or, in the laboratories of science, from Aristotelian theory to paradigm-shifting modes of doing nuclear physics (Kuhn).[50] In California, to go from the sublime to the mundane, what Kierkegaard called the Knight of Faith's "expectancy of the impossible" may be the faith that an earthquake, or end-time rupture, will not happen in Los Angeles or San Jose, at least not today.[51] Ever turning, as befits such a climate, William Lobdell (who became a *Los Angeles Times* religion reporter in a weekly column called "Getting Religion") has gone from lack-faith, through evangelical rebirth in 1989, toward a near-conversion to the sacramental ritualism of Catholicism around 2000, and back again to skeptical wariness in the face of sexual and economic corruption in the church-in-denial.[52]

The frames and conditions of conversion are by no means limited to these polarities, which is meant to be suggestive. More broadly situated, the therapeutic tactics of conversion have proved crucial to twelve-step and other recovery programs, from Alcoholics Anonymous (AA) to weight regimes and ex-gay ministries. Soon after his conversion experience and testimony to a detoxifying conviction of "God as we understand Him," Bill Wilson, co-founder of AA in 1935, read James's *Varieties*. As the ex-alcoholic founder avowed to Carl Jung, who was also interested in the psychology of rebirth, "This book [*Varieties*] gave me the realization that most conversion experiences, whatever their variety, do have a common denominator of ego collapse at depth." Wilson wrote in a letter to Jung that AA "has made conversion experiences—nearly every variety reported by James—available on an almost wholesale basis."[53] Tanya Erzen, in her study of the "queering" and "dequeering" tactics of conversion in *Straight to Jesus,* estimates that there are some three million such twelve-step and recovery programs in the contemporary United States alone: such groups often still depend upon tactics of conversion (using terms like "sin" and "powerlessness" as well as self-surrendering turns to "grace") and presume meanings not all that far from the "primitive Christianity" of the Oxford Group that had influenced Wilson's self-shattering reformation in the 1920s and 1930s.[54] As the eleventh step of AA affirms, "[We have] sought through prayer and meditation to improve our conscious contact with God as we understand Him, praying only for knowledge of His will for us and the power to carry it out."

Conversion as Promised Ideologeme

Conversion assumes a signifying process and varying tactics of "becoming semiotic." Conversion offers the self a new vocabulary and alternative syntax for shaping selfhood, a different story to live by, or "supreme fiction" in which to believe, as an encounter with forces of amplified being. At least that is what the pragmatics of plural conversion means for the model of selfhood in James, for whom the stress is on *varieties* of religious experience, *conversion as well as counter-conversion* in differing contexts, shapes, and modes. His philosophical ancestor, Emerson, had captured this sense of perpetual flux and malleability of a given identity, as he posited (in essays like "Circles" or "Self-Reliance") an American self of ever-capitalizing social space, with freedom and empowerment whereby even objects and ideas can immigrate or new technologies can alter frontiers of possibility.[55] This is expressed once again when the radically self-relying Protestant Emerson affirmed, defying predeterminations of culture and social configuration as a first-fall in "Fate," "We rightly say of ourselves, we were born, and afterward we were born again, and many times."[56] In "Experience," Emerson compounded this influx of semiotic power and will to newness and subjective grace by connecting it to the broader powers of typological conversion and the geographical openness of a Pacific-bound America expanding into world space: "I feel a new heart beating. . . . I am ready to die out of nature, and be born again into this new yet unapproachable America I have found in the West."[57] Land and language conspired to open the quasi-Emersonian American self to a flux of New World becoming and transactional power as languages of incoming newness, troping "limit" or "fate" as a kind of perceptual sin or social distortion: this self is posited within parameters of Manifest Destiny expansionism, yet it is all the more so linked to lines of flight and inner forces of becoming.

In the radically Emersonian conversion, delineated in its shocking self-affirmative force in "The Divinity School Address" of 1838, the subject of grace awakens, or rather crosses over into via "transition," one's own conviction of an unlimited "beatitude." In this awakening to a sense of perpetual miraculousness that comes by finding the *newness* of "God in themselves," "A true conversion, a true Christ, is now, as always, to be made, by the reception of beautiful sentiments." In this mode of receptive empowerment, called earlier in the same talk as throughout his writing career "the religious sentiment," "This sentiment is divine and deifying. It is the beatitude of man. It makes him illimitable." Conversion converts the subject into that which is above the self, and the self becomes younger, born again into newness, as Emerson calls it in the fully performative sentences of "Circles," as "life, transition, the energizing spirit."[58] "Born once is born from the spirit below, which is when you're born. It's the spirit you're born with. Born again is born with the Spirit from above, which is different," as Dylan explained the conversion experience that led him to write his first fully gospel album, *Slow Train Coming.*[59]

As a "promised land" in which covenants of world-renewal become literalized, America has provided contexts of mobility, inventiveness, and indetermination to the self, as discussed by such scholars as Bercovitch, Rorty, Poirier, Sollors, and Bloom. Such understanding assumes an antinomian or, at the very least, pluralist terrain in which experiences of "regeneration" have been *promised as rebirth* to various immigrating constituencies, from the Puritans, through Crevecoeur, to Emerson, Thoreau, and Whitman, down to William James, Maxine Hong Kingston, Jack Kerouac, Albert Saijo, and beyond. This encounter occurs as a world-shattering influx of newness and solitary power in which "the spirit must know itself to be free both of other selves and of the created world."[60] Wallace Steven's deathbed conversion (or counter-conversion from the linguistic play of troping over "The Rock" of native nothingness) in 1955 to the "supreme fiction" of Catholicism, in which he mimes the pragmatist scenario he had already depicted through his aesthetic-worshipping portrait of Santayana in "To an Old Philosopher in Rome" (1955), offers an (unexpected) example.[61]

Bob Dylan's conversion from Judaic piety and existential nihilism on the road to a born-again didacticism in albums like *Slow Train Coming, Saved,* and *Infidels* is a radically American-prophetic instance. Dying to what he took to be the narrow or square life of his father's hardware store, Dylan turned toward modes of beat beatitude in order to become the son reborn into his real life as a poet, exchanging sacral signs, literary prophecies like "Chimes of Freedom" flashing for hung-up people across the world, or folk songs brought back from oblivion in the grave. In a formulation that may fit for this uncanny conversion mode in Bob Dylan, Bloom's antinomian claim affirms that "Freedom, in the context of the American Religion, means being alone with God or with Jesus, the American God or the American Christ. In social reality, this translates as solitude, at least in the inmost sense."[62]

If an "ideologeme" inside the self can be defined as "the smallest intelligible unit of the essentially antagonistic discourses of social classes" and

sign of national/transnational struggles (terms taken from Russian "dialogical" linguistics), this formulation offers a way of reading rebirth texts
as a *parole* within the social, global, and class discourse *(langue)* available
to the context-laden style of a given writer.[63] Conversion takes place
within what a Marxist scholar such as Voloshinov would call an "ideological colloquy" between self and other, and is made possible through these
socially situated utterances of language. In these terms, the mutating "ideologeme" of conversion as the *long-promised rebirth* has found a home of
long duration in the discourse of various Americans, multicultural and
otherwise. American poets like Dylan, and Ai or John Ashbery for that
matter, are always *busy being reborn,* and that many times over the course
of a writing and believing career if blockage and diminishment are to be
overcome in the traumatic loneliness and agonistic destiny of America.
This struggle was so in the modernizing Pacific, as we have observed
through the life of 'Ōpūkaha'ia and shall soon see in Epeli Hau'ofa and
others. The born-again subject achieves self-design, narrative emplotment,
and what we would now call (trying to stabilize the semiotic instability and
play of textual difference) a new "identity." But identity, too, means always converting into, or in relation to, the otherness of differing cultures
and altered selves.

Beyond Asymbolia: Busy Being Reborn from Inner Tombs

Burrowing into traumatic figurations of aesthetic modernism after the
death of God and eruption of horrors like Hiroshima and Auschwitz, Julia
Kristeva tracks the subjective shift from deathlike states of melancholia
and depression, marked by "asymbolia" and the suspension of all meaning, to a return of affect, transliteral becoming, and semiotic plenitude.[64]
Emphasizing the powerful role of trope-ridden language to enact such
transference and change in *Soleil Noir,* Kristeva tracks this process of
"reinscription" in the black-sun unconscious via the tormented conversion
narrative and turn to "forgiveness" acted out in the novels of Dostoyevsky.
"So that the unconscious might inscribe itself into a new narrative that will
not be the eternal return of the death drive in the cycle of crime and punishment," Kristeva urges, "it must pass through the love of forgiveness.
The resources of narcissism and idealization imprint their stamps upon the
unconscious and refashion it" (*Black Sun,* 204). As she describes this turn
to semiotic sublimation in *The Idiot* and *Crime and Punishment,* signs of
sublimated identification can reinscribe the self "in the availability of
love," and this hearing of forgiveness "allows [the self] to be reborn"
(*Black Sun,* 190). Later, Kristeva summarizes this agency as an act of

language-poesis: "*Forgiveness emerges first as the setting up of a form*. It has the effect of an acting out, a *poesis*" (*Black Sun*, 206). The process of "semiotic becoming" in conversion depends upon such an active making and resignifying empowerment in the self, a *poesis* felt as the turn to articulate "semiotic representatives" from within "the economy of psychic rebirth."[65]

In René Girard's anthropological portrayal of triangulated desire and the contagion of European literary models begetting a semiotic imitation doomed to frustration, self-ironizing, snobbery, resentment, hypocrisy, and defeat, "The imitation of Christ becomes [in a capitalistic society of mimetic contagion and rivalry] the imitation of one's neighbor."[66] But if such "deviated transcendency" and conversion-downward can move from social resentment and mimetic rivalry (as in snobbery and romantic love) to modes of "vertical transcendency," the renunciation of socially mediated mimicry will be achieved, as in novels that move toward ascetic irony, such as *Red and the Black* and *In Search of Time Past* (*Deceit*, 61). "This time it is not a false but a genuine conversion" (*Deceit*, 294), Girard concludes, invoking some kind of novelistic *imitatio Christi* as counterworldly norm. "Conversion" here means the turn toward the autonomy of a deromanticized selfhood, achieved by aiming the agonistic energies of conversion toward a higher model/rival/mediator—namely, so Girard claims, the narrative turn (at such a novel's end) toward miming self-abnegating "symbols of vertical transcendence whether the author is Christian or not" (*Deceit*, 312).[67] Rebirth, for Girard's self-altering mode of literary mimesis, offers the promise of absolute release from social violence and abiding resentments of capitalist social being in acts of sacrificial self-abolishment and the turn to changed terms.

On the Road to Catholic-Buddhist Beatitude

As Jack Kerouac describes this power of self-forgiveness and conversion to post-Christian beatitude in the "61st Chorus" of *Mexico City Blues*, a collection of jazz-drenched and meandering musings (published by Grove Press in 1959) that influenced poets like Dylan in his early folk-club days in Minneapolis and Ginsberg in manuscript circulation in San Francisco,

> And all my own sins
> Have been forgiven somewhere—
> I don't even remember them,
> I remember the sins of others.

Kerouac pokes fun at this high state of beat conversion and beatified grace by admitting (later in the same poem), "Powerful Tea you gotta smoke/to believe that," but the affirmation still holds.[68] Believing that Thomas Wolfe's writings were "awakening him to the idea of America as a poem, rather than just a place to work and struggle in," as was the effect of Whitman's writing on Ginsberg later, Gerald Nicosia described how Kerouac in July of 1947, "With his romantic sense of quest . . . picked out one long red line, Route 6, that led from Cape Cod to Los Angeles, [and] it reminded him of the pioneer trails, and he planned to follow it all the way to Denver."[69] Such was the power of this beatitude, as conviction of self-forgiveness, and grace that led to roads of becoming and life-quest, the drive to "spontaneous bop prosody" that would generate the world-altering visions of America as written in the Beat-conversion novel of exalted *and* downfallen beatitude, *On the Road* (1957).

Kerouac's writings, read as a project of beatitude lost, found, or quested for again and again, exists between poles (as Paul Giles has elaborated in *American Catholic Arts and Fictions*) charged with, on the one hand, an "ethnic plenitude lost" (which the Franco-American Catholicism of Lowell, Massachusetts, stood for) and, on the other, "the final plenitude of confessional revelation" Kerouac strove toward as novelistic language via the linotype rolls used to write *On the Road* or the reversions in *Big Sur*.[70] In *Big Sur,* the Zen Buddhism of mountain-minded emptiness prominent in *Dharma Bums* or the notebooks of *Some of the Dharma* or the poetic experiments in consciousness of the *Mexico City Blues* gives way to some kind of alcohol-drenched counter-conversion back to the sacramentalism of his youth, as in this fitful scene in the dark night of Pacific privacy. "I lie there in cold sweat wondering what's come over me for years my Buddhist studies and pipesmoking assured meditations in emptiness and all of a sudden the Cross is manifested to me."[71] This sense of post-Catholic beatitude may have pervaded *everything* Kerouac wrote, early and late. As Kerouac's character Ti Jean notes in the clunky "autobiography" of life in the milltown of Lowell, Massachusetts, *Vanity of Duluoz,* he calls himself "one of the world's secret Jesuits, everything I do is based on some kind of proselytization."[72] This is a huge and mysterious claim for such a world-omnivorous writer. All the Dharma Bum had quested for was to write about Jesus, to become beat but hip and cool, as if speaking and honoring the sacramentalism of the holy name even when displaced into the jazz music and saxophone prayers of Charlie Parker.

On March 4, 1955, at a time when he was coming to think of his unpublished Beat manuscripts, including *On the Road,* as "Pre-enlightenment" work moving toward a more visionary form of counter-conversion, Kerouac wrote Ginsberg of his new miscellany of writings drenched in Buddhist teachings and the meditative quest for enlightenment: "*Some of the Dharma* is now over 200 pages, & taking shape as a great valuable book in itself. . . . I intend to be the greatest writer in the world and then in the name of Buddha I shall convert thousands, maybe millions: 'Ye shall be Buddhas, rejoice!' " In ways compounded of tantra, Zen, and Franciscan piety, the novel *The Dharma Bums* became this conversion text to a vernacularized form of American Buddhism-cum-post-Catholic quest for states of fitful beatitude. "I have been having long wild samadhis in the ink black woods of midnight, on a bed of grass," he wrote to Ginsberg from his sister Nin's house in North Carolina, writing the American sky into the black ink of a Zen-enlightenment quest that would bring many post-Beat Americans, including myself back in square Cold War milltowns of Connecticut, into a kindred quest amid the pop culture clash and the spreading "buddhist [sic] boom."[73]

In a pop prose at times cartoonlike in its mixed languages of ad-speak-cum-dharma-quest, Kerouac captured the vernacular form this American Buddhism would take in commodity-culture in a letter he wrote to Philip Whalen in 1958, the year *The Dharma Bums* and *The Subterraneans* were published:

> I mean 1958 will be great year, year of buddhism, already big stir in ny about zen, allen watts big hero of madison avenue now, and nancy wilson ross big article about zen in mademoiselle mentions me and allen and knows her buddhism good, now with dharma bums i will crash open whole scene to sudden buddhism boom and looks what'll happen closely soon. . . . everybody going the way of the dharma, this no shit . . . then with arrival of gary, smash! watch. you'll see, it will be a funny year of enlightenment in america. . . . i dunno about 1959 but 58 is going to be a dharma year in american . . . everybody reading suzuki on madison avenue.[74]

The drive to become "always converting" never left Kerouac, and informed his huge and important project to write literature as a mode of healing and converting others from sadness, blockage, boredom, lifelessness, and death. If Kerouac drank himself to death by 1969, he saw even this as a line of flight to self-abolished states of beatitude and beat mourning.

"To Be Regenerated"

Drawing on a nineteenth-century vocabulary of religious pluralism, whereby the self is enjoined to produce its set of beliefs according to myriad models, William James depicted "conversion" and "counter-conversion" as moving the *divided self* from habits of inferiority and dread to increased vitality and a felt sense of wellness, health, and wholeness. As James later argued in the ideas-as-dynamogenic-agents schema of conversion in his essay "The Energies of Men," "*Conversions,* whether they be political, scientific, philosophic, or religious, form another way in which bound energies are let loose. They unify us, and put a stop to ancient mental interferences. The result is freedom, and often a great enlargement of power."[75] The important element for the pragmatist James (positing ideas not as metaphysical foundations but as psychological instruments of *change*) was not so much the myriad sources of such conversions, however trivial they would seem to outsiders ["Mr. Fletcher's disciples regenerate themselves by the idea (and the fact) that they are chewing, and re-chewing, and super-chewing their food"], but ideas as *lived hypotheses.*

James was interested in the subjective consequences ("results") of such limit-shattering conversions and beliefs, which are real and efficacious ("They unify us"). Ideas are not represented as foundations but are taken as instruments, signs of direction and purpose, especially as these "dynamogenic ideas" become habitual to the shaping of the self. Even if the turning point of the conversion experience is just that—a trope, a turn, an inner belief in a suggestive fiction—what matters for James is that these beliefs can and do work and that they go on producing motor consequences that awaken the self to deeper resources of energy, renewal, and habits of expanded work, even of greatness. James would take stock in the Russian proverb I learned from a Franciscan monk in the Bronx, "Yes, *pray always,* but keep rowing the boat."

James defined the conversion experience in Lecture Nine of *Varieties of Religious Experience:* "To be converted, to be regenerated, to receive grace, to experience religion, to gain an assurance, are so many phrases which denote the process, gradual or sudden, by which a self hitherto divided, and consciously wrong, inferior and unhappy, becomes consciously right, superior and happy, in consequence of its firmer hold upon religious realities" (*Varieties,* 189). The stress on the timing ("gradual or sudden") and plural sources and consequences in the subconsciousness of the self cannot detract from the Christian ideality informing James's vocabulary: the goal remains "to be regenerated, to receive grace, to experience religion." As William Dean Howells's *The Rise of Silas Lapham* represented through its main character and his middle-class family's quest to secure both economic capital and cultural capital in Gilded Age Boston, the conversion to belief in God could be counter-converted into belief in the grandeur and rewards of Capital, or at least this process of Emersonian self-making could be channeled into or undone by market forces larger than subjective narrative.[76]

Even in a secular era, these speculations on conversion come out of the late-capitalist future with relevance, speaking with "extraordinary insight into the spiritual needs of the modern world."[77] Still, this inward experience is haunted by narrative, by fictionality as trope: conversion can be shadowed by an uncanny sense that the self has come to articulation based on the pragmatic mimesis of a prior literary or evangelical model.

Not only did James's experience of dread and self-division recall the "vastation" experience of his father, Henry Sr.; he treats his own experience as a fictional narrative, citing himself as a French "sufferer" afflicted with religious melancholy and "panic fear" (*Varieties,* 135). Even Saint Augustine, the convert from sexual excess, Platonism, and African paganism, as James's footnote from Louis Gourdon's *Essai sur la Conversion de Saint Augustine* reveals (*Varieties,* 144), had shuffled around the time scheme of his world-transforming conversion to Christianity to make it seem permanent, more a total change then it was. Conversion, for Augustine, is surrounded by the turn and return toward "perversion," as Kenneth Burke shows, the turning of the will back to lesser joys, false loves, and empty gods, and a false autonomy of self-choice in a kind of perpetual delinquency and excess, as so many turns toward transgression.[78] As John Henry Newman revealingly confessed in the self-reflective pages of *Apologia Pro Vita Sua,* in contrast to the Calvinist, who has at some point an achieved certainty of elected sanctification, no Catholic can ever tell the converted from the unconverted subject, so that the once- or even twice-born self is never "saved" in any *lasting* state of grace. For Newman, conversion means being always on the verge of falling back into daily sinfulness and subtle modes of heresy—hence the need for repeated conversion acts where "repent" and "convert" become the same event via the sacramental repetition of penance and the Holy Mass he so tenderly believed in across the consubstantial terrains of Victorian England.[79]

"Act Faithfully" as Turning Point in Metanoia and Metamorphosis

Wary of the affective grounds of grace, Jonathan Edwards was cautious that many of the conversion experiences in the first Great Awakening might have been spurious; reflecting a plot of regeneration gleaned more from mimetic contagion than from inward experience. "The scheme already established in their minds," as Edwards warned, shaped the conversion narrative into a too-neat shape, with a convenient *before and after,* with all the subjective parts adjusted to conform to the *a priori* whole of the twice-born plot.[80] Though the consequences might be the same sanctification, the beatified self of everyday confusion was haunted by this sense of signs gathered from the public air and coding the self with textures of belief, as sense of "reality." Mapping the fitful shape, substance, and semiotics of what he calls "the religious affections" that go into the second-birth experience of conversion-by-grace, Edwards's works, like "Sinners in the Hands of an Angry God" or "A Faithful Narrative of the Surprising Work of God," remain masterpieces of self-abnegating selfhood registering the unstable polarities of the conversion-narrative genre in sermon, autobiography, diary, and private quest as Shepard had done for earlier Puritans.

Burdened with producing a set of beliefs and attitudes in the empirical laboratory of hypothesis and consequence that is each pragmatic self, the self indeed acts *as if* it had self-created these thoughts and moods, *as if* in the privacy of the self the ground and signs of belief had been self-engendered, with all the solipsistic *anguish* of privacy and doubt so well embodied in Emily Dickinson as an exemplary or deconstructive case. "*Act* faithfully, and you really have faith," affirmed William James, for whom feelings followed actions and counted (pragmatically considered) as a *semiotic difference* if these led to change. "So to feel brave, act as if we *were* brave, use all our will to that end, and a courage-fit will very likely replace the fit of fear" or negative "fear-thought"—so went the American pragmatism of James.[81] At the believing extreme of embracing "as if" metaphors of belief for James, a higher self can be contacted, re-generative energies do flow into the ego, and conversion-metamorphosis can happen. It is only a matter of *when,* if the proper subliminal attitude of receptiveness and self-suggestion obtains.

The "turning-point" obtains during a traumatic *crisis* of selfhood in which meaning seems blocked, the will to semiotic self-formation becomes clotted, falls into darkness and silence: "self-surrender has been and always must be regarded as the vital turning-point of the religious life" (*Varieties,* 210). The conversion experience obtains when that which has been felt "divided" (hence, in identity-terms, "wrong, inferior and unhappy") is made "unified" (thus forging a self that is "consciously right, superior and happy"). If only the subjective signs are changed by "so many phrases" of healthy-minded semiotics, as in those of Whitman or Billy Bray and the Pentecostals, the affective benefits can be *real.* That is, these signs work to have "cash-value" as instruments and signs of belief and will through semiotic adherence and choice.

William James was aware (in the wake of Pearcean semiotics) that the change need not be "ontological" or metaphysical but can be *semiotic,* a change not so much of the ground of idealism as toward the choice and mutability of signs.[82] As he later argues, in quasi-Nietzschean fashion, "soul" becomes a matter of interpretive perspective: "When I say 'Soul,' you need not take me in the ontological sense unless you prefer to. . . . Talking of this part [the "soul" as "only a succession of fields of consciousness"], we involuntarily apply words of perspective to distinguish it from the rest, words like *here, this, now, mine,* or *me;* and we ascribe to other parts the positions *there, then, that, his, or thine, it not me.* But a *here* can change to a *there* and a *there* become a *here,* and what was *mine* and *not mine* change their places" (*Varieties,* 195). Conversion can be undone into a counter-conversion, via backsliding into reversion or toward a set of alternative narratives, beliefs, and signs. It is as if the boundaries of consciousness to the self can be changed by altering semiotic perspectives, as the core of the "me" takes in more of the "not me" through representing a change of territory. There is a transformation of tropes with consequences that are real, effecting alterations in the coding of the self.

This habit-altering self need not be converted to a total belief-system—as in Erickson's life-cycle scenario—or away from what we would now call Romantic "self-consciousness" subjected to temporality. As James realized in plural contexts of awakening (like that in Kate Chopin's *Awakening,* her heroine converting to feminist empowerment and erotic flight, if not oceanic self-abolishment), conversion is full of *varieties of religious and nonreligious* ("psychological") experience. A conversion can occur in settings of linguistic nihilism: one can be converted to emptiness, or to a belief in the power of the deconstructive sign, shorn of ontological ground. Emerson was crossing the bare commons on an abyss of signs, close to the sublimity of an antinomian selfhood shorn of all social ties and fixed frames.[83] As Bloom affirms, invoking Gallup polls and William James in *Jesus and Yahweh: The Names Divine,* to bolster claims for a pragmatically Americanized Jesus, the "paradoxes [of Jesus] always have been universal, but his personalism is nineteenth-century American, from the Cane Ridge Revival of 1801 all the way to the circus-like Revivalism of Charles Grandison Finney, precursor of Billy Sunday and Billy Graham. Eighty-nine percent of Americans regularly inform the Gallup pollsters that Jesus loves each of them on a personal and individual basis. That moves me perpetually to awe and to no deconstructive irony whatsoever."[84] This Jesus becomes a force for *auto-poesis,* opening paths to the Over-soul and the forging of love's body as communal polity.

Embracing Multicultural Conversions and New Age Mutations

U.S. minority versions of this conversion-genre of self-formation abound in multicultural or postcolonial contexts. Werner Sollors has called attention to transethnic texts that have proved instrumental to representing the "ethnic conversion experience" of American authors as diverse as Malcolm X, Mary Antin, and Frederick Douglass. Such works take shape by narrating a turn away from self-hatred or racial abjection, toward constructing an "emerging group identity."[85] Narrating the shape of subjectivity via polarities and movements "from . . . to" (from ethnic immigrant to assimilated American, or conversely, in postcolonial contexts, from assimilated American to unmelted ethnic), this strong sense of a conversion typology is "characteristic of the many Sauls who became Pauls in their Damascus of America," as Sollors urges, playing on the Pauline framework (*Beyond Ethnicity*, 32). The shifts and refiguring of the conversion story by U.S. minorities, as well as the embedded frameworks of spiritual typology this story of new birth often depends upon, are given fresh reincarnations in the mobile frames of liberal democracy and have efficacy in the ever-globalizing and minority-languaging United States. As Sollors summarizes the discursive hold of such rhetoric in *Beyond Ethnicity*, "Typological rhetoric may indicate the Americanization of people who use it" (49). Or, as Charles Taylor puts this in *A Secular Age*, as he maps the faith-turns of American religiosity, "one can be integrated as an American [into the "common civil religion"] *through* one's faith or religious identity" more so than through race, ethnicity, or any marker of multicultural difference.[86]

In postnational contexts (impacted by what Randolph Bourne called in 1916 the cosmopolitical romance of a "trans-national America" nourished by ethnic flux [*Beyond Ethnicity*, 183]), such a renewed typology of cultural choice and religious self-fashioning, "can, alternately or at the same time, serve to define a new ethnic peoplehood in contradistinction to a general American identity" (*Beyond Ethnicity*, 49).[87] Even more so, in postmodern and/or postcolonial works of transnational globality and multilingual textuality, such as Theresa Cha's *Dictee* (1982) and Fae Myenne Ng's *Bone* (1993), the materiality of paper, sign, and blood linger and can serve as forces blocking and detotalizing "the 'conversion' of Chinese into 'Americans.'" To invoke the counter-assimilation claim of Lisa Lowe on this recalcitrant historiography of transnational exclusion, "the conversion [to American] can never be complete."[88] San Francisco Chinatown, in Ng's scrappy rendering in *Bone*, remains "a recalcitrant space that cannot be wholly or univocally translated": thus, the *refusal to convert* or *translate* becomes a mode of living outside or at least against U.S. social hegemony via ties to race and counter-languages.[89]

In Shakespeare's New World allegory, *The Tempest* (1610), the "white magic" of Prospero would take over the Caribbean Bermudas by punishing Caliban into modes of conversion and the need to "seek for grace" after the European master-figure had first abjected the island native into a "devil," "savage," natural-born sinner, rapist, and slave. This helped to give conversion colonial efficacy and its postcolonial bad name.[90] The Pacific islands remain tormented by these conversion dynamics. It would come as no surprise that the characters of Albert Wendt's postcolonial Samoa (see epigraph to this chapter) try to flee the London Missionary Society heirs and those "modernaitu" (modern gods) of Western capitalism and its profit-making system. Via counter-conversion to renewed forms of nativism and Pacific becoming, such characters flee their Western-drenched societies to reconnect to Polynesian gods reborn in the lava ("All is well in Lava, so spake the Flying-Fox"), for whom laughter, escape, and self-abolishment call the pidgin-narrator and his Flying Fox accomplice back to "find the self again."[91] Still, no pure nativist, Wendt's Pacific characters mime "existential" codes of heroic resistance to social norms, and his settings are often urban postmodern from Auckland to Jerusalem. Conversion, as Henry 'Ōpūkaha'ia realized in New England, may have been doing what comes culturally to a Judeo-Christian interpreter of the self: Henry took a pocket Bible with him everywhere and read and quoted from it at any free moment.

Lacking in such figures of transcendence that can mediate mimetic rivalry, as far as I can tell, Hawaiian stories often abound in jealous rivalry, treachery, fits, and flights of natural passion, betrayal, and failed transcendence, as in the love rivalries and failed lineages of the twin sisters in *The Legend of La'ieikawai,* as recently retold and illustrated by the artist Dietrich Varez.[92] S. N. Hale'ole had famously published this much-told story in Hawaiian as *The Hawaiian Romance of La'ieikawai* (1863); it was translated into English by Martha Beckwith in 1919 and reprinted in a dual-language edition by Dennis Kawaharada in 1997. The legends of the Hawaiian goddess sisters Pele and Hi'iaka abound in these premissionary patterns of metamorphosis and familial rage and passion.[93]

Conversions Multiply

Yet as our time-honored scenarios of regenerated selfhood from Bible-drenched James to the neoethnic frames of Sollors suggest, this "ideologeme" of conversion has found a free-floating home in the discourse of post-Puritan America. Conversion multiplies and serves as a boomeranging trope of self-fashioning regeneration to encode the self with coherent meaning, in a sociological context of maximum mobility and seeming indetermination, a radical antinomian and pluralist terrain in which "regeneration" has been promised from the Puritans, through Crevecoeur, to Emerson and the Jameses and beyond. According to John Owen King III in *The Iron of Melancholy,* conversion in Puritan-influenced America occurs in the experience of some "wilderness." This means some traumatized terrain of inner darkness and wildness wherein the habitual self becomes *lost* from daily comforts into an unmapped, uncanny, directionless zone of melancholy and compulsion.[94] This was a "kind of aimless weather, doing and undoing, achieving no proper history, and leaving no result," as William James wrote in *Varieties of Religious Experience.* For Henry James Sr., as for his frail-nerved " 'alienist" son, a private experience of "vastation" or "self-dividedness" occurs and puts the self out of itself, in a moment of crisis, which calls for conversion to some larger and socially encoded narrative of felt wholeness.[95] This reflects a latter-day Christian plot by now interiorized as psychology, but still providing a retrospective meaning to self-division. Division must give way to an affirmation, fitfully maintained, and conviction of self-unity and narrative submission.

In the morphology of the American Puritan conversion experience, Jonathan Edwards had lamented that subjective accounts were becoming all too textually predictable, what we would call contagiously *mimetic,* all too alike in one narrative paradigm. This is what Patricia Caldwell calls the linear schematizing of signs into a whole "morphology" that overrides "religious affections."[96] As a result, "many spiritual narratives of the period were not so much composed as recited," as Edmund Morgan put it.[97] The post-Puritan self went on becoming "always converted" into the narrative shape of preexisting texts, miming some totalization of his/her story as one of narrative finality ("he became a Christian," as Henry's tombstone recorded it). This form of American Puritan subjectivity—as a rather *fixed* born-again morphology—was registered as a passage through states of self-loss in "the annihilation of the self, or conversion," often felt as "a severe trauma, and [Cotton] Mather repeatedly calls it a kind of dying."[98]

More broadly framed in existential contexts, the conversion experience can be read as the imposition of narrative on the flux of experience, the inner weather of subjectivity. Narrative imposes what Jean-Paul Sartre called the "totalizing" textual interpretation of a central moment, such as what Sartre-as-biographer portrays as Flaubert's call to the vocation of literature and God and away from a life of law and philistine dictates of his father.[99] Subjectivity can be marked with textual traces bespeaking anxieties of mimetic rivalry and semiotic imitation. Conversion is founded upon the unstable grounds of hyperbole and repression, shifting via metaphor between language and ontology. The result might not be security but uncertainty, the wholeness of signifying *fictionality, mask,* and *trope,* as Neil Hertz contends in his reading of Sartre on Flaubert: "conversion comes to seem [for

Jules in *Sentimental Education*, as he embodies Flaubert's own anxieties] less an act of totalization than what one repeatedly does in despair of totalization."[100] Here, conversion repeats its own temporal (and temporary) design in what John D. Barbour calls a "deconversion" narrative with a beginning, turning middle, and more settled end.[101]

In the "beloved community" vision of Josiah Royce in his Oxford University lectures at Manchester College in 1913, conversion occurs (just *once*) to rescue the puny American democratic self from the subjective flux of ungovernable interpretations and sign-substitutions: conversion provides a beginning, a middle, and an end, a past and a future for the self rooted in extra-narrative "loyalty" to the life-pattern of Christ (as interpreted by the "born-again" scheme of Paul). The subject is interpellated with Charity, via the conventions of the Christian code, from cradle to the grave. The conversion experience transpires in language, as a born-again recoding of the subject. This takes place (to use Royce's terms) as *recognition* by the subject of its language-coded selfhood, which can then turn to the Christian paradigm of Saint Paul as a narrative legitimated by the Beloved Community of interpretants.[102] The corporate mediation of the conversion experience has been stressed as well by Charles Taylor, who would hold out for a James-like charismatic individualism against its formation into religious institutions or dead forms.[103] Charity is not so much subjective transport or what the postcolonial African anthropologist Johannes Fabian calls "standing-in-ecstasy" outside given ethnographic codes, but an interpretation of rebirth as one affirming the self-abolishing code living in the Beloved Community.[104]

Converted to the semiotic code, the self becomes coherent and makes sense and fits into an Anglo-American community of rebirth, via a coherent narrative of past and future patterned on the plot of the timeless and placeless *imitatio Christi*. The mobilized self is not heterogeneous, not lost to itself in time and place, but made whole via narrative—civilized, relocated, de-nativized, reformed by new language and sublimating influx of grace. A life that has been lost in time and confused into multiple interpretation has been found through the autobiography of textual interpretation and the stabilizing of signs. Conversion, as such, can turn into an all too stabilizing and normalizing form and looks all too much like the linchpin of neoliberal colonization. Conversion can turn some subjects to the theocratic support of Empire and what Hardt and Negri call the forces of "armed globalization" and everyday insecurity. "God's warriors," as CNN calls these monotheological advocates for global-cultural warfare, abound.

The ideologeme and mandate of rebirth have found an all-too-American home and affirmed its Manifest Destiny of self-empowerment to cross boundaries and expand, from coast to coast, if not beyond, to globalize its reign at times, spreading across new world and old from Mexico to Korea, like some neo-Roman dispensation.[105] "Americanization" has often resulted in the turn to affirming some version of a *new selfhood arising in a new land,* but the dream can grow prefabricated, overcoded, fixed with neoliberal certitude before the semiotic process has even begun. Even such a revolutionary force as Tom Paine could affirm this quasi-religious vision of American and world renewal, in *Common Sense:* "We have it in our power to begin the world over again. A situation, similar to the present, hath not happened since the days of Noah until now. The birth-day of a new world is at hand."[106] But conversion, even in these climates, threatens to *revert* into a colonizing form.

"My Name Is Lazarus" on Eternal Word Television Network of Irondale, Alabama

For G. K. Chesterton, the colorful "apostle of common sense," the modernist struggle between a desacralized cosmos and will to voice and affirm rebirth, as portrayed in his poem "The Convert," meant a life-altering turn away from liberal "sages" and "the hundred maps" of scientific rationality at the core of global modernity and its open-ended freedom of semiotic becoming. Chesterton here and elsewhere moves toward sacramental commitment, sublime orthodoxy, and a converting ecumene via his turn back to the magisterium of the Roman Catholic Church:

> The sages have a hundred maps to give
> That trace their crawling cosmos like a tree,
> They rattle reason out through many a sieve
> That stores the sand and lets the gold go free:
> And all these things are less than dust to me
> Because my name is Lazarus and I live.[107]

Chesterton's defection from liberal modernity has found devotees not only on Mother Angelica's Eternal Word Television Network (EWTN) but also among scholarly allies as unlikely as Slavoj Žižek and Harold Bloom. *My name is Lazarus and I live* might well sum up the aspiration and goal of many a conversion and counter-conversion search inside the semiotic possibility of Anglo-American modernity, even if the tropes, translations, and tactics would be coded quite otherwise and elsewhere in postcolonial terms. Undergoing a revival within postmodernity, as has that other convert to his own allegory of higher love, C. S. Lewis, Chesterton has become one of the models for neo-Catholic conversion on Mother Angelica's EWTN cable station telecast from Irondale, Alabama, which runs a weekly show hosted by Dale Ahlquist examining Chesterton's work and life as well as an interesting interview show on various Catholic "converts" and "reverts" hosted by ex-Lutheran minister Marcus Grodie called "Coming Home." Since its founding in 1981, EWTN has aimed (following the globalization mandate of Pope John Paul II) "to re-evangelize the baptized" and via this minority use of mass media to *convert the converted* (as it were) back to deeper sacramental commitment.

Conversion evangelism has spread across mainland and oceans, from post-Puritanical New England, to convert and counter-convert (from native beliefs) a sovereign Pacific nation like Hawai'i into space of plural modernity and semiotic becoming. This process of semiotic becoming is far from over, fixed, or closed, as Royce would have it in his "Beloved Community" of one-way becoming. Global evangelism has resulted in an unstable, carnivalesque process of rejection, overthrow, and reversal across "Oceania." As Dennis Kawaharada tracks the contemporary process of reading Native Hawaiian stories, legends, chants, and poems, as "verbal maps" for remembering "storied landscapes," he urges that we achieve "knowledge, understanding, and appreciation of pre-Christian, pre-colonial Hawai'i and closer connection to the land and sea."[108] In other words, the push is toward articulating the *re-nativization* of language, land, and place, miming a postcolonial counter-conversion toward a half-forgotten ecology and premodern geopolitical vision of belonging that dismantles settler colonialism as a surface knowledge and misrecognition. The *re-goded* poems of Haunani Kay Trask and the novels of Rodney Morales and James Houston map failed Americanization, a counterexegesis into modes of Hawaiian and multicultural belief, literary scripts of decolonization and de-conversion.[109]

Conversion and globalization go hand and hand, as cultural critics as diverse as Charles Taylor and Mike Davis have claimed in works on evangelical belief-from-below. As Taylor writes, "The surge of evangelical Protestantism often occurs in contexts where community has broken down, in Third World countries, where people have been pitched into urban life, often in chaotic circumstances and without support systems."[110] In apocalyptic terms, Davis charts the postsocialist rise of charismatic beliefs in slum cities, across countries on the downside of global capital, as across and within Third World formations at home from Compton to Honolulu and faith-torn Mumbai: "Today [on our "planet of slums"], populist Islam and Pentecostal Christianity (and in Bombay, the cult of Shivaji) occupy a social space analogous to that of early twentieth-century socialism and anarchism."[111]

Conversion from below can awaken Christian-socialist agency, not just neoliberalization Empire plot. The Gospels were never quite history or biography, as Bloom has remarked, but were shaped "as conversionary inspiration" across contexts, eras, and modes.[112] Mapping our current religion-drenched polity, the Old Testament–leaning Bloom predicts, "The American Jesus has usurped Yahweh, and may yet himself be usurped by the Holy Spirit, as we fuse into a Pentecostal nation, merging Hispanics, Asians, Africans, and Caucasian Americans into a new people of God."[113] This Jesus, as Bloom troped, has become a *multicultural everything*. This Jesus, I would add, may very well be a beat Indian speaking pidgin.

Moving toward a Postcolonial Poesis of Counter-Conversion

My stress on *poesis* and semiotic mutability aims to open a dialogical hearing of these alternative visions and faith claims, abjected cultures, mongrel languages, and social becoming. Poetics can allow for modes of listening to and for these languages of counter-conversion, what Emerson affirmed was social "aversion," nonconformity, and alternative belief. Not alone in the decolonizing Pacific, Hawai'i goes on coming unglued at the semiotic and cultural-political seams, for example, as Anglo-Saxon names fly off from places and "Dole Street" can conjure an alternative history to that of missionary belonging or white-American settlement.[114]

The closest American literature comes to such consciousness for "Oceania" is the quasi-Buddhist transcendence we get in Edmund Tyrone, renegade son of the Connecticut Irish-American Catholic family of actors, writers, and addicts who took to the sea as space of flight, renewal and self-invention, in Eugene O'Neill's self-portrait in *Long Day's Journey into Night* (1956).[115] As Edmund Tyrone confides to his self-absorbed father, a Shakespearean actor who has turned to Broadway kitsch, on a moonlit night off Buenos Aires in Pacific trade winds off Argentina, he felt a sense of cosmic unity and self-annihilation "like a saint's vision of beatitude":

> I became drunk with the beauty and singing rhythm of it, and for a moment I lost myself—actually lost my life. I was set free! I dissolved in the sea, became white sails and flying spray, became beauty and rhythm, became moonlight and the ship and the high dim-starred sky! I belonged, without past or future, within peace and unity and a wild joy, within something greater than my own life, or the life of Man, to Life itself! To God if you want to put it that way.[116]

With "the veil of things as they seem drawn back as if by an unseen hand," the young quester for post-Irish Catholic beatitude Tyrone (he has just found out he has TB as he recalls blissful nights as a mariner on the ocean) undergoes a kind of counter-conversion from guilt and pain—and Catholic belief system of his family—toward Oceanic Consciousness. Both experiences of this "beatitude" (holy-happy consciousness of unity) that he recounts take place in rocking rhythms of the sublime Pacific.

The spirit, as if craving release from skeptical modernity, did move across ocean waters, and O'Neill gave this vision shape and voice. If O'Neill's project "from the start seemed to know that his spiritual quest was to undermine Emerson's American religion of self-reliance," Edmund Tyrone's flights into Oceanic Consciousness in the Pacific seem radically Emersonian in their solitary crossings into sites and signs of sanctifying immensity, states of "beatitude," by which the Over-Soul could become known.[117] In the next chapter, we shall interrogate emergent forms of over- and underdevelopment of oceanic consciousness in a more contemporary context, the Pacific counter-conversion as reimagined in the postcolonial fiction, ecumenical regionalism, and the cultural critiques of Epeli Hau'ofa's "Oceania," to which we now turn.

CHAPTER FOUR

Writing down the Lava Road from Damascus to Kona

Counter-Conversion, Pacific Polytheism, and
Re-Nativization in Epeli Hauʻofaʾs Oceania

I look at the map of the Pacific.
The American navy calls the Pacific the American Lake.
They have ships in Samoa
Hawaiʻi, Taiwan, the Philippines,
Belau, Kwajalein, Truk
the Marianas, the Carolines.
In Micronesia, there are 90,000 people,
who gives a damn?
The dead are louder in protest than the living.
The living are silent.
Silent.
Silent
Silent
Silent
Silent.

> —John Pule, *The Shark That Ate the Sun*[1]

"We're here to sell lubricants, Bob White, industrial lubricants,
not to save souls . . . get it, son?"

> —Older salesman to younger, Jesus-believing salesman
> in *The Big Kahuna,* 1999

On the Road to Kona

These days of global popular culture, a New Age fascination with exotic-
ness and world music, as well as an all-but-hegemonic Americanism
across the Pacific from Auckland to Tokyo and Suva, a " 'South Pacific'
epiphany" is apt to mean, still, some strong-voiced baritone at the Lincoln
Center choosing to sing "This Nearly Was Mine" instead of "Some Enchanted Evening" to mourn his vision of paradise lost in the far-flung Pacific.[2] *Kahuna* is not just Hawaiian word for *priest,* mana-laden signifier
for the vocation of piety (as we have seen) in Henry ʻŌpūkahaʻiaʾs journey
from Kona to New Haven but has also become Los Angeles slang for

big-time operator.[3] At a deromanticizing extreme of science, university disciplines (like geography, ecology, and archaeology) continue to use islands in the South Pacific (especially Rapa Nui) to signify parables of environmental destruction, deforestation, and cultural collapse.[4] The "Easter" proclaimed in Easter Island, the trope of rebirth Dutch explorers gave Rapa Nui in 1722, has taken on eco-planetary meanings not of rebirth or cultural renewal but of decay, degeneration, and death. Postwar "cargo cults" that had promised to bring in some kind of *white savior* (like his baptizing prophet named John Frum) installed a "road belong cargo" filled with white refrigerators, radios, cigarettes, jeeps, and a Pacific Ocean that had turned into, as John Pule protests (in the epigraph to this chapter) with voices rising from nuclear graves, "the American Lake."[5]

Nowadays, Pacific Island authors and culture-makers figure the epiphanies, tropes, and regenerations of native attitude taking place across the contemporary Pacific otherwise and elsewhere. These visions and countermemories, as I shall explain further, are neither recycled nostalgias of *South Pacific* or Hollywood comedy nor the misdirected millenarianism of a commodity culture or global war.[6] It was as a transpacific visitor to Hawai'i in March of 1993, where he had been invited to give a social-science keynote talk at the Association of Social Anthropologists in Oceania in Hilo and at the East West Center in Honolulu, that Epeli Hau'ofa experienced his life-altering, culture-renewing, and counter-Pauline moment of charismatic conversion. Hau'ofa's much-cited essay, "Our Sea of Islands," delivered as a keynote talk from Suva and Hilo to Honolulu in the spring of 1993, helped to set the new terms, change the affects, and reframe the macrogeography and micropolitics across the postcolonial Pacific region. This essay has come to be called, from its frame-shifting utterance, "a new paradigm for the Pacific."[7] Uncanny and unsettling, Hau'ofa's "holistic perspective" as he calls his critical mode of visionary amplitude and cosmopolitical renewal in "Our Sea of Islands," aims to turn hypermodernized Pacific islanders like himself away from world-system despair and back toward a hugely *oceanic* perception of place, transnational community, islander space, myth, and language. The turn of rebirth was toward opening a more polytheistic and hopeful ecumene he calls, historicizes, and tropes as a New Oceania.

For, this third-coming time around, in what Hau'ofa had earlier more sardonically termed the "Second Coming" of decolonization and the banal repetitions of national mimicry, postcolonial conversion would now mean the life-shattering event of a *becoming-in-reverse,* a turn away from taken-for-granted Christian codes of nation-state labor, versions of bogus independence, or "developmentalist" frameworks of global dependency and neocolonial entanglement in modern worlding that would "stress [Native Pacific] smallness and belittlement." These frames serve to discourage, demoralize, and pacify islanders in the Pacific. "The drive from Kona to Hilo was my 'road to Damascus,'" Hau'ofa shrewdly noted, with an uncanny intertextual figuration of New Testament biblical echoes and (what I have called) *translation-downward* from identity and type to body, historical situation, and world place:

> I saw such scenes of grandeur as I had not seen before: the eerie blackness of regions covered by recent volcanic eruptions; the remote majesty of Mauna Loa, long and smooth, the world's largest volcano; the awesome craters of Kilauea threatening to erupt at any moment; and the lava flow on the coast not far away. Under the aegis of Pele, and before my very eyes, the Big Island was growing from the depths of a mighty sea. The world of Oceania is not small; it is huge and growing bigger every day."[8]

"Our Sea of Islands" enacted, as a speech-act of performative and auto-critique, a way of troping and narrating the nation-leaping and ecological expansiveness of the watery Pacific Ocean across sites like Fiji, Tonga, Papua New Guinea, Hawai'i, and Australia, where this native anthropologist's Pacific formation had, in these neodiasporic terms of interconnection, taken place. Hau'ofa had converted, in effect, from genres of economics and social science to fiction and poetry, with a post-Pauline vengeance that perhaps only a preacher's prodigal son could muster.

Hau'ofa registered this autobiographical experience of counter-conversion via an evocative sensibility for "Oceania," in a vision of place and identity linking the sublimity of the volcanic island on the Big Island to vast waters *(moana nui)* of the Pacific. Tongan offspring of a Pacific Islander missionary to Papua New Guinea and prodigal son of social anthropology as well, Epeli Hau'ofa had become what Emerson has called a strange "crab fruit" of worship and tropological energy in the Pacific.[9] "Islands in a far sea" were reframed into an interconnected "sea of islands" alive with mobility, metaphors, and mappings, generative of action, community, and hope ("Our Sea of Islands," 7) that do not fit the terms or needs of "the American Lake." However, before this new vision of oceanic becoming, like some Saul persecuting the primitive Christians before the second-birth into Saint Paul, Hau'ofa had been aligned (via dependency models) to articulating "MIRAB" forces of containment, denigration, and limitation, if not death, for the interior Pacific: "Soon the realization dawned on me," Hau'ofa confesses at the outset, "I was actively participating in our own belittlement, in propagating a view of hopelessness" ("Our Sea of Islands," 5).[10]

Work by work, turning from social science to poetry and fiction, Hau'ofa would go on to offer uncanny feedback to the ex-colonial powers, from England and America to New Zealand and Japan (which remains Tonga's principal market, for exports from fish to cassava, yams, coconut, and some knitted clothes). Such *conversion* for the interior Pacific to reigning forms of developmentalism remains, to this day, the taken-for-granted ideology or common sense of "globalization." "Echoing paradigms now applied routinely in north-south relations between wealthy and impoverished nations," as David Hanlon and Geoffrey M. White have noted, "a current, almost evangelical view of the [Pacific] region emanating from Australia paints a 'doomsday' scenario for island peoples unless they transform themselves into responsible, productive, and informed citizens of the modern world."[11]

Into such visions of geopolitical redemption via global capitalism, Hau'ofa's "Our Sea of Islands" intervenes with a counter-conversion that turns away from his own earlier political-economic commitment to evangelical developmentalism and doomsday melancholia. "Oceania," so refigured and rescaled from the interior Pacific, becomes a way of building up a new form of Pacific Islander "oceanic consciousness," as Freud et al. had termed this feeling of primordial unity for self and other, but this time as a move toward consolidation from below and as framed in a geopoliticized mode.[12] "Oceania" becomes a figure of transnational "mobility" from below, recalling water-voyaging, jet traveling, and world-enlarging capaciousness as a "world of social networks that crisscross the ocean all the way from Australia and New Zealand in the southwest, to the United States and Canada in the northeast," as Hau'ofa later writes in "The Ocean in Us" (1998).

"In portraying this new Oceania I wanted to raise, especially among our emerging generations," Hau'ofa urges, "the kind of consciousness that would help free us from the prevailing, externally generated definitions of our past, present, and future."[13] From Oakland to Auckland to Suva and Honolulu, in his uncanny and figurative reframing of roots (islands) and routes (oceanic crossings), the *cross* gives way to the "crisscross" of transpacific mobility and diasporic interconnectedness and reciprocity. Oceania becomes not just heritage or blood but a trope of commitment, vision, and will. It is as if, by translation and Pacific-based reimagining, the anticolonial curse delivered by Vanuatu pidgin poet Albert Leomala years ago against the "Cross"—Kross mi no wandem yu / Yu killim mi / Yu sakem aot ol / We blong mi"—had been lifted by this "crisscross" of transnational possibility and native redemption.[14]

Overcoming an inculcated sense of smallness and neocolonial dependency, Hauʻofa's moment of crisscrossing and self-altering counter-conversion, in "Our Sea of Islands," becomes an uncanny signifier and performative speech-act as a re-nativized trope of "rebirth," looking back to the Bible, yes, but (all the more so) troping forward to a new-made religion, poetics, and art across Oceania, one resonant with hopefulness across the postcolonial Pacific future. This turn of rebirth moves toward a poetics of "Oceania" drenched in vision bespeaking new eyes, altered consciousness, a new-ocean, and new-earth. For this joyous moment of vision-making poesis was, for Hauʻofa, his counter-conversion back to native values and ways of seeing that are affirmed on a large scale worthy of such Pacific gods as Maui and Pele, who are recalled.

The belittling vision of the colonized and dependent Pacific nation is overcome ("Our Sea of Islands," 10), as native deities are reinvoked as keepers of this Oceanic *genius loci* ("Our Sea of Islands," 11), and a native sublimity is signified as interconnecting land, ocean, self, and community. Such modes of space and minor transnational linkages are reclaimed, and the Pacific Ocean is *re-worlded* and *re-goded* as an immense formation, "the world of Oceania" as crisscrossed by generations of Polynesian and Pacific Island voyagers and settlers. "This is not dependence but interdependence," Hauʻofa contends via this vision of globalization-from-below, "which is purportedly the essence of the global system" ("Our Sea of Islands," 13). Hauʻofa's protagonist of this grassroots transnational agency is a diasporic Tongan, "twice my size who lives in Berkeley, California," works as a gardener, and shuttles back and forth from the Oakland international airport to Fiji and Tonga with coolers full of t-shirts, kava, sea food, and so on, to help send his son to college: "There are thousands like him, who are flying back and forth across national boundaries, the International Dateline, and the Equator, far above and completely undaunted by the deadly serious discourses below on the nature of the Pacific Century, the Asia/Pacific co-prosperity sphere, and the dispositions of the post-cold war Pacific Rim, cultivating their ever growing universe in their own ways" ("Our Sea of Islands," 15), Hauʻofa affirms.

Becoming the Transpacific Tongan United States

While it may seem odd to invoke a Tongan writer here in this U.S. global or Asian-Pacific context, we should recall that, first, due to the labor diaspora that has amplified in the past fifteen years, there are now more overseas Tongans (93,000+) than there are Tongan residents in Tonga (91,000+); and they often claim to practice the *anga fakatonga* (Tongan way) and alter kinship and status patterns.[15] Second, during the recent pro-democratic, youth, and labor protests in Tonga in November 2006 in which six died, some of the destruction that took place in the Tongan capital of Nuku'alofa was directed against Chinese-owned shops, to such an extent that two hundred Chinese nationals had to be flown out of the country on a plane chartered by Beijing. So, as with the ethnic antagonism directed against settler Indians in Fiji during the coup, although Asia/Pacific may forget the Pacific, the Pacific is not *forgetting Asia,* and we need to deal with these struggles in a timely, situated, and capacious framework. Ethnic figurations become ethical obligation in how we can reframe our globalization models of conversion and the altered lifeworlds they would narrate and interconnect into being, from "villages to "suburbs" or back.

This transpacific diaspora of job-seeking Tongans is so strong nowadays, for example, that some 8,100 live in the San Francisco Bay Area alone, mostly in San Mateo County, where their king (the last monarch in the Pacific) keeps a residence in a wealthy suburb, though most of these U.S. Tongans live in the poorer or middle-class sections of East Palo Alto, San Bruno, and San Mateo. Some 4,000 Tongans now live in Euless, Texas, a Dallas-Forth Worth suburb, and their male offspring have helped turn the Trinity High school football team not just into the state football champion but into the number-one team in *USA Today's* ranking as of November 21, 2008. Perhaps Hau'ofa plays down the huge class divisions and labor factors of his own Tongan diaspora emigrating across the Pacific from Auckland and Suva to Texas and San Mateo, but his vision is magnanimous and would cut across identity divides and offer hope, mobility, and a vision of empowerment to Pacific Islanders. In a three-sentence final paragraph, Hau'ofa concludes "Our Sea of Islands" with a sublime invocation of his spatial-historical trope, Oceania, as he concludes (like some watery Wordsworth) with this parallel-summoning image of regeneration, community, and rebirth in (and of) the Pacific (16):

> Oceania is vast, Oceania is expanding, Oceania is hospitable and generous, Oceania is humanity rising from the depths of brine and regions of fire deeper still, Oceania is us. We are the sea, we are the ocean, we must wake up to this ancient truth and together use [this vision of Oceania] to overturn all hegemonic views that aim ultimately to confine us again, physically and psychologically, in the tiny spaces which we have resisted accepting as our sole appointed place, and from which we have recently

liberated ourselves. We must not allow anyone to belittle us again, and take away our freedom.

To this resacralizing "waking up" to new beginnings for Oceania, "something as revolutionary as perspectival shift," the Indo-Fijian novelist Sudesh Mishra could only respond with a prolonged "OM," lyrically adding from the Hindu Pacific that "the 'O' in Oceania is the 'O' in Om," a sacred sound.[16]

In the Pauline moment of conversion from death to rebirth, the moment of grace conferred ecumenical capaciousness, broke down" the middle wall of partition between us," and made Greek and Jew, slave and free, "no more stranger and foreigners, but fellowcitizens with the saints, and of the household of God" (Ephesians 2:14–19). Saul, a Jew and Roman citizen from Tarsus, encountered the voice of the resurrected Christ on the road to Damascus and became "Paulus," forevermore "made new" and "sanctified" by grace. This production of equality and the casting off of class, race, or gender differences hailed subjects into a new universal singularity, a sublime ecumene, via a world-shattering *event* overcoming cultural confinement and reified deadness (as Alain Badiou has phrased it) in which "differences *carry the universal that happens to them like a grace.*"[17] Hau'ofa, like Amilcar Cabral in a postcolonial sense of altered region, is *re-Pacificizing* the terms and syntax of this conversion experience and making it serve altered ecumenical ends of region-building, communal transformation, and moral uplift.[18]

To sum up the world-shattering Pauline moment of subject-formation into "new man" of world refiguration and rebirth, in the "militant" antiliberal and countercapitalist terms Badiou would use against U.S. Empire, as was earlier discussed, "Paul demonstrates in detail how a universal thought, proceeding on the basis of the worldly proliferation of alterity (the Jew, the Greek, women, men, slaves, free men, and so on) *produces* a Sameness and an Equality (there is no longer either Jew or Greek, and so on). The production of equality and the casting off, in thought, of differences are the material signs of the universal."[19] But in an interior Pacific region that encompasses some 25,000 islands, 7,500 of which constitute the cultural zones of Melanesia, Micronesia, and Polynesia, how can any concept or figure encompass such heterogeneity and overcome all such divisions and differences, so long inculcated (even at the University of South Pacific) via markers of race, nation, language, cultural more, and kinship? How can a vision of *unity,* apart from the discarded assumption of the "Pacific Way" to neodevelopmentalism, somehow emerge to align this contemporary diversity?[20] How could one "reconvert" converted nationals toward

this transcultural, outernational, transracial, and coalitional project to figure place and self as postcolonial creatures of "Oceania"?

As Douglas Borer objected, in a macrostructural response to Hau'ofa's
unifying vision, "The reality is that Epeli's Oceania is characterized not
by a pan-Pacific unity but by intense national and subnational ethnic divisions," a context that the post-coup citizens of Fiji need not have been
reminded of by this American editor of the *Journal of Pacific Studies*.[21]
For others, like Hari Ram (director of the Institute of Social and Administrative Studies at the University of the South Pacific), in "Not by Bread
Alone," Hau'ofa was not just making "specious argument" but reimagining an ecumenical narrative vision offering hope and positive imagination much needed by citizens in Fiji if not in sites of militourism like
Hawai'i and Guam in the American Pacific.[22] For, like those early Pentecostals of Azusa Street in Los Angeles and first-generation converts in the
American South, "Though converts never used the word ecumenism,
that is exactly what they believed the full gospel message offered," as
Grant Wacker writes in *Heaven Below,* "a new dispensation in which old
divisions [of denomination, race, culture, or creed] would be erased."[23]
Oceania as rhetoric, in a sense, evoked others into this counter-conversion
as a call turning to a *New Pacific ecumene.*

Toward a New Pacific Ecumene

Oceania, as such, invokes this New Pacific ecumene, for Hau'ofa, a
strategic mode of refiguring this Pauline universality of address for Pacific
Islanders for whom globalization discourse would hail them into market
dependency, subaltern labor, and secular difference. Oceania, vast, watery, evocative, at core mysterious (like the earlier Papua New Guinea
pidgin-vernacular term "wansolwara" for the Pacific as "one salt water,"
which can be translated into "one ocean, one people"), becomes a strategic way of reframing and forming a critical regional identity. "South Seas,"
"Australasia," "South Pacific" (introduced via James Michener, Rodgers
and Hammerstein, and others during the postwar American hegemony in
the cold war ethnoscape of "militourism"), "Pacific Basin," and "Pacific
Islands" all give way to Oceania as the self-identified signifier of Pacific
choice.[24] But, in this new more postcolonial turn, counter-conversion is
generated from the volcanic earth and sea on the Big Island in Hau'ofa's
"Our Sea of Islands." The new ecumene for Pacific Islander coalition-
building is called "Oceania," and its capacious vagary of definition
becomes a resignifying identity of unity through which Polynesian,

Micronesian, and Melanesian and all such colonial-imposed definitions of race or nationhood could be sloughed off, turned over, or cast away like dead boundary lines, false confinements into smallness, littleness, irrelevance, and global dependency.

At once ancestral and postmodern, *Oceania* is not just livelihood and place but also metaphor and vision: thus, modes of *poesis,* art, literature, culture-making, music, performance, and craft become an active means of generating, transforming, and conveying (across taken-for-granted imperial boundaries) visions of "Oceania" for postcolonial Pacific islanders especially. To accomplish this transnational community-building work of art-vision, Hau'ofa soon switched careers and helped found the Oceania Centre for Arts & Culture, which he has directed since its founding in 1997 at the University of the South Pacific in Fiji. *Oceania,* as Hau'ofa affirms (troping on the transatlantic Caribbean poet Derek Walcott) *is history;* this transpacific Ocean space opens to past and future. Finally, this crisscrossed Pacific, troped into "omnipresent" Oceania, becomes "our most wonderful metaphor for just about anything we can think of."[25]

Part trope, tall story, myth, truth, and joke, Hau'ofa's vision is meant to challenge the imperial aftermath and preemptive claims of Euro-American power. Oceania would refuse the claim of real estate's and war's "forever" as voiced by American Senator A. G. Beveridge, who in an earlier manifestation of U.S. Manifest Destiny in the Pacific had proclaimed in 1900: "The Pacific is our ocean. . . . And the Pacific is the ocean of the commerce of the future. Most future wars will be conflicts for commerce. The power that rules the Pacific, therefore, is the power that rules the world. And . . . that power is and will forever be the American republic."[26] As university president Isaiah Bowman later declared, in 1943, overseeing the formation of the geography department at Johns Hopkins University as an area of study to help American efforts in World War II, "That 'imaginative grasp of space' which science shares with poetry seemed somehow to be impossible to attain until our Army, Navy and Air forces has taken their stations and begun their operations in almost every part of the world."[27]

Site of trade, conversion, rival empires, and many wars, the Pacific region has long served as a strategic part in these "synchronized" international relations. For, as the transregional analysis of the spatial making of "American Empire" by Neil Smith points out, "regionalism was not alien to, but inherent within, the specific vision of twentieth-century U.S. globalism" that took hegemony across the globe after World War II and throughout the cold war.[28] Unconvinced and by now deconverted, Hau'ofa's regionalism would intervene into U.S.-shaped areas and global "region-making" by offering a trenchantly articulated countervision of globalization-from-below.

Fictions of Dependency and Renewal

In two raucous works of fiction, *Tales of the Tikongs* (1983) and *Kisses in the Nederends* (1987), and the visionary essays "Our Sea of Islands" (1993) and "The Ocean in Us" (1998), Hau'ofa has rewritten, mocked, and all but overthrown the narratives of conversion, development, and evangelical Christianity. He does so in order to put them to diasporic counterpurposes, populist subversion, and uncanny and carnivalesque neonative usages in sites like Tonga and Fiji as well as Hawai'i. This pan-Pacific portrayal of counter-conversion and satirical critique gives voice to what Tiko's neonativist organic intellectual Manu calls "over-influence" and affirms community. Hau'ofa's own career had turned away from the epistemic certainties of social science (anthropology), objective modern knowledge, and developmental leadership (he had served as a dean of social science at the University of the South Pacific) in the early 1980s to track the local warping of Christian global modernity by becoming a comic novelist and geopolitical re-imaginer of "Oceania." Miming lyrical, comic-grotesque as well as satirical keys, Hau'ofa underwent a conversion of writing genres, moving from social science to wry language-games, and satirical modes in poetics and literature. "Our Sea of Islands" is a work in this mixed and blurred genre of native troping and high visionary storytelling, as much poetry and postbiblical literary vision as social science or objective truth. For, as R. S. Sugirtharajah has noted of Hau'ofa's postcolonial fiction, the latter makes "profane use of the Bible" in works of ribald overturning and parodic translations of the Protestantism that come to terms with colonialism and its mangled aftermath in the newly independent islands of the Pacific.[29]

This reversion to storytelling modes of representation was occurring even as another major Pacific novelist and cultural critic of visionary importance, Albert Wendt (born in Western Samoa in 1939, the same year as Hau'ofa), had begun to affirm his own tactics of re-nativization, neo-traditional cultural rehabilitation, and a decolonizing mode of "tatauing the Pacific" that his earlier works of fiction, including *Sons for the Return Home* (1973) and *Pouliuli* (1977), had (seemingly) called into question.[30] Wendt's early vision of the decolonizing was dominantly "pessimistic," as Rod Edmond has noted, and even Wendt's "humor, when present, [was] bitter or sardonic" in contrast to the more raucously affirmative politics of laughter Hau'ofa's fiction has unleashed as desublimating tactic.[31]

Contemporary Pacific writing is rife with such paradoxes, tonal shifts, and surprising moves across cultural frames and genres, as I have suggested. Writing fiction to amplify agency from above and below, Hauʻofa's laughter-drenched, re-nativizing Pacific becomes the site of unpredictable counter-conversions, lines of flight, and mongrel becoming, as his characters take the terms and modes of postcolonial British English and hybrid late-capitalist culture into unexpected transformations and translations. Overeducated and well-trained as critical intellectual, Hauʻofa attended primary and secondary schools in the PNG where he was born as well as in Tonga, Fiji, and Australia; his tertiary education took place at the University of New England (Australia), McGill University (Montreal), and the Australia National University in Canberra, where he received a PhD in social anthropology.[32]

Counter-Converting Turns

In this *counter-converting* turn away from genres of social anthropology and political economy to genres of literary fiction, poetry, and comedic satire, Epeli might be considered a Pacific postmodern version of Zora Neale Hurston, who had moved beyond the cultural anthropology of Franz Boas with whom she had trained at Columbia University to create language games, stories, tall tales, and black signifying practices of orature in literary works like *Their Eyes Were Watching God* (1937) and *Dust Tracks on a Road* (1942).[33] Building on oral narrative modes of storytelling and outdoing, as well as biblical forms of sermonizing and allegorizing he had been subjected to in his youth, Hauʻofa described his project in *Tales of the Tikongs* as "an attempt to translate into writing the cadences of sounds as produced in the islands by story-tellers, preachers, orators, people in supplication, people giving orders, arguing, quarreling, gossiping and so forth."[34] Tale and tall-tale signs mingle into satirical hyperbole and truth-masked fantasy; cultural reconstruction via literature becomes a mode of situated and temporalized vision, aware of past injustices and present needs. In another ground-breaking essay, "Pasts to Remember," Hauʻofa intervenes again into the making of normative Pacific time and (by countervision of past and future) attempts to rescue history from its domination by contact-centered frames that (as in the Canberra school of Pacific historians) that (overstressing colonialism as an Enlightenment fate of modern betterment for far-flung oceanic peoples around Australia) had divided time into "two main periods: the pre-contact and post-contact periods," as if Pacific islander time (or space-making) began with the coming of Westerners with their clocks, maps, compasses, globes, canvasses, and stories of white redemption.

In contact-centered history, the main agents will always be "explorers, early traders, missionaries, planters, colonial officials and regimes, and so forth."[35] The postcolonial history-making is heading in another direction, one more tied to the pressures and needs of Oceania as a coalitional formation wrought in, for, and from the region: "we Oceanians must find ways of reconstructing our past that are our own," Hau'ofa urges. "Non-Oceanians may construct and interpret our pasts or our present, but they are their constructions and interpretations, not ours."[36] *Oceanian,* the *Oxford English Dictionary* tells us, had become a common term for a Polynesian or for any native of Oceania, at least by 1831, so Hau'ofa is hardly inventing these terms out of some Pacific void.[37] If this redefining asserts a will to power over textual interpretation, history, identity, and community, Hau'ofa has read his Nietzsche and his George Orwell (as well as his Roger Keesing, Patricia Grace, and Haunani Kay Trask); his vision of Oceania as time-space construct is careful to avoid the hegemonic tendencies and racialized exclusions of the dominant forms of Hegelian ocean-making. In this new poetics (or mimetic theatrics) of representational power, Hau'ofa continues in "Pasts to Remember," "we must clear the stage and bring in new characters," not just keep on telling history as centered in Captain Cook or Jack London, say, but history as revoiced and retied to "ordinary people, the forgotten people of history" in their modes of grassroots survival.[38] History can no longer be equated to *fixed* conversion and one-way belief in linear progression, history as "equated with progress toward capitalist utopia, the dream of the wretched of the earth."[39] Even chant and poem can help to transmit this countervision of Pacific place-making and history-shaping, for as any dancer of Hawaiian hula or chanter of *ole* knows through gestures, energy lines of *mana,* and native naming, as in the song lines of Australian Aborigines, "Our natural landscapes then are maps of movements, pauses, and more movements" and, all the more amazingly, "Sea routes were mapped on chants."[40]

Black sheep, profane, re-nativizing yet postmodern hybrid neonative and proud of it, Epeli Hau'ofa is the postcolonial missionary offspring from Tonga and Oceania who would go on writing (amid all this postcolonial ferment) back to empire and against the neoliberal good sense of social science norms and its disciplinary tactics of area studies formation. As the set of interconnected stories and carnivalesque satire driving *Tales of the Tikongs* shows, Hau'ofa also wrote back against a reactive Pacific Islander *nativism-by-fiat.* Early and late, Hau'ofa challenges and undermines any elitist will to enforce the recuperated traditionalism of post-colonial national regimes trying to break with Britain but seeing, again and again, the installation of what he mocks as "The Second Coming" of worse state regimes and sad patterns of neocolonial dependency being formed within the globalizing ideology of the "Glorious Pacific Way." In activating his turn away from forms of social science discourse toward fiction, satire, sermon, and Oceanic-based imagery, Hau'ofa was launching forces of globalization-from-below. These forces of populist mockery support and reflect the carnivalesque overthrow of the elite Pacific Rim-players and its generic deformation (especially by those biblical codes of the "Sabattarians," his name for the dominant form of Wesleyan Methodism that reigns still in Tonga).

In Hau'ofa's view of Tonga (as *Tiko*), the people have converted the Protestant work ethic into a Pacific regime of play, relaxation, mockery, transgression, and escape. The Methodist stress on grace and moods of forgiveness and sanctification has all but abolished the codes and regimes of law and "works," to such a preposterous extent (in Tiko translations) that any sin can be forgiven (such as ripping out the page from the Bible with the Ten Commandments to use it for cigarette paper), or worse, people can sin outrageously in order to invoke the pleasures and profits of forgiveness, as the chain-smoking and Moses-dreaming Ti shows in "The Wages of Sin." Such Pacific practices and translations downward from the Christian ethos into body, place, and everydayness can lead to a bountiful hedonism and anarchism that is quite endearing and tactical, as Hau'ofa affirms between the lines of his geospecific allegory. Tiko may not be Tonga but could be any islander culture working in the aftermath of colonialism and in the wake of neoliberal globalization that renews subordination, this time in a multicultural transnational key.

By becoming comic novelist and geopolitical re-imaginer of the post-Christian Pacific, Hau'ofa's fiction serves, in effect, to rewrite the Pacific conversion-and-development story and to put it to contemporary counterpurposes and native uses. The postcolonial Pacific this ex-scientific author portrays is a crossroads of conversions and counter-conversions, as the native and modern interfuse, antagonize, refuse, and seem to become undone in a politics-drenched space Hau'ofa calls (reclaiming for large-scale indigenous comings and goings the French geopolitical category), *Oceanía*. Converted to Christianity, for example, the hero of "Bopeep's Bells" records a malformed Tiko conversion to forms of self-aggrandizing capitalism. The conversion motif, as "A Pilgrim's Progress" more ludicrously shows in this Pacific male adolescent versioning, can be tied into glandular progression from forms of childhood submission and workaday asceticism, into modes of eroticism, then back into a latter-day ascetic in middle age.

Oceanic Kisses across Asia-Pacific

This counter-conversion in the Pacific is carried to a grotesque, Rabelesian, profane extremity in *Kisses in the Nederends,* where in the fictional island of Tipota (as a barely disguised Fiji), Oilei is led to cure his festering, fistulated anus (which Hau'ofa himself had suffered from 1981 to 1985) by the recuperated narcissism propagated by the "holy yoga" Fijo-Indian sage, cosmic meditator, and New Age guru Babu Vivekanand, who advises communicants from the interior Pacific Basin to the Pacific Rim to worship their own abjected body: "It is only when you are able to lovingly and respectfully kiss your own anus, and those of your fellow human beings, that you will know that you have purified yourself of all obscenities and prejudices, and have overcome your worst fears and phobias. You will then be able to see with utmost clarity the true nature of beauty, which is the essence of the unity and equality."[41] If Christianity found the sublime in the humble and spiritual in the lowly, as in the Beatitudes of the Sermon on the Mount, and Christ hung out with publicans, sinners, and black sheep of various sorts, Babu Vivekanand takes this universalizing compassion to an Asiatic New Age extreme. The guru finds back in front, mouth in anus, sacred in the profane, and the visionary in the excremental in some kind of cosmo-democratic leveling into Oceanic Consciousness and yogic unity. In the middle of the Cold War amid the nuclearized Pacific testing sites, he even urges the presidents of the United States and the Soviet Union to kiss each other's arse at their next summit meeting (*Kisses in the Nederends,* 103–104).[42]

Similarly, Babu urges converts to his new world religion to form a circle and kiss the rear end of the fellow believer in front of him or her. Babu trumps (and even desublimates) Jesus in his power of creatural love and dirty beatitude: "The great teacher, Jesus of Nazareth, once told his disciples to behave toward the least members of society as they behaved toward him. We must behave likewise toward our anuses . . . [and become] able to lovingly and respectfully kiss your own anus, and those of your fellow human beings," Babu sermonizes (*Kisses in the Nederends,* 100–101). Surely this renegade son of a minister is having fun with the beatitudes and pieties of the Bible, taking the Augustinian mandate "to love and do as you will" to a preposterous New Age incarnation in this Indo-Fijian guru of holy love.[43] As Hau'ofa summarizes Oilei Bomboki's antipilgrimage to enlightenment via loving the anus in self-other communitas, "His arse had been preached at, prayed upon, exorcized, breathed into and out of, sung and danced. It had been exploded, jabbed, blown, hummed, needled, steamed, smoked, carved, discarded, transplanted, race-transformed, sex-changed, nosed and kissed back to life" (*Kisses in the Nederends,* 152). All in all, this is a comic emplotment of profane renewal that recalls Hau'ofa's own region-wide search across Asia/Pacific for a cure: the searcher has been born again in the body, "nosed and kissed back to life." If Christian beatitude had been humbled into lowly human forms as a carpenter, servant, and body-healer, Babu found this holy love a bit too repressive, ascetic, and refined for his anal-centered jubilations.[44]

By novel's mock-jubilant end, Marxism and Communism, not to mention a guilt-ridden Christian work ethic of the ascetic body, have been supplanted by "the Pan Pacific Philosophy for Peace and the Third Millennium [which] will shake the twenty-first and beyond" with its all-embracing mandate, "Kiss my arse!" (*Kisses in the Nederends,* 153). Transnationalizing the yoga of God-union into a New Age commodity and cure, Babu situates his work at the center of a counterglobalism through redemptive yoga practices, emanating from little Fiji: "Fiji's the hub of the South Pacific, and the Pacific will soon be the hub of the world" (*Kisses in the Nederends,* 118). In his Pan Pacific Philosophy of Peace, Babu, as his disciple Bulbul promotes this Asia-Pacific transnational community of the One Infinite (which is secretly funded by the CIA and Russian money), has got the Pacific Rim grandeurs, a ruse of imperial-expansionism, and that an ominous case of New Age neo-Indian indigeneity as global/local cure for capitalist misery. The guru-racket is hard to tell from the health racket or the aid racket; in their interior Pacific incarnations, they are another version of the ideology of the "Pacific Way" Hau'ofa unmasks and critiques as an elite-class disguise for domination and profit.[45] Traditional healing in Tipota, as with evangelical Christianity in Tiko, is hard to tell from entrepreneurial aggrandizement, propagated by the educated elite, at the expense of the Pacific poor. In this, Hau'ofa mocks his own formation as a Pacific Rim university intellectual and sides with the people.[46]

In its Swiftean desublimations of high and low, body and spirit, sacred and profane, *Kisses in the Nederends,* outrageously, *ends* by affirming the end (anus) over the beginning (the logos of the mouth) and thus gives a Pacific countercultural meaning to T. S. Eliot's "Little Gidding" from the High Anglican and doctrine-drenched *Four Quartets,* which serves as the novel's (seemingly pious) epigraph:

We shall not cease from exploration
And the end of all our exploring
Will be to arrive from where we started
And know the place for the first time.

Needless to say, this postcolonial overturning of the conversion trope into a mongrelized circus of misreading and bogus translations of the scared into the profane is *not the* conversion-to-logos and grim Anglican pilgrimage to the "word within the word" that "Old Possum" Eliot had in mind, like some sad Saint John amid the ruins of world war, for his global Anglican ecumene. Working outside the high church of the global center, the novelist is desublimating the pious text. Hau'ofa situates this conversion drive within the contemporary Pacific of postcolonial nativism and neoliberal globalization. This vision of redemption depends upon the interlinking of cultural and commodity flows from New Zealand and Fiji to Taiwan and India and thereby exposes and calls into question some of the preposterousness, profiteering, and desperation at play in the peripheral fields of these postmodern lords. Official ecclesiastical forms, legal cover stories, nuclear testing, nativist coups, and state pieties are subjected to clowning and critique and what Rod Edmond calls "antipodal inversion." Degradation, in this Bakhtinian mode of sacred overthrow, transubstantiates all sorrow, decay, ecological waste, and bodily misery into laughter and social release.[47] New Age forms of tourism and global enlightenment are given uncanny portrayal, through the Asia/Pacific allied grassroots pairing of Babu and Oilei, as Hau'ofa (as it were) takes the bikini off the nuclear geopolitics of the Bikini Atoll and desublimates the suffering yet surviving Pacific islander body.[48]

But counter-conversion to any purist brand of Pacific nativism is also foreclosed here, for Hau'ofa in his pre-"Oceania" vision of neocolonial dependency, whose Manu (bird) character seems a residual crank haunting Tiko with postcolonial melancholia, a force of negation and rejection, and whose flight back to the gods and precolonial beliefs of native Tiko/Tonga is forced, lonely, and willed. Manu's neo-nativism is not a communal option in Third World Tiko, where a battered British bicycle or broken-down Toyota seems a luxury item, just a singular revolution backwards. When forms of nativism and cultural traditionalism are adopted, as in the government offices of "The Second Coming" or the oral-history research projects of "The Glorious Pacific Way," the result for nation-makers of Tiko is stifling, as when office workers are urged to swear in native Pacific tongues, or Ole Pacificweiskei loses his collection of oral documents but becomes a global grant-seeker and fraudulent office builder, as a Pacific Rim beggar whose culture has become that of the "Fraud Foundation." Although Pauline-like in his moment of conversion, Hau'ofa is more like a Rabelais or Saint Francis in the grandeur of his heart and his commitment to caring for, yet mocking, his people, community, and place of Oceania.

If English is a Pacific language and has been one of the main vehicles of communication for over two hundred years, as Albert Wendt has often affirmed (he has written novels for decades in this language, although his play *The Songmaker's Chair* [2003] now contains much untranslated Samoan), it should come as no surprise to hear British English in Hau'ofa's fiction and to feel the hegemony of Christianity everywhere, in myriad sects and in the everyday life of Tiko/Tonga. For Tonga, those "Friendly Islands" happened upon in 1773 by British navigator James Cook, is now considered to be one of the strongest Christian countries in Polynesia.[49] The Wesleyan Mission that had earlier dominated, along with the Roman Catholic Church, has seen myriad splinter formations from the Free Church of Tonga and the Church of Tonga. There are now many Christian denominations, and social status is commonly reckoned by one's position and involvement in the church and its extensive organization: church and family forms and practices flow into one another, help shape everyday life, as Hau'ofa shows to a comic extreme.

Since 1970, Tonga has achieved political independence, although it has remained within the Commonwealth (again, something that *Tales of the Tikongs* makes light of as a malformed version of Anglo-globalism-cum-neocolonial dependency as the "second coming" of British and Australians into administrative power). Paul Gilroy has called this mood (after Fanon) the turn toward postcolonial melancholy, but it here gives way to postmodern lunacy and conviviality, on a global-local scale of transnational affiliation linking Pacific Rim plunder to Pacific Basin complacency and complicity. Visions of regeneration and rebirth are shadowed by these spectral and uncanny forms of degeneration and disintegration, humorous but also ominous signs for the Pacific Island future regimes, as Hau'ofa has re-imagined this ex-British Pacific and Asian/Pacific present over which the U.S. regimes of Empire preside.

Tonga Goes Online and Offshore

Given the ongoing shift toward these regimes of globalization, to shift contexts from semidistant allegory to the all-too-near material present, the actual Pacific island nation of Tonga has fared no less perilously (than Tiko) in its recent attempts to globalize government revenues,

amplified by selling passports to cash-ready Asians, especially those anxious over Hong Kong's reversion to China in 1997. Not Tonga's island
land or cultural sovereignty but its investment dollars have disappeared
into "a mysterious company that has now vanished," as BBC News put it
in October 2001.[50] Tonga, on this uneven global playing field, has become an unwitting agent in its own financial displacement. The South
Pacific kingdom launched a compensatory law suit in San Francisco,
hoping to recover some of the $26 million it had lost in investment
schemes directed by Jesse Bogdonoff, a Bank of America employee (literally turned court jester) who talked the Tongan king into investing his
kingdom's low-interest checking account into his own Wellness Technologies along with an insurance-buyout company in Nevada called Millennium Asset Management and a dotcom start-up that has since dot.gone
into bankruptcy. Instead of investing to repair local highways in Tonga,
the diasporic king (living in an upscale San Francisco suburb in Silicon
Valley, near the Hearst family) played the Internet frontier under the
tutelage of his court jester and soon squandered the tiny ex-British kingdom's surplus budget in offshore speculation. Bogdnoff was one of those
global players, American-style, who drop in and out of the Pacific when
it suits their national and private self-interest. The king would have done
well to listen to his own "fool" and former secretary, Hau'ofa, or to read
Tales of the Tikongs in Atherton.[51]

Thinking about filing a countersuit for character assassination, our
discredited U.S. jester admitted that he had "people in Tonga calling for
me to be thrown underground and cooked like a pig" and blamed the
lawsuit not on residual primitivism but on rival factions in the postcolonial government and the loss on market forces.[52] Nothing of this failed-
globalization strategy bordering on opera buffo, or what we might
call *Pacific Rim disillusionment fatigue,* would surprise the readers of
Hau'ofa's *Tales of the Tikongs,* which had modeled Tiko's comic en-
tropy, development failures, and Protestant ethic working in reverse on
his native Tonga, where he had once served as the king's secretary. If the
local can overthrow and reverse colonial and neocolonial schemes of ex-
primitive appropriation in Hau'ofa's satirical fiction, global offshore
powers can gobble up local capital and dismantle transpacific world
dreams of global aggrandizement, as here under the management of an
American businessman "who impressed the Tongan king so much that
he issued a royal decree proclaiming him official court jester" (BBC
News). The inter-Asian currency crisis of 1997 made this instability of
late-capitalist investment all too clear, from Seoul and Bangkok to Kuala
Lumpur.

Asia in the Pacific, the Pacific in Asia

Whatever the turn of America to Asia or the Pacific Rim, there is still a need to articulate the Pacific as transnational and transcultural space of uneven flows and conjunctions, as Hauʻofa documents. Regional frames and area knowledge need to include and respond to neo-indigenous, ex-aboriginal, and Native Pacific perspectives on the transnationalizing of the Pacific: how do these various peoples now respond to the transformation of the Pacific into regional coalitions and communities of "Asia/Pacific" or "inter-Asia" forces and peoples? What role can culture or a culture-based politics play in this geopolitical struggle for equality and for resources and recognition? We culture workers in the so-called Asia/Pacific region of hyper-transnationality-cum-decolonization need not only to deal with land-based claims and national identity issues of imagined Native Pacific community, but also to theorize—and to culturalize as well—the makings of a transnational and/or transcultural Pacific from multiple angles of native vision. Can Asia or the dominant U.S. formations hear the Pacific, or the Pacific enlist Asia to some kind of critical dialogue? Will anybody in Paris or London need to read another Pacific work after having awarded the Booker Prize to Keri Hulme's *bone people* over two decades ago?[53]

If, following upon the state-centered dialectics of conquest in Hegel, we still see the ocean as capital's main transnational conduit; we need to see that the transpacific oceanic imaginary does not just belong to transnational capital. Hauʻofa has figured "Oceania" as counterformation in big, interconnected, and upbeat terms that are nonexpansionist, as seafaring is seen as a kind of network building or writing on and across the water. His works like *Tales of the Tikongs* would serve to counter and mock this capitalizing ocean with fables of antidevelopment and satires of failed development, as the Protestant work ethic flips over into a Pacific ethos of mockery, play, leisure, prayer, joke, and dream. Yet in this era of so-called Internet democracy, which is booming in sites like South Korea, of the "Korean Wave," and China, of the 2.5 billion consumers, how can the mounting "digital divide" and technological unevenness be overcome? Singapore is wired with a half million computers, versus Papua New Guinea (Hauʻofa's birthplace) with less than 1 percent on the World Wide Web. By many accounts and most of them gloomy, the Pacific Islands are entangled in a web of globalization forces, many of which emanate from Asia via Manila, Tokyo, Taipei, Hong Kong, Singapore, and more. The global tourist industry enlists further sites of fascination—even as automobile, garment, and mining industry expand in offshore networks across the Pacific—with nostalgias for "the South Pacific."

"One of the most striking characteristics of contemporary globalization in the Pacific Islands is its increasingly Asian complexion," Terrence Wesley-Smith remarked in a special issue of *Contemporary Pacific* devoted to "Asia in the Pacific."[54] The Maori, ghettoized in Alan Duff's novel *Once Were Warriors* (1990), for example, resent the successful Chinese restaurant owners as much as the ex-British white settlers whose suburbs elude and encompass their native claims to the land and priority of history. The resentment against such "market-dominant minorities" who are best capitalizing on globalization aggravates nations and regions, in strange new rehearsals of the colonial past. This reaction to globalization awakens ethnonationalist forces, from South East Asia to Latin America, Central Europe, Western Asia, and Africa. This is the reactionary climate Amy Chua warns against in *World on Fire* in ethnophobic terms of border guarding that would challenge the neoliberal faith in free markets, invocations of democratic teleology, or give the lie to counterformations like Hau'ofa's "Oceania" made-from-below by grassroots transnationalism.[55]

Challenging Hau'ofa's vision of a regenerative Pacific, Eric Waddell has demurred, "For many of us Hawai'i is no longer part of the Pacific. It has been swamped by Asia and dragged to continental North America." And though this well-respected geographer at the University of the South Pacific recognizes the Native Hawaiian activist challenge to this in figures like Haunani Kay Trask, Waddell adds cautionary humor to the "Oceania" trope of bigness, power, and unity as so much "positive thinking": "In spite of your optimistic voice, I feel you almost believe it yourself Epeli."[56] If capitalism offers a "world on fire," aggravated after the East/West civilizational divides of 9/11, Hau'ofa would counter with fires of Pele, mockery of Manu, and visions of reciprocity from the Pacific to oppose the amorality being installed and validated by market forces of border-crossing financialization.

The globalization agenda of neoliberal market forces from Asia and North America show little interest in small places (like Pacific islands) or culture-based claims (like a coalition built around Polynesians and allied cultures). The second or cybernetic wave of globalization, following upon colonial patterns, would incorporate island territories into the global economy in terms that suit the dominant powers and their institutions, such as the International Monetary Fund, the World Bank, and the Asian Development Bank. And yet, from the Pacific of Patricia Grace to the Caribbean of Edmund Brathwaite, island nations can serve as canary in the coal mine of globalization, crying out that they are threatened with indigenous and ecological extinction. As Hau'ofa has warned, in a survey of various forms of Pacific regionalism taking hegemony over his vision of "Oceania," "The development of APEC [Asia Pacific Economic Cooperation] will affect our existence whether we [Pacific islanders as the 'hole in the doughnut' for Pacific Rim geo-powers] like it or not. We cannot afford to ignore our exclusion because what is involved here is our very survival."[57]

Regional visions of Asia/Pacific or inter-Asia cannot afford to forget or ignore internal Pacific dynamics, counter-conversions, and contradictory claims of precapitalist aboriginality, communal alternatives, and antimodern memory. *Asia/Pacific* and *inter-Asia* do not just belong to the "imagined community" of transnational capital and the astronaut class of frequent flyers; they cannot just sublate Pacific into Asia. We can seek the antagonistic synergy of Asia/Pacific forces, flows, linkages, and networks. To the post–Cold War United States, Asia refracts into a hugely contradictory space of dynamism, danger, threat, and promise. This region remains, in postcolonial ways that would challenge dominant forms, the site of a civilizational battle for self-definition at the very least. "The inventing and reinventing of signs [like "Indian" or "Islam"] familiar to the popular imaginary and then articulating them to a higher form of universalism," as Kuan-Hsing Chen has urged in his staging of the battle between Samuel Huntington and Ashis Nandy for the definition of civilizational regions, "is to regain the confidence to 'at least' beat the West in cultural imagination."[58]

We cultural producers can go on dreaming, or (better said) shaping into prefigurative realization, another transnational and transcultural Asia/Pacific region, not some ocean-submerged continent bespeaking exploration and expansion for marines, politicians, and tourists to claim as site of adventure and metropolitan life-writing (region as "absorbed" into Euro-American geography). The Pacific region might become a site where, as Henry 'Ōpūkaha'ia had foreshadowed, *aloha* and *mana* might reign as forces of coalition and redemption.[59]

Oceania as Transnational Belonging

Although this body of Hau'ofa's fictional work is small, it remains a caustic, cosmopolitical, and compelling representation of global-local dynamics in the contemporary decolonizing Pacific. Kindred at times in recuperated aboriginality and orature to the Pacific-based novels of Keri Hulme, John Dominis Holt, Sia Figiel, Robert Barclay, and Albert Wendt, if less in style and voice, Hau'ofa's carnivalesque mode of popular storytelling, as Susan Najita has suggested, can "provide self-conscious retellings of the history of popular resistance to colonization, multinational capital, and to the proposed marginalization of Pacific islands in the age of globalization."[60] Hauʻofa offers a comedic vision of people and place with generosity, heart, self-mockery, and expansive capaciousness, putting (global) megatrends and (local) micropolitics into contentious global/local dialogue.[61]

Hauʻofa intervenes into prior understandings of conversion and counter-conversion and makes strange the taken-for-granted discourse of globalization from above and from below. He offers Pacific translational feedback to the Protestant work ethic and to the very vision and language of redemption and vocation that had been irrevocably spread into the Pacific with the coming of Captain Cook and the generations of missionaries, traders, and offspring of Empire who, like the American (in "Blessed Are the Meek"), "likes to walk tall, even though he may be short, and . . . occasionally takes a giant step or two for mankind even though mankind may not have asked him to." However, as caustic soothsayer Manu replies, offering unasked-for Pacific feedback to this bombastic American, "Good luck to him, says Manu, and may he live long, what with the energy crisis, rising unemployment, falling Skylabs, policing human rights, and carrying other heavy global responsibilities befitting a member of the Greatest Nation on Earth" (*Tales of the Tikongs*, 68). While the Pacific is no "Western Asia" region in terms of its threats and challenges to post-9/11 global hegemony, blundering global powers like the United States and United Kingdom would do well to hear this interior or "minor" vision of globalization and counterredemption from below.[62] "The sea has no interior frontiers and is not divided into people and territories," as Elias Canetti once urged; it is all-embracing and (surging beyond crowd and hordes) pulls all into its watery universality; this is what "Oceania" means at its most capacious extremity in the way Hauʻofa uses it to do geopolitical, ecumenical, and region-making work in our own time.[63]

As writer and organizer, Hauʻofa stands at the forefront in shaping counter-converting visions of Pacific-based *poesis*, as we go on working out implications that Albert Wendt had started voicing in his speech-act performance of a New Oceania some thirty years ago: as Wendt affirmed in "Towards a New Oceania," "I belong to Oceania—or at least, I am rooted in a fertile part of it—and it nourished my spirit, helps to define me, and feeds my imagination."[64] Oceania becomes an ecumene of transnational belonging, evoked via the metamorphosis of writing, one that activates powers of semiotic becoming, social transformation, and altered selfhood, yet stays tied to joys of invention, place, and transoceanic renewal. Oceania signifies a new birth.

Kava Rising

Not to be outdone by Albert Wendt or, for that matter, by Edward Said, nor to remain too tied to Christian figurations of Saint Paul and the ethnographic prognostications of Marshall Sahlins, Hauʻofa ends his ocean-crossing vision of Pacific time-space as routed with this uncanny— perhaps semidrunken—invocation of a "homeland" situated not in Tonga or Papua New Guinea but in Fiji, where he now lives, works, and crafts his visions of expansion, mobility, and ascent:

> Wherever I am at any given moment, there is comfort in the knowledge stored at the back of my mind that somewhere in Oceania is a piece of earth to which I belong . . . We all have homelands: family, community, and national homelands. And to deny human beings the sense of homeland is to deny them a deep spot on Earth to anchor their roots. Most East Oceanians [as in Hawaiʻi or Tahiti] have Havaiki, a shared ancestral homeland that exists hazily in primordial memory.

Hauʻofa turns, via forces of countermemory and counter-conversion, to anchor his earthly paradise in worldly specifics of Pacific place, memory, half-dream, trope, and body, tying Fiji to Vaihi and Havaiki like a neo-Dante prefiguring his own afterlife in the Pacific: "Every so often in the hills of Suva, when moon and red wine play tricks on my aging mind, I scan the horizon beyond Laucala Bay, the Rewa plain, and the reefs of Nukulau Island, for Vaihi, Havaiki, homeland. It is there, far into the past ahead, leading on to other memories, other realties, other homelands."[65]

The tactical skill of this passage is not just the scale-shifting of its spatiality but its reconfigured temporality as in a phrase conjuring the speaker's staring "far into the past ahead," making "the past" come out of the "far" future and yet appear on the horizon ("ahead"). By the figures and syntax of his quasi-sermonic essays, Hauʻofa would stake claims for the regeneration of a New Oceania. In Hauʻofa's version of the Pacific region, "the soul we have [that] came from Vaihi," as his much-anthologized poem "Blood in the Kava Bowl" depicted, the colonial oppression and economic misery about which the white professor at the ceremony keeps reminding the Pacific islanders as they share the kava cup in a circle can be overcome, if only in the hybridized transactions of postcolonial unity founded "on the shit of the cows Captain Cook brought":

> The kava has risen my brother,
> drink this cup of the soul and the sweat of our people,
> and pass me three more mushrooms which grew in Mururoa

on the shit of the cows Captain Cook bought
from the Kings of England and France![66]

In Hau'ofa's translation of the Eucharist and Logos into a down-to-earth kava bowl ceremony, the white anthropology professor "tastes not the blood in the kava / mixed with dry waters that rose to Tangaloa." This postcolonial knowledge-maker fails to perceive the hugely important *turn back* to Oceania as regional and ecumenical site, namely as the ancestral homeland (like Vaihi and Hawaiki) for the presencing and return of myriad Polynesian gods and totems who are *still there,* in Tonga as in Fiji, New Zealand, and Hawai'i, *co-present* at the event of world globalization.

CHAPTER FIVE

Regeneration through Violence

Multiple Masks of Alter-Becoming in the
Japanese/American/African Poet Ai

I came not to astonish
But to destroy you. Your
Jug of cool water? Your
Hanker after wings? Your
Lech for transcendence?

  —Galway Kinnell, "The Supper after the Last"

I didn't just read the Bible, I lived it.

  —Ai, "Charisma"

The ghosts [of mixed-race people in the Old West] are out there.
There are still things being hashed over today that began back
when, on the Trail of Tears, for instance. If you tap into your ancestors, if you tap into the ghosts of these ancestors, they are still
doing things. They are still saying, "Granddaughter, I want you
to look into this for me."

  —"A Conversation with Ai"[1]

Mimetic Becoming

More than sentiment, ritual, or ideology, religion means the pluralized
modes of tapping into life force and, potentially for any American subject,
the world-shattering or even violence-drenched power of life becoming. But
as Victoria Nelson has urged, theological speculation and the remaking/
unmaking of American religiosity and masks for reborn selfhood takes
place very often in shadowy frontiers and spectral genres as in a "subzeitgeist" of popular culture or more machinic realms of experimentation and spirit replication—like a 45 record, genre film or subliterary Goth
genre, radio studio, a website zine site, or avatar-ridden computer video-
game—more so than in temples, mosques, churches, cathedrals, or houses
of God-worship as such.[2] A computer video game (now on sale at

Wal-Mart for Christmas) has become ominously American "endtime" in its narrative terms and roles for players, who play death and rebirth games along masked lines of self-altering projection: it is called "Left Behind: Eternal Forces" and is driven by a "Convert or Die" dynamic at the crude fantasy core in which to score "spirit points" the player must convert non-Christians or kill them.[3] Another cyberspace fantasy of self-projection called "Second Life" is giving "rebirth" and "avatar" strange new meanings, as video games come into their own as potential masks of alter-becoming, sites of attaching with cyborg lovers, or imagining the patterns of self-death and life-change.[4]

Mapping the rise of American Empire from its earlier raw industrial-capitalist formation into global power, Henry Adams outlined a huge shift in American everyday life and urban spaces to new mores and modes of psychic empowerment, as machine-worship and Trust-incorporation, post–Civil War, had (seemingly) supplanted Christ, Madonna, or godhead as motivating forces across American modernity. In this "cultivation of occult force," affirmed Adams standing uplifted and baffled before the electromagnetic sublimity of the Dynamo, the mind could nonetheless tap into "the subtlest of all known forces." A modern believer could by such means once again activate "the old occult of fetish-power," no longer as materialized in a sad wooden cross or the grand stone cathedrals of Europe, but as aggregated into industrializing modes of machine power and materialized in cities like Chicago, Pittsburgh, San Francisco, and New York.[5] Atmospheric forces, electromagnetic auras, halos, and the potentiality of cosmic power would now and again leak into, and pour out from, the commodity-form or the machinic uncanny, as Walter Benjamin constellated in European capitalist cities: "Not what the moving red neon sign says—but the fiery pool reflecting it in the atmosphere."[6] The sacred was overcome and occluded perhaps, yet spectral forces and even messianic messages went on leaking out from these new mimetic technologies and the everyday objects of capitalist culture. The "excarnation" of spirit forces, as Charles Taylor differently urges, is hardly a fait accompli of Euro-American modernity.[7]

Given the large-scale and world spreading forces of mimetic replication, these machines can help the modern self activate powers of "aura" or "shock" and multiply what Michael Taussig calls "the born-again mimetic faculty of modernity," by instigating that "crucial circulation of imageric power between these [Enlightenment] sorts of selves and these [postcolonial native] sorts of anti-selves."[8] The born-again mimetic of conversion would be born again, in these multiplying world contact scenes of mana-encounter, into the mimesis of counter-conversion and imperial dissent as we have seen across Oceania. This stress on born-again contact scenes leads us to the powers and transformations of mimetic mimicry, as force of self-alteration and history making, that drives the frontier-haunted poetry of Ai beyond buffered selfhood and disincarnated matter: poem (mask) by poem (mask), Ai reopens American frontier history with cunning wit and uncanny powers of conversionary imagination and traumatic incarnation. Rebirth is seldom a solitary or one-way act for this singular poet: transfiguring "bios" (biological life) into "Zoë" (spiritual being), Ai shows that the drive (and it is often less a desire than a *drive* in her American figures and masks) to becoming "born again" is like "turning a horse into a winged creature," as C. S. Lewis once described the mutation process. Ai's converted masks of selfhood cannot hide the trauma, costs, egomaniacal force, or sheer sacramental violence that often mars this "transformation" into new self.[9]

Consider, as another subterranean context for the poetics of masking in Ai, this gnostic text on conversion called "Converts":

A Jew ("Hebrew") makes a Jew whom we call a convert
   ("proselyte").
A convert makes no convert.
Some are and make others like them,
while others simply are.

This passage from "The Gospel of Philip" inspires doubts that the born-again experience can be conveyed from one self to another, that another self can be turned into a convert across religious or ethnic borders: "A convert makes no convert"; they just exist in gnostic knowledge, estranged otherness, and "simply are."[10] No wonder such a text was banished from the early-Christian canon; its word is closed in on the self, unavailable to others via evangelizing deed or acts of community. But such a gnostic scripture might help us all the more so to understand the American rebirth formations in the alter-making mimesis of Ai's poetry, wherein each poem mimes and records "the mask" of remade self, in voices alive with regenerative energies and changes, haunted by race, transgression, and frontier burdens, as we shall discuss.

Born and Reborn as "Ai"

Early and late, from the blood-soaked deserts of Arizona to the fire-fallen towers of New York City, Ai's poetic ghosts speak the terms of raw ego-survival from what she calls (after a haunted blues lyric by Chester Burnett) the "killing floor" of America's race-torn history. Her voices of dramatic monologue now and again come back from their data-specific afterlife, dripping blood, violence, transfiguration, solipsism, and prophetic insight, to haunt, mourn, awaken, and indict the semi-amnesia of America's neoliberal Empire. This is poetry of nonidentity yet one that is everywhere speaking minoritized burdens of frontier history, suppression, spectral suppression, death, and trauma. What Zapata blazons out, as Tex-Mex revolutionary, from the crazed afterlife of "Pentecost" in *Killing Floor* (1979), can be said by many of Ai's visionary personae taking U.S. repossession:

> Boys, take the land, take it; it's yours.
> If you suffer in the grave,
> you can kill from it.[11]

Each poem is figured as dramatic monologue of self-transfiguration, ecstasy, and self-becoming. Hailed and castigated for this unnerving mastery of mimetic alterity, as "the queen of poetic monologues," Ai's "cleansing soliloquies," as Donna Seaman has observed in a prescient review, "give voice to pain both personal and communal."[12] History and fiction mingle into a radically interiorized, at times gnostic vision.

The poet has written of her self-willed identity as "Ai"; her project (in *poesis*) becomes one in which the self is masked and rendered anonymous via this conversion into personae on the edge of death and rebirth. "Ai is the only name by which I wish, and indeed should, be known," she affirms. "Since I am the child of a scandalous affair my mother had with a Japanese man she met at a streetcar stop, and I was forced to live a lie for so many years, while my mother concealed my natural father's identity from me, I feel that I should not have to be identified with a man, who was only my stepfather, for all eternity."[13] As she explains this reinvention of herself as "Ai," her poetic identity begins to resonate with cross-racial conflict and uncanny connections revealed (and concealed) in mask-making feats of resymbolized identification. By way of biography, we know that Ai was born in Tucson, Arizona, in 1947; her father (who abandoned his family) was Japanese and her mother was "a Black, Choctaw Indian, Irish and German woman from Texas." Deepening the roots of mongrelized identity as the empowering materials of raw writing, Ai went on to receive a BA in Oriental Studies from the University of Arizona and an MFA in Creative Writing from the University of California at Irvine. She has been married to the poet Lawrence

Kearney and is known for flamboyant readings on the U.S. poetry circuit.

Ai's Will to Transcendence

There is a compelling rhetorical analysis of this American "lech for transcendence," as Galway Kinnell calls it in the opening epigraph from his poem "The Supper after the Last," that is read as a mono-drama of self-refiguration and conversion from impotence by Kenneth Burke in his essay "I, Eye, Ay—Concerning Emerson's Early Essay on 'Nature' and the Machinery of Transcendence." Burke's compacted pun of a title is meant to enact the way the God-hungry Emersonian ego, the American poet's first-person I, is changed through the self-transcending vision of the imaginative eyeball, his ocular eye, into a cry of cosmic affirmation, some world-shattering ay.[14] The puny democratic ego converts irrelevance, failure, smallness, and social blockage into states of empowerment and material release, via other-becoming and over-coming. For Burke, as we have seen in his discussion of Saint Augustine's *Confessions*, language becomes used as a "symbolic action" for the turning, returning, diverting, detouring will to convert and become reborn into change, on the turning path to redemptive becoming.[15] Emerson, in more radically American Protestant terms of inner freedom and singular abyss-crossing, takes this given apparatus of rebirth even further, as I shall touch upon once again below as I have done so in the Introduction and Chapter 3 in this study.

To read the myriad figurations of death, rebirth, and self-preservation—those ancestral "ghosts" of Oklahoma, Texas, California, and Arizona alluded to above—given voice through Ai's poetry, early and late from *Cruelty* (1973) to the current post-9/11 terrors of *Dread* (2003), nobody ever fully *dies* on this genocidal American frontier: they are reborn as life-haunting specters of visionary castigation, vengeance, revelation, and (above all) survival.[16] Like Joe McCarthy, from Ai's 1986 collection *Sin,* their desire is unsatisfied and unrelenting, as even in death the ego vaunts: "I'm an American / I shall not want. / There's nothing that doesn't belong to me."[17] If, as Elias Canetti warned, "The moment of *survival* is the moment of power," such voices of survival and semiotic becoming haunt the present with afterlife. Ai, in an agonistic poetic sense, becomes that figure of exultation and uniqueness, a voice surrounded by the dead, heroic, or otherwise: "[She] is stronger. There is more life in [her]. [She] is the favored of the gods."[18]

Whether Japanese, African, American, or all of the above and more as an ever-masking poet of death, trauma, and rebirth, "the phonetic irony of Ai's mono-moniker," as Ray McDaniel theorized her three-decade-long career, "has always been her consistent identification with a project that defeats identity."[19] But given this will to mimetic mimicry, formal repetition, and evasiveness into alter-becoming mask, who is Ai under the myriad masks of her poetry that would defeat any given identity? Ai, the self-abnegating pen name of this contemporary American poet, Florence Ogawa Anthony, suggests the concern of her poetic project: the attempt to transcend her ego, a place-holding I, through acts of transcendental vision and self-refiguration that allow the assuming of a masked identity, another's I and eyes, and yet affirm the power of her own identity over the world of ordinary selfhood, social determination, and death. Ai survives myriad ghosts of America's racial history and native genocide. If one were to add to Burke's Emersonian formula for poetic identity the "aiee" of sexual ecstasy, as well as that of the Japanese word "ai," which means "love" and gives her this cross-cultural pen name, one would have a sense of the range and personae of *voice* in the poet called Ai. Here, too, lie the dangers of her symbolic quest to transcend/become reborn beyond given personality *(bios)* entailed as "Ai."

In her dramas of voice-othering, somebody commonly must die as sacrifice. The stage of Ai's history is bloodied with these transformations of self into alterity; there is no rebirth, she shows again and again, without destruction, annihilation, and death. Even Jesus, in Ai's quasi-gnostic version of redemption in "A Mother's Tale," from *Sin,* uses the body of blessed mother Mary as a vehicle of translation/transition into his own transfiguration, wounding, and surmounting of the bloodied body itself (*Vice,* 68):

> that suffering is her inheritance from you
> and through you, from Christ,
> who walked on his mother's body
> to be the King of Heaven.

Cruelty, Ai's first book (1973), was acclaimed for its array of poetic masks expressed in a terse, highly charged language of emotive force: she allows dwarfs, sharecroppers, prostitutes, crazed and jilted lovers, child beaters, warriors, and ordinary persons in various states of ecstasy and grief to have their ungenteel say. *Bios* and *Zoë* clash inside her radically creatural embodiments.

As David Wojahn notes of this harrowing project to voice mimetic alterity, Ai has refunctioned this soliloquizing voice-form into "striking contemporaneity," as if "a Browning monologue [was] rewritten in the terse manner of Sam Shepard." Ai is a "religious poet" and rightly so, for

Wojahn, but "the deity she envisions is wrathful and she seems to identify with such a figure," or at least she identifies with the figure of Lazarus (coming back from the dead) more than any Jesus of perpetual forgiveness, mercy, or creatural tenderness.[20] Her godhead is seldom a "be passersby" figure. The resurrection of the James Wright figure, in "More," speaks to this endurance and proletarian empowerment over death (mingling Lazarus into a river-rising Jesus), as Wright rises up from factory-town and Iron Belt misery of America, rebirth (if only in afterlife) from dirty fluids along "this icy water called Ohio River" (Vice, 64):

> I'd float past all the sad towns,
> past all the dreamers onshore
> with their hands out.
> I'd hold on, I'd hold
> till the weight,
> till the awful heaviness
> tore from me,
> sank to bottom and stayed.
> Then I'd stand up
> like Lazarus
> and walk home across the water.

In "The Testimony of J. Robert Oppenheimer," in Sin, the force of nuclear annihilation again figures this power of rebirth and spectral survival, as the scientist affirms after the techno-triumph at Los Alamos and Hiroshima, "Oh, to be born again and again / from that dark, metal womb, / the sweet, intoxicating smell of decay / the immanent dead give off / rising to embrace me" (Vice, 78).[21] In "Jimmy Hoffa's Odyssey," from Fate (1991), Hoffa's specter survives alien abduction and oblivion and returns to haunt his political creations: "I am coming back / to take my place on the picket line, / because, like any union man, / I earned it" (Vice, 101).

The Beat comedic genius of Lenny Bruce, in "Boys and Girls, Lenny Bruce, or Back from the Dead," longs for "that state of grace / when performer and audience fuse" (Vice, 104) and so returns from a heroin overdose to proclaim (like some broken-down yet exalted American Jesus of street beatitude at the Hungry I) his theatrics of redemption-via-art: "and like some hostage savior, I'm here to stay / till everyone's sanctified / in laughter" (Vice, 106). In "General George Armstrong Custer: My Life in the Theater," from Fate (1991), Custer directs the sacralized violence of his own "civil war" campaign against a more global will to native obliteration and global domination:

but I kill for
the spectacle, the operatic pitch
of the little civil wars
that decimate from inside,
as in Belfast, Beirut, or Los Angeles.
where people know how it feels to be
somebody's personal Indian (*Vice*, 108)

Custer's global overextensions of Indian-hating into Empire-building, as Richard Drinnon (troping on Melville) called this drive to hegemony over native forces and nature, as theatricalized by Ai, are meant to be cautionary tales to contemporary U.S. globalization as Empire.[22] Facing Indian land if not the indigenous Pacific, Custer becomes another death-driven Ahab, propelled by Manifest Destiny visions of white redemption "into another breach / from which there is no deliverance" (*Vice*, 109). Caught up in such visions of self-transcendence, even James Dean becomes a Christ-figure in his speeding Porsche, through which "I reenact my passion play" as a line-of-flight into glamorized infinitude beyond death along the forlorn highways near Paso Robles that remain haunted still (*Vice*, 115).

In the everyday terms of transfiguration from *Cruelty* (1973), a truck-stop prostitute in "Everything: Eloy, Arizona, 1956" offers her body as some kind of redemptive altar for violent abolishment and sexual release:

He's keys, tires, a fire lit in his belly
in the diner up the road.
I'm red toenails, tight blue halter, black slip.
He's mine tonight. I don't know him.
He can only hurt me a piece at a time. (144)

And in "Hangman," the fields of Kansas are illuminated by a seemingly sacred act of public execution, which transfigures the whole landscape:

He places his foot on the step going down
and nearby, a scarecrow explodes,
sending tiny slivers of straw into his eyes. (124)

"The silos open their mouths" to receive the bloodshed of this full moral harvest of American violence, which is performed in the name (the Lebanese worker thinks) of an ideal cause of regenerated "brotherhood."

In *Killing Floor* (1979), which won the Lamont Prize, Ai's cast of masked characters began to go upscale, global, and allusive, self-dramatizing an array of literary, mystical, political, and historical figures. Ai in effect gives voice to an emerging cast of romantic visionaries like Mishima and Trotsky, heroes at political poles of fascism and revolution, yet who are voices of body-altering social violence sharing the quasi-Americanized will ("lurch") to storm their way into eternity or to die trying. Both of these early books were feats of poetic empathy as symbolic transactions of a protean negative capability by which the ordinary identity of Ai is (seemingly) transcended and she enters another self, if only through the figurative time and the symbolic agency of the poem. Ai (and her I) becomes a voice of eloquent nothingness, blasted and re-shaped, and yet she sees beyond the body's confines of given ("fated") identification, as Emerson had urged upon the imperial ego of the poet on that errand of redemption in the American wilderness and self-diminishments of industrial capitalism. As the voice of crazed colonialist Lopé de Aguirre announces in "The Gilded Man," searching for his El Dorado in promised lands of these Americas:

> Urzua is dead. Guzman is dead. There is no Spain.
> I'm hunting El Dorado, the Gilded Man.
> When I catch him, I'll cut him up.
> I'll start with his feet
> and give them to you [his daughter] to wear as earrings.
> Talk to me.
> I hear nothing but the monkeys squealing above me. (48)

Even God must give way to this visionary will-to-power over wilderness, as Ai presents this drive thus: "God. The boot heel an inch above your head is mine." Nature lovers in Keats and Emerson are bypassed by voices of visionary projection that would remain moral, or at least regenerative. But can one make the Nietzschean claim for this death-confronting mask that Ai has effaced herself and overcome moral judgment and historical material via this refigured ego?

Karl Malkoff has traced the collective ambition in postconfessional American poetry to transcend the autobiographical ego back to sources in Anglo-American Romanticism: to Keats on the negation of the ego through ventriloquized voice; to Browning in his dramatic monologues; to Yeats and his doctrine of the mask; to Pound with his mastery of Personae; to Eliot and his geriatric alter ego, Prufrock.[23] A haunting statement of this romantic project to use poetry to transcend the ego remains the letter on poetic identity that Keats wrote to Richard Woodhouse (Oct. 27, 1818):

> As to the poetical Character itself (I mean that sort of which, if I am any thing, I am a Member; that sort distinguished from the Wordsworthian or egotistical sublime; which is a thing per se and stands alone) it is not itself—it has no self—it is everything and nothing—It has no character—it enjoys light and shade; it lives in gusto, be it foul or fair, high or low, rich or poor, mean or elevated. . . . A Poet is the most unpoetical of anything in existence; because he has no Identity—he is continually informing and filling some other Body.

Through acts of imaginative empathy, the poet informs the body and voice of another's character: the ego (or I-voice) would be *negated* through the language of the poem and changed into the perspective of someone else. The confessional ego of the poet may not be vehicle of the sublime, as in Wordsworth or Whitman; but others can be, whether they be high or low class, rich or poor, mystical or profane, tame or wild, Beat or square, if portrayed in this drama of semiotic alter-becoming and postcolonial otherness as will to freedom.

"I Am Nothing, I See All"

Looking back into American Romanticism for origins of Ai's attempt to transcend the personal ego, we are confronted with a more extreme and culturally determining case of this will to transcend ordinary identity and proclaim the morphology of death-and-rebirth. Consider Emerson's *locus classicus* passage on crossing into self-beatitude in *Nature* (1836): "Standing on the bare ground,—my head bathed by the blithe air, and uplifted into infinite space,—all mean egotism vanishes. I become a transparent eye-ball; I am nothing; I see all; the currents of the Universal Being circulate through me; I am part or parcel of God."[24] The vehicle of transcendence in Keats is other people whereas in Emerson it is the power of nature as energy influx, but the goal of these two poets is much the same: to overcome the ego and yet to *see all* in some revelation of an interconnected totality of energy and sign linking Godhead and will. As extreme advocate of self-reliance, Emerson could not bring himself, in this self-empowered nexus of the Oversoul, to depend upon another's character for his vision of God; but his larger goal is Keats's romantic one, to annihilate the ego through some self-transcending vision that the poem performs. In such works of mimetic energy-exchange, as Emerson urged in "Fate," the poet is "born and afterward we were born again, and many times," as we have seen.[25] This is what I am here calling Ai's "alter becoming" agency, her "unselving" to use that term from rebirth psychology that William James discussed as a passageway to amplified life, altered subjectivity, and what Jackson Lears has called the "polytheism" of his religious pluralism.[26]

In Emerson's provocation to incarnate and give voice to the godhead in the self, in which "we learn that God IS; that he is in me" ("Circles"), God is not dead or (worse) reified into stale material forms, but lives, moves, metamorphosizes, and speaks in the very self as instantaneous stream of power, trust, and beauty.[27] Articulating again and anew this semiotic conviction of prophetic/poetic speaking as "God without mediator or veil," in this extreme form of Protestant conversion, "Yourself [become] a newborn bard of the Holy Ghost—,—[you] cast behind you all conformity, and acquaint men at first hand with Deity."[28] You are both a God in nature and a weed by the wall, when the Influx falters, as in "Circles" or (worse yet in the overdetermining negations of this blessed selfhood) "Fate." This is a one-on-one with the godhead taken into Pentecostal extremity of present-tense assumption no church (not even according to codes of *sola scriptura* nor *sola natura*) could house or sustain: "It is the office of the true teacher to show us that God is, not was; that He speaketh, not spake."[29]

The end result of this conversion, as an essay like "The Poet" makes clear, is a heightened *access* into semiotic plenitude in which nature and all the world glistens as trope, radiant with correspondences, converted into fire and glass: "The condition of true naming on the poet's part, is his resigning himself to the divine *aura* which breathes through forms, and accompanying that."[30] In the conversion experience, nature converted into resource, and the whole world stared back at the poet with the aura of beatitude recuperated into a language whose "speech is thunder."[31] Writing at the core of his spirit Influx, Emerson was the first of many American Protestants to "pragmatically displace Jesus by their kinetic reliance upon the Holy Spirit" eruptive as newness and creative empowerment in the self.[32] Ai is working in this tradition but altering it, by releasing the racial and historical repressions and trauma that haunted white sublimity. Indeed Ai's ethnic ethos as poet helps to refigure the "American sublime" genre of transcendentalized appropriation and returns the repressed to any quasi-Emersonian poetics of the self-overcoming and nature-using capitalistic will.[33]

On De-Selving

At first glance, Ai's poetry appears *de-selved*, as if the autobiographical identity of Ai has been negated through an act of dramatic objectivity that is often astonishing. Consider this much-anthologized lyric in a share-cropper's voice, from "Cuba, 1962":

> When the rooster jumps up on the windowsill
> and spreads his red-gold wings,
> I wake. thinking it is the sun
> and call Juanita, hearing her answer,
> but only in my mind.
> I know she is already outside,
> breaking the cane off at ground level,
> using only her big hands.
> I get the machete and walk among the cane,
> until I see her, lying face-down in the dirt.
> Juanita. dead in the morning like this.
> I raise the machete—
> what I take from the earth, I give back—
> and cut off her feet.
> I lift the body and carry it to the wagon,
> Where I load the cane to sell in the village.
> Whoever tastes my woman in his candy, his cake,
> tastes something sweeter than this sugar cane;
> it is grief.
> If you eat too much of it, you want more,
> you can never get enough. (*Cruelty*, 32)

The violent act in "Cuba" of the farmer's dismemberment of his dead wife becomes for Ai an act of visionary cruelty; through grief, the farmer is storming his way into eternity and sublime utterance. Magical-realist in mode and Martí-like in its ties to other Americas, the voice of transfigured grief in the poem is not Ai's, not that of the poetic ego confessing its own desires and needs, but the voice of a Cuban cane farmer whose proletarian station in life does not withhold the capacity for sublime perception, the metaphor that Juanita is one with the cane she picked.

That the voice in "Cuba, 1962" has moved beyond self into "another world," a realm of the great souls, is clear from a comment Ai herself makes in her *Ironwood* interview: "The character speaking in 'Cuba' seems to me a character with 'heart,' a character larger than life, no matter how insignificant his own life is."[34] In other words, the voice of a humble character is capable of conveying in simple language glimpses a vision-opening ecstasy that tradition would call the sublime, a term that is a useful way of describing the structure of "Cuba" as it builds from description to climax and silence. Ai has effaced her ego in the character of another being who mounts to glimpse transcendent perception through some act of "cruelty" but also of love and sacrifice.

"It's transcendence—that's what I'm striving for in all these poems: no matter what the characters go through, no matter what their end, they mean to live," says Ai about her own project of regenerative becoming in *Killing Floor,* justifying the violence and vision as parts of one whole (*Ironwood,* 34). Similarly, she says that she aims to cross "the line that separates the ecstatic visionary from ordinary life" by creating characters who have, in her imagination of them, done so: Aguirre, Zapata, Mishima, Ira Hayes, and more. *Sin* contains voices of the Kennedy brothers, Mary Jo Kopechne (as some bitter party girl), Elvis, and President Lyndon Baines Johnson, as well as that of an anonymous mass murderer of Atlanta's black youth. *Greed* gives voice to Marion Berry's "Self Defense," black rioters in South Central Los Angeles, J. Edgar Hoover (twice), Jack Ruby, and a witness to the horrors of the Marcos regime. *Dread* at once allows John F. Kennedy to speak from beyond the grave and gives voice to psychic detectives (as some figure for the poet), and several figures speak their pathos and survival in the aftermath of the World Trade towers' ruination.

Reimagining Frontier History as Masks

As scene of mimetic alter-becoming, history is fair game for American-visionary transfiguration. From workers to movie stars and presidents, acts of cruelty and violence can be (for Ai) a means of vision, an enlarging and self-ennobling of the ego by that "ecstatic visionary" consciousness and will to rebirth beyond bare selfhood. Even a poor farmer can pass beyond himself through greatness of soul, not so much ethos as pathos, a quality that Ai can find anywhere, as did democratic Emerson and dramatistic Keats, in the souls of others marooned in the profane. It appears that in the poetry of Ai, then, the ego of the poet has died and been replaced by a fictive I, a *mask* that is not the poet's own compound of desire and grief. Her lyrics are notable for the range and depth of their negative capability, for their entry into the voices and beings of a virtual circus of masks, a cast of characters diverse in origin and voice. Is not almost every character given to some act of violence (hence her titles, *Cruelty, Dread,* and *Killing Floor*) in which either the self or another person is mutilated from ordinary identity and normal consciousness? Hence, Ai's preoccupation, Dylan-like, with radically Americanized visions of *Fate, Greed,* and *Sin.*[35] We do need to see that mystical violence is often symbolic, as if some recurring means to sacramental transformation of the ego. Her characters, masks for Ai via this semiotic becoming, would awaken the movement to higher consciousness, become forces of ecstatic vision just this side of the body's slipping into that annihilation that we call death. Poems, for Ai, are vehicles of this semiotic becoming into voices of alterity: each poem is a kind of mimetic technology of rebirth and spirit influx.

Lurching into Transcendence

Violence is not just Ai's theme; it inheres in the very form of the poem as dramatic monologue; it drives her to try to see beyond the fated body into states of "sin" and "dread." What we have is allusive expression in dramatic voice of Ai's will to transcendence and "visionary ecstatic" consciousness. An Americanized "lurch into transcendence," as I have been elaborating, comes out of (1) Christian-Puritan, (2) frontier, and (3) ethnic sources in the contradictory American self, which Ai symbolically represents and stages.

Left and right, from fascist to revolutionary will, all her characters could utter the mystical self-affirmation that Yukio Mishima (Ai's mask) makes at the climax of his ritualized suicide:

> I start pulling my guts out,
> those silk red cords,
> spiraling skyward,
> and I'm climbing them
> past the moon and the sun,
> past darkness
> into white.
> I mean to live. ("Nothing but Color")

Such a spiral upward beyond space and time or good and bad may finally have nothing to do with the mask of the historical Mishima. One of the best analyses of Ai's mytho-poetic restaging of history into so-called fictions in terms of her own poetic project in endless monologues, remains a reading done by Stephen Yenser in a review of *Killing Floor,* where he writes of the historical distortions toward symbol in "Nothing but Color": "Someone better acquainted with Mishima's life might pronounce on the cannibalism, but anyone will be puzzled to find that the hara-kiri in this poem occurs in the speaker's garden, whereas Mishima's took place in the office of a general at an armed forces base."[36] Does the power of the imagination allow the poet to appropriate another's life to her own and even symbolically to restage his death? Yenser's analysis of Ai's version of Trotsky in her title poem is even more compelling: "In the first section she seems to have Trotsky plead for exile (in fact he even had to be carried to the train) and in the third she has him sitting in a bed-room at a 'mirrored vanity' and putting on his wife's maquillage when he is struck from behind (he was in his study, not in front of a mirror, reading an essay the killer had just given him). Are the facts not bizarre enough?" As Yenser implies, Trotsky seemingly becomes a cipher in Ai's will to mystical transcendence, but are not the data and dialectics of history and sheer human otherness too important for such a trope to live on and be meaningful?

Ai's characters in *Killing Floor* do share (her) thematic obsessions: novelists, socialists, revolutionaries, foot soldiers, war heroes, conquistadors, all are struggling to enter that blissful state of consciousness that Lopé de Aguirre calls El Dorado (gold land) or Vera Cruz (holy cross) in "The Gilded Man," the poem about the ruthless quest for the spiritualized lucre of the New World, which finishes *Killing Floor* on a note of sublime terror. Such a climax of ecstasy, which we have seen in detail in "Cuba," is characteristic of the form of any Ai lyric. Her characters (like Mishima or the crazed leader of mass apocalypse at Waco) would enter some consciousness of transcendence traditionally called *the sublime.* Her worldly means to this end is violence, barely ritualized acts of cruelty, obsession, and love, as in Lopé de Aguirre's murder of his own daughter, Vera Cruz, after his quest for El Dorado has failed:

> I unsheathe my dagger. Your mouth opens.
> I can't hear you.
> I want to. Tell me you love me.
> You cover your mouth with your hands.
> I stab you, then fall beside your body.
> Vera Cruz. See my skin covered with gold dust
> and tongues of flame,
> transfigured by the pentecost of my own despair.

Such "pentecost" figures are not icons of resurrection and beatitude but what Kenneth Burke was wont to call "transcendence downward," a descent into the body and tragic suffering.

Through Aguirre's project of desire and despair, his own mutilating passion, Ai nonetheless gives voice to American transcendental violence at its bloodiest and most sensational. She adheres (via vision and critique) to that Puritan and frontier myth central to American possession of the land that Richard Slotkin calls "regeneration through violence." Through violence and the will to death and rebirth, Ai's voices would possess and enact this visionary frontier. They open a space of powerful vision that would alter if not overcome American frontier history. She becomes, through such voices of sacralized violence, at once a symptom and critique of this will to U.S. Empire.[37] As the speaker of biblical apocalypse puts it in a showdown with the state at Waco, Texas, "I didn't just read the Bible, I lived it" (Vice, 199).

Ai's Poetic Autobiography

In writing about other characters like Kawabata, Bruce, Wright, Mishima, and Trotsky as symbols of would-be regenerative violence, Ai has annihilated her own ego, and she has overcome others with separate histories and drives. Historical biography is reduced to poetic autobiography, as if characters from history were legends in some Book of Saints as narrated by the poet Ai. If she writes "For the Ghosts" (as one of her dedications claims), she does not write as them; consequently, the act of poetic empathy has become morphology of death-and-rebirth in which history means symbol, and many of the symbols (ego-masks) are too alike. The tones of the voices get predictable, as are the visionary plots, especially in *Killing Floor,* where the characters are no longer unique as they were in *Cruelty.*

Her third collection, *Sin,* and subsequent collections do help to remedy this predictability of theme and form, her repetitive thematics of violence and the sacred, if her symbolist method is to progress beyond its prior resolutions. As a prologue to such poems, which go on mingling fact, gossip, trope, dream, headline, joke, legend, and myth, *Vice* now carries on its title pages this elaborate, virtually Shakespearean disclaimer for Ai's dramatic monologues as what she calls "fictions":

> These dramatic monologues are 100 percent fiction and are merely characters created by the poet. Some of them project the names of "real" public figures on to made-up characters in made-up circumstances. Where the names of corporate, media, public, or political figures are used here, those names are meant only to denote figures, images, the stuff of imagination; they do not denote or pretend to private information about actual persons, living or dead, or otherwise.

Whether this works as legal or biographical defense, Ai's dramatic mono-logues are exciting, stunning in detail, and one might even say intoxicat-ing in the sublime sense that both poet and reader are caught up in another's will to ecstatic vision and alteration. Ai is a poet genuinely gifted in her goals and verbal means. Yet her "tyrannous eye" of self-hood, which Emerson urged for the American poet in the wild tropes of "The Poet," can mask the poet's masked "mean egotism," which would manipulate or disguise nature, culture, and character into a "colossal ci-pher" for what John Ashbery terms in *Three Poems* that latter-day mon-odrama of self-salvation.

The world of other beings can become mere "cipher" to such tyranny of the will to re-imagine nature in one's own beloved image and need. Another human being is too separate, too other, too delicate a biology of consciousness, to wind up as a cipher in a song of the visionary self. Ai, who first suppressed her own ego in poetry, has so much taken over voices in her poems that nothing is left on the stage of history but her vi-sionary imagination. Still, this is often done in a cleansing act of renewal and insight, re-enacting the return of repressed forces and subaltern terms. Overall, Ai is engaged in a project representing challenges to racial codes and uncanny forces of American Empire.

The violence that preoccupies Ai has a sacred goal: she wants vision, self-transcendence, and mystical insight as her poems and comments show. Such a transfiguration through bloodshed is captured in the lines from Charles Simic that open *Cruelty:*

> Whoever swings an ax
> Knows the body of man
> Will again be covered with fur.

As Burke argued in his analysis of Emerson's *Nature,* there can be both *transcendence upward* and *transcendence downward:* man can become a saint or god (as Aguirre would), or he can become an animal or savage (as the ax-swinger in Simic's poem would). He is bios becoming Zoë. By presenting voices of low vision, like rapists and child beaters, and voices of sublime vision, like Kawabata and Mishima, Ai would transcend *both* downward and upward, as if each violent character shared the same vi-sionary need to see beyond the body.

Is the violence of Mishima akin to that of the wife beater? By *Killing Floor* it becomes clear that the victims who must be sacrificed for the sa-cred personae to occur are other human beings who must give up their identities in Ai's drive to articulate the will to the sacred in art, politics, life.[38] Need the communist visionary Trotsky become a bloody, glamorous figure of self-transcendence on a par with Hollywood's Marilyn Monroe ("She Didn't Even Wave")? Or a murderous punk like "The Kid"? Has history become a warehouse of *reborn personae?* Critical doubts may linger. And yet, if we historicize Ai's will to transcendence, situating her project in relation to the Romantic dialectics of self-transcendence, we comprehend this *all-too-American* will to abolish history into vision and to sublimate violence and liquidation into Empire.

Kenneth Burke, in his analysis of transcendence in Emerson, reads its language as a process in which there is not only a victim but a *passage,* a movement from here (nature) to there (spirit), by means of a poetic trope (for Emerson, metaphor). Almost all the masks of Ai are informed with such a "lurch toward transcendence" and rebirth, a will to go beyond the body and ordinary consciousness, be it through ecstasy or death. (*Killing Floor* is filled not only with murders but also with suicides.) Her means are what Burke would call "tragic": what gets left behind is not so much a concept or term (Emerson, for example, passes from nature as commodity to nature as spirit), but a human victim who must be sacrificed through some cruel act of love, as in "Cuba," where the wife becomes a victim of the husband's urge to express his proletarian rage and grief. This can make for poetry at its most tragic and sublime. As Norman O. Brown once affirmed in his commitment to embrace *metamorphosis,* as the masked power of releasing revolutionary energies of desire, and the will to rebirth (in "Revisioning Historical Identities"), "Revisioning as I have experienced it is not a luxury but life itself, a matter of survival; trying to stay alive in history; improvising a raft after shipwreck, out of whatever materials are available."[39]

If the plot of poetry is to use "language as symbolic action" (Burke) or to turn history into a force of metamorphosis (Brown), then the plot of Ai's symbolizing has one visionary goal: to get beyond identity and selfhood. With so much visionary violence in *Vice,* the stage gets strewn with corpses as in a revenge tragedy, but without much dramatic presentation of motives and values as in Eugene O'Neill. Nevertheless, as Fredric Jameson has shown in his Marxian rereading of Burke in *The Political Unconscious: Narrative as a Socially Symbolic Act* (1981), symbolic action remains an action as an imaginative *praxis* wrought upon the contradictions and occluded forces of history as a means to resolve them by re-interpretation. The idealized violence figured into Ai's poetry is that of American history in its march over the wilderness and the racial other, something that she must feel deeply as one of marginalized ethnic origins.

If we grant such a method, what then is her genre? Are we purged of violent emotion, as in tragedy, or absorbed into the ecstatic consciousness of the visionary poet, as in the sublime? I think that in Ai's poetry it is the latter structure of emotion that prevails: we are caught up in another's vision of regenerative aggression and must imagine some transfiguration of means (the body) taking place if we would, like Kawabata, seize the image of "this moment, death without end." As Burke remarks of Emerson, such poets storming the sublime "can select just about anything, no matter how lowly and tangible, to stand for it," the "overall term-of-terms or title-of-titles," which is everywhere and nowhere, in everything and in nothing: that flitting of vision Ai calls El Dorado (a place), death (a state of ego loss), or God (the union of souls beyond the body).

There is killing, racial genocide, and cruelty on the floor of Ai's poetry, yes—killing both literal and symbolic as a means to transfigure the body into something other and visionary, which is the goal sought by Mishima, for example, in his ritual suicide in Japan. But Ai's vision of poetry is also so concerned with transcendence, using other characters to get beyond self and body, that (a bit like Southwestern-frontier novelist Cormac McCarthy) she assumes violence as a universal and unconscious premise, as if violence as a means of vision were a fact of postfrontier American life. Violence may be, as Malcolm X once put it, as American as apple pie; for, as Ai phrased this defense of her poetic preoccupation (in a 1999 PBS radio interview by Elizabeth Farnsworth), "I think violence is an integral part of American culture, and I set out to deal with it, actually." She refuses explicitly to moralize this violence, but her imagination would validate its use for visionary ends, a dangerous (and deeply American) myth indeed. Ai's atavism is not so much subjective as structural, the reflex of a poetic sensibility responding to a climate of idealized warfare from Hiroshima to the Persian Gulf to Lebanon or Los Angeles.

For Ai, the violence is a mystical given of her art, a given of American history all the more so; she might well find another argument from cultural mythology to justify this concern with the body mutilated and transfigured, with the symbol of Christ crucified as sacred victim and savior. Ai was raised a Catholic (she wrote her first poem at age twelve, pretending to be a Christian martyr who was going to die the next day—her first vision-hungry monologue). A deeply interiorized Roman Catholic sense of the Incarnation as a bloody, sacred fact might well be influential upon her own poetic imagery, which would link violence and vision, as in the lines that close "Guadalajara Hospital" on a brutal note: "Virgin Mary, help me. Save me! Tear me apart with your holy, invisible hands." Such a dismemberment of the body as a sacred act occurs, symbolically, in the very act of Holy Communion; and Ai's poetic images often would aim in this direction of the body engorged, brutalized, and transfigured in the *Agnus Dei* ceremony of grace. Ai's poetic commitment to some quasi-Catholic "doctrine of the Real Presence" abides, even if this Eucharistic commitment is displaced into everyday transactions and events.[40]

Still, the overriding justification for the violence in Ai's work has been alluded to: the all-too-American preoccupation with regeneration through violent means, a central mythos of the confrontation between Indian and Christian cultures and ideologies. In Puritan and frontier narratives, a hero emerges, like Daniel Boone, whose violence against the Indians and animals is yet a sacred act seeking possession of the land: "an American hero is the lover of the spirit of the wilderness, and his acts of love and sacred affirmation are acts of violence against that spirit and her avatars."[41] However deep his plot of initiation through projected darkness, the physical conditions of American history give this myth special prominence for American writers. Ai is reworking this American mythology when she would attempt to connect violence of the body with regeneration of the spirit.

Ai's poetry is so deeply interiorized in its images and rawness of other-devouring drives that one must still ask whether the violence is there as masked sensation or as historical sign. I admit that one would at times have to answer the former (as in Bob Dylan); but the literal dimension of the bloodshed in her imagery cannot be casually dismissed. Another motive must haunt Ai. As a person of mixed-ethnic origin, Ai might well explore and expose, through poetic symbols, the violence wrought against her ancestors by the murderously abstract Christians. In this view, her poetry would become an attempt to understand the visionary violence of religious and political fanatics, through masks, which reveal and conceal her autobiographical interests. The violence is not hers but exorcizes via willed repetition the violence of a racist and of class-structured America betraying democratic ideals. Her body becomes the site of an ongoing *wound*—yellow, black, and ready to draw blood. The ghosts of history rise up to speak. The stigmata of American history haunt its rebirth, from cradle to grave and back.

Even though Ai's dramatic monologues are wrought as solitary ceremonies of vision, violence, and transfiguration, they are haunted by the death-and-rebirth dynamics of the Great Awakening crowds at Crane Ridge Kentucky in 1801, as Canetti has described this *drama of reversal* as being "slain" by the incoming spirit of the self-shattering Holy Ghost:

> When the fallen came to themselves they were changed people. They rose and shouted "Salvation!" They were "new-born" and ready to begin a good

and pure life; their old sinful existence was left behind them. *But the con-version could only be believed in if a kind of death had preceded it* [empha-sis mine].[42]

Ai's conversion is haunted by these traumas and passages between vio-lence, grace, death, and rebirth.

Alter-Becoming Violence

The sepia photograph on the cover of *Killing Floor* is a case of such semi-otic masking of the self in an image that both reveals and conceals Ai. Her cover of a young girl with a rifle, gun, and bandoliers of bullets staring at the reader was explained away by Ai, during an InterArts Hawaii sympo-sium on her work, as an interesting costume, as if she picked this one suit to wear without any special moral or political significance. Clothing, however, like language, does not work like this: each *parole*/sign takes place within a system of langue that gives that single act meaning by dif-ference. It is as if Ai, like an Isabel Archer, wants absolute freedom from social systems of identity-signification that would claim that a child with a gun is a revolutionary in appearance (she is called Rosebud Morales in the text); that Trotsky stands for distinct political positions that cannot be falsified at will; that even the most self-reliant ego wears fashion-coded clothes and talks a language of others. Ai wants the masks of *Killing Floor* and *Vice* to be arbitrary, beautiful, doomed in a singular way. Yet myriad monologues of *Vice* reveal that Ai has reached an extreme and yet keeps going with her project in history-harrowing ways.

Ai would enact the symbolic language of poetry as if it could function in latter days as the symbolic language of religion and redemption-via-performance (as in her poem on Lenny Bruce). Her cast of characters hungers for visionary breakthrough. As Ai commented on *Killing Floor,* "I'm dealing with past and present mystical beliefs—that line that sepa-rates the ecstatic visionary state from ordinary life—and saying 'look, it is as simple as lifting your hand, this passage into another life.' "[43] Noth-ing is got for nothing in the shift from *bios* to *Zoë,* following the Emer-sonian hard principle of *compensation* ruling in poetry as in life: and Ai's passage into other lives is not all that simple or idealistic, as this chapter has attempted to map. Nevertheless, Ai's goal remains the visionary one in which art would serve a quasi-religious "function of transcendence" or force of newness in a secular age that devalues symbolic language as the mimetic machinery of othering except in shamans or pagans.[44]

Ai's characters, although often historical, pass beyond the facts and literal documents of biography (which she does admit to using as the starting-point of her poems, as in her comment on the poem in the "abducted" voice of Jimmy Hoffa). But they become poetic heroes, saints, and missionaries for the project of seeing beyond, legends of a mystical consciousness encompassing, as by a film, our fall into limits of the ordinary and historical real. As if rising up from what Victoria Nelson calls the subzeitgeist of neogothic culture, Ai's symbolized personae want to get out of time, lurching beyond the mortal body and its repetitions, to pass beyond mere selfhood. When she depicts this will to transcendence, Ai alters history into symbols of the self, as religion long did in American culture with cures of self-transcendence via rituals of sacrifice, sacrament, and an incarnational language of the logos.

In a three-fold way, Ai suggests the (1) frontier, (2) Christian, and (3) ethnic-racial sources of this American will to transmogrify the ego into something sacred, if by the dismantling of otherness. Such an ambition may be endemic to American poetic self-conceptions and the will to perpetual rebirth as "Redeemer Nation," given the transcendental mantles of Emerson's "Poet" and a pro-imperial incarnation in Whitman, not to mention the mimetic of conversion this study has traced. This drive to self-transcendence and the death-and-rebirth of ordinary selfhood informs the masks of Ai, as survivor of trauma and abjection. Ai's poems are ways into rebirth and what she calls, in her interiorized portrayal of J. Robert Oppenheimer, "the third eye of History" (*Vice*, 79). Each Ai poem, violence-and-vision drenched, "takes its place in the landscape of horrors that comprise for Ai our recent American legacy."[45] From the disasters of Hiroshima to the ruins of 9/11, this is the horizon of Ai's trauma, vision, and survival as American poet. In a time of "white heat" and neonativism, which would scapegoat nonwhite immigrants and multiethnic settlers as nonbelonging newcomers, we need to hear claims of these ghosts whose voices had been here long before this Empire told itself dreams of innocence and global redemption.[46] Ai brings the violence back home as some kind of religious sacrament of alter-becoming, enacted as sacred hunger and postcolonial release.

The Maori novelist and poet Witi Ihimaera has a poem laced with devastating ironies of indigenous history, lost sovereignty, and Eucharistic Christianity called "Dinner with Cannibals." We sit down to a dinner with chandeliers, red roses, dinner jackets, and claret as the white visitor begins to eat with "manners [that] were impeccable / Not one sweet morsel of me dropped / From his lips." Soon we realize who is the violent one ("cannibal") in this "contact zone" of colonial re-imagining, where selves (as in the rebirth appetites of Ai's monologues) consume others to savor the "body and blood" of sacred sacrifice on this transoceanic frontier:

He was a gourmet of impeccable sophistication
"That was much better than Aboriginal or Red Indian"
He said. And I have never liked the taste of Hindu or Pakistani
Too much curry in the diet taints the flesh
"You are a repast quite delicious
Almost like Samoan, less fatty than Tongan"
So saying he proceeded to the main course [to eat the Maori
    host].[47]

CHAPTER SIX

Becoming Jeremiah inside the U.S. Empire

On the Born-Again Refigurations of Bob Dylan

I consider myself a poet first and a musician second. . . . I live
like a poet and I'll die like a poet. I've always liked my stuff.
And you have to please yourself in any area of life.

> —Bob Dylan, as quoted in Robert Shelton,
> *No Direction Home*[1]

But even here the impact of [American popular] music is of a
quite different order than as an aspect of conquest or conversion

> —Simon Frith, " 'And I Guess It Doesn't Matter Anymore':
> European Thoughts on American Music"[2]

Oh child, why you wanna hurt me?
I'm exiled, you can't convert me

> —Bob Dylan, "We Better Talk This Over"
> from *Street Legal*, 1978[3]

Conversions against Empire

Reigning forms of born-again Christianity in the United States can make
submission to fundamentals of family, shopping mall, state security, sexual identity, and corporatized nation seem mandated by a *call-on-high*
from—that hypernormalized citizen of Constitutional law—God. If subterranean beliefs or spectral resurrections still echo, the air-waves get
filled with mediated terms of political invective and high-level gossip,
what the apostle Paul called "vain jangling."[4] It's as if born-again conversion meant little more than a lifestyle change into flag-waving conscription, voice flattened into signifiers of caustic whiteness and gospel of
wealth: target audience, say, for Fox News television.[5] An SUV passes me
by on Interstate 5, near Los Angeles, with a bumper sticker literalizing
scriptural inerrancy, as if biblical prophecy can become U.S. social policy:

"God said it. I believe it. That settles it."[6] The "Last Day" novels, selling in millions like evangelical hotcakes, ratify an end-time vision of a polity on the verge of being lifted into nuclear rapture and global rage, with the preterite elect saved by apocalyptic convictions from *Revelations* and the rest *left behind* to mourn and burn.

In the Columbia rock video that came out in the late Cold War years of 1983 for Bob Dylan's reggae-influenced song "Jokerman," to the post-Beat contrary, the prophetic curse of visionary denunciation that is uttered against our contemporary *Sodom and Gomorrah* ("ain't nobody there would want to marry my sister") is hard to dissociate from an ecoscape of nuclearized death the U.S. Empire inflicted upon Hiroshima not so much to end as *begin* hegemony by superpower. This Jokerman trickster-figure looks like some crossover of Dick Tracy's skull-and-bones Joker and that taunting president who presided over the binary redemption of U.S. good and U.S.S.R. evil at that time, Ronald Reagan. For the belief-structure of President George W. Bush that admits little sense of sin, self-doubt, or historical wrongdoing, as Calvin Trillin mockingly notes in "Presidential Eating Preferences" for his weekly *Dunciad* poem in the pages of *The Nation*, "He won't eat crow. No crow. No, not a bite. / He's never wrong, cause Jesus makes him right."[7] God, in this U.S. fundamentalist turn toward messianic globalism, has come to be spelled (as one Democratic wag put it) *GOP.*[8] God becomes another name for *global warrior* or *conversion by the sword*, rebirth into dogma.

By contrast with these right-leaning affirmations, James Baldwin's Afro-American Baptist son once urged after becoming a "man-child, bestial, before the light that comes down from heaven," the conversion experience can signify a world-shattering experience inside the ghetto, as he looks out on a twice-born Harlem inside the American Babylon: "And the avenue [Lenox], like any landscape that has endured a storm, lay changed under Heaven, exhausted and clean, and new."[9] Or as Baldwin signifies this black-conversion through the fugitive experience of Village jazz, in "Sonny's Blues," sorrow can get lifted up from streets of "ruin, destruction, madness, and death," as the junk-sick jazz pianist "was giving [blackness] back, as everything must be given back, so that, passing through death, it can live forever."[10] In pop cultural dispersal, auras of the sacred can be displaced into what Dylan calls "Visions of Johanna" on the radio, just as demons of theological rumination get cast into neogothic genres of cinema, internet, or "faux Catholic" fiction: in poems of our climate, infinity goes up on trial again and again.[11] These are techno-related instances of regenerative immanence and "occult force" surging up from urban sidewalk, freeway dirt, and river water as much as across American airwaves. The passion of Christ haunts the making of this polity, then as now, as beat shepherd.[12]

From Hawai'i to Minnesota or Tonga and New England and beyond, as this study has urged, terms of Judeo-Christian rebirth can get translated, spiritually transliterated, and push beyond entrapment into Empire, so that the being born again looms ahead of the techno-present, say, comes out of a mouth-harp or an airplane. Dylan once taunted the left-coast audience at the Santa Cruz Civic Auditorium, opening his "never-ending" concert on March 16, 2000, with a Southern white-gospel tune cranked out in a gruff voice as if spoken from a beat cross on Pacific Avenue, as if chorus, prophecy-drenched Dylan, and audience comprised some theo-primitivist collective in the Roman wilds: "I am the man, Thomas, I am the man / Look at these nail marks here in my hands." This country-gospel song sets up an immanence of the spirit, conjures the return of blood, hand, voice, and nail to an audience filled close to doubting Thomas.[13] Dylan has long questioned the direction of U.S. national progress toward formations of Empire, atomic power, and global war, as in his ballad "Señor (Tales of Yankee Power)" from *Street Legal* (1978), "Señor, Señor, do you know where we're headin'? / Lincoln County Road or Armageddon?" Back then, it might have seemed we were closer to a suburban street named after Honest Abe lined with car dealerships than locked in some binary battle for global domination and civilizational supremacy. If one were waiting for some invisible republic of the spirit to be reborn as a polity called America, then a huge change would have to come in, and singers like Sam Cooke and Bob Dylan would make sure that the Holy Spirit was not a life force blown away in late-capitalist winds but an abiding presence in heartbeat and the soul.

We stand as a global polity, post-9/11, facing a time of political insecurity and economic terror when an evangelical talk-show host on the 700 Club can advocate the assassination of the twice-elected president of a pro-labor government in Venezuela as an ethical option.[14] Dylan's song of imperial warning is set near Mexico and ends in disconnected cables and overturned tables fading with a bitter Jeremaic lament, "This place don't make sense to me no more / Can you tell me what we're heading for, señor?"[15] No wonder the post-NAFTA America portrayed in *Masked and Anonymous* (2003) collapses into Third World immiseration, and the streets of Los Angeles look like a merger of San Quentin and a banana republic. Even in Hollywood movies from the 1930s and 1940s, with zany plots of remarriage and domesticity, the eruption of the sacred in the ordinary or fits of Emersonian optimism were *never that far off,* however, as Stanley Cavell has noted of the musical genre: it plays "on the idea of the ordinary world as a step away from ecstatic harmony (a feature especially notable in the routines of Fred Astaire, which so characteristically take their rise from events and objects of everyday life—a walk along a river or down a train platform, taking shelter in a pavilion in the rain, roller skating, golfing, swabbing a floor, tripping over overstuffed chairs)."[16] In our popular culture, as Dylan early learned, America can itself go up on trial again and again.

This counterimperial vision of America as what has long been called the "invisible republic" of the spirit, to invoke Greil Marcus's trope for "the old weird America," is now and again portrayed in terms of deliteralized faith, spectral leaps into beat presencing, and profane illumination.[17] Writing like some neo-Beat "Isaiah among the lumpenproletariat," the novelist Denis Johnson captures this quest to incarnate Pentecostal eruptions in novels and poems of unhoused sacramentalism—works in which religious seekers may find revelations in a pop tune, highway sign, jukebox, cheap frame houses, or a drugstore window.[18] This drive for altered states of conversion becomes tormented, profane, and routed on the road to beatitude across some no-man's-land like that of the drugged-out drifter in *Jesus' Son,* who crosses highways of disconnected prophecies and broken translations in the heart-land. His post-Beat characters seem to be seeking some "lost testament" of *gnosis* as outlined in Johnson's work on crazed American religiosity, *Seek:* "Or does it seem [in this America] we've been abandoned here unredeemed, confused, trying to decipher a strange new text?—a Third Testament cobbled together out of bits and pieces of the other two and interpretations that don't bear much examination."[19]

Beaten-down forms of redemption—a thief on the cross (or worse), for example—figure in Johnson's novel, *Already Dead,* as a migrant farm worker drifts from job to job, community to community, in lost corridors of the west until she winds up on "the Lost Coast" of Mendecino County, California, where forms of dislocated religiosity and belief find a home. As Carrie explains her patchwork code of New Age Christianity to a surf bum drifter she treats as a random force of salvation, met on the roadside,

> Where do you get your religion?
> From the road. From the radio. TV sometimes.
> You're not a member of a church?
> The road is a church.[20]

In Azusa Street Awakenings in Los Angeles, the Holy Ghost might speak in tongues of visceral redemption, socialist challenge, mongrelized idioms of class dialectics-cum-garage poesy. "Equally heretical, the Pentecostals sometimes seemed to confuse Biblical eschatology with Marxist theory," as Mike Davis outlines in *Dead Cities,* "as when Sister Galmond prophesied a great "War of Labor against Capital."[21] Haunted blues-poet Robert Johnson staged this spectral unrest spreading into techno-forms (in his last Dallas studio session of June 27, 1937), which no bus or train ride across the land could ever cure, "You may bury my body, ooh / down by the highway side / so my old evil spirit can catch a Greyhound bus and ride."[22] Pentecostal socialism lives on as such in these survival tactics for the downtrodden, on the other side of high-capitalist modernity and its cash-flow gospel of the preterite elect.[23]

In another latter-day quest to affirm some "invisible republic" built of spectral lyrics and occulted folk tones written in the American vernacular weirdness that would "many times" outflank and undermine an America-becoming-empire through subterranean reclamation, Greil Marcus invokes the voice of a *Village Voice* music critic who hears (in Dylan's 1967 basement tapes) a subterranean theology issued outside of workaday time, "like some bootleg gospel of Christ, ellipsis as parable."[24] Rebirth energies are heard between pores of blues records, rail sounds, dust rolls, Sunday quiet, or gospel tunes: elliptical, evasive, half out of reach—never buried or forgotten but, like Guthrie, an ancestor to choose or be chosen by in margins of official history. Dylan subjects Guthrie to figurative recall in which repetition becomes "a future-directed retrieval of the past," an afterlife in which offspring can carry ancestors into the future (as Baudelaire did for Poe) and the dead can live on as cultural transmission in the folk-son.[25] Such works comprise this "Invisible America" of alter becoming, housing tropes of conversion and counter-conversion, forces of resurrection, insurrection, life-experimentation. They contribute to making a "prophetic America" shaped and judged by covenantal terms.[26] Rebirth and self-metamorphosis become a mandate, in the lyric subject, to redeem the nation from falling into a Roman Empire of false gods and broken promises, as I shall discuss.

Tambourine Man by the Beat Pacific

Digging into (or *digging* in the Beat sense as well) the left-coast mythos of San Francisco as a "swarming locale" and "port of recall," Robert Duncan, in *Roots and Branches* (1964), played upon San Francisco's nearness to the Asia/Pacific Orient and Charles Olson's "mythic sea," wherein the Ahab-ego in *Moby-Dick* had met its end and something new would rise up:

> . . . Here
> our West's the Orient,
> our continent the sea.[27]

Facing west from California toward oceanic horizons of animistic aura, the early Bob Dylan, in his most Pacific-based poem (written at Joan Baez's home in Carmel in 1964) of natural immensity, "Lay Down Your Weary Tune," waxed full of cosmic melodies, strands of mythic recurrence at Carmel, symphonic invocations, in a lyric call to turn from the history-weary anguish of war and battle into oceanic-consciousness. Its refrain, "lay down your weary tune, lay down lay down," turned from history to sublime pantheism, Big Sur water-worship: "The ocean wild like an organ played, / The seaweed wove its strands . . . no voice can hope to hum."[28] Dylan, seeking a vernacular vision-quest, was not about *to lay down his weary tune* as a poet or song-maker. A muse-figure from that early era and place, Joan Baez of the quasi-angelic voice and leftist leanings early recognized his *drive*—over many burnt bridges—"to live and die like a poet."[29]

While most would agree that Robert Allen Zimmerman from the Mesabe Iron Ranges in upper Minnesota took the name "Bob Dylan" from the Welsh poet Dylan Thomas, rather than from a Jewish-Russian uncle Dillon as he was wont to avow like some neo-hillbilly in the city,[30] we could also affirm (as Dylan told *People* magazine in 1975) that his name change "was given to me—by God" in a moment of "inspiration."[31] This name-change or conversion *mask* (assumed around 1958 in Minneapolis) converted "Bob Dylan" to believing in his own power as a poet and mythmaker able to speak for or against American culture. The new name of reborn identity inscribed an allegory of self-formation into his willed vocation of *poesis*. Indeed, the name *Dylan* comes down from Welsh folklore and means "darkness," signifying a night born at the beginning of the world and nourished across the Atlantic Ocean waters to become "son of the wave," the darkness split off from "Lyewellyn," twin brother of light.[32]

Later, when Gemini-born Dylan—given to "exile," doubleness, surrealist allegory, mask, and modes of dirty Beat alienation—turned to affirm (via his later conversion) the light of Jesus-as-Messiah, Joel Selvin was not alone in mistakenly castigating "Bob Dylan's God-awful Gospel" and his *turn/return* to God as a fateful betrayal of poetic vision-quest. "Years from now, when social historians look back over these years," Selvin warned, "Dylan's conversion will serve as a concise metaphor for the vast emptiness of the era."[33] Dylan, fabulist of self-myth as homemade son of Woody Guthrie, Dylan Thomas, Rimbaud, Brecht, Ginsberg, and God, had been at that point "overtaken by the myth of Christ," which modern poetry itself (as Robert Duncan once advised) is supposed—in all its nihilist severity and postmodern de-creation—to defend you from as belief.[34] Dylan became a poet of U.S. "holy aggression" who aimed his poetry at cleansing the good of the accretions that had come to encumber visions of redemption or democratic possibility in his declining and Mammon-worshipping homeland.[35] "We walk by faith not by sight," said Saint Paul and a world cast of thousands, which for a poet like Dylan means self-refiguration via the leaping power of imagination, grace, and trope. Cultural critics still find it easier to grasp Dylan's turn from folk modes to electric guitars at Newport 1965 than to accept Dylan's conversion as a poet to "born-again" Christianity as such.[36] Conversion signified for Dylan not so much emptiness as renewed semiotic *plentitude* and states of poetic becoming, as we shall see. Reinvention of the self, as an American mandate to make it new and be *always converting if not converted,* became Dylan's core affirmation of freedom and the will to change.[37]

A Faith Long Abandoned

It's HIM through YOU. "He's alive," Paul said. "I've been crucified with Christ, nevertheless I live. Yet not I but Christ who liveth in me." See, Christ is not some kind of figure down the road. We serve the living God, not dead monuments, dead ideas, dead philosophies. If he had been a dead God, you'd be carrying around a corpse inside you.

Jesus put his hand on me. It was a physical thing. I felt it. I felt it all over me. I felt my whole body tremble. The glory of the Lord knocked me down and picked me up.
      —Bob Dylan in New Zealand[38]

"I practice a faith that's been long abandoned / Ain't no altars on this long and lonesome road," Dylan later affirms on *Modern Times* (2006), in the blunt final track called "Ain't Talkin," which surveys the "cities of the plague" and a homemade Empire that "will tear you away from contemplation" and "crush you with wealth and power" at the (near-seeming) world's end. "Man of Constant Sorrow" was not just a song from folk traditions; it became a mask the youthful Dylan crafted into a way of telling his broken romances, wanderlust in the Midwest, even messianic longings. Later, in electronic autonomy of poetic imagination, "Mr. Tambourine Man" became an anthem of gnostic knowing, amplifying a way to defeat time, social determination, and empire, "with all memory and fate driven deep beneath the waves" until the spell of poetic enchantment ends at daybreak. The beaten-down Jesus became, for Dylan as Man of Sorrows, "the man who died a criminal's death" opposing high priests of ritualized piety as well as the worldly forces of Caesar. As born-again minister Billy Graham once advised a political leader, who sought assurance of salvation during the Vietnam war, "We are not saved because of our own accomplishments, I am not going to Heaven because I have preached to great crowds or read the Bible many times. I'm going to Heaven just like the thief on the cross who said in the last moment: 'Lord, remember me.' "[39]

Via relentless processes of *conversion* and *counter-conversion*, Dylan's will to activate metamorphosis as a life principle abides at the core of his gift as a didactic poet of American prophecy and denunciation, as he goes on daring (right in the face of an Empire's ever-expanding global power) "to write his autobiography in colossal cipher" and to render (as Emerson demanded) "America [as] a poem in our eyes."[40] Emerson speaks here of Dante but he also provokes Whitman and countless voices from John Ashbery to Anne Waldman to emerge as poets. Along these self-relying lines, the greatness of Bob Dylan as poet of cultural myth-making implies that he embodies an array of voice-masks from secular love *(eros)* to sacred love *(agapē)* and back again: early and late, his poetry moves (across our immiserated "modern times") from states of lack-love, social abandonment, and male rage to more redemptive or prophetic states of U.S. imperial critique. As a love poet at all points believing in "romantic love as salve and salvation," as Courtney Haden observed in her keen review of *Modern Times,* the never-ending performance of Bob Dylan on the road to caritas is also haunted by "a desire to atone," and "sin" abides as a category of his prophetic worldview.[41] With a poet's "mercury mouth in the missionary times," as *Blonde on Blonde* put this, Dylan as writing self could survive death, disaster, divorce, voice-loss, and disintegrations of poetic mask several times over. Dylan's mask as "Dylan" was a first version of self-empowerment and inner belief in embracing off-beat semiotic feats of self-becoming. For, as Elias Canetti affirmed of such masked "transformations," "The working of the mask is mainly outwards; it creates a *figure. The mask is inviolable and sets a distance between itself and the spectator.*"[42] John Pareles also gets at this force of masked identification and poetic transformation in Dylan, when he remarks of *Time Out of Mind* on the *Charlie Rose* show, "He gets his religion from Hank Williams' 'I Saw the Light.'" From such songs, Dylan borrowed masks of becoming and empowerment.

Such Dylanesque turn-arounds of poetic imagination, mask, white face, and mercurial myth can be lifelong or sudden, as in line shifts or across a single album, period, or song. This much we do know, as the collaged video for "Series of Dreams" by Meijert Avis wonderfully captures in its wry portrait of Dylan-as-multiplicity set over the grave of Jack Kerouac and haunted by messages from Rimbaud, Dylan Thomas, Allen Ginsberg, Son House, and a motley cast of soul-shaping thousands.[43] A bedraggled love song like "Bye and Bye" from *Love and Theft* (2001) can shift from casual tonalities like "breathin' a lover's sigh" and banal couplets made of "sugar-coated rhyme" to close its two-timing romance with world-shattering stanzas embracing the fateful turn to conversion, all but Pauline in the fierceness of its will to social renewal and agon (*Lyrics,* 585):

> I'm gonna baptize you in fire so you can sin no more
> I'm gonna establish my rule through civil war
> Gonna make you see just how loyal and true a man can be.

What might seem a throwaway line from this love-weary song, "I'm not even acquainted with my own desires," captures the power of the unconsciousness to shatter codes of romance or social stability (*Lyrics,* 585). This accords with the Pauline account of desire under the law, "what I would [do], that do I not; but what I hate, that do I" (Romans 7:15). For Dylan in *Saved,* "sin" is fatally Adamic to desire: "it run[s] in my vein" (*Lyrics,* 430). In lyrics blasted open, and fragmentary voice becoming discontinuous, masked, and ironic, Dylan is still talking what American poet Rodney Jones calls the *salvation blues.*[44]

Reborn in Time: "Be Always Converting"

Back in 1981, after *Saved* and *Shot of Love* had already drawn fiercely binary lines between the *saved-and-fallen* across the whole canon of his earlier poetics, Dylan openly recounted a "rebirth" experience that had taken place in 1978 even as his life was going well, and he was touring the land, that night holding a silver cross in a motel room in Arizona. Dylan affirmed the core of his conversion experience in the following starkly Pauline terms: "Jesus did appear to me as King of Kings, and Lord of Lords. . . . I believe every knee shall bow one day, and He did die on the cross for all mankind . . . they call it reborn . . . it changes everything. I mean it's like waking one day and can you imagine being reborn, can you imagine turning into another person? It's pretty scary if you think about it. . . . It happens spiritually, it don't happen mentally."[45]

In the mode of prophetic vision materialized on *Slow Train Coming* and *Saved,* Dylan had begun to drive a wedge between taken-for-granted worlds of "sin/grace, corruption/goodness, with no room for anything in between," aggravating via such a mask of certitude "the strife of Christ against the empire of Satan," as abolitionist William Lloyd Garrison had done, for example, in this American Jeremiad mode of prophetic denunciation-cum-liberation.[46] Some of Dylan's seemingly Hal Lindsey-drenched prophetic rants (influenced by apocalyptic works of Cold War ideology and antimodernism, like *The Late Great Planet Earth* [1970]) are still hard to listen to, or accept, as trope-claiming-to-be-historical-truth. These hectoring rants and sermons are aimed to be unsettling and agonistic to the core, unless you are one of the raptured preterite of the self-declared American elect, as when Dylan rails against those living in "East-Coast bondage," slaves to desire and death, from dusty Tulsa to that insurance capital, Hartford.[47] But the "self" or masked voice animating this archive of death and rebirth, as if following some *Dylanesque dynamic of metamorphosis* and perpetual self-remaking via adherence to *poesis,* has been *born and later born again, and that many times.* "His habit of crossing genres may explain his habit of crossing religions," as Alex Ross once affirmed, meaning that Dylan's will to metamorphosis may have motivated his quest for religious conversion rather than the other way around.[48] Norman O. Brown captured this dynamic of poetic-becoming in his retranslation of the Greek text from Romans 12:2 into post-1960s American English: "And by ye not conformed to this world [*be nonconformists*]; but be ye transformed [*metamorphose yourself*] by the renewing of your mind."[49]

This will to rebirth was expressed, in terms of nonconformity to commodity-culture, when Emerson affirmed, denying the predeterminations of culture, biology, class, and social status he had invoked as the nemesis of self-relying power and the godhead in the self, namely "Fate": "We rightly say of ourselves, we were born, and afterward we were born again, and many times."[50] Dylan's commitment to these states of self-reliant becoming and adverting antagonism to American conformity to market forces was brought out in Martin Scorsese's PBS bio-documentary *No Direction Home* (2005), wherein Dylan (his speeded-up voice mimicking his Beat mentor Jack Kerouac's "spontaneous bop prosody") not only aligns his Village self to the Beat aesthetics of those "mad to live, mad to talk, mad to be saved, desirous of everything at the same time" personae from *On the Road,* but the mercurial songwriter also affirms his quest as "poet song-writer" to stay "constantly in a state of becoming" that never at all stays fixed in form, language, or set number.[51] Being beat, in this sense, meant being beaten down and blasted open to love's death and the soul's traumas: on the road to poetic beatitude and highways and byways of vision Dylan has been seeking to give gruff voice to, album by album, all along the line.

Reborn to Protest

I think all of my stuff is protest material in some kinda way. . . . Protest is anything that goes against the ordinary and the estab-lished. And who's the founder of protest? Martin Luther.
    —Bob Dylan to Kurt Loder, *Rolling Stone* interview, 1984[52]

Even before Dylan's rebirth experience in 1978, from songs that have be-come "crypto-biblical classics," as *Mojo Magazine* called "This Wheels on Fire" (*Lyrics,* 299), to surrealized tales of Abraham being tested by a taunting pre-liberal God on Minnesota's "Highway 61 Revisited" (*Lyrics,* 178), Dylan prefigured his religious obsession with Messiah im-ages, dustbowl pilgrims, glory-bound trains, and folk embodiments as outcast suffering. Even a song full of agonistic rage, trying to overcome resentment in the NYC urban folk scene as in "Positively Fourth Street," centers around (or *against*) a liberal antagonist losing faith, or one who "had no faith to lose" to begin with (*Lyrics,* 184). The language of the Bible implodes inside and all over the pages of Dylan's lyrics, early and late, as the Byrds recognized with their electric versions of *Ecclesiastes* on "Turn, Turn, Turn," to go with their pop-hit rendering of Dylan's "Mr. Tambourine Man." They took Dylan's poems into a realm of tran-scendence and vision-opening mode, "with all memory and fate driven deep beneath the waves" beyond any literal-minded resentment. As touched on in Chapter 2, "Turn, Turn, Turn" implies the *turning away from* and *turning toward* God that is implied in the Latinate verb form *convert:* its genius loci of electronic forms, Roger McGuinn, the founder of the Byrds in Los Angeles, would also be drawn to faith-forms in gospel and white country as well as Scots ballads.

Refiguring the terms and syntax of song prosody, Dylan brought *rebirth*—and radical defamiliarization—to the very form of what a folk or rock song could be or do, as Johnny Cash captured in his defense of

Dylan in *Broadside* in March 1964: "Near my shores of mental dying. Grasping straws and twigs and drowning," Cash wrote in Dylanesque echoes of poetic rebirth, "Worthless I, But crying loudest, Came a Poet Troubadour, Singing ... a hundred thousand lyrics, Right as Rain, Sweet as Sleep."[53] Early on, Dylan reflected biblical-based figurations in his folk album days in New York City, as in preaching songs from *Bob Dylan* for the first studio sessions of Columbia Records in 1962, including "Quit Your Low Down Ways" (*Lyrics*, 35) or "I'd Hate to Be You on That Dreadful Day" (*Lyrics*, 37), with their sinners, broken covenants, men of sorrows dying in forlorn graves, graves made by Jesus, or even more so as in this appeal to Messianic time in the Civil Rights-haunted gospel tune "Long Ago and Far Away" (*Lyrics*, 24):

> To preach of peace and brotherhood
> O, what might be the cost!
> A man he did it long ago,
> And they hung him on a cross.

Biblical precedents to brotherhood endure across social contexts; the song makes distance near and blasts images from the past into the future, as it laments and mocks the rejection of Jesus's message of communal caritas.[54] The folk-blues highway trope, as Michael Gray urges, houses a Bunyan-like pilgrim quest in Dylan's early days of protest and civic justice.[55] "Father of Night," from *New Morning* (1970), is Hebraic in its liturgy-like rhythms of divine worship: "Father of minutes, Father of days / Father of whom we most solemnly praise" (*Lyrics*, 268).

"Despite his pose as Woody Guthrie-type country drifter," as Camille Paglia noted, "Dylan was a total product of Jewish culture, where the word is sacred," and his "sensitivity to language, [and] mastery of irony and satire" reflect a commitment to the word as prophetic utterance however surrealistic, crypto-subjective, or masked-and-anonymous the poet's formulations became over decades of albums and concerts.[56] Vulgar and hybrid, a music wrought of vernacular empathy and "made out of cultural intermingling, the uprooting and rerooting of people" like Dylan's Jewish relatives from Russia and the Midwest, popular music was tied to "a sense of religiosity, a sense of collective uplift," as Simon Frith notes; and Dylan (early and late) embodied vernacular forms he learned from precursors as diverse as Jimmy Rogers, Ma Rainy, Hank Williams, Son House, Victoria Spivey, and Blind Willy McTell.[57] Dylan could be local and vernacular, in this mixed-U.S. sense, and yet have what

Frith calls a larger "cultural resonance" that, like Methodist morphologies of conversion, had crossed the Atlantic and beyond the Mississippi.

Being Born Again Is a Hard Thing

> Jesus put his hand on me. It was a physical thing. I felt it. I felt it all over me. I felt my whole body tremble. The glory of the Lord knocked me down and picked me up. . . . Being born again is a hard thing. You ever seen a mother give birth to a child? Well, it's painful. We don't like to lose those old attitudes and hang-ups. Conversion takes time because you have to learn to crawl before you can walk. You have to learn to drink milk before you can eat meat. You're reborn, but like a baby. A baby doesn't know anything about this world and that's what it's like when you're reborn. You're a stranger. You have to learn all over again. God will show you what you need to know.[58]

Yet the pilgrim's "highway" in Dylan's life-figurations twists from romantic to sacred love, if not back again several times, and shape-shifted the terms of this cultural resonance: "I know all about poison, I know all about fiery darts / I don't care how rough the road is, show me where it starts" (*Lyrics*, 428), as he avows to the lover-become-Jesus in "What Can I Do for You?" "Dylan's conversion to Born Again Christianity is the last step down a long road he's been traveling for years," Michael Gray avers, as Dylan turns from the torments and Sara-love in *Blood on the Tracks* and death-in-life traumas of *Street Legal* to the Jesus-love and blood-of-the-lamb imagery in *Saved* and *Shot of Love*.[59] From the "flesh-colored Christs that glow in the dark" of "It's Alright Ma (I'm Only Bleeding)" on *Bringing It All Back Home* (*Lyrics*, 156) to "that sign on the cross that worries me" of *The Basement Tapes* (*Lyrics*, 300), even this *pre-conversion* Dylan is haunted by the presence (or absence) of the sacred, the allure of a transromantic love, the quest for a path between the cynicism of "the joker" and mean will-to-power of "the thief" (*Lyrics*, 224). With Dylan, we could say of his poetic strength asserted against standard Judeo-Christian beliefs and covenants, that (as Andrew Marvell affirmed of Milton's Protestant will to revelation by *sola scriptura*), "he would ruin (for I saw him strong) / The Sacred Truths to Fable and Old Song."[60] In lyrics of beatitude, lifting the downtrodden into the exalted and released, Dylan sides with *trope over truth*, rendering "conversion" into a process signed with grace, sin, and flux, more than convicted affirmation.

The leap across the abyss via intertextual refiguration, moving from the profane to the sacred or the vernacular voice to American apocalypse and back again, is expressed in caustic lyrics as in "High Water (For Charley

Patton)," which cranks up a Delta blues idiom to evangelical hyperbole: "The Cuckoo is a pretty bird, she warbles as she files / I'm preachin' the Word of God / I'm puttin' out your eyes" (*Lyrics*, 591). The forked-tongue of the trickster voice (figured by the cuckoo bird) is vanquished by logocentric mandates affirming baptism-by-truth troping hard rains into cosmic Flood: "Thunder rolling over Clarksdale, everything is looking blue." Folk blues and gospel idioms were never that far apart, as the music of a Dylan precursor like Blind Willie McTell shows. "Born in Time," refusing the fallen will's ruination into time and body, registers love's damages burned into destiny of romantic selfhood, "where we were born in time" (*Lyrics*, 548).

Male Specters and Female Emanations

The grim landscape of the Midwestern "North Country" and American-populist affiliations would prove enduring, to be sure, as the prose-poem "My Life in a Stolen Minute," handed out as a program note for Dylan's concert at New York's Town Hall in April 12, 1963, made palpable, with its on-the-road claims to encompass the Whitmanic polity, its folk ties to Duluth, and its "iron country" class-claims to "making my own depression" and "hitch [hiking] on 61—51—75—169—37—66—22."[61] By the time this shape-shifter, Robert Allen Zimmerman (born May 24, 1941), was self-renamed Bob Dylan and had all but shorn his folk-masks and Popular Front identifications with the dust-bowl proletariat and those cast off by the side of the road to the American dream of equality, prosperity, and state justice, he put on a proliferating array of Blakean masks of Male Specter and Female Emanation (in his myriad lyrics) to speak from the torments of romantic love and broken spiritual quest.

Blood on the Tracks is the fullest version of that psychic dramaturgy, as Sarah turns from being emanating Muse of poetic glory in "Sad Eyed Lady of the Lowlands" to becoming the spectral male's worst enemy, blocking his works, refusing his projection of divine or poetic aura. The figurations of woman-as-muse turn from the death-dealing Isis of self-disintegration charted in "Isis" (cowritten with Jacques Levy) to the Beatrice figure of enhanced vision called "Precious Angel," whose redemptive call "under the sun" is leading the poet "On the way out of Egypt, through Ethiopia, to the judgment hall of Christ" (*Lyrics*, 404). Album-length works from *Infidels* to *Love and Theft* push this uneasy dynamic of romantic love and quest for conversion to higher levels of metamorphosis and self-becoming. In "Up to Me," as the male hounds the earth after the woman of his dreams, run off from a mere postal clerk to an affair with a man in an officer's club (the class torment is still there), Dylan portrays the blinded jealousy, male possessiveness, and lust that has been blocked or abandoned. The jealous male sees through a glass darkly, turns from one profane love to the next, as songs measure failure in such stanzas of desire and lack:

> We heard the Sermon on the Mount and I knew it was too
>   complex
> It didn't amount to more than what the broken glass reflects
> When you bite off more than you can chew you pay the penalty
> Somebody's got to tell the tale, and I guess it must be up to me.

The broken glass reflects the rage and misery of broken love and shattered covenants. Contrast these muse battles with the conviction of "Love Minus Zero/No Limit," wherein the woman "doesn't have to say she's faithful / Yet she's true like ice, like fire." *Faithful* puns on romantic loyalty and sacred vision, loves sacred and profane, here as elsewhere.

The wages of compulsive desire and male need are shown to incite an endless round of song and empty quest, in sin-driven drives for romantic completion, "life [become] a pantomime" of male specters and female emanations (*Lyrics,* 348–349). "Idiot Wind" registers a death-dealing male rage against this rejection, "You're an idiot, babe / It's a wonder that you still know how to breathe," in a refrain that is crudely a misogynist's curse (*Lyrics,* 336).[62] "Simple Twist of Fate" suggests that such desire, sensual need coded as poetic-and-romantic fate, can take on trappings of a mistake or, worse, *sin.* "People tell me it's a sin / To know and feel too much within" (*Lyrics,* 334), to believe that a twist of fate is spiritual calling or covenant of sacred imagination. On the tormented *Desire,* as if naming the plight of self-blinded love in the album title itself, "Oh Sister" overcomes the broken covenant as the voice calls out for a confederation of male and female in transromantic quest: "We grew up together / From the cradle to the grave / We died and were reborn / And then mysteriously saved" (*Lyrics,* 362).

But the failure to *deconvert* from forms of the male will's bondage is revealed in the bypassed song from *Blood on the Tracks,* "Call Letter Blues," which opens with the singer walking all night, "Listenin to them church bells tone," and ends with the mother run off from family and male need, both caught in an endless round of desire, betrayal, suffering: "Well, I gaze at passing strangers / In case I might see you. . . . But the sun goes around the heavens / And another day just drives on through" (*Lyrics,* 350). In "Abandoned Love," which is a crucial sequel to "Sarah," that hymn to a "radiant jewel, mystical wife" who is abandoning him to his own self-love and poems (*Lyrics,* 369), Dylan reverses his sense of being abandoned into a rejection of love's "ball and chain" as a clown's purgatory. The song ends in mutual rejection: "Once more time at midnight, near the wall / Take off your heavy makeup and your shawl / Won't you descend from the throne where you sit? / Let me feel your love one more time before I abandon it" (*Lyrics,* 371).

It seems here, in terms of self-refiguration, that the male lover is the one *doing the abandoning,* as if maintaining mastery over love's muse and queen. The spiritual forces have also abandoned him to his own pain, selfishness, and rounds of desire's hunger: "My patron saint is a-fightin with a ghost / He's always off somewhere when I need him most / The Spanish moon is rising on the hill / But my heart is a-tellin me I love ya still" (*Lyrics,* 371). With *Saved,* the lineaments of "Covenant Woman" will try to get beyond such loss and emptiness by the appeal to eternal covenants, shared quest, and gospel precedents all along the line, from family to self to community and globe in ecumenical embrace become didactic, apocalyptic, hard to take as poem.

That visionary balladeer of apocalyptic desire, William Blake, had foreshadowed the romanticist's plight of poetic emanation and spectral male need in three related poems of cryptic intensity from around 1800, "William Bond," "Crystal Cabinet," and an untitled poem (from the Notebooks of 1800–1806), which opens in the middle of crazed psychic space:[63]

> My Spectre around me night & day
> Like a Wild beast guards my way,
> My Emanation far within
> Weeps incessantly for my Sin.

Fending against this figuration of jealousy/vengeance, Blake's imagination scapegoated (and tried to transcend) as Female Will, the poet cannot prevent the lover-turned-rival's murdering of his new poems and future loves, this blockage of his creative power and love-flows seven times:

> Seven of my sweet loves thy knife
> Has bereaved of their life.
> Their marble tombs I built with tears
> And with cold and shuddering fears.

In "Seven Days," an unreleased lyric from *Desire,* Dylan for once wills repetition and associates the repeated number *seven* with the seven days it will take for the return of an old lover from out of his midwestern past, as if to heal the wounds and broken loves of the present: "Seven days, seven more days that are connected / Just like I expected, she'll be comin' on forth / My beautiful comrade from the north" (*Lyrics*, 376). One tactic of Dylanesque memory aims toward willed *discontinuity* and breaks with the past, as in the D. A. Pennybacker film title *Don't Look Back* (1967), taken from the beloved woman's credo in "She Belongs to Me": "She's got everything she needs / She's an artist, she don't look back" (*Lyrics,* 143). On the other hand, as Dylan adopts the muse of folk, Bible, and blues recovery, over and again there is also a drive toward *lived anachronism.*

The Blakean poet quests after his Emanation figure in love song after love song, in rounds of desire, sorrow, and death, being born and cast down into time again and again until (later in the same poem) he can cast off this Specter's blocking his vision of eternity and can "turn from Female Love" and the "Infernal Grove" of sexual desire as a mode of fleshly overcoming prefigured by Jesus-the-Imagination: "Throughout all Eternity / I forgive you, you forgive me. / As our Redeemer said: / 'This the Wine & this the Bread.'" Entrapments of sexual desire in "Crystal Cabinet" (the male lover seeks to consummate romance with a woman-within-woman as if in some infinite purgatorial abyss [505] of babylike regression) give way to the bondages of adulterous love in "William Bond." In this auto-ballad, William Blake becomes the love-blinded figure William Bond, whose Angels and Fairies of providential imagination flee the poet and his multiple love for the pitiful recovering of his cold, sobbing, tomb-like wife, Mary (*Lyrics,* 511–512).

An epigrammatic poem (*Lyrics,* 494) from Blake's Notebooks of 1800–1806 captures that path beyond romantic love to spiritual love that the poet would urge in longer poems on the Specter/Emanation dialectics (such as "Milton," wherein the epic poet like some rock star has a "Six-fold Emanation" of wife and daughters and muses scattered across deep space [515]):

> Each Man is in his Specter's power
> Until the arrival of that hour
> When his Humanity awake
> And Cast his own Spectre into the Lake.

The push is from tormented romantic love to sacred love, wherein "Eternal Lineaments" of Jesus-the-Imagination begin to shine through the male bondage ("Milton," 584–586). Bondage to the Emanation is, at least lyrically, overcome. As Leonard Cohen put it, in one of his somnambulant lyrics of broken love and lost covenant, "Ah, they don't allow a woman to kill you, / Not in the Tower of Song."[64]

As Dylan puts his conversion from forces of romantic bondage in "Abandoned Love," a key work, "I march in the parade of liberty / But as long as I love you I'm not free / How long must I suffer such abuse / Won't you let me see your smile one more time before I turn you loose?" (*Lyrics*, 371). Even in such a crucial work as "Like a Rolling Stone," the lyric (*Lyrics*, 167) doubles the speaker into male denouncer and female agent of cool arrogance, what Ricks calls a sin of Pride, so the poet enacts on-the-road desire even as he turns from codes of false knowledge and ego-smugness and tries to renounce states of bondage by images of poetic adversion.[65] The terms of "figurative self-writing" that John D. Barbour used to describe Saint Augustine's conversion quest as he "deconverts" from romantic love to love for God might stand for Dylanesque states of love-quest on albums like *Street Legal, Desire,* and *Blood on the Tracks,* as he turns from "The Sign on the Cross" to search for his soul in women. "Metaphors of thirst and hunger, bondage, mental confusion, bodily disease, and physical motion (wandering, distance from God, rising and sinking)," Barbour urges, "vividly render the soul that has turned away from its ultimate loyalty."[66] Dylan, in these tactics of psychic refiguration, becomes heir to Saint Augustine, who haunts his dreams and methods of soul-quest on *John Wesley Harding* (1967), a title that recalls not just the name of Texas desperado John Wesley Hardin (1853–1895) but also the itinerant Methodist "rebirth" figure of John Wesley (1703–1791), who spread his message of grace to the Americas when Georgia was still a British colony.

Searching for a Precious Angel

In "Precious Angel," from *Slow Train Coming,* moving self to the contrary side of belief and sacred affirmation, the female lover is the bringer of light, vision, and the kind lineaments of redemptive imagination herself: "Precious angel, under the sun / How was I to know you'd be the one / To show me I was blinded, to show me I was gone" (*Lyrics*, 403). The born-again lineaments of this tutelage are rendered as evangelical fellowship. Dylan's push beyond the bondage of living "under the law" of desire/transgression, or the countercultural allure of Buddha or Mohammed as alternative belief system figures like Jack Kerouac or Paul Bowles were drawn to, is broken by an imagination-freeing vision of higher love through "the Man who came and died a criminal's death" (*Lyrics*, 403). The "spiritual warfare and flesh and blood breaking down" that Dylan portrays ties polity and psyche into a drama of struggle and desire, a conversion plot of binary allegiance in which "Ya either got faith or ya got unbelief and there ain't no neutral ground" (*Lyrics*, 403). The struggle for liberation is akin to the one Blake described in his preface to "Milton," where he affirms of the poet's battle, "I will not cease from Mental Fight, / Nor shall the Sword sleep in my hand: / Till we have built Jerusalem, / In England's green and pleasant Land" (*Lyrics*, 514).[67] For Dylan, working in the Jeremaic-genre of *Slow Train Coming,* this battle between love and death, a turn from decadence or a renewed calling to global redemption, would mean an agonistic battle for nothing less than the soul of a nation. That was why, on another more crudely physical level to gain power in the politics of love and life's battles for soul survival, Michael Ondaatje once advised me, Dylan has practiced the art of *boxing* all these years and contexts from Mexico City and Waterbury, Connecticut, to the Lower East Side of Manhattan.

As he reflected back on masking in the first volume of his autobiography, *Chronicles,* Dylan reveals the reach of his theo-poetic vision toward some New Jerusalem, as songs brought him to envision an altered America: "There was nothing easygoing about the folk songs I sang. They weren't friendly or ripe with mellowness. They didn't come gently to the shore. I guess you could say they weren't commercial. Not only that, my style was too erratic and hard to pigeonhole for the radio, and the songs, to me, were more important than just light entertainment. They were my preceptor and guide into some altered consciousness of reality, some different republic, some liberated republic."[68] "City of Gold," an unreleased gospel tune from *Saved* (later recorded by the Dixie Hummingbirds), captures some of these lineaments of this Americanized *civitas dei:* "There is a City of Hope / Above the ravine on the sunlit slope / All I need is an axe and a rope / To get to the City of Hope" (*Lyrics*, 434). Axe and a rope might lead to this New Jerusalem, if it aims to be built in Los Angeles. For, as the Dylan-centered movie *Masked and Anonymous* will render around the poet "Jack Fate," it is a long way from a Third World-like Los Angeles of imprisonment to this "City of Hope" with its community of light, love, hope, peace, and spiritual gold. At the core of Dylan's vision remains the paradox that (in the terms of George M. Marsden), "America was simultaneously Babylon and God's chosen nation," sublime in the grandeur of democratic vision yet fallen into betrayal and condemnation as poems like "Jokerman" or "Blind Willie McTell" pronounce.[69]

Before and After

It's on that world-shattering album, *Slow Train Coming* (1979), which divides Dylan's history into *before/after*, that the poet turns toward a full-fledged Jeremiah voice. As such, he is recalling a traditional post-Puritan genre wherein the sermonic voice laments the greatness of America, the redemptive possibility of America as fallen into imperial betrayal. In the Hebrew tradition Dylan would know intimately from his bar mitzvah days, prophetic voices like those of Jeremiah, Ezekiel, and Isaiah are endowed with power to render "poetic oracles" that bespeak "prophecies of doom for Israel; prophecies of doom for the surrounding nations [like Babylon]; prophecies of restoration for Israel."[70] The Doomsday sermons Dylan laced his concerts with from 1978 to 1980 challenged the countercultural pieties of his American-liberal audience. These are transcribed in the pirate text *Saved!: The Gospel Speeches of Bob Dylan:* "You can go and see Kiss and rock 'n' roll all the way down to the pit!," he exclaims, dividing the audience into "two kinds of people . . . saved people and lost people," and later predicts a war in the Middle East.[71]

In a song like "Neighborhood Bully," from hectoring domains of *Infidels* in the Reagan era of binary formulations, Dylan comes dangerously close to Zionist affirmation that Israel "made a garden of paradise in the desert sands" (*Lyrics,* 468), has been turned into the slaves and outcasts of Empire from Egypt and Rome to Babylon, and needs to fend off rival claimants (like Palestine?) to this nation-divided earth. The inside sheet to this album shows Dylan sifting sands on Mount Olive over history-tormented Jerusalem. Still, for Dylan, speaking these "poetic oracles" of prophecy, as for Bob Marley, the United States has become analogous to the latest Roman Empire on earth. To talk about "poetic oracles" in a latter-day American context, Dylan masked as Jeremiah laments the fall to empire, the lost City of God. Dylan feels that fallen sense about the Vietnam War and the reign of Reaganomics all through *Infidels* (1983), especially on "Jokerman." *Infidels* reflects an American buildup of violence and the luxurious life in the 1980s that was founded in hegemony as world superpower, becoming the new Rome.[72] Dylan laments that America has lost itself somewhere along the road to global hegemony. Later down the Reagan decade, he speaks about living inside what has become an "empire burlesque" and himself (as rock star) being a clown inside this global empire of commercial music. In effect, he urges that big record companies, MTV, and contemporary music offer commodity entertainment. The Jeremiah complex reflects upon misguided subjects who must "serve somebody," meaning the reign of capital in Empire Burlesque, as foreshadowed in the masters and slaves of "Dear Landlord" or "All along the Watchtower" as allegories of blindness on *John Wesley Harding.*

Belief-drenched and ever preaching to the lost, abandoned, or blinded, Dylan is also a *trickster poet* in his approach to conversion and counter-conversion, in his visions of love sacred and profane. Dylan is a trickster poet in the sense that he speaks in ironic metaphors, veiled tongues, proliferating masks, and enigmatic parables. If "saved," he crosses through states of dark vacancy and dread that "feel like my soul has turned into steel" ("Not Dark Yet" [566]). Living "in another world where life and death are memorized," as if before the foundations of this profane world, Dylan speaks in "Dark Eyes" (*Lyrics,* 502) of those blocked from any vision of redemption in this era of *Empire Burlesque* we are still living through. Working out his salvation publicly "in fear and trembling," he speaks poetry beyond any audience reductions to literal meaning, as if calling to some muse figure inside himself, in figurations sacred and profane. The poet baptizes this *muse* (often the "you" in a love poem) with an angellike woman's name, *Angelina:* "farewell Angelina / the sky is on fire / and I must go" (*Lyrics,* 161). Dylan comes back to "Angelina" as the muse abandons him for another male lover (portrayed as a kind of Satan) "trying to take heaven by force" (*Lyrics,* 457):

> When you cease to exist, then who will you blame
> I've tried my best to love you but I cannot play this game
> Your best friend and my worst enemy are one in the same
>
> Angelina. (*Lyrics,* 456)

Sometimes he calls this muse-figure Sara, as when he reincarnated her as covenanted woman of the "warehouse eyes" in *Blonde on Blonde* (1966). As Harold Bloom had illuminated Dante's refiguration of Beatrice, poetic imagination overrides historical accuracy or doctrinal affiliation. "Since her advent follows Dante's poetic maturation, or the vanishing of Virgil the precursor," Bloom affirms, "Beatrice is an allegory of the Muse, whose function is to help the poet to remember."[73] The Muse opens a passageway, beyond romantic desire or marital torment, to remembering what Blake calls a figure of "Jesus the Imagination," where poet is speaking to a cast of spiritual entities walking inside a dream world, caught up in a dramaturgy of survival, saving, or being saved.

In a lyric like "Jokerman" from *Infidels,* Dylan is "standing on the waters casting your bread" (*Lyrics,* 463) and speaking to a violence-torn land become Sodom and Gomorrah, and the audience either gets it poetically (the Jesus-like quest for redemption amid all the macho egomania) or they don't. Dylan is really talking about a redemptive vision and resisting what he takes to be an antichrist of Empire. The moralizing voice of persecution turns back upon the poet, who tries "keeping one step ahead of the persecutor within," shedding off false masks and dead layers of sin (*Lyrics*, 463). Invoking the *Book of Leviticus* and *Deuteronomy* to denounce a land where "the law of the jungle and the sea" now rules, the "Jokerman" poet (no trickster voice here) outlines a prison-driven America of death, captivity, and destruction, on the verge of some violent apocalypse: "Nightsticks and water cannons, tear gas, padlocks / Molotov cocktails and rocks behind every curtain / False-hearted judges dying in the webs that they spin / Only a matter of time 'til night comes steppin' in" (*Lyrics*, 464). Jokerman, trying to forget memory and fate like his predecessor self-figure, "Mr. Tambourine Man," tries to escape by dancing over the dark void of the West Indies: "Jokerman dance to the nightingale tune / Bird fly high by the light of the moon / Oh, oh, oh Jokerman" (*Lyrics*, 464).

Forty Miles of Bad Road

Dylan's work offers a complicated vision even when he's all but deconstructed religious beliefs, counter-converted from his own convictions, whereby they seem to be falling apart. When questioned about her son's seeming renunciation of his Judaic background and roots in his turn to affirm Yeshua, the Christian messiah, Mrs. Beatty Zimmerman observed, "When [Bobby] was a child in Hibbing, he would go to all the churches. He was interested in all religions."[74] Later, on the other side of postmodern nihilism, Dylan says in *Time out of Mind* (1997), his "heart's in the Highlands gentle and fair" (*Lyrics*, 571), in some dreamy Scotland where ballad-making poets like Burns or Van Morrison can escape into a green afterlife; he is almost dead and walking around with "dark eyes" (*Lyrics*, 502) on the other side but looking back at his own existence. There is the lurking sense, still, that Dylan has pushed a bad set of beliefs into an extremity of paranoid egotism and macho rage and shredded them up like a used mask.

A song like "Nothing Was Delivered" confesses to having failed to bring any kind of truth or redeeming *good news* and ends in a failure of insight and turn to domestic banality just this side of Poor Richard: "Nothing is better, nothing is best / Take care of your health and get plenty of rest" (*Lyrics*, 296). That emptying out of didacticism or claims to *born-again* transformation are later reiterated in "Mississippi," from *Love and Theft,* voiced as a sense of blocked space and failed promises: "Got nothing for you, I had nothing before / Don't even have anything for myself anymore / Sky full of fire, pain pourin' down" (*Lyrics,* 581); he is redeemed only by the later claim that though the ship of self be sinking, "I've got nothing but affection for all those who've sailed with me." "Not Dark Yet," from *Time out of Mind,* had captured this same sense of stasis and defeat, reversal of temporal triumph, in the fine last stanza, "I was born here I'll die here against my will / I know it looks like I'm moving but I'm standing still," and its claim of vacancy, "Don't even hear the murmur of a prayer." The body itself is fallen down: "Every nerve in my body is so vacant and numb / I can't even remember what it was I came here to get away from" (*Lyrics,* 566). The room confines; movement from London to Paris and across oceans seems empty. In a poem aggrandizing romantic desire like "I Want You," the poet jests that "the saviors are all fast asleep" (*Lyrics,* 196), so that lover's libido can be given its aura-emanating due. Jugglers outnumber believers in songs from those desire-fueled days of carnivalesque overturning in *Blonde on Blonde* (1966), as "Obviously Five Believers" affirms (*Lyrics,* 209–210).

In "Shelter from the Storm," Dylan (along with his theater of lovers and muses, sacred and profane) turns himself into the self-crucified Messiah in a landscape of doom, dread, poison, death, and exhaustion, as "She walked up to me so gracefully and took my crown of thorns / 'Come in,' she said, 'I'll give you shelter from the storm' " (*Lyrics,* 345). Amid such misidentifications and projected auras, it is no wonder that the poet longs for a new start, if not a new life, a way to begin the god-quest anew: "Well, I'm living in a foreign country but I'm bound to cross the line / Beauty walks a razor's edge, someday I'll make it mine / If I could only turn back the clock to when God and her were born / 'Come in,' she said, 'I'll give you shelter from the storm' " (*Lyrics,* 346). This was taking romantic love as far as it could go by the burden it places on allegorical embodiment and libidinous projection of spirit-aura.

An unreleased lyric from *Slow Train Coming,* "Ain't No Man Righteous, Not One," plays upon the Pauline messages of sinfulness and need for grace but comes as close as Dylan ever comes to uttering the core of his religious convictions. The Messiah is not the self so "unacquainted with my own desires" (as admitted in the later lyric "Bye and Bye" [585]) but higher and above, if *trusted inside.* This cut-to-the-chase sermonic lyric ends, after admitting to have "done so many evil deeds in the name of love, it's a crying shame" and emptying out the self of vaunted glory, in a poetic voice close to black-gospel vernacular and street-wise *Romans* (*Lyrics,* 418):

When I'm gone don't wonder where I be
Just say that I trusted God and that Jesus was in me
Say he defeated the devil. He was God's chosen Son
And that there ain't no man righteous, no not one.[75]

"Things Have Changed," from *Time out of Mind* (used in the sound-track to the loopy writer-as-pilgrim movie *Wonder Boys*), looks back on such romantic hunger and the arcs of failed quest, this longing to forget the self in otherness and capricious affairs (*Lyrics*, 574), with wry acceptance of this "bad road" as a path to self-abolishment:

I've been walking forty miles of bad road
If the Bible is right the world will explode
I've been trying to get as far away from my self as I can.

Shape-Shifting Poet

If Dylan has become a shape-shifter in his work, as if committed to some *trickster* mode of irony more than any *born-again code* of certainty, we could assert (in mythological terms) that this poet is a classic Gemini of double selfhood. As Harold Bloom explains being overinfluenced by any past, which Dylan overcame with the blitheness of a Kerouac or Emerson, "Influence is *Influenza*—an astral disease."[76] In other words, Dylan challenges, interiorizes, and overcomes influence, embracing anything that might motivate his power to change, which means he embodies *both* belief and deconstruction of belief (or love) as its lived antithesis. As performative artist, upon whom a U.S. global audience has put a prophet-like burden (since the 1960s) to offer authentic voice and to speak "truth" to powers of business and government, as in "Dear Landlord," he does adhere (over the course of his poetic career) to antimodern modes of "Evangelism" even if masked, ironized, disavowed, and troped.[77] This remains so, however myth-undermining and trickster-like Dylan gets as a poet.

The source for this "trickster" voice of enigmatic defiance and cryptic otherness may be that God of "bad news incarnate," meaning the "Yahweh" of the Old Testament or first covenant whom Bloom has described as a King Lear-like poet of trickster-like complexity who has doom, grief, torment, death, anxiety, and evasion on his Jewish mind, above all, for his Chosen People: "His voice gone, Yahweh may still be visible [in the scriptures of the Tanakh], but only as [the prophet] Daniel's Ancient of Days [whom Blake renamed the vengeful "Nobodaddy," nobody's

Daddy], akin to the robust trickster of the J Writer's saga [of Yahweh in the books of Genesis and Exodus]."[78] Like the J Writer, Dylan can be a trickster-poet masking voice into cryptic utterance, putting on and casting off masks of selfhood like tattered cowboy suits or dead letters.

Whether this trickster-like Dylan-as-poet of evasive irony, parable, and allegory has become converted into a "Jewish Christian" or a "Christian Jew," or some strange *amalgam* known only to his innermost self, it may be safest to conclude as did Wikipedia in its recent "List of Converts to Christianity" that Dylan is a "popular musician" whose "current religious status [is] disputed."[79] There is also Dylan's public support of Jewish sects in the later 1980s on telefests for Lubavichers and Chabad groups. He would also sing the Christological gospel tune "In the Garden," from *Saved,* at fund-raising concerts for these groups if only to complicate and mask the Judeo-Christian affiliations in his conversion or commitment to Christ as Messiah. As a poet, Dylan always surrounded his claims to conversion rebirth with trickster-like ironies and gambler masks that kept him anonymous, mobile, unfixed; that is to say, nonreducible to any literal, dead-letter meaning. Conversion against the determinations and false gods of Empire (like Mammon and Moloch) meant for Dylan a basic right to live free and open as poet before God.

Born Again as Trickster Poet

In the conversation we had when he [Dylan] visited [to play new songs from *Empire Burlesque*] a couple of weeks ago, there was a great deal of judgmental Jehovaic or "Nobodaddy"—"nobody daddy up in heaven"—a figure of judgmental hyper-rationality. There's this judgmental Jehovaic theism in his recent work, and he said, "Allen, do you have a quarrel with God?" and I said, "I've never met the man" and he said, "Then you have a quarrel with God." And I said, "Well, I didn't start anything!" So he still has a fixed notion of divinity, and I think that's a mistake, as a non-theistic Buddhist, that any solidification of the ideal God like the ancient Jews warned against—naming the name of God—is a mistake.

 —Allen Ginsberg in 1985 using Blakean, Hebraic,
  and Buddhist terms to describe Dylan's conversion[80]

An evangelical-cum-hellfire album like *Saved* or the belief-drenched claims of *Slow Train Coming* or *John Wesley Harding* can be grasped in antagonistic terms: the poetic word affirms, "I believe in you even though I be outnumbered" (*Lyrics,* 405) by forces of anti-logocentric doubt or its mode of liberal wishy-washiness. Dylan's response of agonistic transmission is conveyed, to invoke another example, in "Tangled up in Blue" (*Lyrics,* 332), in a reader-response of fire-and-blood coming out from "every one them words" of what must be Dante's poetry: "Then she opened up a book of poems / And handed it to me / Written by an Italian poet / From the thirteenth century / And every one of them words rang true / And glowed like burnin' coal / Pourin' off of every page / Like it was written in my soul." This generosity of poetic excess and spiritual vision pours into later generations, as Dylan has transmitted from "Song to Woody" onward, in which the poet honors predecessors and enters into that prior "basement tapes" world, in humility of spirit, courting vernacularized sublimity: "I'm seein' your world of people and things / Your paupers and peasants and princes and kings" (*Lyrics,* 5). Guthrie's hillbilly phrasings are mimed, and his class terms echoed in ballad terms, but with this distancing effect differentiating the eras and roads of Cisco, Sonny, Leadbelly, and Woody from his own middle-class comfort in the Midwest, "The very last thing that I'd want to do / Is to say I've been hittin' some hard travelin' too" (*Lyrics,* 5).

Guthrie's Depression-era poetry, as Dylan later recounts, had opened up sources to his sublimity, helped to put his youthful self in command of language powers and belief in the imagination to build on this tradition, to add something new, by converting to its causes and codes: "That day I listened all afternoon to Guthrie, as if in a trance and I felt like I had discovered some essence of self-command, that I was in the internal pocket of the system feeling more like myself than ever before" (*Chronicles,* 244). From these Dinkytown folk-club origins in the Midwest, right near the vaunted Highway 61 in Minnesota, Dylan begins to chart a detailed cartography of his own American poetic imagination that will lead him into—and beyond—the artistic mastery of mixed white and black singers like Guthrie, Jimmy Rodgers, Muddy Waters, and Howling Wolf: "Highway 61, the main thoroughfare of the country blues, begins about where I came from . . . Duluth to be exact. I always felt like I'd started on it, always had been on it and could go anywhere from it into the deep Delta country" (*Chronicles,* 240). Another more experimental poetic cartography of self-formation leads him to East Coast and West Coast, on-the-road like a Dharma Bum across the highways of the United States, via beatnik and hipster linkages to Greenwich Village in New York and to North Beach in San Francisco. But this Delta *crossroads* leading him north/south to "Mississippi" flood-lands and a vernacular is the crucial landscape, as *"Love and Theft"* and *Modern Love* rephrase in borrowings from Muddy Waters and John Lee Hooker to Chuck Berry and Frank Sinatra.

Becoming *trickster poet* has to do with powers of being a typological "troper," and the troper, as a maker of poetic syntax and cultural visions, means becoming the projector of tropes-as-identifications, myriad masks and personae for the underlying Jeremaic self.[81] If a poet aims to become a cheesy folk singer, or a Nietzschean blues singer for that matter, one will have to project the self into various *songs as masks and genres,* as small audiences saw Dylan do in his Village days in coffee houses and smoke-filled bars, where he looked like a choir boy or baby beatnik more than the gruff Dave Van Ronk, who was a New York City product more than a creature of bluegrass hill; just as Rambling Jack Elliot came not from western highways but from the Jewish suburbs of New York City.[82] If forces of reaction and disillusionment would now destroy the radical energies of our 1960s United States, Dylan was a part of this same constellation in his "rolling stone" energies of dynamism-from-below. A young quasi-Beat folk song writer in Dylan's early days in the Village called David Cohen had changed his name—at Dylan's urging in 1963—to David Blue. He secured a contract with Electra, *David Blue* (1966), and went on to record several albums, but by his death in 1982 he was all but forgotten.[83] The name-change or "mask" had no career-shattering impact for David Blue, as it did for Zimmerman-becoming-Dylan. Mark Brend registers the effect that "Dylan's epoch-defining *conversion* to electric rock" (emphasis mine) on *Highway 61 Revisited* as it left "American troubadours" from Greenwich Village to North Beach, including Blue, Tim Buckley, Tom Rush, and Fred Neil, struggling to find their own folk-rock groove.[84] Dylan's mask was one of defiance and threat, and is still. A Blakean *agon* drives and animates the Dylanesque soul.

Dylan could affirm in a borrowed blues of macho renunciation, "She's gone and I don't worry, I'm sitting on top of the world" in the archive of *World Gone Wrong* (1993), and at that moment he has to project himself into a Delta situation to become that song; it is not him, but he has been through that. He becomes Blind Lemon Jefferson, Blind Willie Johnson, or the Clancy Brothers, by "white face" and "black face" song-masks throughout his career; and (at the core) he mimics the folk persona and quest of Woody Guthrie *until he becomes his own mastery.* A believer in the American poetic vernacular mode and Beat beatitude of which Dylan has been an extraordinary embodiment since the early 1960s, equal in some ways to Whitman, Kerouac, Eliot, Ginsberg, or Blake in scope and social-visionary relevance, I would still have to agree with the skeptical Louis Menand that "You can't find the road that gets you from 'Hell Hound on My Trail' [Robert Johnson] and 'This Land Is Your Land' [Guthrie] through 'Pirate Jenny' [Bertolt Brecht] to 'Sad-Eyed Lady of the Lowlands' " nor even more so to a work of masterful postcolonial hybridity like the Marleyesque biblical "Jokerman."[85] Like many a poet before him, from Sappho and Whitman to Ginsberg and Ai, Dylan breaks open the forms and tracks an emergence into his/her own originality. He covers the veils of his voice or points to a shifting array of terms and sources (as in *Chronicles*). For this parabolic empowerment, we can only "see through a glass darkly" as Saint Paul advised the born again or the lost in *Corinthians*.

A self-ironizing song from the early-conversion days like "The Ballad of Frankie Lee and Judas Priest," from *John Wesley Harding* (1967), fuses and later polarizes the two voices of gambler and Judas-priest (teachers and priests are quite often *negative* forces of limitation and soul-death blocking the "crimson flames" of vision in Dylan, like those "mongrel dogs who teach" the young to fail in "My Back Pages" [126]). Dylan can create a ballad of warring voices, overturning both libido and superego, until each trickster-like figure flips over into the other or both get lost in some whorehouse of desire, need, and greed. Each lone self (the narrator warns at the end) might "go mistaking Paradise / For that home across the road" (*Lyrics*, 226). "Frankie Lee and Judas Priest" is a "ballad" of spiritual-carnal entanglement, but the lyric also dead-ends and blocks interpretation at key points, with the line "nothing was revealed" speaking to that refusal to reduce to any fixed meaning.[86]

Dylan's quest for poetic beatitude implied passing through states of restlessness, soul-death, mobility, blindness, drive, and endless antagonisms of desire from start to finish. *Judas Priest* (as one name for this trickster voice) haunts Dylan like the satanic tempter of Jesus in the desert, offering Frankie the pleasures of power, money, the world, women, and flesh— quite a paradise in its 1960s survey of Blakean desire-as-redemption. Frankie is no Jesus figure, to be sure, as he dies feasting over his surfeit of flesh consumption and erotic worldliness in that false-paradise house of whoredom, with no resurrection in sight. This Frankie never makes it to paradise, so he cannot be any kind of Jesus, not even a gnostic, flesh-denying one. If anything, the song fits the carnal Pauline rebuke in Romans: "those who live by the flesh will die by the flesh." So it is a pre-born-again song, thus pointing to where Dylan would need to go, as poet of visionary affirmation, into the powers of rebirth overcoming the ordinary self via the spirit: imitating the beatitudes (high spirit in lowly form) of a messiah who is no "Judas priest" or false prophet, just as Dylan would himself become no messiah. Andy Gill interprets this ballad so that Judas Priest is connected to Dylan's manager at the time, Albert Grossman; but Dylan would never be that historically reductive, in allegories masking the spirit in the flesh of Hollywood-like mansions.[87]

So what Dylan did was to create a whole myriad caste of people, that quasi-Shakespearean carnival of Pound and Eliot in "Desolation Row" (*Lyrics*, 181), from the village liberals heading for a fortunate-fall from prior assumptions in "Like a Rolling Stone" (*Lyrics*, 167) all the way up to his vision-quest in "Every Grain of Sand" (*Lyrics*, 451), from the Christological terms of *Shot of Love*, which is a more Dante-like belief song. The trickster figure plays out these enigmatic extremities of mask as he/she embodies characters, experiences, beliefs, codes—a range of voices and attitudes, which is what gives Dylan cultural resonance. Burt Bacharach writes beautiful Dionne Warwick lyrics about loss of love and domestic emptiness; even "Alfie" touches on states of doubt and belief questioning the sexual hedonism of the era. But Dylan can also write vision-opening lyrics about the quest for redemption and embody a Jeremiah-like rage against American imperialism and capitalism, as in "Jokerman" (*Lyrics*, 463) or "Thunder on the Mountain." Dylan is not speaking to that Albert Hall audience in London 1965 as a raging punk; he's elsewhere as a poet: he goes out there, like some rope thrown across the abyss, positing the metamorphosis of selfhood and soul as imagination and visionary risk. The audience gives him various doses of appreciation, rage, and contempt and they can call him *Judas Iscariot;* but Dylan (like Blake, Saint John of the Cross, or Dante) abides on another plane of poetry and vision, and fans are either with him or not "with ears to hear and eyes to see."

Given Dylan's career of four decades, we face a relentless metamorphosis of vision and imagination, but at the core there abide gifts of newness and incoming power in the prosodic ability to associate line-by-line, stanza-to-stanza. That's a trope, in Emersonian terms, where the writer transitions (*turns* language) from one thing to the next leaping domain, as in the abyss-crossing line "Beauty walks a razor's edge, someday I'll make it mine," from *Blood on the Tracks,* as he "bargains for salvation" and the woman/Muse "gave me a lethal dose" (*Lyrics*, 346). He even tries, preposterously, in that crucial poem of love-and-identity-death, worthy of the God-void in the gnostic theologian Valentinus, "to turn back the clock to when God and her were born" (*Lyrics*, 346). In Jeremaic terms of poetic genius going back to his first three albums released on Columbia (*Bob Dylan* [1962], *The Freewheelin' Bob Dylan* [1963], and *The Times They Are A-Changin'* [1964]), a cultural-based analysis of his poetic vision would conjure him embodying many of the Civil Rights energies.[88]

The leftist tradition of Joe Hill, a protest music that was Dylan's prosodic starting point, as it was for Woody Guthrie, sought to croon a genre of working-class protest song the Village could identify with as

American neo-ethnic. Dylan did not stop there as a poet and songwriter. Indeed, he did that folk-masking mode quite well but soon transformed himself into a rock 'n' roll Rimbaud kicking out the stops of form and flow of line-to-line thinking, whereby he would evoke surrealistic visionary-quest lyrics, the greatest of which may be "Tambourine Man" or (as Greil Marcus reaffirms) "Like a Rolling Stone."[89] Dylan kept going: he went all the way to Blake, Saint Paul, and Dante. Still, he kept going into autonomy of vision and syntax, so then we can track his becoming a U.S. Jeremiah; or he is writing (more warrior-like in his affirmation of Messiah than Man of Sorrows) the neo-Psalms of David in the American vernacular grain. When the audience confronts this kind of *range*, in a poetic compound of vision and irony, we are talking about a writer who has become a mongrel Shakespeare for this time, voicing nation-shaping dramaturgy and allegorical complexity of subject, belief, and time. He may borrow from *Confessions of a Yakuza*, but he enacts tropes from the Over-soul.

In a fit of semi-Judaic rage and/or bewilderment, Dylan had questioned in his denunciation of American exceptionalism, in "With God on Our Side," "whether Judas Iscariot / Had God on his side" when (as if fulfilling some gnostic plan) Judas betrayed Jesus Christ with a death-of-the-soul kiss (*Lyrics*, 86). Dylan knows, too, as in his gospel songs touching on Doubting Thomas, that confirmations via materialized vision and signs of wonder are often given "to unbelievers, heretics, and Jews," who would doubt any kind of Real Presence: "Thomas, because thou hast seen me, thou hast believed: blessed are they that have not seen, and yet have believed," as a spectral Jesus put it in John 20:29.[90]

Love Allegories, Soul Quests

Conversion implies that there is a *before-and-after* Dylan, and so the other side of early Dylan is the *Slow Train Coming, Infidels, Shot of Love*: all of that canon I have been calling *post-Blakean redemptive* in its terms and range. He made a scriptural white-gospel album called *Saved* (1980). He pushed toward *refunctioning* (to use Brecht's term for work in genre-transformation and cliché-estrangement) the whole gospel tradition like some cross between Saint Augustine, Blind Willy McTell, and Sam Cooke when he sang sacred do-wop lead for the Soul Stirrers. At the extremity of this symbolization of self and polity, poetry's quest is to offer not just a vision of *profane love*, but also a vision of *sacred love* as quest for *caritas* and *agape*. When Dylan says, sounding a bit like the ice-cream-smooth

Bing Crosby, "Love is all you need, it makes the world go 'round / Love and only love, it can't be denied. . . . take it from one who's tried [to deny it]" (*Lyrics*, 240), from the hillbilly-like domestic comedy that is *Nashville Skyline* (1969), the term "love" will take on sacred implications in the Dylan intertextual canon, just as the "you" he is singing to is often not just an ordinary woman but, via the *allegory of love,* a Muse or figure of godhead.[91]

Dylan encounters this tradition of love-allegory and Beatrician woman-worship through Dante, though as he proclaims (self-mockingly toward his own macho will to power over women) in "Thunder on the Mountains," from *Modern Times,* "I've been sittin' down studyin' the art of love / I think it would fit me like a glove / I want some real good woman to do just what I say / Everybody got to wonder what's the matter with the cruel world today." It sounds like Dylan has been studying Andreas Capellanus's *Art of Courtly Love* to learn medieval love-quest manners, to go with Ovid's *Art of Love* and the Coasters' "Book of Love," if not the Kama Sutra. Turning from the embers of romantic love, which (all too often) leave him behind in states of wounded narcissism, Dylan makes his quest for *love-as-caritas* overt in the burnt-out Los Angles urbanscape of "Something's Burning Baby," from the Reagan-era denunciations of *Empire Burlesque* (1985), when he laments toward the close (taking self-humiliated pages out of Saint Paul's Corinthians), as if speaking to some female Lazarus who refuses to be reborn,

> We've reached the end of the road, baby, where the pasture
>   begins
> Where charity is supposed to cover up a multitude of sins. . . .
> You can't live by bread along, you won't be satisfied
> You can't roll away the stone if your hands are tied.
> (*Lyrics,* 501)

Charity will cover the multitude of sins, post-Blakean lovers have to learn (from 1 Peter 4:8), perhaps over and over again like a sad macho case of blind willing. *Charity suffereth long and remains kind,* or tries to (1 Corinthians 13:4). This is the mandate to rebirth and recovery from automatisms of desire, sin, and death, in the Pauline model of conversion that Dylan had proclaimed in *Saved.* But where does this romantic male-misery come from, *the Dylan angst?* There seems to be a rage that he has had all along driving his overthrow of imagery and belief. Part of this drive perhaps has to do with a prophetic self-marginalizing "Jewishness" that drives and haunts him, something Bloom tracks in his contrast of a personalized Yeshua-become-Jesus with the caustic Old Testament Jehovah, in *Jesus and Yahweh: The Names Divine,* which takes its mana-giving subtitle from Blake's poem "The Gates of Paradise," wherein the "Son of Morn" (Jesus) triumphs over the nighttime deity of anger and traumas of first reckoning (Jehovah).

Dylan's lyric anger may also have to do with the way he, like a scape-goating misogynist, projects auras of his imagination of darkness-and-light (as if becoming his Welsh namesake Dylan) on women, via this Blakean framework of desire and counter-conversion from romantic love. The poet of the will to sexual possession will feel betrayed when women turn out to be human and lost from charity. When these "An-gelina" figures turn back from trope into an ordinary woman or fall in love with somebody else, he is full of rage and contempt for such betrayal—and he *writes more poetry.* From *Blood on the Tracks* and *De-sire* to *Time out of Mind, Love and Theft,* and *Modern Times,* such is the allegorical burdens the flesh-and-blood women in these love songs must carry, as refigured into Dylan's lifelong "allegory of love," as C. S. Lewis outlined this tactic in medieval love. Given Dylan's *tropological drive toward the male love lyric-cum-animistic muse,* he seems to shed an ex-cess of anger and rage.

"Positively Fourth Street," "Crawl out Your Window," and Mister Jones in "Ballad of a Thin Man" are all early rage-filled love songs. Dy-lan also has a tenderly didactic song, "Trust Yourself," meaning we should not listen to someone outside the god-self of poetic beatitude: that has been one of his post-Emersonian messages all along. To follow your own vision is to follow your poetry, even if people tell you it is un-timely or derivative or all in the past. While others might project upon a rock star auras of the *second coming* or mantles of prophesy and re-demption, the poet-as-trickster has to do with ironical transformations and allegorical states of turning language, transmuting states of love into self-figuring of despair; states of vision into crossings of emptiness. Alle-gory is more the rule than any sustained doctrinal affirmation or theo-logical fixity. Even Christianized, Dylan's trickster voice speaks for this "Judas Priest" energy of a godhead spilt into forms of darkness and light; Dylan is willing to be an Orpheus figure who descends into hell to find vision, courses states of damnation to find salvation. Dylan will disinte-grate fixed-identity in his mask-making process but has to come out of this drama of salvation and go on his own ruination-quest again. In this calling to self-altering mimesis and rebirth through masks and journeys to beatitude and redemption, Dylan remains a *romantic* poet in the most literary sense of this term.

"Love and Theft"

The degree of "love and theft," to use that Eric Lott phrasing that Dylan later borrowed to stand for his own art, is huge in any Dylan song or album. He is always miming and borrowing from the voices in the archives and tombs of the American vernacular songbook, giving his ancestors and precursors rebirth and renewal through such honoring. As a poet, Dylan almost always covers all trails and homages (debts, influences, spectral honoring, and recalls from the tombs of American or even Pacific Rim vernacular history) by making the resulting songs and spectral genres into something strange, mongrelized, raunchy, and *magpie-new*. Behold all things are becoming lyric and new—that is his special pleading here in this confederation of kindred spirits.[92] There is also the larger problem of *blackface,* as a mode of miming the blues of those who suffered for their racial abjection, which no white person can ever claim however subaltern the ethnicity or class.[93] Masking is identified all the more so with a period of Dylan's life where he was tormented about his marriage breaking up. When listeners would seek to negotiate the quasi-Jungian period of *Desire* (1976) and *Street Legal* (1978), there abides a whole crazed Beat carnival of soul-masks, stanza by stanza. These become psychic projections of self and soul onto others: animus/anima struggles as in a monodrama of the soul's masking. Dylan breaks through as reborn poet with *Slow Train Coming, Shot of Love,* and above all *Infidels* in 1983, which may be the most spectacular album of all, both musically and creatively: each song exhibits a mix of vision, politics, rage, and tenderness that is, decades later, still cathartic and awesome. With its cover quoting from Jeremiah and its photo of Dylan holding shifting sands at the Mount of Olives, *Infidels* endures as Dylan's post-Beat vision of beatitude in the love-scarred and vision-blocked Holy Land: saints and sinners turn into one another in these songs, as devils and angels stand watch over world spaces yet baffle the poor citizens in their greed, lost loves, violence, and need.

Perhaps the most revealing speech Dylan has made was given during the Grammy Awards of 1991: he came on stage and looked blasted, not in the sense that he was on drugs, but just broken apart by fate and age. Finally, he was honored with a Grammy Award for his lifework, and he said: "My father was a poor man, he didn't have much to give me or say to me, but he did tell me this: [reads] 'It is possible to be so defiled in this world that your own mother and father will abandon you. And if this happens God will always believe in your own ability to mend your own ways.' " What he is talking about, finally, is the soul's drive to *trust yourself.* Dylan implies here a very Emersonian formulation: to trust in yourself is at once to trust in the power of God *to remake or heal you. Be opened,* he says, to change and mask, to the freeing powers of alter-becoming, to beatitude.

This is what this study would imply by the titular mandate, *be always converting.* As Todd Haynes shows in *I'm Not There* (2007), however, it might take at least *six* accomplished actors and a worldly cast of poets, prophets, gamblers, and thieves to play the masks of just one Dylan. And—for me at least seeing Dylan's poetic as a serious and lifelong commitment to the forging of a poetics and politics of rebirth for self, nation, and world—that colorful and deft biopic of a movie does not even come close to the innermost complexity of the psyche and the polity, and gets lost, finally, in some postmodern funhouse of mask, pose, mimicry, irony, and code. Rebirth, for Todd Haynes, seems in the end just another Hollywood pose. But for Dylan, as for Martin Luther King, Jr., or Norman O. Brown, rebirth was a mandate to perpetual renewal ("a change is gonna come") for nation, polity, and soul "born by the Mississippi River in a little tent" as Sam Cooke so movingly put it during the Civil Rights era in his anthem "A Change Gonna Come" as a Dylanesque transracial coalition, embracing practices of freedom and social change.

The first trickster act had occurred when he changed his name from Zimmerman to Dylan. So that is, further, his way of rejecting his small-town family: I am not becoming Dylan Thomas; *I am Bob Dylan.* When people would ask him about his family, Dylan would say (i.e., lie) that he was in a carnival for ten years and never went to college. Seemingly, he never wanted to admit that he was from a warm Jewish family who ran a hardware store and that he went to the University of Minnesota for half a year and played in little music clubs or that he hitchhiked his way to New York City totally broke. So he did follow some "Dharma Bum" vision of dirty beatitude to New York City and renamed himself "Bob Dylan" and he became that trickster persona—"I am Bob Dylan"—as if by this self-fashioned mask he was rejecting his biological father, leaving his Jewish, lower-middle-class origins and the blockages and traumas of the North Country to follow his vision of selfhood, vocation, and destiny into the coastal cities. I say, "as if he was leaving" such materials and concerns, but clearly these origins haunted and informed his work, in a strong sense, from start to finish.

By *Slow Train Coming,* folk masks and Beat postures held in abeyance, Dylan *really was following Christ* as poetic-spiritual master in the self. Dylan would affirm in "Precious Angel," "You were suffering under the law / You were telling [your husband] about Buddha, you were telling him about Mohammed in the same breath / You never mentioned one time the

Man who came and died a criminal's death" (*Lyrics,* 402), proclaiming rather overtly his willed allegiances to Christ as messiah and his overcoming of the Hebraic law. For post-Rolling Stone Dylan of Beat mobility and libidinal freedom, that choice against the repetition-compulsions of desire and drive was an ego-shattering act of submission and change. By the lineaments of such Christological rebirth, Dylan went on affirming that he was *not* following Muktananda or some Zen master (as I had done across the 1970s in Berkeley and Honolulu), that he was *not* following any New Age inner-authority as guide to liberated desire, even great ones like Alan Watts or Shinryu Suzuki. Rather, this religion-saturated poet of theo-poetics and perpetual self-making was submitting to "that man named Jesus." Such rawness of commitment and belief alienated many, and he was often booed coast to coast. Elvis Presley, like Hank Williams, could make a white-gospel album, singing country hymns to Jesus on Sun Records for his mother. Dylan was committing his mercurial works to Bible-based language, producing music that was starkly evangelical and coded with new terms of grace and the lineaments of death-and-rebirth. Many (especially West Coast liberals) found that *contemptible.* They booed Dylan, for example, on the Beat stages of San Francisco, where Dylan had earlier found, in the 1960s, a second home. Conversion sounded prescientific, antimodern, even nationalistic, backward, banal, bossy, and irrelevant to our secular age. Dylan was not just going electric at Newport and in Greenwich Village; he was going Christological, covenantal, messianic, way beyond the terms of any given neoliberal hegemony.

The poetics of vision is an *aversive* path, if one is following this path to inner authority. That choice is crucial to Dylan's vocation as poet of post-Beat beatitude: the "Jesus freak" (as detractors called him with postcolonial contempt) and the spiritual-master identification remain important, life-altering, socially engaged, resonant with a before-and-after shape. For Dylan is still following the "Tambourine Man" mandate, and that means embracing the plenitude and vastation of this muse of becoming and ecstatic-poetic vision. As poet and songwriter, Dylan is driven *to produce production,* as it were, to use a Deleuzian phrasing— but not to serve Columbia Records because the market demands he needs a new album now. Dylan creates to live and he is driven, album by album, to create beauty and seek out poetry and song via some never-ending tour of masked performance and soul-studio production.

If this poet of rebirth has often gone back and done traditional lyrics from the folk or blues grain, for self-renewal, Dylan's mind inhabits a tapestry of national if not world forms, and he seemingly knows every lyric form, protest song, ballad, pop tune, or love lyric, as his XM radio show reveals. Dylan becomes a whole *production studio* in the self: he is like Shakespeare, who knew any dramatic form as actor, writer, stagehand, and director. In *Modern Times,* Dylan has written, produced, and performed the whole work. Dylan's language gift—as Christopher Ricks has demonstrated in terms of rhyme, allusion, and prosodic wit—is keen and extraordinary, and would put Dylan at the top of any list of great songwriters. But, as a poet of rebirth, Dylan dives into and renews the white gospel mode, like a Whitman or a Blake crossed with Sam Cooke, John the Revelator, and Ma Rainey.

In *Time out of Mind,* in the dark-night of the soul portrayed via "Not Dark Yet," with his "soul turned into steel," Dylan laments at the end that he "can't even hear the murmur of a prayer" (*Lyrics,* 566), meaning that faith/rebirth is somewhere over in the distance, where people are praying and the poet is in his own abyss of darkness, like soul-dead saints or lesser mere humans. Fading star in a full-length black leather coat, at times he is just an aging, postfeminist drifter in a coffee bar asking for hard-boiled eggs (sexual puns intended) from a sullen, Erica Jong–reading waitress in Boston town in "Highlands" (*Lyrics,* 571–573), whose drifting narrative of the soul reads like a sexual lowlands as well. In such works, Dylan has fallen upon an inability to sustain any reborn state. He creates a kind of *anti-poetry,* at such times, as if shredding his own tropes, masks, and convictions in a feat of de-creation worthy of Wallace Stevens, Baudelaire, or Poe.

Perhaps, his "current religious status disputed," Dylan has gone from being Jewish to becoming Christian and back again, a trajectory of belief, faith, rebirth, death, and irony nobody else might want to or even could follow as soul's morphology in becoming. Dylan's path to conversion may not be everyman's, in its dynamics of renunciation, mask, and change: this poetics performs contrarian energies of "adversion" as a credo for American poets. "Always being converted," as Thomas Shepard had urged in earlier Puritan contexts, Dylan awakens powers of faith and imagination as conviction to trust your God-relying, quasi-gnostic selfhood, so as to find a way forward along lines of creative flight/fight. In the late 1970s, I once asked Norman Hindley, a poet from Rhode Island who teaches at Punahou High School (Barack Obama's former school) in multicultural Honolulu, whether he "liked the lyrics" on *Slow Train Coming* from the Christian-era work. Hindley looked at me rather dumbfounded: "Like them? Man, that's like *having open heart surgery!*"—meaning one can listen to "Precious Angel," and this one song might transform your existence in the light of its convictions. "We walk by faith not by sight," as Saint Paul urged, which for a poet means embracing world-transformative powers of imagination and trope. So the people who can hear such theo-poetic meanings of troped truth in Dylan *really hear them:* "and some sweet day, I'll stand beside my king."

Dylan's masks of denunciation, critique, and covenant are linked not just to Afro-Baptist sources of outrage like Martin Luther King, Jr., Ozzie Davis, or Frederick Douglass (as they might be in Cornell West, say), but all the more so to those raging, burnt-out Puritan-Judaic figures like the Old Testament's Amos in Greil Marcus's *The Shape of Things to Come,* who connects "Highlands," from *Time out of Mind* (1997), and "High Water (For Charley Patton)," from *"Love and Theft"* (2001), to omens of U.S. misdirection and downfall.[94] Though not shorn of love or hope, Dylan's poetry since *Time out of Mind* and *World Gone Wrong* conjures death, elegy, bad weather, and ruination, as if seeing in a glass darkly the falling towers of the World Trade Center or the flood-tides rising and the displaced peoples of Hurricane Katrina. He evokes (as if by blasted allegorical fragments) the "portrait of an American who has used up his country," as does Philip Roth in *American Pastoral* (1997), wrenching his innocent protagonist and his deconverted daughter into the wilderness of "the indigenous American berserk."[95]

In his reading of Philip Roth's trilogy on Nathan Zuckerman as American Jeremiah mapping the hollowing out of its prophetic codes and citizens, Greil Marcus makes a shattering connection to a latter-day Dylan album kindred to *American Pastoral*'s subjects of brokenness. "Only Bob Dylan, in 1997 [when *American Pastoral* was published], with *Time Out of Mind,* a state-by-state, city-by-city guided tour of an America that has used itself up and a portrait of an American who has used up his country, comes close to occupying the same territory; and Roth stayed longer."[96] Dylan's conversion into "the indigenous American berserk" would never stand stable as such but would be subject to reversal into fits or stanzas of *prophetic blessing.* Marcus gets at this tonal instability outlining song as American vernacular prophecy coming back in a time of need.

Some critics would see Dylan not so much as a *Jeremiah* but a *Terence* for a neo-Roman U.S. Empire.[97] If skeptics think the man has a rasping nonvoice just this side of the graveyard, or that Dylan is some con-man of faith-postures, stolen masks, folk and blues rip-offs, minor poet borrowing, and male need advertising rerun rock love-lyrics on an iPod, so be it. "His old raspy incoherent voice was a sad and bitter way to see him live," said one disgruntled concertgoer after a Dylan performance at Genentech in South San Francisco.[98] Most would agree with Greil Marcus, Paul Williams, and Ricks that Dylan is a gifted poet, a master in terms of pedagogical multiplicity, truth-quest, tropological play, openness, and performance.[99] His crabby voice says as much about his lifelong role as teacher. As Gilles Deleuze, philosopher of anti-Oedipus, Nietzschean activism and God-intoxicated energies in Spinoza and Kerouac, affirmed,

> To encounter is to find, to capture, to steal, but there is no method for finding other than a long preparation. . . . How proud and wonderful—and modest—is this Bob Dylan poem. As a teacher, I should like to give a course as Dylan organizes a song, as astonishing producer rather than author. And that it should begin as he does, suddenly, with his clown's mask, with a technique of contriving, yet improvising each detail. The opposite of a plagiarist, but also the opposite of a master or a model. A very lengthy preparation, yet no method, nor rules, nor recipes. . . . You are no longer an author, you are a production studio, you have never been more populated.[100]

The self in this neoliberal climate of everyday mobility and value flux, where objects immigrate and technologies arise and get undone often in the same generation, lives in free-floating anxiety as in despair, unwilling to believe in one conversion experience of understanding (or wisdom) that never quite comes or that seems momentary, belated, or deferred. Dylan shows that the self is made known through abiding in encounters with higher forces whose meaning remains the will to humble the self to grace and open the heart to charity. *Always being converted*, as well as writing love poetry about this quest to achieve states of post-Beat beatitude, Dylan all but never loses this tender Augustinian conviction from *Nashville Skyline*: "Love is all there is, it makes the world go round. . . . You just won't be able to do without it / Take a tip from one who's tried" (*Lyrics*, 240).

Born Again in Modern Times

The tradition-drenched songs on *Modern Times* (2006) are full of half-echoes, talking ghosts, flood tides, fires, thunder on the mountains and spirits on the sea, visions rising up from slavery days and Muddy Waters and Slim Harpo down to Marian medieval traditions of prayer and hymn and what Dylan admits (in "Thunder on the Mountain") come from a lifetime "studyin' the art of love." The late-style lyrics are full of what he calls "an ancient presence" and renew his lifelong quest for love and visionary redemption. Hardly Chaplinesque in its love-and-death masks and oblique prophecy or in its techno-embrace of 1950s-like studio tactics, *Modern Times* might well just as well be called *Modern Love*. It is that keen as a psychodrama of male love and female psyche (soul), once again, as George Meredith once called his own Victorian sonnet collection of tormented marital love portraying polarizations and impossible unions.[101]

Sacred and profane loves, masks of *eros* and *agape,* intertwine and unravel from song to song in Dylan's *Modern Times.* Ten well-wrought lyrics show the way forward and conjure a way that leads back to a "sweet voice [that] calls out from some old familiar shrine," as he puts it in the anciently named "Spirit on the Water," in riffing on the gospel-blues prophecies of "God Moves on the Water" by Blind Willie Johnson and Son House's "John the Revelator." "I don't need any guide, I know the way," Dylan affirms in "Thunder on the Mountain," rebuking Dante—or Woody Guthrie—for those ex-mentor needs. At sixty-five and just starting to express such multigeneric haunting, "I'm beginning to believe what the scriptures tell," he sings in "Nettie Moore" crooning belief over the gravesite of friends like "Albert," perhaps his Falstaffian ex-manager Albert Grossman. Dylan mimes what he calls, in a *Rolling Stone* interview by Jonathan Lethem (his phrase half-echoing the *vox clamato in deserto*), that voice of "the individual crying in the wilderness," which he heard on records of the 1940s and 1950s. "I'm talking about artists with the willpower not to conform to anybody's reality but their own," Dylan affirms in self-reliance (tapping into what Emerson termed "God-reliance"). He goes on to cite sources from the pop vernacular to the American sublime: "Patsy Cline and Billy Lee Riley. Plato and Socrates, Whitman and Emerson. Slim Harpo and Donald Trump. It's a lost art form."[102]

If Dylan is speaking in tongues as a poet, the audience must have ears to hear the impact of lines like "I'm gonna make you come to grips with fate" from "Nettie Moore" or (more mysteriously as soul-allegory) "Well, I got up this mornin', saw the rising sun return / Sooner or later you too shall burn," as he says in the struggle toward Mutual Forgiveness that is the tormented marital-love lyric "Rollin and Tumblin."[103] An embrace of "blackness" in all senses, "Nettie Moore" is based on a Delta slave song but redone in terms of a didactic project as American-vision reformation. It is moving, but all of the songs on *Modern Times* are like that, conjuring scraps from the past into something clear and purposeful. There is no playing around on this late-period album, no throwaway lines, just haunting lines like his reference to Saint Herman's Church in "Thunder on the Mountain," where he "said my religious vows," or those Marian echoes of Saint Mary's bells in "Beyond the Horizon."[104] To call this borrowing *theft* is to miss the *love and honoring* not just of ancestors but also of that which abides as sacred beatitude.

Modern Times registers the motley inheritance of voice and genre Dylan has made new in his quest to confect a vision of "cultural resonance" for these "modern," dazed, half-fallen, secular times: "riches and redemption can be waiting behind the next bend in the road," Dylan affirms this in between the lines, as he conjures American new-millennial hopes for "1000 years of hope" beyond the fallen towers of 9/11, the Great Mississippi Flood of 1927, proletarian immiseration (see "Workingman Blues #2"), blight, and the New Orleans hurricane (in "The Levee's Gonna Break"). Such songs go on mixing *Revelations* and old-time Delta blues, and thus can offer, as Joe Levy noted of this album's turn beyond end-time or *Left Behind* revelations, "an odd promise of redemption—the river brings not just death and destruction but baptism and rebirth."[105] Ecological ruination is alluded to in *Modern Times,* as when Robert Johnson's line, "blues falling down like hail," twists into acid rain in Nettie Moore's black Delta landscape, "Blues this morning fallin' down like hail / Gonna leave a greasy trail," in a riverscape "out of whack" with God and nature as John the Revelator sits down, mourns, and weeps as "Lost John." (Or perhaps this "lost John" is Jack Kerouac, whose grave and persona Dylan *always* honors.)

A Voice That Calls

Years ago they used to say I was a prophet. I'd say, "No, I'm not a prophet." They'd say, "Yes, you are a prophet." "No, it's not me." They used to convince me I was a prophet. Now I come out and say, "Jesus is the answer." [And now] they say, "Bob Dylan? He's no prophet." They just can't handle that.

—Bob Dylan to an Omaha, Nebraska, audience, 1980[106]

Working (once again) against the U.S. right-wing fundamentalist grain of this *Empire Burlesque* and prophetic literalization of Judeo-Christian logos, Dylan's poetics of metamorphosis and counter-conversion, given the intertextual framework to his Jeremaic prophecy, quests for sacred love, and poetic becoming via mask and pose, could have it no other way, walking like some Blake or a guitar-carrying Dante in a mystic garden "in the last outback at the world's end."[107] The last lyric, "Ain't Talkin'," is a vision-quest poem coursing through "cities of plague," which opens (like Blake's "Crystal Cabinet" or Dylan's own quasi-medieval ballad, "I Dreamed I Saw St. Augustine"), "As I walked out tonight in the mystic garden / The wounded flowers were dangling from the vine / I was passing by yon crystal fountain / Someone hit me from behind." Earlier, "Spirit on the Water" is more Judaic in its Old Adamic sense of perpetual sinfulness than any "American Adamic" claim (as in "Song of Myself") to embody renewal, as paradise is scarcely recovered for post-*Saved* Dylan on any steady basis in "born again" truth-claims: "I wanna be with you in paradise / And it seems too unfair / I can't go to paradise no more / I killed a man back there." Freedom means release from fixed selves or moribund beliefs. His pilgrim is like a vagabond from *The Big Sleep*.

There is *thunder on these sublime mountains,* latter-day Dylan affirms, for the Holy Spirit still walks across the water in these ancient-but-new songs, and "the rising sun returns" from all this midnight "Rollin' and Tumblin'." The happiness of the male singer "on the Santee's dancing tide" in "Nettie Moore" is broken and lost forever when on a sunny day in autumn "came a trader from Louisiana bay, / Who gave to master money, and then shackled her with chains!," bringing misery and endless lament to Nettie's husband left on the plantation. In Dylan's "love and theft" (or *blackface*) reforging of this slave song into his own masked act of American compassion, death-bed lament, and transhistorical redemption, "The world has gone black before my eyes," a haunting line of cross-racial identification he repeats as refrain and closing lament that means more than mere "darkness" or the failing vision of old age. Dylan's version of "Nettie Moore" becomes the most moving song on *Modern Times:* a feat of empathy and self-metamorphosis, turning the profane into sacred and back again. (No Henry Timrod writes like this.) Out of all this "blackness" or end-time vision, Dylan as Beat-pilgrim croons to long-lost slave girl Nettie Moore, "Today I'll stand in faith and raise / The voice of praise."[108] Dylan yet again, as in W. T. Lhamon's reading of blackface masks in *Raising Cain,* mediates between blues culture, white-folk aspirations, and late-modernist culture of the Village and North Beach that animated beatitude-quests and fusions with outlaws, workers, and vagabonds, converting such masks into what Cecil Brown calls "a kind of hillbilly blues" of the highest visionary order.[109]

With Dylan, we bargained for salvation amid the nihilism of our time, and he gave us a lethal—life-saving—dose. Converting against Empire, Dylan's songs of prophetic beatitude, such as "Blowin' in the Wind," can still inspire street-protesters in present-day Taipei fighting for Taiwan's independence to declaim, in Dylanesque Chinglish, "How many rocky roads must the people of Taiwan walk, before really achieving democracy," as David Yaffe noted in a twist upon global nonsynchronicity.[110] Maybe Pope John Paul II was up ahead of this will to late capitalist nihilism and the transience of commodified life we take for granted,

when he noted of the song's wind-breath-spirit imagery at a Dylan concert for youth in Italy in 1997, "The answer is blowing in the wind, it's
true, but not in the wind which disperses everything into swirls of nothingness, but in the wind that is the breath and voice of the Spirit, a voice
that calls and says: 'Come.' "[111] As a poet of rebirth, Dylan's "Visions of
Johanna" have turned into Visions of the Madonna, American style, beat
yet undaunted.[112]

Epilogue: Conversions through Literature

Writing Transpacific Becoming from Connecticut to Hawaiʻi and Asia/Pacific

> It is pleasant to see the emigrants when they swarm up Broadway
> from the ships, stop in front of [New York City's Trinity]
> Church, which they take to be a Roman Catholic Church on a
> small scale, and kneel before it on the pavement, thanking their
> God for bringing them safely to land.
>
> —Anonymous correspondent to
> *United States Democratic Review,* 1853

> Our roots can go anywhere and we can survive, because if you
> think about it, we take our roots with us. . . . [Y]ou can go back
> to where they are and they can be less real to you than they were
> three thousand, six thousand miles away. . . . The essential thing
> is to have the feeling that they exist, that they are somewhere.
>
> —Gertrude Stein, "A Conversation
> [with John Hyde Preston]"

> For aside from what could be brought back as cargo, he carried
> everything else in his mind.
>
> —John Yau, "Marco Polo"[1]

"Be Not Conformed"

U.S. liberal democracy still constrains the "puny democratic subject," as Alexis De Tocqueville once called him/her, into marked forms of value-making and post-Christian vocations of success, life risk, and self-empowerment—within some eternalized marketplace of value, commodity, job role, and form—along a certain line of upward social mobility, agonistic competitiveness, life-risk, and what has been called if things go well for such a career-driven pilgrim the Anglo-modern project of *self-fashioning*.[2] This capitalist dynamism often makes and mars what we take to be the very vocation to beatitude, conversion, and rebirth. Never driven to praise melancholic saintliness as William James was in his own father and a cast of a hundred thousand modernists, the ever-reborn optimist Emerson captured this immense drive to self-fashioning as an American globalization imperative radiating out, across town, city, and region, to far corners of the post-British Earth, in the pages of his late essay "Success" (which might have led "rolling stone" Bob Dylan to hold that upside-down sign "Try to be a SUCKCESS," in Beat alleyways of the film *Don't Look Back* [1967]):

> Our American people cannot be taxed with slowness in performance or in praising their performance. The earth is shaken by our engineries. We are feeling our youth and nerve and bone. We have the power of territory and of seacoast, and know the use of these. We count our census, we read our growing valuations, we survey our map, which becomes old in a year or two. Our eyes run approvingly along the lengthened lines of railroad and telegraph. We have gone nearest to the Pole. We have discovered the Antarctic continent. We interfere in Central and South America, at Canton and in Japan; we are adding to an already enormous territory. Our political constitution is the hope of the world, and we value ourselves on all these feats.[3]

The whole world, Emerson saw, from Canton to Tokyo and Lima and across the Atlantic, the Pacific, to the Indian Oceans, seems amenable (in thin reckoning) to hugely American appetites for "success" in engineering, industry, space exploration, culture, and even art. For Emerson, as he had affirmed in his 1854 moral protest against "The Fugitive Slave Law," the decisive precept remained the converted and converting conviction that "*self-reliance, the height and perfection of man, is reliance on God.*"[4] Emerson, more than the punishing Foucault, abides at the capitalist-poetic core of this world-saturating disciplinary apparatus of American self-formation and alter-becoming. By now, as well, many more have caught a case of what Dylan called (self-beatified in the druggy basements of North Beach and Greenwich Village haunts) those "Subterranean Homesick Blues."

Still, in following the vocational voice to go on the road toward beatitude of figures like Bob Dylan, Ai, Jack Kerouac, William James, and Henry Obookiah and the mandate to become "always converting, always converted," I would mime the transplanted roots of that radical language-experimenter Gertrude Stein, as well, commuting back and forth over the Atlantic between William James and Picasso. Or embrace the multitudinous Gilles Deleuze who advocated the "God-intoxicated" theopoetics of Spinoza in believing *(theoretically affirming)* that an American writer works across multiple languages and sites, and thus aims to plug his puny self into a range of minor energies, commotions, transcultural fluxes, and alter-becoming shapes, not just prefabricated or given as norms or forms tied to Paris, New York, or London. "The line of flight is creative of these [minority-] becoming. Lines of flight have no territory," affirmed Deleuze as he lauded the deterritorializing flows in de-oedipalizing desire as a force of continental, national, and oceanic crossing (*Dialogues*, 50). For, amid the tame possibility and dreams of market fulfillment, we can still *convert from*, advert, revert, be turned around, "Create the opposite dream: know how to create a becoming-minor."[5]

Writing as a life-force bent on this quest for amplified being—witness F. Scott Fitzgerald's "crackup" and breakdown into anonymous-being in the aftermath of the Stock Market crash in the 1930s—still carries out the conjunction of fluxes, linking to a multiplicity of forces through which creating life might escape from the resentment of persons, societies, and identity-reigns.[6] One of Deleuze's semicrazed examples is from the Pacific: "Captain Ahab has a whale-becoming" (*Dialogues*, 44). Or, in the case of this Henry-imitation we have been tracking, the move would not be one of *becoming Ahab* or *pursuing Herman Melville* across the Pacific, as if chasing that "robust tutelary ghost"[7] of U.S. epic narration within canonical texts of national subject-formation. In Frank Lentricchia's *Luchesi and the Whale,* this drive across Melville's Pacific constitutes the protagonist Luchesi's desire to achieve conversion through writing, for this ex-Catholic subject, in a beaten-down quest to rewrite American literature as path to self-dispossession. The "wings" Luchesi eventually sprouts lead him back, finally, not to the Pacific but across old oceans and lands of Europe to "roots" in Italy and a transatlantic epiphany of opera, language, hunger, and eros. Pushing into the dark heart of *Moby-Dick* shorn of audience, plot, job, and family, Luchesi finds nothing to take possession of but a self-wrought imperative to keep on writing and experimenting with words: "Write. To write. Without object."[8] No *Ishmael-becoming* is evoked, though that may seem a worthier postcolonial cause, if *conversion to literature* as a metamorphosis into newness is still called for.

Connect/I/cut

Here we have been tracking "conversion" into American minority-becoming, a becoming minor Hawaiian, a countercultural mode of becoming otherness within the white conversion apparatus at Yale College, Amherst, and Andover Academy or worse: "A minority never exists ready-made, it is only formed on lines of flight, which are also its ways of advancing and attacking" (*Dialogues*, 43). We are once again invoking the all-but-forgotten evangelical voice of Hawaiian Henry, as if spoken from the ground and grave of a renewed transoceanic tradition, as translated into a *world-becoming figure* of Hawaiian-American-global import. "He who is transplanted, sustains"—that is the motto of my scrappy home state of Connecticut, and it is meant to affirm the Puritan community of the elected elite, led by Thomas Hooker, that broke away from Massachusetts and transplanted to Wethersfield, Windsor, and Hartford in 1636 to found a new colony. Growing up the son of Lebanese immigrants in the Naugatuck River Valley mill town of Winsted, Ralph Nader learned a set of frugal, hardworking, patriotic, bleak, and pedagogical values he still credits with forming his life code and will to become a productive citizen on the American left.[9]

Yet it was this sense of *"Connect/I/cut,"* from the routed outset, as Deleuze once rewrote this U.S. state name, that called out for flight and or breaking away for *newness to happen.*[10] This motto of diasporic affirmation could apply to incoming and outgoing others as well, from Henry 'Ōpūkaha'ia and John Ledyard to Wallace Stevens, who had emigrated to Connecticut and would "live in the tradition which is the true mythology of the region," a set of values Stevens linked to hard work, material scarcity, frugality, taciturn character, and enterprising energies. "There are no foreigners in Connecticut," Stevens oddly affirmed. "Once you are here, you are—or you are on your way to become—a Yankee."[11] Becoming reborn as Yankee subject, tangled into a work ethos, as was Henry 'Ōpūkaha'ia, in many ways that went beyond becoming a Congregationalist minister in native formation. Others, from Puerto Rico to Canton and El Salvador, would have to learn the cues and codes or be all but abolished in the Wasp-Anglo exclusions and social molestations still in place.

Affirming the will to "liberty" still to be found in these United States and the discourses and contexts-of-becoming available to its postwar subjects, Marcelin Pleynet once noted that, here, in this climate of geographical becoming and semiotic plenitude, "You can always leave a milieu, abandon a discourse to enter another."[12] *Conversion,* as I have invoked the term in its material, figurative, and semiotic "turns," would now and again tap into these plural energies of newness, alteration, renewal, ingenuity, and open-ended possibility. But conversion these days, under the by-now-dominant formations of the internet and microelectronic technologies, may have more to do with "data conversion" on the market or a simplistic "language conversion" in which all terms and codes can, by one-to-one equivalency, be translated ("converted") and encoded from one sign into another sign, whether from French, Chinese, Latin, or Hawaiian, say, into the Anglo-global language of English. This is not the *spirit* as seen in a glass darkly, nor even the *letter,* haunting what "conversion" means as a power of life-becoming, semiotic change, and empowerment via enhanced forces as I have been invoking the term, from Henry ʻŌpūkahaʻia to Ai and Bob Dylan. *Conversion* registers a life-affirming transformation of the mind and spirit advocated in "nonconformity" to such worldly givens, racial fixities, or market mores of Empire.

"And be not conformed to this world [*be nonconformists*]; but be ye transformed [*metamorphose yourselves*] via the renewing of your mind," to once again invoke that compelling sentence on conversion from Romans 12:2 as translated from Pauline Greek into a post-1960s force of "apocalypse and/or metamorphosis" by Norman O. Brown in his last book by that same grand mandate of a title.[13] Even in the more starkly *dialectical* figurations of "conversion" in *Brecht and Method,* Fredric Jameson captured the mutability-effect haunting the *poesis* of modernist experimentation as what he called a "quasi-religious conversion," even a "deconversion" power as he rightly terms it, calling the self toward experimental mandates of social mutation and stylistic shift (as in Brecht's turn, through it all, to critical Marxism, or Eliot's conformation to belief-systems affixed to the Church of England). Modernism is driven by the dynamism of these defamiliarizing changes, "in which we are called upon . . . to convert to its dominant ideology, and to learn its codes, to absorb its structure of concepts of values, in some relatively exclusive way which, in our literary enthusiasm, tend to block off an approach to other rival literary codes and languages, until at last we are deprogrammed in disabusement, and reluctantly deconverted."[14]

Invoking Brecht's methods in this postmodern time of global stalemate and leftist defeat by capital, Jameson (who seemingly never suffered bouts of "deconversion" from what earlier generations of ex-communists had called *The God That Failed*) recalls spectral modernism as a power to self-change and socialist becoming, as a mandate to aesthetic transformation, and as an abiding commitment to seek utopian life-experimentation.[15] Many other postmodernists, from Michael Taussig in *Mimesis and Alterity* to Victoria Nelson in *The Secret Life of Puppets,* as I have earlier touched upon, would invoke Walter Benjamin to do this kind of counter-visionary work of "deprogramming" within the material shocks and profane spaces of these late-capitalist cities and malls. Angus Fletcher invokes the endlessly experimental "environmentalism" of Walt Whitman's "language experiments" to do some of this work toward embracing democratic possibility and powers of trope-laden openness.[16] Some of the "deprogramming" needed nowadays may have more to do with *relocating,* or *resituated imagining* (as here in the American Pacific or sites closer to Asia and Oceania), decentering the taken-for-granted normality of a postcolonial Empire by moving outward and across national or regional boundaries toward *democratic world-possibility*. Gayatri Spivak, advocating that we challenge and pluralize the given late-capitalist formations of Asia-Pacific and continental Asia via a "critical regional" turn to articulate "other Asias," nonetheless takes a more ascetic turn away from worldly advocacy: "I am not out to convert the world."[17]

There is a pilgrimage-like memoir by Nancy M. Malone called *Walking a Literary Labyrinth: A Spirituality of Reading*. She's a capaciously well-read Ursuline nun of keen empathy who had a midlife problem with alcoholism and what quasi-medieval poets like Gerard Manley Hopkins and Dylan Thomas used to call *wanhope*. She painstakingly develops a kind of "lectio divina" approach via "slow, attentive, repetitive reading" of key passages in a whole range of works, sacred and secular, from Augustine to Gordimer and Atwood. Malone presents politicizing takes on Harvard Divinity School in the late 1960s and probing details on Bridgeport and the Bronx. Literature deepens the inwardness (via reading, meditating, praying, loving) and what she calls her rebirth as an "exchange of selves" that it advocates and enacts. At the core of her quest abides the conversion experience of recuperated interiority to a "God [who dwells] in you, as you."[18] "When, in my forties, I began to realize what the experience of conversion and finding one's true self might mean, I thought with some pique: it's not fair," she writes. "You spend your whole life becoming who you are only to find out that you have to change, radically."[19] *Conversion*, for this Catholic offspring, remains an open-ended process of self-refiguration, a mandate to seek enhanced life, to exchange selves, and "to change, radically." Malone kept on becoming routed and altered in her deeply Catholic and widely read selfhood even though, like Emerson, she stayed *rooted* in one New England place.[20]

Our roots can go anywhere, perchance back and forth across the Pacific; and we can survive border-crossing becoming, as Gertrude Stein suggests (writing from Paris to Oakland and New York City) in the epigraph to this epilogue. A voice of outernational possibility and self-altering mimesis may be *torn from the stomach* of global forces, local codes, and national enclosures. Yet here we are, in the postmodern shadows of hypercapitalist globalization, financial risk, regional transformation, and mass insecurity spreading across post-9/11 nation and globe, still chasing the spectral ghost of Henry 'Ōpūkaha'ia. We pursue such a force if only to hear his *still small voice* of minority-becoming call with some literary resonance (translated "afterlife," transliteral restoration) that is *great within one*, as Haydn Carruth once urged, as if opening self toward a Pacific-diasporic force of becoming and outernational self-formation through strong dynamics of conversion, metamorphosis, and refiguration of the self. As Jack Kerouac wrote, linking his on-the-road quest from Lowell, Massachusetts, and French-Canadian English into the becoming-writer force and small-town dreams of Thomas Wolfe and Saint Francis, he sought from his teenage days to plug his beatitude-driven career into the romance of vast American space (all those roads going west became his mandate to mobility) and sheer inventiveness and thus "[to] make somehow a new tradition for himself, derived from his own life and from the enormous space and energy of the American life," to forge his conversion-into-writer.[21] To become saved was more an open road challenge and life-quest than a settled certainty, meaning an embodied and risky energy of experimentation that has led back and forth the country as across into Asia, Latin America, Northern Africa, and the Pacific. Sixteen million Hispanic Americans, for example, now claim to be *born-again Christians,* according to a recent poll by the National Hispanic Christian Leadership Conference, an ever-amplifying configuration.

Mad to Be Saved . . .

The only people for me are the mad ones, the ones who are mad to live, mad to talk, mad to be saved, desirous of everything at the same time, the ones who never yawn or say a common place thing, but burn burn burn, like fabulous yellow Roman candles exploding like spiders across the stars.
　　—Jack Kerouac, *On the Road,* 1957[22]

Perhaps, given the waning hopes of leftist melancholy that haunt our feats of self-formation and alter-becoming, we now face a right-leaning conversion into a U.S.-centered "machtpolitik" and the biopolitics of a quasi-imperial government given over to power politics of terror, surveillance, market domination, and authoritarian exceptions to law, democratic modality, or creed. We might at times agree that ours is a time of *"techno-medievalism"* more than any looseleaf postmodernism or New Age animistic panorama as such.[23] If Bob Dylan arrives with enigmatic overviews of this downfallen yet still redemptive nation in *Modern Times* five years after 9/11 (when *Love and Theft* had ominously appeared in September 2001) to offer semiprophetic denunciations, along with more scaled-back terms of vision, love, compassion, and hope ("For the love of God, you ought to take pity on yourself," says the voice in "Thunder on the Mountain"), no God or politico arrives to rescue us from this global malaise, this ongoing battle between civilizations and conversion codes. Each day we face a militant entanglement into monotheistic conversionary codes, Muslim, Christian, Jewish, Hindu, who knows what else. *Conversion by the sword* still escalates and haunts what we have been tracking here as the free choice of "semiotic becoming," mobility, border-crossing risk, and the turning and counterturning dynamics in embracing and regenerating *conversion by the word*.[24] "Convert or die" nonetheless haunts the will to convert and live, from Hawai'i and India to Afghanistan, South Korea, Orange County, and Rome. *Blessed are the poor in spirit* still, even when the powers that be cast them out down-and-out into the streets, alleys, or deserts in this planet of slums. Blessed are those who mourn, even when their health plans are abolished and their pension plans and job security hung out to dry in the capitalist winds.

"Conversion," in these viciously binary terms of faith-war and self-death haunting the world market, might mean the forcible conscription into a suicidal bombing mission spelling catastrophe, ruin, or death for thousands: we ourselves might credibly be cast as *the global Infidels* and the death-of-God forces of secular domination, as America was called on BBC News today (September 11, 2006), by an array of prayerful world citizens, from Pakistan and Baghdad to South London, speaking in memory and praise of what happened on 9/11/2001 when the Twin Towers fell into ruination. Wall Street and the Pentagon may have been blasted with market blowback and the deadly Cold War revenge of a "holy war" ire motivated by another monotheism whose *Satan,* so these bombers said, *was the United States*. We might now realize what William Empson meant when, in the context of two world wars and spread of Maoism across China, where he was teaching English literature, he retreated from the antagonistic monotheisms of the West or East into modes of literary "ambiguity" and embraced the counter-converting force of self-emptying consciousness: "I think Buddhism much better than Christianity because it managed to get away from the Neolithic craving to gloat over human sacrifice"[25]—as if Buddhism, in Japan, China, and India, had not known war and bloody sacrifice across the same twentieth century.[26]

Right now in the Middle East, Africa, and China, there may be grinning and over-earnest South Koreans there "quietly introducing Jesus to Muslims," Korea having sent some twelve thousand Christian missionaries abroad from Korea as "imbued with the fervor of the born again," a mission to convert second only to the United States and ahead of Britain in this evangelical movement gone global. And these converted Koreans "proselytize, not in their own language, but in the local one or English," as Norimitsu Onishi has outlined.[27] Fearless grassroots evangelists are said by the *Asia Times* of Hong Kong to recruit some ten thousand Chinese everyday to accept Jesus as their savior. Still, the flow of forms and tactics becomes crisscrossed and altered. As Whitman blithely projected in "A Broadway Pageant," celebrating the arrival of the Japanese delegates to New York in 1860, "Commerce opening, the sleep of ages having done its work, races [will be] reborn" and cultures made new in transpacific flows and Asian contact zones.[28] The notion of being "born again" as such has become entangled, across the twentieth century (as in writers like Kerouac, Gary Snyder, Mary Austin, and W. S. Merwin), with "rebirth eschatologies," meditation tactics, and divergent technologies of death-and-rebirth drawn from Buddhist, Amerindian, Egyptian, and Magna Graecia sources and "smaller scale societies" of mythic plenitude like the Trobriand Islands.[29] The Grateful Dead, as left-coast gothic example from San Francisco pagan transfusions, took their countercultural and post-Christian name from the Egyptian Book of the Dead.[30] Mort Sahl, playing on those all too divergent meanings of being "born again," wondered out loud at the Monterey Jazz Festival in 2007, "I don't believe [that the U.S. president is born-again]. If he had a chance to be born again, why would he come back as George Bush?" As a mongrelized punk band crooned (or croaked) at a drunken Waikiki club in Honolulu in the late 1980s, as I still recall the crazed lyrics, "Who wants to be born again, man/ It's bad enough to be born once, Uncle Sam."

Assuming no posture of American Innocence or self-virtue in "Honest with Me" from that cautionary album of 2001, *Love and Theft,* Dylan all the more desperately asserted against the domination of Empire and New Age therapies, but caught all up in it, "I'm here to create the new imperial empire / I'm going to do whatever circumstances require / I care so much for you—didn't think that I could / I can't tell my heart that you're no good," wherein the "you" of the song he is lamenting for falling off, backsliding, and betrayal is not so much a woman but a figure of idolatry hard to tell from a nation fallen into betrayed promises and broken covenants by becoming-Empire.[31] As love-allegory, Dylan's "Dirt Road Blues" may have more to do with sorrows over this national lament against imperial entanglement, not just moaning for a broken heart, on *Time Out of Mind:* "praying for salvation laying round in a one-room country shack" (560).[32] As this enigmatic poet of self-possibility and renewal puts this end-time assessment and imperial blight in "Things Have Changed,"

> I've been walking forty miles of bad road
> If the Bible is right, the world will explode
> I've been trying to get as far away from myself as I can.

Given ego drives to sinfulness and misrecognition, there comes this Dylanesque appeal to mutual forgiveness and charity as lover's code: "I hurt easy, I just don't show it / You can hurt someone and not even know it /

The next sixty seconds call feel like an eternity" (574–575). If *things have changed,* some tactics to get beyond these cycles of revenge and will-to-death may remain the same since the coming of Christ to war-torn Palestine and that saddest of holy sites, Jerusalem, two millennia ago: Mutual Forgiveness endures as path to Peace, Joy, and Eternity.

Ernst Bloch, refusing the hopelessness of Cold War containment, yet mocked the American belief in messianic rapturism and its will to decode *realpolitik* via evangelical affirmation and national blessing: "God arrives next Tuesday at 11:25 A.M. at the Illinois Central, hurry there to welcome him!"[33] We all may need this kind of deprogramming via mockery or caustic lament. In a disturbing Hollywood movie on U.S. end-time thinking and beliefs set in the Middle American heartlands of all this, *The Rapture* (1991), a small-town quest for Christian "rapture" via literalization of an American Apocalypse comes closer to a death-drive shredding self, family, and town apart more than to being any kind of born-again awakening to God, peace, or conversion to caritas. This U.S. end-time Gabriel, manifesting as domestic epiphany of Revelations, spells *global bad news* from Texas to Israel and Iraq (not that, in my reading of the Taliban, I could side with that mode of conversion, stripping the mountains of Buddhist faces, burying videos in graves). Auto-critiques like John Perkins's *Confessions of an Economic Hit Man* might not help us understand the sacrament of penance ("confessions") or Mutual Forgiveness, but in the wake of 9/11, as Perkins recounts his turning-point toward shame and redemption, such narratives could unmask the damages that global regimes of investment do in sites across the marketized globe, as all that is sacred becomes the sin or techno-plunder of earth, resource, currency, and otherness.[34]

Pacific Turnings

As a region of geo-strategy and militourist haven, the Pacific Ocean has long figured as such an ocean-space of history, war, imperial rivalry, and bloodshed: the U.S. continental vision of frontier expansion and homesteading hit some dreaded limit, faced a quasi-orientalist decreation, abyss, or unknown space. David Palumbo-Liu summarizes this transpacific dynamic and Jeffersonian dream of passage-to-India as allure (still beckoning via Mainland China) of huge inter-Asian markets: "The defining mythos of America, its 'manifest destiny,' was, after all, to form a bridge westward from the Old World, *not just* to the western coast of the North American continent, but from there to the trans-Pacific regions of Asia."[35] But to be sure, Pacific Man, as Charles Olson called Melville and his transoceanic ephoebe, served as figure of innovation, power, alter-connection, life-surging promise: for, as John Steinbeck lyricized on the edge of Monterey Bay, the Pacific was where life "gathered and scattered," became "a poem, a stink, a grating noise, a quality of light, a tone, a habit, a nostalgia, a dream."[36]

"It took me a long, long time to get over the idea that the Pacific Ocean was going to be more important in our history than the Atlantic. If I ever got over it," born-again New Englander Robert Frost struggled to admit in "A Poet's Boyhood," far from his Orient-facing queer birthplace, San Francisco.[37] Kerwin Lee Klein summarizes "two centuries of conflict be-tween competing visions of American empire," such that the Anglo-global "Old World" vision of an America tied back across the Atlantic to Eu-rope for values had yielded to a more Pacific-based mapping linked to Asia and the Pacific Ocean as Basin and Rim:

> In [this] Jeffersonian vision America faced west across the mythical over-land passage to India. Lewis and Clark converted mythic anticipation into physical reality, and by the early nineteenth century Manifest Destiny had won out.[38]

With the U.S. frontier "closed" and ocean vastness beckoning many a rough rider, Frost, in "Once, by the Pacific," created a Bible-drenched poem of cautionary between-the-wars reckoning to fill this "last ocean" of the American Pacific with a Jehovah-like figure of darkness casting omens of civilizational battles coming up, between East and West, as so many blinded struggles for domination on the edge of America, world-apocalypse.[39]

Complex and unstable in transoceanic mix, the Pacific has long proved a space of "acculturation in two directions," as the French ethnographer Maurice Leenhardt avowed of Melanesian Christianity while theorizing (and working in) these contact zones and off-spaces of mongrel transla-tion that made the sacramental native and the Native Kanaka a polycul-tural creation of newness coming into and going out from the apparatus of global modernity.[40] Our literatures and theories of Pacific literature should try at the very least to be adequate to that grounded situation of uneven global/local entanglement and translation, however far from the "world literary space" of recognition bestowed by the "consecration," translation, and annexation systems of Paris, London, Barcelona, Berlin, and New York.[41] In charismatic revivals spreading, once again, across parts of Papua New Guinea, as Joel Robbins shows in his ethnography of Christianity as lived critique and social vision, the people of this Melane-sian Pacific are still in the process of seeking Baptist rebirth, and the work ethic, (as he says) "becoming sinners."[42] "Multiplicities" is another Deleuzian term I would invoke for such a social-linguistic assemblage of emergent energies and alter-becoming read as a force for and as *counter-conversion.*

As this example only begins to suggest, the interior Pacific has long been lived in by its own politics, counterclaims, death-traps, drugs, radios, videodromes, tourist feedback loops, and forces of negation and complicity as well, the very thick of meaning and contestations of politics and rival meanings the modern ego is longing to escape from in all existential angst.[43] The Pacific has served as world-space for these "encounters" and creative-becoming, an array of good/bad entanglements in the Deleuzian sense, activating life-forces of self-transmutation and an other-multiplied ontology via affects of altered being and multiple connection, not all of them the white-colonial "poison" of "relational decomposition" or the spelling out of native death.[44] As with the "Calibanization" of English and nation-language activated by the Caribbean poet Edward Kamau Brathwaite, for Joe Balaz the pidgin of Hawaiian Creole English (preserving strong ties to Hawaiian language and values more so than to standard or "haolified" English) becomes a subversive poetic means (see his all-too-raunchy love poem, "Lapa Poi Boy,") by which "English is not so much broken, as broken into," as Nathaniel Mackey has described this reclamation of place, polity, and poetic in the West Indies, as "a struggle for turf [that] is taking place in language."[45] "Good encounters" in the transcultural Pacific or West Indies would amplify ideational activity and prod powers of becoming and composed self-transformation out into the world: take the self out of a state of mute opacity and social stalemate.

"When I lie on the beach there naked, which I do sometimes, and I feel the wind coming over me and I see the stars up above," the aging Marlon Brando once mused on a Pacific island, "and I am looking into this very deep, indescribable night, it is something that escapes my vocabulary to describe. Then I think, God, I have no importance, whatever I do or don't do, or what anybody does, is not more important than the grains of sand that I am lying on, or the coconut that I am using for my pillow. So I really don't think in the long sense." This is what Marlon Brando asserted on the Larry King Show, on CNN, about his lotus-eating attraction to live like a huge Buddha—or Kurtz—in the South Pacific, where he set down roots sporadically, family-love gone wrong after the making of *Mutiny on the Bounty* in 1963.[46] In these postures, Marlon Brando is no "quiet American" of lethal idealism, mute opacity, world destructiveness, white bromides, or social stalemate like some Graham Green-like failed U.S. idealist in *The Quiet American,* or Willard from *Apocalypse Now*

Redux. More like John Ledyard, Marlon Brando's mutineer's island of American Pacificism in *Mutiny on the Bounty* leans toward a utopian pole of mutual cohabitation and shared bliss in libidinal-becoming.

Still, the contemporary Pacific is much more than tropical backdrop or epistemological end-game for a Westerner hero's oversaturated nihilism, where (like, say, Paul Theroux) he can project his own outsized longings to escape from social roles and ideological determinations, to escape into some palmy sandscape from the burden of thinking and acting and from Actor's Studio interviews, if not from language and selfhood altogether. The voices of rivers petitioned for as spiritual possession and mana-force in Steven Edmund Winduo's poetry collection *Hembemba: Rivers of the Forest* are *not* those of Langston Hughes, William Butler Yeats, Marlon Brando, or Muddy Waters.[47] Although these modernist figures do flit in and out of Winduo's English-language poems as mentors, running through the book is all the more so the counter-converting quest to speak as Lo-mo'ha, a spirit voice and mana-quester in Nagum Bokien culture (his native language). Many of these poems are situated in the river-crossed region of East Sepik Province, Papua New Guinea, where Winduo takes his pride of birth and starts his journey of Pacific-crossing, estrangement, and return. This book is Winduo's contemporary lyric record of this journey outward, as disorientation, and as return to the Pacific as a cosmopolitical site.

Among Winduo's *tok-pisin* poems written in terse Creole English, "Klostu Mi Les" captures the loss and agony that drive Winduo across the ocean in quest to heal the agony of postcolonial and modern nation-making: "Dispela wokabaut belong me" begins the stanza of the transpacific walkabout, which reads in (diminished) translation:

> This long walk of mine
> Began from a distance
> On the way I met difficulties ["planti heavy"]
> My shoulder carried the burden
> My journey to end
> My ancestor's curiosity
> When they first saw the sea

All rivers lead beyond the forest toward Pacific crossings in Winduo and lead back, fitfully, to a sense of ancestral connection and the loss of spirit-place as motive for poetry and song. As he writes in another poem of diasporic journey from the forests and across oceans in "Taim Mi Raun" ("In My Walk"), "This search goes beyond my own life," meaning this journey of estrangement and return belongs to his ancestral people and their unevenly modernizing nation of Papua New Guinea in the minor Pacific modes. Winduo's poetry reflects large-scale counter-conversions taking place across the Pacific, metamorphosing the South Pacific into "Oceania" at one transoceanic extreme and into sites of pre-Christian or pagan polytheism at the other more place-based extreme in a postcolonial dialectic (as it were) of *routes* and *roots, shoots* and *wings,* turning and returning modes.

California Dreaming Still

"If a man is going to California, he announces it with some hesitation; because it is a confession he has failed at home," was how Emerson castigated those Gold Rush seekers of 1849, who were leaving New England and hitching their destiny to a western star—California or the Pacific Northwest—as he reaffirmed his own stance of *self-reliant willing* as rooted in the unhumiliated ground of Concord, Massachusetts, as a beatific site where the Over-soul of God might make its visitations of universal being and the troping language of imagination and poetry.[48] Dwelling in syntactical openness and ontological surprise, Emerson (as does Nancy Malone) abandoned the self to that mode of American becoming, *routing in place,* whereby (as Stanley Cavell puts it) "achievement of the human requires not inhabitation and settlement but abandonment, leaving."[49] The self could stay in place, if even opaque to itself and socially stalemated or, as Deleuze once mused, activate drives to *Connect/I/cut.* For Donald Hall, Hayden Carruth, and more mainstream poets of American modernism, New England is still "elegy land," forever mulling over its stony earth into "second growth" as elegy and pastoral, as if summoning Frost and Eliot to rise decorously from the dead.[50]

But that was not the heady mood in August of 1967, when I left the sodden valleys of Connecticut industrial towns for a different life and vision of post-Beat beatitude amid the vision-redemptive spaces of San Francisco, California, and a life of western-becoming there, later, in Berkeley. I come from the western part of Connecticut, the Nutmeg State of Yankee commerce, and grew up playing basketball and learning Catholicism and ethnic tolerance in the Naugatuck Valley there. Aside from the antic larger-than-life actress Rosalind Russell of *Auntie Mame* (1957) and *His Girl Friday* (1940) Broadway-to-Hollywood fame who (along with Katherine Hepburn of Hartford) seemed to influence the freedom-minded Connecticut women, my "Brass City" hometown of Waterbury, Connecticut, is notable as the birthplace for contemporary U.S. forces of conservative reaction, like ex-CIA director and Republican senator Porter Goss, as well as manic-depressive figures of agonistic creativity, such as the elegant poet Hayden Carruth[51] and the singular baseball player and Chicago announcer Jimmy Pearsall.[52] (The 1957 movie *Fear Strikes Out* starring Anthony Perkins was based on Pearsall's nerveridden struggles and outfield antics for the Boston Red Sox.) Another Waterbury by-product, Michael McGivney, born into a large Irish-American immigrant family on Railroad Hill in 1852, became a Catholic priest and later founded the Knights of Columbus in New Haven to help laborers, widows, and orphans across the Naugatuck Valley secure insurance, health care, and support.[53] These were mentor figures of corporeal aesthetics that went beyond Western Connecticut origins to become forces of creative becoming and social change, materialized personae of imaginative power.[54]

Where I come from, amid the white spare churches of Congregationalism on the green or the rising styles of Catholic and ethnic multiplicity that dotted the neighborhoods of many a Connecticut mill town, the "holyness people" were apt to be called the Holy Rollers with their talk of latter rain, living out the full Gospel, Spirit-filled talking in tongues that just gave the Sunday church-going people a headache. The signs and wonders of these other churches—"drunkards delivered, eyes restored, unlettered folk speaking foreign languages they had never studied"—sure sounded impressive, as did the claim, "If speaking in tongues accompanied Holy Ghost Baptism on the Day of Pentecost, why not now? Indeed, if then, why not always and everywhere?"[55] Reading spirit-drenched essays of Emerson years later in college, such a primitivist deduction of present-tense biblical revelation made perfect sense to me, indeed seemed the only way to go forward toward an Americanized baptism into spirit-filled words and worlds of new creation. These little churches of the holy spirit were not so much "signing off," as Emerson feared in the 1830s, but "coming out," with crazy literalist names from Azusa Street to Bishop Street Zion Baptist, which I passed on the way to Saint Thomas School, closed down in 1997, which now houses under its aging bricks (fittingly enough) a Pentecostal church.

Hitching my own wagon to some western star of open possibility and geographical becoming, I had moved westward under the sign of *Highway 61 Revisited,* the *I Ching,* Meher Baba, *Howl,* and San Francisco's street paper *The Oracle* and went on to undergraduate and graduate degrees in English at UC Berkeley, where I was founding editor (under poet/scholar Josephine Miles) of the *Berkeley Poetry Review* in 1974.[56] Since that time I have been teaching literatures in universities in Hawai'i, Korea, Taiwan, Massachusetts, and California. Perhaps, as my colleague in Humanities at UC Santa Cruz James Clifford once observed, my life-work and writing have been organized around a kind of anti–Manifest Destiny journey from east to west and along lines of flight that comprise sites of "Asia/Pacific" and "un/American" spaces like Hawaiʻi and Taiwan or the DMZ haunted spaces of Seoul. These are motive forces shaping my life as a literary vocation, calling to the life-transformations provoked by forces as what I have been calling "semiotic becoming." If you stay long in or along the Pacific, you become a part of it; see the world from those formations and sites, even if you take New England values and codes with you as an abiding core. "The New England spirit has been nurtured in the American atmosphere," Charles W. Eliot had advised an aspiring poet in 1919, as he cautioned his cousin T S. Eliot that he might lose that "finest New England spirit" if he stayed too long abroad "in the English atmosphere" (as had, in his view, the expatriate Henry James).[57]

Moving to the West Coast in California and Hawaiʻi, literature became for me a conversionary experience of empowerment and linkage to literary performatives, an awakening to Emersonian/Deleuzian forces of self-becoming and amplified creation. My first experience of this had centered on a famous passage from Emerson's "Nature" that is resonant with the transition into God-relying empowerment, a passage that is both about crossing a bare commons and that also *enacts* that crossing into the "Over-Soul."[58] This passage was being taught from a bulky, white canonical *Norton Anthology of American Literature* in a large, restless lecture class on American literature at UC Berkeley in 1968 by the most unlikely of Emersonians, Frederick Crews, who was known at the time as a Freudian critic of Hawthorne and now for his anti-postmodern skepticism and appeals to empirical knowledge. But as Professor Crews read out and speculated on these Emersonian passages with liminal empathy and uncanny insight, I was *taken out of myself* into something I can only call the linguistic Over-soul of literature looming in all its transcendental afterlife and aftermath-of-becoming. That was how it felt, at least to me, in the campus chambers in that introductory American literature one day in 1968.

This was a more valuable experience than any psychedelic glimmers of transcendental experience I had courted with, in the Fillmore and Winterland ballrooms, via hallucinogens and rock concerts, in the Boston and San Francisco post-beatnik scenes I was part of. This Emersonian "Over-soul" passage on self-reliant (cum-God-reliant) conversion was for me a *vocational call* to forces of transcendental-becoming, a worldly dialogue with the huge transhistorical nexus of American literature of which Emerson, Crews, and potentially Rob Wilson were parts and particles in some quasi-literary godhead, being called into the *poesis* of language and the great linguistic Over-Soul that is American literature as such. Conversion was not so read as salvation but as experimentation, trope, and mask: the life-call to adventure, poesis, and risk, all of which goes under the sign of becoming. This to me is what "becoming an English major" meant in the heady energies, cultural politics, and wild leftist affluence of the West Coast in 1968.

This calling into the metamorphosis-powers of literature and mimetic birth into life-altering possibilities of poetry is what William Everson calls (in his "Santa Cruz Meditations," given later in Porter College at UC Santa Cruz) the turn to "charismatic vocation" as rooted in motions toward visionary "westwardness" and a quasi-sacramental awakening to body, place, and calling.[59] Like Frederick Exley, I had found my "Emersonian calling" to literature amid a sea of undergraduate humanity. When this spirit of creativity and will to newness is implanted in the unwashed subject as a quasi-literary calling to newness and the "influx" of beatitude at the core of being, it casts out wanhope and lacklove from the puny democratic soul, overcomes what William James termed *fear-thought,* those "Sad Passions" that lead to blockages, shames, doubts, chains of inferiority, resentment, and inaction.[60] Such passages implant a will to newness, conversion into the powers of the linguistic Over-soul that writes through and beyond the small given self of everyday subjection. This, too, is what I have tried to show by affirming the love-and-belief-drenched poetics in Bob Dylan.

Before this *conversion through literature,* as I would now trope this turn, I had begun writing in journals and poetic scraps to piece my life together, haunted by the muses of Dylan Thomas, Bob Dylan, Jack Kerouac, William James, the Beatles, and Marguerite Duras. I kept going each day, following the path of trauma/bliss and this life sentence of "becoming a poet/scholar," "becoming Asia/Pacific," becoming he whom the self- and faith-relying Emerson or the Over-Soul had intended me to be. (When I crossed this huge country in 1967, I kept a dog-eared copy of *Varieties of Religious Experience* in my jeans pocket, with a tattered black-and-white photo of Emerson from the Sunday pages of the *Boston Globe*—I still keep these "sacramentals" near my writing desk.) For I am still learning to tap into this life force or godhead as I go, in dialectic of self-loss and quest for utterance and bliss. Influences on this trajectory of self-formation remain the agonistic texts of Nietzsche merging critical theory into poesy; the prophetic blues of a "Jokerman" named Dylan/-Zimmerman/Jeremiah; Emerson; Jo Miles in her brilliant Zen way; Ulrich Knoepflmacher; Jack Spicer, the one and only; the Pauline scriptures recoding the good news of Jesus; Kerouac's Buddha prayers; Scottish and Italian grandparents from Jura and Naples; the Judaic dramatician Mrs. Rabinowitz, who taught me Shakespeare in eighth grade at Sprague Grammar School in Waterbury; and a cast of thousands better than I will ever be. "For I and it are less than the least of God's mercies," George Herbert so tenderly—and with absolute self-abolishment—phrased his life-work on *The Temple; or, Sacred Poems and Private Ejaculations* on his death-bed, sending the unpublished manuscript to an old friend, Nicholas Ferrar, in 1633.[61]

The underground America quested for, as climate of rebirth, stands for an "invisible republic" tied to forces of mongrel becoming and minority transformation. "This is not exactly a people called upon to dominate the world," as Deleuze affirmed of this United States from below. "It is a minor people, eternally minor, taken up in becoming-revolutionary," at least for multitudes of immigrants, beat-pilgrim souls, and libertarian forces of creative enunciation.[62] I recognize the openness of this politics and will to transformation and *auto-poesis* in Bob Dylan. "The poet was always—would always be—in the process of being reborn," as Susan Sontag once urged.[63] This quest for rebirth, in the American climates, is embodied by Ed Sanders in his collage-poem *1968: A History in Verse*, which collates modes of libidinal transformation, high and low—scatalogical music of the Fugs, drug festivals and concerts, flyers, advertisements, posters, be-ins, street protests, flights, poems, letters to editors, little magazines, sit-ins, hallucinations, media spectacles—adding this wry proviso like that of a "masked and anonymous" poet:

> A writer is never right enough
> for the right
> left enough for the left
> pure enough for the pure
> nor poor enough
> for the poor of heart.[64]

Crossing *routing* with *dwelling* as sites of metanoia, we can once again invoke the "Gospel of Thomas" as a beaten-down yet beatified mandate to keep moving down the road of spiritual becoming: "Yeshua said, Be passersby."[65] The slide-guitar evangelist Blind Willie Johnson caught this gnostic pilgrimage through a blues-glass darkly in the late 1920s, portrayed as a journey from dying Empire (self) to enlivened spirit (soul): "My mother often told me, angels bonded your life away / She said I would accomplish, but trust in God and pray / I'm on the King's

Highway, I'm travelin' everyday."[66] Amid this real estate tract of a nation, people still bury statues of Saint Joseph to help them sell a house.[67]

Conversion as Minority Becoming

Caught up in a diasporic journey into creative-becoming and torn from the place of birth and its social compulsions, moving between California and Hawai'i as well as teaching in Korea and Taiwan, I keep on questing. Since the late 1970s, I have become part of a movement at Bamboo Ridge and tied to a project of techno-poetics at *Tinfish,* aggravated by the Internet, film, and pop music. Susan Schultz, postmodern poet-scholar and editor of *Tinfish,* once observed in a review of *Reimagining the American Pacific,* "This is the autobiography of a white critic's conversion into the local."[68] Needless to say, *conversion* has become for me a loaded term of willed force and a commitment to living across the Asia/Pacific and New England nexus.

In such global and local contexts, I have been ruminating in the epilogue to this study of the poetics and politics of conversion, trying to reframe and personalize questions of minority literature in this era of Empire and globalization. Partly I have been doing so by evoking contexts linking these energies and forms of minor writing to the autobiographical trajectory of myself (Scottish/Italian and New England *wings* across the Pacific), as well as movements in postcolonial Hawai'i and "Oceania" as localist (*roots* via place-based imagining and ethnic and indigenous culture), which I have been a part of for some thirty years and writing about these past decades. Why follow such *forces of minority-becoming* when major forms call? In the U.S. field of modern sports, there are the major leagues and minor leagues of baseball. The only goal of a minor league player is to get into the major leagues; the minor leagues are too small, too underpaid, too close to the farm leagues and bush leagues of ordinary play or amateur irrelevance for a player to want to stay there.

But "minor literature" is not like this in tactic or intent; overcoming shame and abjected habits of taste, minority literature need not wish to take on a major function so as to serve the majority culture of canon (unless it has gone wrong) of Empire; it wants to express "becoming-minor," as Deleuze has put it in his study of Kafka as "minor" writer: to become deviant, mongrel, nomadic, small, local, in ways that challenge state forms of identity and canons of what the nation and national language is. Even Dylan does this, say, by performing his "never-ending concert tour" in nowhere *minor-league* ball parks like Pawtucket, Rhode Island, or New Britain, Connecticut, just as *Modern Times* climbs in the U.S. Billboard

charts, or not. John Ashbery, a canonical poet of postmodern indetermi-
nacy and "flow chart" forays into democratic syntax, as Angus Fletcher
shows, roots his experimental writing in a cast of "minor poets" who form
what he calls "other traditions" that enable his desubjectified poetry more
than the canonical personae of Pound or Eliot.[69]

The major most often feeds upon minor expression and, at times, may
fear it like a pidgin speech that mocks and warps the reign of standard
currency. It stutters and rasps like Bob Dylan singing, or half-speaking,
the blessing of a refrain to "Nettie Moore." It is what minority groups
construct inside of a major language like English, Spanish, Chinese, or
German—not an essence but a movement, a tonal position of unrest, ag-
itation, a nervous mode of "deterritorialization" that (at its best) out-
flanks the workings of the capitalist market, social regulation, and
identity-making. Politicized by necessity, minority literature emerges tied
to collective enunciation, energies, and aspirations of counter-conversion
forces fed up with being excluded, dominated, considered as substan-
dard, illiterate, or underdeveloped. Minority literature develops alternative forms, practices, and outlets of circulation (like Bamboo Ridge Press,
subpress collective, or Tinfish Works in Hawai'i) that are the equal to
major leagues and languages; the major leagues of literature may try to
get into the minors, but they have been locked out or abandoned by the
minority forms.[70] Pascale Casanova's model of the *world-literary-system*
portrays this global-local relationality, but upside-down, as in a "world
gone wrong" where the center always rules.

To invoke the diasporic affiliation in Jessica Hagedorn: "I'm not interested in just writing 'an American novel.' . . . Though I've been living in
America for 30 years now, my roots remain elsewhere . . . back there [in
the Philippines]."[71] More so than British English today, "American English" has become a global language for fracturing and fusing activity, a
globalizing language expanding the territory of global capital and the
power of Americanization, yes;[72] but also a language of creolization that
is being driven toward "deterritorialized" energies at multiple points,
which is to say it is worked over and transformed daily by minor expression, "necessarily worked upon by all the minorities of the world." So
Jameson theorizes globalization as a "deterritorializing" force transforming market forms, far and near,

> The first and most fateful deterritorialization is then this one, in which what
> Deleuze and Guattari call the axiomatic of capitalism decodes the terms of the
> older precapitalist coding systems and "liberates" them for new and more
> functional combinations. . . . [T]here comes a moment in which the logic of

capitalism—faced with the saturation of local and even foreign markets—determines an abandonment of that kind of specific production, along with its factories and trained workforce, and, leaving them behind in ruins, takes its flight to other more profitable ventures [such as new forms of financial speculation shorn from land and place]. . . . Globalization is rather a kind of cyberspace in which money capital has reached its ultimate dematerialization.[73]

American English is becoming Konglish, Singlish, Ebonics, and Hawaiian Creole English, amplifying immixtures at the global-local interface.[74] Minority literature helps articulate this "borderlands" interface, forging a language where past and future mix and different gods can co-exist. Minor writing is not just what a social minority writes; it is a writing that aims to do something different that may be risky, off, vernacularized, impure, unpredictable in voice and cultural-political vision. Milton Murayama does not aspire to become Chang-rae Lee, nor does Joe Balaz write like W S. Merwin on Maui. To invoke Deleuze/Guattari on "becoming minor" in the full, decolonizing sense: "To make use of the polylingualism of one's own [major] language, to make a minor or intensive use of it, to oppose the oppressed quality of this language to its oppressive quality, to find points of non-culture or under-development, linguistic Third World zones by which a language can escape, an animal enters into things, an assemblage comes into play" (*Kafka,* 27). While no one would claim born-again Dylan as a poet of postcolonial islands like Bob Marley or Joe Balaz, he did once admit that his song "Jokerman" "kinda came to me in the [Caribbean] islands. It's very mystical. The shapes there, and shadows, seem to be so ancient. The song was sorta inspired by these spirits they call *jumbis.*"[75] So that Christ and the jumbis can live on and *co-exist* in the minority becoming of such Dylanesque poems.

Maybe F. Scott Fitzgerald in the wry wisdom of "The Crack-Up," amid all the creative and destructive forces marring self and society, put it best as vocation to beatitude under such conditions of risk, breakdown, lostness, and life-quest: "I was always saving or being saved."[76]

At the Edges of the Pacific

At the edges of the Pacific Ocean, or writing near the techno-creativity of the DMZ and Seoul, I am still learning to embrace the blasted-open dialectics of representing global and local contact from writing inside/outside Asia/Pacific, and inside/outside America, as these regions, localities, fragments, and nations have come to share an entangled fate of *global becoming.* To invoke that ancient poet of unhousedness and semiotic risk, John Ashbery, "The Task" of conversion through the mongrel powers of *poesis* may still be one in which,

> there are reaches to be attained
> A last level of anxiety that melts
> In becoming, like miles under the pilgrim's feet.[77]

The converts ("pilgrims") I have looked at in this study—from a minister like Henry ʻŌpūkahaʻia to poets like Ai and Bob Dylan or a novelist like Epeli Hauʻofa—have come through strange waters and dwelling sites of the spirit from the Atlantic and the Pacific to the Mississippi and the Connecticut Rivers and been washed in vision and metamorphosis, leaving their homelands of the heart for hinterlands of the spirit in New York City, San Francisco, and New Haven that circle back to the beginning and embrace transformations without end. These are what I have been calling theo-poetic quests and projects of semiotic becoming that open (as Ashbery puts it touchingly) "like miles under the pilgrim's feet." Better change via *poesis*, risks of counter-conversion and outernational becoming, than a nation closed in on itself, caged in fear, as portrayed by Fanny Howe in a land where "cars whir and curse" past abandoned houses, all-but-dreamless before promises the open-road once stood for:

> This America is a wonderful place,
> one immigrant said. If it's in a cage, then it's safe.[78]

If we live in a time of global terror when warring civilizations would do techno-medieval battle and exact blood for blood, when geopolitics can get done in quasi-religious garb on CNN news to justify military forays as missions for freedom, we need not be conformed to this "worlded configuration."[79] In these days of "crazy weather" and what Al Gore documents is global heating and eco-ruination, perhaps a love affair with the planet is taking place between death-drive forces conjoined to bring us all into "end-time" grasp and, as media tactic, to accept the fundamentalized terms of world loss as *realpolitik*.

Not to end this study of theo-poetics with a worldly *cage* or a mean little *curse*, I want to turn back (and move forward) to a counterworlding image of an *airline* wrought from grassroots poesis and dustbowl gospel idioms, Woody Guthrie's "Airline to Heaven."[80] This heavenbound plane comes back from the dead, from the pen of Bob Dylan's prophetic precursor. "For a dead man," as an *International Herald Tribune* reporter wryly noted, "Woody Guthrie has been awfully busy lately."[81] It is a work of counter-conversion, coming out from the future, rediscovered by British singer-songwriter Billy Bragg and the American band Wilco on *Mermaid Avenue.* Like "This Morning I Am Born Again," it conjures hope and beatitude for the broken-down in a world gone wrong, as on the soundtrack to Dennis Johnson's beat-quest novel, *Jesus' Son:*

> There's an airline plane
> Flies to heaven everyday
> Past the pearly gates
>
> If you want to ride this train
> Have your ticket in your hand
> Before it is too late
>
> If the world looks wrong
> And your money's spent and gone
> And your friend has turned away
>
> You can get away to heaven
> On this aeroplane
> Just bow your head and pray
>
> Them's got ears, let them hear
> Them's got eyes, let them see
> Turn your eyes to the lord of the skies
>
> Take this airline plane
> It'll take you home again
> To your home behind the skies
>
> Well a lot of people guess
> Some say no and some say yes
> Will it take some and leave some behind?
>
> But you will surely know
> When to the airport go
> To leave this world behind
>
> Oh a lot of speakers speak
> A lot of preachers preach
> When you lay their salary on the line
>
> You hold your head and pray
> It's the only earthly way

You can fly to heaven on time
Fly to heaven on time

Them's got ears, let them hear
Them's got eyes, let them see
Turn your eyes to the lord of the skies

Take that airline plane
It'll take you home again
To your home behind the skies

Your ticket you obtain
On this heavenly airline plane
You leave your sins behind

You've got to take this flight
It may be daytime, might be night
But you can't see your way if you're blind

Them's got ears, let them hear
Them's got eyes, let them see
Turn your eyes to the lord of the skies

Take that airline plane
It'll take you home again
To your home behind the skies

Notes

Introduction: Conversions against Empire

1. Hillel Italie, "Turkish Novelist Orhan Pamuk Wins Nobel," *San Francisco Chronicle,* Oct. 12, 2006, A1. On such Asian and European synergies and oppositions, see Orhan Pamuk, *Istanbul: Memories and the City,* trans. Maureen Freely (New York: Knopf, 2006).

2. Along another trajectory, in *American Catholic Arts and Fictions: Culture, Ideology, Aesthetics* (Cambridge: Cambridge University Press, 1992), Paul Giles has written a far-ranging study of authors including Kerouac, Fitzgerald, O'Neill, and McCarthy and filmmakers and artists including Hitchcock, Scorsese, Warhol, and Altman, whose work is shown to refract Catholic sacramentalism, analogical poeticism, and a religiosity that drenches everyday capitalism in auras of beatitude lost and found.

3. See Erik Davis, *The Visionary State: A Journey through California's Spiritual Landscape* (San Francisco: Chronicle Books, 2006), 9. As Davis writes of his quest for conversion, "By the time school beckoned me east, I had met and broken bread with teen witches, born-again surfers, Hare Krishnas, wandering Christian mendicants, Siddha yogis, est seminar leaders, psychedelic Deadheads and a spindly metaphysician who taught English at my junior high and read my aura after class" (8).

4. It was while holidaying at the Bush family's inner sanctum at Walker's Point in Kennebunkport, Maine, that George W. reportedly "found God," after Southern Baptist minister Billy Graham spent a summer weekend there in 1985 (accessed via BBC News online, June 29, 2007). Graham, so-called pastor-in-chief, has served as spiritual counselor to the last eleven U.S. presidents with varying degrees of alliance and confidence, close in the case of the two Bushes, LBJ, and Nixon but distant in the case of Kennedy and Truman. See Nancy Gibbs and Michael Duffy, "The Political Confessions of Billy Graham," *Time,* Aug. 20,

2007, 40–47. The postconversion Bush later maintained, to his more Episcopalian mother, "that only born again Christians were eligible for entrance" to heaven, a view minister Graham countered with a more severely Calvinist sense that "no one should try to play God" in the maze of his or her own sinfulness (44).

5. Colin Wilson, Rogue Messiahs: Tales of Self-Proclaimed Saviors (Charlottesville, VA: Hampton Roads, 2000), 41. Wilson exposes the messianic fakery, sexual exploitation, and abuses that conversionary religiosity can take in cult figures like David Koresh and Reverend Jim Jones as well as the "gospel of free love" that came out of the Great Revival of 1832.

6. As John Rajchman phrases the terms of what he calls an "empiricist conversion," while discussing the immanentist philosophy of Gilles Deleuze as linked to Spinoza and William James, this experience of life-risk can be "found in American pragmatism, which substitutes experimentation for salvation." See The Deleuze Connections (Cambridge, MA: MIT Press, 2000), 19.

7. See Sara Miles, Take This Bread: A Radical Conversion (New York: Ballantine Books, 2008).

8. See Isaac Gewirtz, Beatific Soul: Jack Kerouac on the Road (New York: New York Public Library, 2007), 162. "Souls on the Road" was one of over a hundred titles considered (75), suggesting the close affinity of Beat with the quest for Buddhist-Catholic "beatitude."

9. Charles Taylor, A Secular Age (Cambridge, MA: Harvard University Press, 2007), 6.

10. Taylor, A Secular Age, 755; see also chapter 20 on "Conversions," 728–772.

11. Quoted in David Van Biema, "America's Unfaithful Faithful," Time, accessed online, Feb. 28, 2008. See also Alan Wolfe, "Pew in the Pews," Chronicle of Higher Education, accessed Mar. 21, 2008 online, on this denominational "churning" as contemporary norm.

12. Taylor, A Secular Age, 732.

13. Ibid., 761–765.

14. Ralph Waldo Emerson, "Experience," in Ralph Waldo Emerson: Essays and Poems, ed. Joel Porté, Harold Bloom, and Paul Kane (New York: Library of America, 1996), 485.

15. Journal entry for June 9, 1838, in Selections from Ralph Waldo Emerson, ed. Stephen E. Whicher (Boston: Houghton Mifflin, 1960), 89.

16. For a "planetary" portrait of these cross-fertilizing religious exchanges across a global system of "deep time" in Emerson and Thoreau et al., see Wai Chee Dimock, Through Other Continents: American Literature across Deep Time (Princeton, NJ: Princeton University Press, 2007), chapters 1 and 2. She notes that the minor transcendentalist Bronson Alcott "was doing nothing special" when he tried to borrow from the Boston Athenaeum library these books of world religion as a kind of comparative literature: Collier's Four Books of Confucius, History of China (by the Jesuit), the Kings of Confucius, the Vedas, the Sama Vedas, Vishnu Parana, Saadi, Firdusi, the Zendavesta, and the Koran.

17. See Terry Eagleton's introduction and commentary to *The Gospels: Jesus Christ* (London: Verso, 2007), 173, which portrays Jesus as a "tortured political criminal" and links this awareness of redemptive struggle against empire to "the revolutionary act which the Gospels know as *metanoia,* or conversion" (xxvii–xxviii).

18. Ralph Waldo Emerson, "Experience," in *Emerson: Essays and Poems,* 485.

19. I discuss de Tocqueville's paradox of a "puny democratic ego" drawn to modes of aggrandizement linking self, nation, land, and a democratized "sublimity" in chapters 6 and 7 of *American Sublime: The Genealogy of a Poetic Genre* (Madison: University of Wisconsin Press, 1991) on Walt Whitman and Wallace Stevens.

20. Quoted in Grant Wacker's fine study, *Heaven Below: Early Pentecostals and American Culture* (Cambridge, MA: Harvard University Press, 2001), 257, as testimony of an "anonymous zealot" to such Holy Ghost healings, last days, latter rains, and tongues.

21. Grant Wacker, in *Heaven Below,* discusses Sister Aimee Semple Mcpherson's "standard pentecostal absolutizing [as] the tendency to ratchet every issue into one of ultimate morality" (33). As another voice from the *Apostolic Faith* in Kansas phrased this charismatic inspiration in 1913, the "Holy Ghost does not put us out of business; he puts us in business" (op. cit., 33).

22. See Chapter 4, which maps these crucial postcolonial dynamics that go on reframing the space, time, and mores of "Oceania" from Papua New Guinea to Hawai'i Nei. Chapter 5, on the poet Ai, offers an uncanny refiguration of the whole U.S. frontier ethos as expansion into a "killing floor" of racial if not spiritual genocide.

23. The Bob Dylan song that (for me at least) bluntly expresses this brazen, pull-no-punches Christology abiding at the core of his "born-again" poetics in 1978 is "Ain't No Man Righteous, Not One" from that album of Jeremaic denunciation, *Slow Train Coming.* See Bob Dylan, *Lyrics: 1962–2001* (New York: Simon & Schuster, 2004), 418.

24. As Dylan tells *Rolling Stone* while elaborating on the archaic specters and generic ragpicking of his album *Modern Times* (accessed online Aug. 20, 2006), "The 60s belong to me, I own them, you want them?" If this means "living outside the law to be honest," Dylan shows that charity still rules in the loves of this native American son, burnt bridges and wasted Rim cities notwithstanding on an album of burnt-out fields like *Empire Burlesque.*

25. Eagleton, *The Gospels,* xviii.

26. "The term translated [from Mark 1:15] by the moralizing 'repent' is *metanoiete* derived from two words, *meta* (beyond) and *nous* (mind). Jesus is urging his hearers not primarily to change their behavior but to go beyond the mind that they now have, to see things in a new way, to adopt a different attitude [via self-renovating faith, God-trust]": Robert Barron, *The Priority of Christ: Toward a Postliberal Catholicism* (Grand Rapids, MI: Brazos Press, 2007), 165–166. See also Robert Barron on "conversion" as metanoia in *And Now I See: A Theology of Transformation* (New York: Crossroad, 1998), 4.

27. Susan Harding, "Speaking Is Believing," in *The Book of Jerry Falwell: Fundamentalist Language and Politics* (Princeton, NJ: Princeton University Press, 2001), 38. She argues, rightly so as I see it, that these "folk interpretive practices are best described as [a] poetics [of faith], not [a] hermeneutics [of suspicion]" (294 and 124).

28. Michael Ragussis, *Figures of Conversion: "The Jewish Question" and English National Identity* (Durham, NC: Duke University Press, 1995), 2.

29. See Paul Gilroy, "Bold as Love?: Jim's Afrocyberdelia and the Challenge of the Not-Yet," *Critical Quarterly* 46 (2004): 115.

30. Dylan, *Lyrics: 1962–2001*, 224.

31. The key study of this "covenant nation" on quasi-Hebraic lines of biblical typology, whereby the "city on the hill" community of redemptive American nationhood falls into a betrayal of covenants and backslides into imperial entanglement with Rome and Babylon, remains the typological reading of this far-reaching genre by Sacvan Bercovitch, *American Jeremiad* (Madison: University of Wisconsin Press, 1980). See also the perdurance of these theo-poetic modes of figuring nationhood during the Enlightenment and early Republic eras, in Ernest Tuveson, *Redeemer Nation: The Idea of America's Millennial Role* (Chicago: University of Chicago Press, 1980); and Conrad Cherry, *God's New Israel: Religious Interpretations of American Destiny* (Chapel Hill: University of North Carolina Press, 1998).

32. On postcolonial identity-fashioning as responsive to global capitalist needs and shifts from labor to professional class culture, see also Paul Gilroy, *After Empire: Melancholia or Convivial Culture?* (London: Routledge, 2006), particularly chapter 2, "Cosmopolitanism Contested."

33. I also see this study as aligned to the confederative poetic-scholarly project of Eric Lott, *Love and Theft: Blackface Minstrelsy and the American Working Class* (New York: Oxford University Press, 1993); and Eric Lott, " 'You Make Me Feel So Young': Sinatra & Basie & Amos & Andy," in *This Is Pop II: Papers from Experience Music Project* (forthcoming, Harvard University Press). See Chapter 6 in this volume, on Dylan, as well as the epilogue, on the multiethnic working-class Connecticut towns of possibility and dread.

34. My colleague in anthropology at the University of California at Santa Cruz, Susan Harding, has outlined the American vernacular terms of this Bible-based belief system in sermons, public speech, videos, TV broadcasts, and direct mailings, in *The Book of Jerry Falwell*. On the "dominion theology" driving strands of the U.S. right to civil—if not global—domination via this will toward a theocracy of cultural conservatism that remains antiscience and antihistory while it is also being fully pro-wealth, see Michelle Goldberg, *Kingdom Coming: The Rise of Christian Nationalism* (New York: Norton, 2007). On Sinclair Lewis's anti-imperialist warning uttered from the Midwestern Main Streets of the 1930s that "When fascism comes to America, it will be wrapped in the flag and carrying a cross," see Chris Hedges, *American Fascists: The Christian Right and the War on America* (New York: Free Press, 2007). The election of 44th U.S. President Barack Obama means at last that, as Sam Cooke and Bob Dylan have urged all along, a real social

"change has come" and the blight of no-nothing darkness upon the land can begin to end.

35. Norman O. Brown, *Apocalypse and/or Metamorphosis* (Berkeley: University of California Press, 1991), v, 183, 196.

36. As Barry Bonds put it after hitting his 756th home run to break Hank Aaron's record on August 7, 2007, for the San Francisco Giants, "Muhammad Ali has always meant a lot to me—there was no greater person, except maybe God." When asked in May 2001 about his home-run prowess, Bonds— an avowed Christian, in the middle of steroid accusations, who often points heavenwards after he hits one out at Pacific Bell Stadium—said, "The balls I used to line off the wall are lining out (of the park). I can't tell you why. Call God. Ask him," See "756: Alone at the Top," *San Francisco Chronicle,* Aug. 8, 2007, A7.

37. *The Autobiography of Malcolm X,* as told to Alex Haley (New York: Ballantine, 1965), 169, 199, 201.

38. *The Autobiography of Malcolm X,* 340.

39. Barack Obama, *Dreams from My Father* (New York: Three Rivers Press, 2004), 86.

40. See the discussion of dietary regimes, across various contexts, from Puritan ascetic to Christian therapeutic and self-healers like Mary Baker Eddy to the countersecular food regimes of the Nation of Islam, in R. Marie Griffith, *Born Again Bodies: Flesh and Spirit in American Christianity* (Berkeley: University of California Press, 2004). Griffith contrasts the antipork regime of Louis Farrakhan (156–158) with the flesh-loving Father Divine who saw corporal weight and large bodies as the "tangibilization" of God in fat men and women (143–146).

41. On pragmatically Americanist challenges to social forms of these self-relying influxes of beatitude and faith (selves "becom[ing] organs of the Holy Ghost" [412]) transforming overdeterminations, see Ralph Waldo Emerson, "Fate," *The Conduct of Life* (1860), in *Emerson: Essays and Poems,* 781. Overcoming belatedness through this semiotic model of self-reliance as God-reliance, Emerson becomes a perpetual son of American religious newness and invokes the "brave text" of Paul from 1 Corinthians 15:28 in "Circles" (409) to back up this will to conversion and comradeship in the Over-Soul: "Then shall the Son be subject unto Him who put all things under him, that God may be all in all." On this transliteralism of grace, see Alan Badiou, chapter 7, "Paul against the Law," in *Saint Paul: The Foundation of Universalism,* trans. Ray Brassier (Stanford, CA: Stanford University Press, 2003).

42. In reviewing the anthology edited by Mary Eberstadt, *Why I Turned Right: Leading Baby Boom Conservatives Chronicle Their Political Journeys* (New York: Simon & Schuster, 2007), Stephen Metcalf shrewdly notes, "These [essays] aren't in any recognizable sense 'journeys.' They're conversion narratives"; *New York Times Book Review,* Aug. 5, 2007, 23. For a scathing portrait of the turn to "boomeritis" as an accommodation to conservative hegemony in New Left, public intellectual, and critical theory circles, see Eric Lott, *The Disappearing Liberal Intellectual* (New York: Basic Books,

2006), who explores, for example, Cornell West's post-Marxist and less radically prophetic-Christian turn to a centrist Clintonism in chapter 4.

43. Steve Turner, "John Lennon's Born-Again Phase," *Christianity Today*, Sept. 10, 2007, accessed online. In the spring of 1977, Turner contends, Lennon privately claimed he had become a born-again Christian, but by 1979 defined himself as a "born again pagan" bound to Yoko.

44. Badiou, *Saint Paul*, 77. Badiou's terms of "militant" materialization would challenge the soft hegemony of neoliberalism, as when he urges that "Christ's death *sets up an immanentization of the spirit,*" (69). Beyond these Pauline reflections on the power of grace overcoming regimes of law, the crucial passage on born-again dynamics in the New Testament remains John 3:3–5, a passage I shall return to in this study: "Except a man be born again, he cannot see the kingdom of God. . . . Except a man be born of water and *of* the Spirit, he cannot enter into the kingdom of God." Twice-born means fully born.

45. John W. O'Malley, *Four Cultures of the West* (Cambridge, MA: Harvard University Press, 2004), 58.

46. See the "Moloch" curse in the inferno section of "Howl," Allen Ginsberg, *Howl and Other Poems* (San Francisco: City Lights Books, 1957), 21–23. A more lethal form of Mammon become war-god, Moloch is opposed to "spectral nations!" rising up against the "blind" empire of capital, war, and death. On the formation of this "spectral nation" in Bob Dylan, The Band, Robert Johnson, Dock Boggs et al., see also Greil Marcus, *Invisible Republic* [or as reissued and retitled, *The Old, Weird America: The World of Bob Dylan's Basement Tapes* (New York: Picador, 2001)]; and in a post-9/11 intervention into the grim or terrorized terms of American subject-formation under the Bush 2 regime, *The Shape of Things to Come: Prophecy and the American Voice* (New York: Farrar, Straus, and Giroux, 2006).

47. Although he does not explore American theo-poetics in his latest study of the religious imagination and its sublime mood and mode, Harold Bloom's *Jesus and Yahweh: The Names Divine* (New York: Riverhead Books, 2005) may be—obliquely to be sure—the most Emersonian approach to the Bible of the American imagination. For Bloom, provoking dominant modes of American Pentecostalism belief stressing the Holy Ghost moving in the self, the Book of James is oddly more interesting in its injunctions than the Gospel according to Saint Paul or tears of Saint Peter, not a view shared by many.

48. This work-sanctifying "Jesus in the cash-flow" modality of subject-formation mapped by Max Weber as a configuration of spiritualized capitalism in the United States of America cannot be forgotten as it is infused all over our cable television stations and on the cover of *Time* magazine: see *The Protestant Ethic and the Spirit of Capitalism,* trans. Talcott Parsons with an introduction by Anthony Giddens (London: Routledge, 2005), 69ff. This labor of "protest" and capitalized conversion of immigrants from shame, exploitation, and racial stigmatization into successful, upwardly mobile Americans is given an innovatively ethnic interrogation in Rey Chow, *The Protestant Ethnic and the Spirit of Capitalism* (New York: Columbia

University Press, 2002). (On the Pacific Rim, South Korea is perhaps the strongest version of this "born-again" formation into global modernity on a quasi-Americanized model.)

49. Emerson, "Power," in *Emerson: Essays and Poems,* 808.

50. Régis Debray, *Empire 2.0,* trans. Joseph Rowe (Berkeley, CA: North Atlantic Books, 2004), 23. Further references will occur parenthetically.

51. Régis Debray, *God: An Itinerary,* trans. Jeffrey Mehlman (London: Verso, 2004), would track the contemporary "God Bless America" ideology of prophetic nationhood (cum global redeemer) as it migrated across the Atlantic with Columbus et al. to New England Puritanism down to the U.S. Constitution (200–205). For Debray, this "redemptive" mandate is epitomized in a 1952 Supreme Court decision, "We are a religious people whose institutions presuppose a Supreme Being" (270).

52. Juliana Spahr, "January 29, 2003," in *this connection of everyone with lungs* (Berkeley: University of California Press. 2005), 50.

53. Robert Fogel, *The Fourth Great Awakening and the Future of Egalitarianism* (Chicago: University of Chicago Press, 2000), tracks periodic waves of American religious fervor and revivalism and contends that we are in the midst of a fourth "awakening" that began in the 1960s. On the myriad forms of what William James called "over-beliefs" animating our "gnostic" New Age Revivalism and populist theo-poetics, see Harold Bloom, *Omens of Millennium: The Gnosis of Angels, Dreams, and Resurrection* (New York: Riverhead, 1996): "American religionists of our indigenous varieties more frequently return to the older belief in the resurrection of the body, and many among them indeed, like the ancient Gnostics, already have experienced resurrection in this life" (165). Whatever his animadversion against "cultural studies," Bloom is doing important American cultural studies work by unpacking what he calls the poetic imagination of "the American Religion."

54. Herman Melville, *The Confidence Man: His Masquerade* (New York: Norton, 1971), 168. Melville's mock-Emersonian character, Mark Winsome, cannot tell the difference between faith and fraud, parable and life, as here he also is being duped by the devil on this ship of fools and fops.

55. Bob Dylan, *Chronicles,* vol. 1 (New York: Simon & Schuster, 2004), 150, 153, 161, 188. Dylan's fourth chapter ("Oh Mercy") is the only one in *Chronicles* that deals, even obliquely as allegory, with his "born-again" experience and its subjective consequences for his core poetics of perpetual transformation.

56. Ibid., 188, 164.

57. As a website (http://womenofthebeat.org/MaryNorbetKorte) devoted to Korte's work as poet and ecological activist urges, "It surely is an incredible act when a former Catholic nun, who had devoted her entire life to God, became a liberated Beat writer. Mary Norbert Korte was born in 1934 to an extremely Catholic family in eastern San Francisco, who encouraged Mary to join the convent right after high school, which she did obediently, entering St. Rose Convent in San Francisco at the age of eighteen in 1952. While in

the convent, she earned a masters degree in a specialized field of Silver Latin. At this point, Sister Mary Norbert was indeed a true nun—devoting her life to God and the convent." In 1965, Sister Mary Norbert was "called" outside of the convent, as Brenda Knight portrays this "Beat" turn: "She attended the Berkeley Poetry Conference and heard the readings by Robert Creeley, Jack Spicer, Charles Olson, Robert Duncan, Gary Snyder and Allen Ginsberg." Hearing their work moved Sister Mary enormously, and she was awakened into a new type of devotion. Sister Mary felt just as comfortable with the Beat community as she did at the convent. "She remembers being the only nun in attendance and was treated as rather an exotic, but very warmly welcomed." See Brenda Knight, *Women of the Beat Generation: The Writers, Artists, and Muses at the Heart of a Revolution* (Newberry Port, MA: Conari Press, 1998), 258. See also Ronna C. Johnson and Nancy McCampbell Grace, eds., *Girls Who Wore Black: Women Writing the Beat Generation* (New Brunswick, NJ: Rutgers University Press, 2002). My mentor in graduate school in the English Department at UC Berkeley, the poet-scholar Josephine Miles, was taken to be one of these radical "Beat" women by the *Evergreen Review* et al. for her work nurturing poets as diverse as Jack Spicer, Robert Duncan, Ron Silliman, A. R. Ammons, Allen Ginsberg, Denise Levertov, Robin Magowan, Arthur Sze, and, ever gratefully, me; see *Women of the Beat Generation*, 39–45.

58. I thank Julie Brower in the Literature Department of the University of California at Santa Cruz for this reference to this post-Beat poet of Franciscan integrity and global vision. She and Mary Korte stand for this "genius loci" of place (like Everson, who taught large-sized courses on "the vocation of the Poet" at Porter College in UC Santa Cruz from 1971 to 1982), serving as a force of Northern California post-Beat poetics for me, what Jack Kerouac called in post-Catholic terms his on-the-road quest for Beat, beaten down, and beatific "beatitude." See *Women of the Beat Generation*, 257–267.

59. Newman's impact on writers like Muriel Spark, Edith Sitwell, G. K. Chesterton, and Graham Greene and the turn from modes of secular modernity to Roman Catholicism in twentieth-century Britain is elaborated on in Joseph Pearce, *Literary Converts: Spiritual Inspiration in an Age of Unbelief* (San Francisco: Ignatius Press, 2006), 293ff. See also Charles Taylor, *A Secular Age,* chapter 20; and Paul Elie, *The Life You Save May Be Your Own: An American Pilgrimage* (New York: Farrar, Straus, and Giroux, 2003), on Thomas Merton, Dorothy Day, Flannery O'Connor, and Walker Percy as exemplary converts ("pilgrims") within American modernity.

60. Harold Bloom, "The Gospel of Thomas," in *Where Shall Wisdom Be Found?* (New York: Riverhead Books, 2004), 259.

61. Bloom, *Jesus and Yahweh,* 5. "Yeshua of Nazareth," in Bloom's vision of Christianity's post-Judaic "revisionary warfare against Moses" (82) and God-the-Father Yahweh, all but disappears into affirmation as Godhead in the son, whereby late becomes early and the monotheistic precursors of this Messiah are sublated into "law" and "form" and dead-letter ritual. These revisionary ratios are taken to plural extremes in the conversionary designs

of American Protestantism, Mormonism, and Baptist salvationism and so on, acting out this transmutation. New Testament writing is seen as a "Belated Covenant" (11) making the world "new," from Saint Paul to the church fathers et al., thus overcoming indebtedness, law, anxiety, and guilt through "polytheistic" affirmations of grace and Holy Spirit. These latter-day gospels overcome precedents by sublating charismatic "prophets," like Jeremiah or David, into prefigurative announcements of the Messiah. Bloom's much-admired Yeshua-become-Jesus fulfills the laws of Jehovah; in a phrasing Bob Dylan might admire, Jesus thus "remains the Jew-of-Jews" (13) and becomes in act, text, and embodiment "the greatest of Jewish geniuses" (26).

62. Dylan, "Precious Angel," in *Lyrics, 1962–2002,* 403.

63. Doug Zachary, biographical statement in Maxine Hong Kingston, ed., *Veterans of War, Veterans of Peace* (Kihei, HI: Koa Books, 2006), 598.

64. Michael Denning elaborates on these democratic-populist values as comprising an American "substitutive counter-concept," circulating in the leftist populism of Steinbeck, Guthrie, and Leon Samson as opposed to any state-styled "socialism," in *The Cultural Front* (New York: Verso, 1996), 431. (Pete Seeger would be a latter-day figure of this left-leaning populism, as would Bruce Springsteen in our own era of American Empire protest and counter-community.)

65. Bloom, *Where Shall Wisdom Be Found?,* 268.

66. Bloom, *Jesus and Yahweh,* 11.

67. Ibid., 82–85: a reading of the Gospel of John as a work of literary agonistics overcoming claims of Moses and Abraham to originality, redemptive priority, and textual authority, as done in New Testament revisions of Judaic law, sin, and death by the rebirth patterns in Saint Paul. Stressing the power of *works,* the Gospel of James becomes the most authentically Judaic text in Bloom's New Testament overreading.

68. For a wonderful portrait of the life and poetics of King David as a kind of *Sopranos* figure from Jewish New Jersey, see Robert Pinsky, *The Life of David* (New York: Schocken, 2005): "a superman, if that term includes super-concentrated human failings" (179).

69. For more on these configurations, see Chapter 6, on Dylan's multiple conversions and trickster-like masking, a process that rises to a higher level in *Modern Times* (2006), which came out to charges of plagiarism in the pages of Empire's daily bulletin, *The Wall Street Journal.*

70. Nathaniel Mackey, "Other: From Noun to Verb," in *Discrepant Engagement: Dissonance, Cross-Culturality, and Experimental Writing* (Tuscaloosa: University of Alabama Press, 2000), 275.

71. T. S. Eliot, "Choruses from 'The Rock,'" in *Selected Poems* (San Diego: Harcourt Brace, 1958), 120.

72. Eliot, "Choruses from 'The Rock,'" 113.

73. On Eliot's conversion as a mode of cultural conservation and high-church centralism in England, in the context of myriad antimodern Catholic conversions, see Joseph Pearce, *Literary Converts: Spiritual Inspiration in an Age*

of Unbelief (San Francisco: Ignatius Press, 2006), 263–266. This Anglo-Catholic turn of "conversion" away from countercultural forces of liberal modernity is memorably registered in Malcolm Muggeridge, *Conversion: A Spiritual Journey* (London: Collins, 1988); on the contemporary turn rightward away from modes of postmodern relativism and tacit nihilism toward renewed orthodoxy, see Colleen Caroll, *The New Faithful: Why Young Adults Are Embracing Christian Orthodoxy* (Chicago: Loyola Press, 2004).

74. While the left-leaning journalist Oriana Fallaci and Pope Benedict XVI would disagree on many a cultural and political position in Italy, Europe, and the world, they share in their public pronouncements the conviction that Islam has become the main source of "holy war" *(jihad)* driving the religiously motivated violence and conversions to terrorism across the Middle East. In the Pope's case, this view has been challenged in many sites of the Muslim ecumene erupting in furor over the pope's invocation (at an address concerning violence, faith, and unreason at the University of Regensberg on Sept. 12, 2006) of an "erudite" Byzantine Christian emperor who contended, "Show me just what Muhammad brought that was new, and there you will find things only evil and inhuman, such as his command to spread by the sword the faith he preached."

75. This neutralization of resistance and what I am calling the languages of "counterconversion" takes place in modernizing Japan with the coming of the Asian and Pacific War: see Masao Miyoshi, *Off Center: Power and Culture Relations between Japan and the United States* (Cambridge, MA: Harvard University Press, 1991), 20. In the postwar period of increased democracy and more fully elaborated selfhood, Miyoshi also sees "an ironic repeat performance of conversion" to forms of state and corporate collectivism (21). On "reconversion" policies of the Hindu right directed against Indian Muslims during the globalization tensions of the 1980s, see Arjun Appadurai, *Fear of Small Numbers: An Essay on the Geography of Anger* (Durham, NC: Duke University Press, 2006), who connects such state-managed conversions to a will to ethnonational "purity" and completion (70–71).

76. Emulating their Protestant mentors from the United States, South Korea now has an estimated twelve thousand Christian missionaries abroad, the world's second largest source of Christian missionaries after the United States; and these aggressively evangelistic formations are coming into contact with hostile resistance in Muslim-dominated sites like Afghanistan: see Choe Sang-Hun, "Taliban Seize Members of South Korean Church," *International Herald Tribune,* July 20, 2007, online edition (accessed July 20, 2007).

77. This is based on a declaration of the United Nation Commission on Human Rights, drafted by the International Covenant on Civil and Religious Rights and propagated as a legally binding treaty. On the rise of such "minority" rights, see Appadurai, *Fear of Small Numbers,* 64–65.

78. Bob Dylan, *Lyrics,* 232.

79. Robert Hass, "Regalia for a Black Hat Dancer," in *Sun under Wood* (New York: Ecco Press, 1996), 58, describes a U.S. quest romance framed (in Ko-

rean temple-space and market) around twin "emptinesses—/ one is desire, another is the object it doesn't have" (50).

80. William Burroughs, letter of Jan. 23, 1957, *Letters of William S. Burroughs: 1945 to 1959,* ed. Oliver Harris (New York: Pan Macmillan, 1994), 349–350.

81. On this post-Beat reimagining of transpacific regionality and linkages to Buddhist beliefs, see Timothy Gray, *Gary Snyder and the Pacific Rim: Creating Counter-Cultural Community* (Iowa City: University of Iowa Press, 2006); and Josephine Nock-Hee Park, *Apparitions of Asia: Modernist Form and Asian American Poetics* (New York: Oxford University Press, 2007), who discusses Ezra Pound's "conversion to Confucianism" and Italian fascism during World War II, as well as Gary Snyder's later countercultural turn to Zen Buddhism, watersheds, ocean commons, Han Shan as beat guru, and the wilderness ecologies of the Pacific Rim.

1. The Poetics and Politics of Henry 'Ōpūkaha'ia's Conversion

1. Martha Beckwith, *Hawaiian Mythology* (Honolulu: University of Hawai'i Press, 1976), 85; William S. Chillingworth, "Requiem," *'iwi* 1 (Dec. 1998): 146; Edwin W. Dwight, *Memoirs of Henry Obookiah* (Honolulu: Woman's Board of Missions for the Pacific Islands, 1990), 33.

2. Edith H. Wolfe, "Introduction," in *Memoirs of Henry Obookiah,* ix–x. Hereafter cited parenthetically as *Memoirs.*

3. Samuel M. Kamakau, *Ruling Chiefs of Hawai'i,* rev. ed. (Honolulu: Kamehameha Schools Press, 1992), 246.

4. Kamakau, "Roman Catholicism in Hawai'i," in *Ruling Chiefs of Hawai'i,* 324. Entry from the Hawaiian newspaper *Ke Au 'Okua,* Mar. 18, 1869.

5. For a discussion of broader American-pragmatic dimensions of this conversion and counterconversion dynamic, see Chapters 3 and 4.

6. See Albert J. Schutz, *The Voices of Eden: A History of Hawaiian Language Studies* (Honolulu: University of Hawai'i Press, 1994), 256. Hereafter cited parenthetically as *Voices.*

7. These dynamics of outer-national becoming and cross-cultural translation will be discussed more fully in Chapter 2.

8. Mary Kawena Pukui, *Ōlelo No'eau: Hawaiian Proverbs & Poetical Sayings* (Honolulu: Bishop Museum, 1983), 180, proverb 1673.

9. This trope of "priest to priest" is not my contemporary anachronism: Christian-derived terms such as "curate," "pastor," and "bishop" were used by the narrators of Captain Cook's expeditions (e.g., John Ledyard) to describe Polynesian "kahunas" as "priests." See also Gananath Obeyesekere, *The Apotheosis of Captain Cook: European Mythmaking in the Pacific* (Princeton, NJ: Princeton University Press, 1992), 162. When Cook met the Lono-priest Koah on his fatal visit to Kealakekua Bay during the Makahiki ceremonies, for example, he wrote, "we soon found he [Tou-ah-ah] belonged to the Church, he introduced himself with much ceremony, in the course of which he presented me with a small pig, two coconuts, and a piece of red cloth which he wrapped round me." See journal entry for Jan. 17,

1779, in *The Journals of Captain Cook,* ed. Philip Edwards (London: Penguin, 1999), 605.

10. See Noenoe K. Silva, on these discrepancies of translation from Hawaiian to English in contexts of Anglo-global conversion and modern governmentality, *Aloha Betrayed: Native Hawaiian Resistance to American Colonialism* (Durham, NC: Duke University Press, 2004), 32–37.

11. Gavin Daws, *Shoal of Time: A History of the Hawaiian Islands* (Honolulu: University of Hawai'i Press, 1974), 104. Hereafter cited parenthetically as *Shoal.*

12. Also see the vernacular usages of "kanaka" for all Pacific natives in Herman Melville's *Typee: A Peep at Polynesian Life* (1846) (London: Penguin, 1972). For example, Karakoee is an "Oahu Kannaka" sailor who speaks "broken English" and is so crafty, cosmopolitical, and powerful ("tabooed") in the Marquesas that he helps to negotiate the captive American sailor Tommo's release from "captivity" to an Australian vessel (*Typee,* 328–333).

13. Joseph Puna Balaz, *Dats How Dem: Pidgin Poems and Stories* (forthcoming); this poem was earlier published in '*Oiwi: A Native Hawaiian Journal* 3 (2003).

14. Charles Nordhoff, *Nordhoff's West Coast: California, Oregon, Hawai'i* (London: KPI, 1987), 23. Further references will occur parenthetically.

15. On Twain's pro-plantation journalism on Hawai'i as linked to California, see Rob Wilson, "Exporting Christian Transcendentalism, Importing Hawaiian Sugar: The Trans-Americanization of Hawai'i," *American Literature* 72 (2000): 521–552.

16. A different way of situating this contemporary Hawaiian literature would be the framework of "Oceania" as elaborated in Paul Lyons, *American Pacificism: Oceania in the U.S. Imagination* (London: Routledge, 2005), who challenges A. Grove Day's liberalist project, Bamboo Ridge settler multiculturalism, and the nationalizing telos of any "American Pacific" as such.

17. Marshall Sahlins, *How "Natives" Think: About Captain Cook, for Example* (Chicago: University of Chicago Press, 1995), 87.

18. Quoted in Ibid., 87. By a twist of literary fate that shaped later images of the Pacific, Charles Nordhoff's grandson, Charles Bernard Nordhoff (1887–1947), would go on to become the coauthor (with James Hall) of *Mutiny on the Bounty* (1932). The trilogy based around the rivalry of Captain Bligh and Fletcher Christian became *the* blockbuster romance of the Pacific for millions of readers and moviegoers, from the 1930s through the 1960s, and helped project an image of British sovereignty, grandeur, and legitimacy across the Pacific. See Greg Dening, *Mr. Bligh's Bad Language: Passion, Power, and Theater on the Bounty* (Cambridge: Cambridge University Press, 1992), 339–367. I would claim that Bligh's fable of mutiny ruled until the Hollywood musical of American cross-cultural romance, *South Pacific,* took postwar global sway.

19. Owen Chase, *Shipwreck of the Whaleship "Essex"* () (New York: Lyons Press, 1999), 4.

20. Hawaiians have a mocking expression for a native who mimics foreign ways of whites instead of appreciating the knowledge and food (ways) of their own culture: "He Hawai'i 'uwala Kahiki," meaning "an Irish-potato Hawaiian" (see Mary Kawena Pukui, Ōlelo No'eau, 66, no. 570).

21. See Deborah Lee and Antonio Salas, eds., Unfaithing U.S. Colonialism (Berkeley: Dharma Cloud Publishers, 1999).

22. See Hattori's poem in Ibid., 10.

23. See Chapter 4 for more on these postcolonial dynamics in Epeli Hau'ofa's post-Christian work, for example.

24. See Dana Takagi, "Forget Postcolonialism: Sovereignty and Self-Determination in Hawai'i," ColorLines 2 (1999): 6; and Dana Takagi, "The Selling of Statehood in Hawai'i: Interview with Marion Kelly," ColorLines 1 (1998).

25. On re-nativizing tactics across the postcolonial Pacific, see James Clifford, "Indigenous Articulations," in The Worlding Project: Doing Cultural Studies in the Era of Globalization, ed. Rob Wilson and Christopher Leigh Connery (Berkeley: North Atlantic/New Pacific Press, 2007), 13–36.

26. See Kyle Miura and Jon Leong, "Reconciliation and Healing from U.S. Colonialism in Hawai'i," in Unfaithing U.S. Colonialism, 46.

27. See Brij LaV. Lal and Kate Fortune, eds., The Pacific Islands: An Encyclopedia (Honolulu: University of Hawai'i Press, 2000), 305.

28. An American missionary tract from 1818 written by two ministers to Bombay, Gordon Hall and Samuel Newell, carries the expansionist title The Conversion of the World: or the Claims of Six Hundred Millions and the Ability and Duties of the Churches Respecting Them. See Mary Zwiep, Pilgrim Path: The First Company of Women Missionaries in Hawai'i (Madison: University of Wisconsin Press, 1991), 13I. If English missionary efforts reigned into colonial reaches of India, Ceylon, and Tahiti, Americans in the Pacific knew that the British civilization project had been challenged and all but demonized by the death of Cook in Hawai'i. On Tahiti considered as the London Missionary Society's "most promising" nation to launch conversion in the Pacific from 1797 to 1840, see Rod Edmond, Representing the South Pacific: Colonial Discourse from Cook to Gauguin (Cambridge: Cambridge University Press, 1997), 226.

29. James Clifford, Person and Myth: Maurice Leenhardt in the Melanesian World (Durham, NC: Duke University Press, 1992), 3.

30. Hiram A. Bingham, excerpts from A Residence of Twenty-One Years in the Sandwich Islands, in A Hawaiian Anthology, ed. Gerrit P. Judd (New York: Macmillan, 1967), 22 and 26.

31. See Sally Engle Merry, Colonizing Hawai'i: The Cultural Power of Law (Princeton, NJ: Princeton University Press, 2000), which deals with Anglo-American law codes in the years 1820–1852, especially given modes of Western governmentality under the republicanizing rule of Kamehameha III.

32. Bingham, who became the unofficial leader of the pioneering mission to Hawai'i, recorded his abjecting impressions of native subjectivity, drives to sinfulness, and polytheism, in A Residence of Twenty-One Years in the

Sandwich Islands (1847), after he left Hawai'i in 1840 due to his wife Sybil's illness with consumption (see Zwiep, *Pilgrim Path*, 298–304), never to return. His globe-trotting offspring, Hiram Bingham, a professor of archaeology at Yale, who seems to have sprung not just from American missionary conviction to the global South but from *Raiders of the Lost Ark*, would claim to "discover Machu Piccu" for American science and ethnography in 1911, with native Peruvians (invisibly) right there: see Neil Smith, *American Empire: Roosevelt's Geographer and the Prelude to Globalization* (Berkeley: University of California Press, 2004), 76–78. The earlier Bingham *saw the natives* but as children of lesser gods, who needed to be "saved" from their original sin and (king or no king) from myriad forms of adultery.

33. See Klaus Newmann on experimental modes of retelling Pacific colonial history: "Starting from Trash," in *Remembrance of Pacific Pasts: An Invitation to Remake History,* ed. Robert Borofsky (Honolulu: University of Hawai'i Press, 2000), 73.

34. On messy, residual modes of articulating "indigeneity" in the Pacific, see also James Clifford, "Taking Identity Politics Seriously: 'The Contradictory, Stony Ground . . . ' " in *Without Guarantees: Essays in Honor of Stuart Hall,* ed. Paul Gilroy, Lawrence Grossberg, and Angela McRobbie (London, Verso, 2000), 94–112.

35. On modes of sacralizing hagiography, contagion by alterity, and fits of drunken excess haunting African ethnography and social science at the edges of the system-making, see Johannes Fabian, *Out of Our Minds: Reason and Madness in the Exploration of Central Africa* (Berkeley: University of California Press, 2000).

36. See Slavoj Žižek, *The Fragile Absolute* (London: Verso, 2000), 121 and 130.

37. Melville, *Typee,* 266–267. Further references will occur parenthetically.

38. The first editions of the *Memoirs* listed no author's name, ascribing the copyrighting of the text to the Reverends Lyman Beecher and Joseph Harvey and suggesting (by elision of white authorship) that the text was written by Obookiah as ex-native memoir. Later editions were rightly credited to the Reverend W. W. Dwight, first instructor of the Foreign Mission School (*Memoirs,* 96, 98).

39. Gauri Viswanathan, *Outside the Fold: Conversion, Modernity, and Belief* (Princeton, NJ: Princeton University Press, 1998), xvii.

40. On this quest to recuperate indigenous knowledge-modes and methods, in genres of epistemic representation from literature and history to social science, see the Maori-based critique by Linda Tuhiawai Smith, *Decolonizing Methodologies: Research and Indigenous Peoples* (London: Zed Books, 1999). For more dialogical Western approaches to Pacific history-making, gender constructions, and aesthetics, see also Anne Salmond, *The Trial of the Cannibal Dog: The Remarkable Story of Captain's Cook's Encounters in the South Seas* (New Haven, CT: Yale University Press, 2003); and Patty O'Brien, *The Pacific Muse: Exotic Femininity and the Colonial Pacific* (Seattle: University of Washington Press, 2006).

41. On Henry's "celebrity because of his conversion to Christianity," see the Americanizing telos of conversion as elaborated in Gerrit P. Judd, *Hawaii: An Informal History* (New York: Collier, 1961), 42.

42. See Jeffrey K. Lyons, "*Memoirs of Henry Obookiah:* A Rhetorical History," *Journal of Hawaiian History* 38 (2004): 35–57.

43. Nicholas Thomas, "Colonial Conversions: Difference, Hierarchy, and History in Early Twentieth Century Evangelical Propaganda," in *Remembrance of Pacific Pasts,* 246.

44. Viswanathan, *Outside the Fold,* 3.

45. See Nicholas Thomas, *Colonialism's Culture: Anthropology, Travel, and Government* (Princeton, NJ: Princeton University Press, 1994), 190.

46. Margaret Fuller shared Melville's skepticism toward the missionary work of conversion in the Pacific of the 1840s and (in a review of *Typee* in 1846) urged ladies' sewing societies outfitting American foreign missionaries to read *Typee* "while assembled at their work." See Ann Douglas, *The Feminization of American Culture* (New York: Avon, 1977), 125 and 139.

47. As Stephen Greenblatt contends in *Marvelous Possessions: The Wonder of the New World* (Chicago: University of Chicago Press, 1991), "Christian universalism—the conviction that its principal symbols and narratives are suitable to the entire population of the world—commits it to the unconstrained circulation of its mimetic capital" (186, fn. 2). Such mimetic technologies generate "engaged representations," relational and contingent upon historical usage (12), and can lead both to the appropriative dynamics of colonization and to countereffects of "marvelous dispossession" (150).

48. Schutz, *Voices of Eden,* 94.

49. See Helen Geracimos Chapin, *Shaping History: The Role of Newspapers in Hawai'i* (Honolulu: University of Hawai'i Press, 1996), 5.

50. On the subjective new beginning and deracialized community formed through grace above law, see Alain Badiou, *Saint Paul: The Foundation of Universalism,* trans. Ray Bassier (Stanford, CA: Stanford University Press, 2003), 77.

51. As Maurice Leenhardt learned from immersion inside discrepancies of cross-cultural translation and the world-transforming poetics of place-based conversion, "Ethnology was essential to the comprehension of cultural-spiritual change and could make Christianization less authoritarian, more a part of the reciprocal interaction of texts" (see Clifford, *Person and Myth,* 107). As Clifford shows, Leenhardt sought a nonconquest mode of conversion and writing ethnology, in the process scaling back and transforming French overseas colonialism (77). On divergent cross-cultural translations of "conversion" and sacred rituals and things in contemporary global-local contexts, see also Fenella Cannell. ed., *The Anthropology of Christianity* (Durham, NC: Duke University Press, 2006).

52. See Paul De Man's "de-canonizing" theorization of Walter Benjamin's theory of translation, in *The Resistance to Theory,* ed. Wlad Godzich (Minneapolis: University of Minnesota Press, 1986), 83–97, 97.

53. On tactics of cross-cultural translation and tactics of pidginization, see Yunte Huang, *Transpacific Displacements: Intertextual Travel in Twentieth-Century American Literature* (Berkeley: University of California Press, 2002), 115–137. On "mediation" as a translational discrepancy in diasporic contexts of postcolonial belonging, see Radha Radhakrishnan, *Diasporic Mediations: Between Home and Location* (Minneapolis: University of Minnesota Press, 1996).

54. Obeyesekere, *Apotheosis of Captain Cook,* 73.

55. This and related passages are discussed in a cross-cultural framework of mutual miscomprehension by Obeyesekere, *Apotheosis of Captain Cook,* 72.

56. Here I am troping upon what Rey Chow calls "the unbearable lightness of postcolonial, postmodern ethnicity," which has replaced what she calls the Weber-like mandate to become a form of protesting, racialized labor in the global system of U.S. capital. See *The Protestant Ethnic and the Spirit of Capitalism* (New York: Columbia University Press, 2002), 191.

57. On recurring Christian revivals in Hawai'i, see Arrell Morgan Gibson, *Yankees in Paradise: The Pacific Basin Frontier* (Albuquerque: University of New Mexico Press, 1993), 274–275; and Daws, *Shoal,* 99–102.

58. Titus Coan, *Life in Hawaii: An Autobiographical Sketch (1835-1881)* (New York: Anderson D. F. Randolph, 1882), 50.

59. Dibble is discussed in Rob Wilson, *Reimagining the American Pacific: From South Pacific to Bamboo Ridge* (Durham, NC: Duke University Press, 2000), 193.

60. I thank Katharine Norwood for calling my attention to her missionary-ancestor's text and pondering its obsessive work-regime and racialized and gendered patterns of spatial segregation with me: see *The Journals of Cochran Forbes, Missionary to Hawai'i 1831–1864* (Honolulu: Hawai'i Mission Children's Society, 1984), 65, 158.

61. The *Empress of China* reached Macao and Canton after a six-month voyage from New York in 1784 and opened the American Pacific to commerce. See Samuel Eliot Morison, *The Maritime History of Massachusetts, 1783–1860* (Boston: Houghton Mifflin, 1961), 45. The first ships from America to China contained the valuable cargo of ginseng from the hills of Massachusetts or the Midwest (see Morison, *Maritime History,* 44). See also Andrew C. Kimmens, ed., *Tales of the Ginseng* (New York: William Morrow, 1975), 60, 197. Chinese demand shifted to extraction cargo like Hawaiian sandalwood and Oregon seal furs, with huge ecological impacts. Hawaiian sailors and the national economy were involved in these global transpacific exchanges.

62. See Tom Koppel, *Kanaka: The Untold Story of Hawaiian Pioneers in British Columbia and the Pacific Northwest* (Vancouver, BC: Whitecap Books, 1995); on this Hawaiian diaspora, also see work on Hawaiians in the Pacific Northwest and on Hawaiians working in leather tanning along the California coast in 1840 as portrayed in Richard Henry Dana's *Two Years before the Mast* (New York: Penguin, 1986), 202–230. Such Kanaka seaman "often received new names and went through other initiations (like the rites of Nep-

tune when they first crossed the equator," as did the common sailor Obookiah (David A. Chappell, "Diaspora," in *The Pacific Islands: An Encyclopedia,* 109).

63. Morison, *Maritime History* 1, 43–44.

64. Hiram A. Bingham, excerpts from *A Residence of Twenty-One Years in the Sandwich Islands,* in *A Hawaiian Anthology,* 23–24.

65. See Zwiep, *Pilgrim Path,* 13.

66. On extranational multiculturalism and divergent uses of the Puritan ethos of self-disciplined "restraint," see the following innovative works in cultural studies by C. L. R. James: *Mariners, Renegades, and Castaways: The Story of Herman Melville and the World We Live in* (Hanover, NH: University Press of New England, 2001); and *Beyond a Boundary* (Durham, NC: Duke University Press, 1993).

67. "The Far East seemed closer to Salem than to any other American town when Ernest Fenollosa was born there in 1853," as Van Wyck Brooks writes in his biography of the great American orientalist and co-inventor of Imagism, in *Fenollosa and His Circle* (1962); quoted in Huang (*Transpacific Displacements,* 27), who foregrounds the process of "transpacific displacement" by which meanings fed back and across the Pacific and led to modes of linguistic mimicry, ontological affinity, and transcultural transformation.

68. In another transhistorical Puritan connection worthy of Thomas Pynchon, the main biography of Elihu Yale is written by the namesake, grandson, and heir to the Hawaiian missionaries from New England: see Hiram Bingham, *Elihu Yale: The American Nabob of Queen Square* (New York: Dodd, Mead, 1939). Gauri Viswanathan discusses this as a belated work of imperial "hagiography," in "The Naming of Yale College: British Imperialism and American Higher Education," in *Cultures of United States Imperialism,* ed. Donald Pease and Amy Kaplan (Durham, NC: Duke University Press, 1993), 102. Viswanathan shows that Yale's fortune is tied to its Asia/Pacific outreach for capital and souls, linking India to New Haven and London.

69. See Paul Gilroy, *Against Race* (Cambridge, MA: Harvard University Press, 2000), 122–123.

70. A "*pahoa* [is a] short dagger, sharp stone especially as used for a weapon, stone battle-axe": see Mary Kawena Pukui and Samuel H. Elbert, *Hawaiian Dictionary* (Honolulu: University of Hawai'i Press, 1986), 300.

71. See Newmann, "Starting from Trash," 72.

72. See Pukui, *Ōlelo Noʻeau,* 30, proverb of Kupanea's quest for new life.

73. For this post-Puritan dynamic, see Chapter 2.

74. See Sahlins, *How "Natives" Think,* 67–68, 133–134, on the demotion of Lono priests; on clashing Hawaiian genealogies in the Kū versus Lono lineages, see 256–263.

75. On "hanai" practices of adoption common to Hawaiian culture, see Mary Kawena Pukui, E. W. Haertig, and Catherine A. Lee, *Nānā I Ke Kumu* [Look to the Source], vol. 2 (Honolulu: Hui Hanai, 1972), 36.

76. Stephen L. Desha, *Kamehameha and His Warrior Kekuhaupi'o* (Honolulu: Kamehameha Schools Press, 2000), 450. Translated from the Hawaiian by Frances N. Frazier. Further references will occur parenthetically.

77. See Gibson, *Yankees in Paradise*, 277. The scholarly labor and cultural translation did continue: Hiram Bingham Jr. (1831–1908) served as a missionary in Micronesia and translated the Bible into Gilbertese. See Lauru Piercy, *Hawai'i Truth Stranger Than Fiction* (Honolulu: Mutual Publishing, 1985), 113.

78. See Etienne Balibar and Immanuel Wallerstein, "Is There a 'Neo-Racism'?" in *Race, Nation, Class: Ambiguous Identities* (London: Verso, 1991), 18.

79. Ibid., 21.

80. Thurston Twigg-Smith, *Hawaiian Sovereignty: Do the Facts Matter?* (Honolulu: Goodale, 1998), 28. Twigg-Smith is writing an updated pro-missionary history and claims (23) that Albertine Loomis gives "the most complete and accurate" chronicle of Henry Obookiah's life. See Loomis's fictionalized account of the American missionary presence, *Grapes of Canaan: Hawai'i 1820* (Honolulu: Hawai'i Mission Children's Society, 1969), 11–25.

81. Asia and Pacific were conjoined peripheries in the missionary geography of New England: at Bradford Academy, for example, Henry had boarded with the family of Deacon Hasseltine and the family of Reverend and Mrs. Adoniram Judson, who were the first missionaries sent out by the ABCFM in 1812. The Judsons (assigned to do missionary work in Burma) yet became Baptists en route to India and severed their ties with the ABCFM (*Memoirs*, 102). This was a version of what I will be calling *counter-conversion* and *deconversion* (see Chapters 2 and 3).

82. Timothy Dwight (1752–1817), grandson of the influential writer of the Massachusetts conversion experience, Jonathan Edwards, was also one of the Connecticut Wit poets, whose poem "Greenfield Hill" (1794) conveys an impression of Connecticut as a prosperous pastoral theocracy of republican virtue. Dwight was president of Yale from 1795 to 1817 and helped to install a modern curriculum and strict theology at the college. Given such familial examples, it is no wonder that Henry was admired for "dili[gence] in his literary studies" (*Memoirs*, 69), at a time when the languages of poetry and theology often merged into the same study. (I call this "theopoetics.")

83. Thomas, "Colonial Conversions," 244.

84. On the disavowal of sameness through the colonial production of such fetishized stereotypes as "lazy native" and "savage," see Homi K. Bhabha, *The Location of Culture* (London: Routledge, 1994), 66–122.

85. On tactics of mimesis and contact with "forces of alterity" that serve to challenge colonial relationships, see the cross-cultural claims for power sharing and reversing in Michael Taussig, *Mimesis and Alterity: A Particular History of the Senses* (New York: Routledge, 1993), 68. Taussig makes "mimesis" mean not just representation but *contact* with the sacredness and life-force of the other, a use that fits the mimicry powers of Henry 'Ōpūkaha'ia.

86. Fabian, *Out of Our Minds*, xii.

87. Sahlins, in *How "Natives" Think*, uses this term as scholarly rebuke for the way Gananath Obeyesekere's *The Apotheosis of Captain Cook* "turns Hawai-

ian history into pidgin anthropology" and reduces Hawaiians into agents of "universal empirical rationality" in their transactions with Captain Cook (14–15). As I use the term here, Henry's "pidgin anthropology" results from his using native thinking in comparative contexts of cultural give-and-take and informancy to explain New England to Hawai'i and vice versa.

88. Greenblatt, *Marvelous Possessions*, 104.
89. Chapin, *Shaping History*, 16.

2. "Henry, Torn from the Stomach"

1. W. S. Merwin, *The Rain in the Trees* (New York: Knopf, 1988), 62.
2. Vico is translating the language and naturalized mythologies of "indigenous" Greco-Roman history as seen (in his early-modern era) in space and time, by cultivating "two eyes, poetic chronology and poetic geography"; *New Science: Principles of the New Science Concerning the Common Nature of Nations*, trans. David Marsh (London: Penguin, 1999), 225, 338. I benefit from Paul Bové's readings of Vico's *On the Study Methods of Our Times* as a critical methodology opposed to knowledge forms in the humanities or sciences that would ratify terms and values of Empire: the critique and historicization of tropes and beliefs becomes crucial.
3. John D. Barbour, *Versions of Deconversion: Autobiography and the Loss of Faith* (Charlottesville: University of Virginia Press, 1994), 22. On the uncertainty in Puritan conversion and the need for public testimony of a "turn" toward repentance and grace, as evinced in the fifty-one "confessions" recorded between 1637 and 1645 by Shepard from members of his own Cambridge congregation, see Patricia Caldwell, *The Puritan Conversion Narrative: The Beginnings of American Expression* (Cambridge: Cambridge University Press, 1985), 66–80.
4. Kenneth Burke, "Verbal Action in St. Augustine's Confessions," in *The Rhetoric of Religion: Studies in Logology* (Berkeley: University of California Press, 1997), 63 and 77.
5. Ibid., 63.
6. Bob Dylan captured this "returning" power of conversion, in stark lineations of *John Wesley Harding* (1968): "I dreamed I saw Saint Augustine last night / Alive as you or me / Tearing through these quarters / In the utmost misery . . . Searching for the very souls / whom already have been sold." See *Lyrics: 1962–2001* (New York: Simon & Schuster, 2004), 223. See also Chapter 6.
7. William James, "Conversion," lecture IX, in *The Varieties of Religious Experience* (New York: Penguin, 1985), 209.
8. James, *Varieties of Religious Experience*, 177. See also Edwin Diller Starbuck, *The Psychology of Religion: An Empiricist Study of the Growth of Religious Consciousness* (New York: Scribner's, 1899), wherein he tracks a process of "unselfing" that can lead toward a "new worth of the self" after conversion (134).
9. James, *Varieties of Religious Experience*, 175–176. See Barbour, *Versions of Deconversion*, 73–74.

10. See David Hempton, "Reconversion: A Fresh Look at Faith and Doubt," *Christianity Today* 13 (July–August 2007): 9, on this "crisis of doubt" and turn away from "secularism."

11. This is further elaborated in Chapter 3, which explores the semiotics of conversion.

12. See the preface to this work of co-translated songs and sayings from traditional Mohawk and Samoan cultures, James Thomas Stevens and Caroline Sinavaina, *Mohawk/Samoa: Transmigrations* (Oakland, CA: subpress collective, 2005), 9: canoes, bark patterns, food stuffs, baskets, drums, birds, and funeral songs fly across original sites as meanings "transmigrate" across contexts and eras, linking the Pacific Ocean and Niagara Falls sites to native mores and resurgences.

13. Edwin W. Dwight, *Memoirs of Henry Obookiah, A Native of Owhyhee, and a Member of the Foreign Mission School; Who Died at Cornwall, Connecticut February 17, 1818, Aged 26 Years,* ed. Edith Wolfe (Honolulu: Woman's Board of Missions for the Pacific Islands, 1990), 33. Hereafter cited in the text as *Memoirs*.

14. Milton Murayama, *Dying in a Strange Land* (Honolulu: University of Hawai'i Press, 2008), 145. The latest novel from this master of the Hawaiian Creole English idiom of pidgin, which recounts the death of the Oyama parents in Hawai'i and in California, is a novel of artistic self-formation registering how Murayama made himself into postcolonial novelist through residence and "apprenticeship" in New York City and San Francisco though he wrote of nothing else but Hawai'i.

15. Eastman's *From the Deep Woods to Civilization* (1916) is discussed in chapter 5, "Christianity and 'The White Man,' Religion,' " in Barbour, *Versions of Conversion,* 93ff.

16. See the reformulations of Pauline universality and "becoming subjective" through grace that shatters Judaic law and Greek logos and counters the empire of Roman—and American liberal—value domination elaborated by Alain Badiou, *Saint Paul: The Foundation of Universalism,* trans. Ray Brassier (Stanford, CA: Stanford University Press, 2003), 72.

17. Henry's uncle was "a high priest of the island," and "taught him long prayers, and trained him to the task of repeating them daily in the temple of the idol" (*Memoirs,* 2). His status and power were recognized by the man who murdered Henry's parents, who later let him stay with his uncle: "The man did say but little, because my uncle was a priest" (*Memoirs,* 4).

18. See Gananath Obeyesekere, *The Apotheosis of Captain Cook: European Mythmaking in the Pacific* (Princeton, NJ: Princeton University Press, 1962), 51.

19. See Gavin Daws, *Shoal of Time: A History of the Hawaiian Islands* (Honolulu: University of Hawai'i Press, 1974), 42–67, 72.

20. Mark Twain, *Letters from Hawaii,* ed. A Grove Day (Honolulu: University of Hawai'i Press, 1975), 215, 237. Twain wrote this report from the infamous Kealakekua Bay as a journalist for the Sacramento *Union.*

21. Twain, *Letters from Hawaii,* 238.

22. See David A. Chappell, *Double Ghosts: Oceanian Voyagers on Euroamerican Ships* (New York: M. E. Sharpe, 1998).

23. Mitchell Robert Breitwieser, *American Puritanism and the Defense of Mourning: Religion, Grief, and Ethnology in Mary White Rowlandson's Captivity Narrative* (Madison: University of Wisconsin Press, 1991), 179.

24. Ibid., 141.

25. Ralph Waldo Emerson, "The Conduct of Life" (1860), in *Emerson: Essays and Poems* (New York: Library of America, 1996), 883.

26. Ralph Waldo Emerson, "Power," in *Emerson: Essays and Poems,* 806.

27. Twain, *Letters from Hawaii,* 237.

28. Ibid., 53.

29. Ibid., 237–238.

30. James Michener, *Hawaii* (New York: Random House, 1959).

31. On the missionary project in Hawai'i, see also LaRue W. Piercy, *Hawaii's Missionary Saga: Sacrifice and Godliness in Paradise* (Honolulu: Mutual Publishing, 1992), 7.

32. Larue W. Piercy, *Hawaii Truth Stranger Than Fiction: The True Tales of Missionary Troubles and Triumphs Fictionized by Michener* (Honolulu: Mutual Publishing, 1985), 3–4.

33. On *catachresis* as "abuse" and purposeful misapplication of metaphor, see Richard A. Lanham, *A Handlist of Rhetorical Terms: A Guide for Students of English Literature* (Berkeley: University of California Press, 1969), 1 and 21.

34. To this day along the beaches of Waikiki, many a tourist takes Michener's book *Hawaii* more as literal history than as American settler myth or multicultural fantasy.

35. 'Ōpūkaha'ia's conviction of "aloha" (love) remains a crucial Hawaiian value to this day, despite tourist appropriations of this reciprocal and mana-laden spirit of person, kin, language, and place: see the amazing archive of Native Hawaiian wisdom and pedagogy on such values, Mary Kawena Pukui, ed., *Ōlelo No'eau: Hawaiian Proverbs and Poetical Sayings* (Honolulu: Bishop Museum, 1983), 45.

36. As suggested in the introduction, I would situate a postcolonial Christian figure of bicultural belonging (like Henry) as an outsider to the "dominion theology" of the U.S. right, as outlined in Michelle Goldberg, *Kingdom Coming: The Rise of the Christian Nationalism* (New York: Norton, 2007). In this study, I am linking conversion with the multiple affiliations emanating from below and migrant linkages attaching change to "the multitudes" against the "armed globalization" forces of Empire, as elaborated (with Pauline-cum-Marxist echoes) in Michael Hardt and Antonio Negri, *Multitude: War and Democracy in the Age of Empire* (New York: Penguin, 2004), 92–227.

37. *Memoirs of Henry Obookiah,* notes by Edith Woolf, 97.

38. There is an uncanny Hawaiian proverb that Mary Kawena Pukui and Samuel H. Elbert recount in their co-edited *Hawaiian Dictionary* (Honolulu: University of Hawai'i Press, 1986), 354: "Ua holo 'o Hanale, komo mai 'o Keoni Pulu," translated as "Henry is run off, John Bull has come in" (said when one is full—when hunger, which sounds like "Henry" is gone, but

when John Bull, which sounds like "full" has come in). See also Mary Kawena Pukui, Ōlelo Noʻeau: Hawaiian Proverbs and Poetical Sayings, 20, proverb number 162, which explains how hunger (Hanale) makes the fingers move to the mouth like one or two running horses (representing one or two fingers scooping poi).

39. This was done for the Hawaiian Sunday School but published by the American Tract Society of New York.

40. Albert J. Schutz, The Voices of Eden: A History of Hawaiian Language Studies (Honolulu: University of Hawaiʻi Press, 1994), fn. to p. 95.

41. See the poem appended to this study written by Rob Wilson, one of many poems written since ʻŌpūkahaʻia's death in his honor; see also, for example, one of the first poems on this tropical native conversion, "Hail! Isles of the South! your redemption proclaim" (Memoirs, 95). This hymn to Henry ʻŌpūkahaʻia went along with the Psalms, Ten Commandments, and Acts of the Apostles in early Hawaiian schools: see Samuel M. Kamakau, Ruling Chiefs of Hawaiʻi, rev. ed. (Honolulu: Kamehameha Schools Press, 1992), 270–271.

42. In contrast to Todorov's native-colonial encounter as one of monological technologies, I am ascribing the power of self-fashioning representation and writing to native converts in Hawaiʻi who seize and transform powers of poesis (verbal remaking and figuring-forth). See Tzvetan Todorov, The Conquest of America, trans. Richard Howard (New York: Harper, 1984), 156–159.

43. See Nicholas Thomas and Richard Eves on the uneven dynamics of "white nativism," native degeneracy, and narratives of failed enterprise in Bad Colonists: The South Seas Letters of Vernon Lee Walker and Louis Becke (Durham, NC: Duke University Press, 1999), 140–144.

44. Victoria Nalani Kneubuhl, Hawaiʻi Nei: Island Plays (Honolulu: University of Hawaii Press, 2002), 28. Further references will occur parenthetically.

45. Jack London, Tales of Hawaii, ed. A. Grove Day (Honolulu: Press Pacifica, 1964), 59.

46. Susanna Moore, I Myself Have Seen It: The Myth of Hawaiʻi (Washington, DC: National Geographic, 2003), 6. London's summary of American colonization is quoted on 97. Moore's chapter called "The Gentry" refers to the genealogy of this American novelist (whose works include the novels In the Cut and My Old Sweetheart) as a white-settler offspring (see 123–165).

47. On Melville's struggle with this Anglo-American discourse and captivity fantasy of native cannibalism in the post-contact Pacific, see Geoffrey Sanborn, The Sign of the Cannibal: Melville and the Making of a Postcolonial Reader (Durham, NC: Duke University Press, 1998), 4–6. On broader white mythologies and meanings of cannibalism across the Pacific, see Gananath Obeyesekere, Cannibal Talk: The Man-Eating Myth and Human Sacrifice in the South Seas (Berkeley: University of California Press, 2005).

48. For an emergent pedagogy of counter-American identity-formation applied to postcolonial Hawaiʻi, see Morris Young, Minor Re/Visions: Asian American Literacy Narratives as Rhetoric of Citizenship (Carbondale: Southern Illinois University Press, 2004).

49. Amitava Kumar, *Bombay London New York* (New York: Routledge, 2002), 179.

50. See Walter Benjamin, "The Task of the Translator," in *Illuminations*, trans. Harry Zohn (New York: Schocken, 1969), 71, a translation process upon which I am placing a "minority-becoming" stress in the Pacific.

51. Dennis Kawaharada, *Storied Landscapes: Hawaiian Literature and Place* (Honolulu: Kalamaku Press, 1999), 35.

52. Elias Canetti, "The Survivor in Primitive Belief," in *Crowds and Power*, trans. Linda Stewart (New York: Noonday Press, 1998), 251.

53. Simon During, *Secular Magic* (Cambridge, MA: Harvard University Press, 2002), 11.

54. Breitweiser, *American Puritanism*, 166; see also chapter 4, "The Strangers," on white/Indian mimesis and binary shifts of hospitality to hostility.

55. Kalani Akana, "Da 23rd Psalm," *Tinfish*, no. 14 (May 2004): 70.

56. Wallace Stevens, *The Palm at the End of the Mind: Selected Poems and a Play*, ed. Holly Stevens (New York: Vintage, 1990), 363.

57. Harold Bloom, *The American Religion: The Emergence of the Post-Christian Nation* (New York: Simon & Schuster, 1992), 32.

58. Philip Roth, "The Conversion of the Jews," in *Anthology of American Literature*, vol. 2, ed. George McMichael et al. (Upper Saddle River, NJ: Pearson, 2004), 1833.

59. Elizabeth M. Deloughrey's *Routes and Roots: Navigating Caribbean and Pacific Island Literatures* (Honolulu: University of Hawai'i Press, 2007) reads Wendt's *Black Rainbow* (1992) as a figuration of Maori urban indigeneity and links his narrative tactics of postmodernity to reflexive concerns with resistance and coalitional politics of indigeneity across scales of city, nation, land, and ocean. Such a thick-descriptive focus can bring out the many "postcolonial" contexts in which a profound Pacific novelist like Wendt reflects and refracts a whole range of discourses in his deft, uncanny English. See also Paul Sharrad, *Albert Wendt and Pacific Literature: Circling the Void* (Manchester, United Kingdom: Manchester University Press, 2003), on Wendt's proliferating vision of Pacific place, ocean, and peoples.

60. Epeli Hau'ofa, *Tales of the Tikongs* (Honolulu: University of Hawai'i Press, 1994), 92.

61. Paul Theroux, *Hotel Honolulu* (Boston: Houghton Mifflin, 2001), 373.

62. On states of religious feeling forming the basis of individuality and the "conversion experience" later hardening into more institutional modes as "religion," see Charles Taylor, *Varieties of Religion Today: William James Revisited* (Cambridge, MA: Harvard University Press, 2002), 7–19.

63. Frederick Exley, "The Nervous Light of Sunday," in *The Vintage Contemporaries Reader*, ed. Marty Asher (New York: Vintage, 1998), 18–19. In this displacement of American religious states into more secular and literary modes, Exley will later come to realize his own "sinfulness" by rereading American literature, specifically guilt-ridden novels of Hawthorne. As cure for this utter alienation from the ordinary, Exley awaits what he terms an

"Emersonian calling" as writer of American redemption: he wants to be re-born as a writer and is.

64. Exley, "The Nervous Light of Sunday," 13.

65. Albert Saijo, *OUTSPEAKS: A Rhapsody* (Honolulu: Bamboo Ridge Press, 1997), 109, 197.

66. See D. Mahealani Dudoit, "Carving a Hawaiian Aesthetic," *Ōʻiwi: A Native Hawaiian Journal* 1 (1998): 22, on the Hawaiian-centered evocation of past modes as a way of creating future culture, "going forward into the past." The transnational, translinguistic vision of a "mongrel" Pacific generated by writing across genres, cultures, bloods, and languages is sketched in Rob Wilson, *Pacific Postmodern: From the Sublime to the Devious* (Honolulu: Tinfish Works, 2000). See also Juliana Spahr, "Connected Disconnection and Localized Globalism in Pacific Multilingual Literature," *boundary 2* 31 (2004): 75–100; and Joan Retallack and Juliana Spahr, eds., *Poetry and Pedagogy: The Challenge of the Contemporary* (New York: Palgrave Macmillan, 2005), in which these "minor" experimental languages can effect changes in pedagogy in the Pacific, as in Morris Young, "Beyond Rainbows: What Hawaiʻi's 'Local' Poetry Has Taught Me about Pedagogy" (105–125).

67. Ralph Waldo Emerson, *Society and Solitude*, ed. Edward Waldo Emerson (Boston: Houghton Mifflin, 1904), 21.

68. Emerson, *Society*, 20.

69. Larzer Ziff, *Return Passages: Great American Travel Writing, 1788–1910* (New Haven, CT: Yale University Press, 2000), 5, 17–57; see also American travelers with "western" coastal or Asia-Pacific ties challenging orientalism, including Bayard Taylor, Richard Henry Dana, and Mark Twain.

70. On history "as done-to" Pacific islanders, whose creative agency is often over-looked in these "fatal contact" narratives of colonization-cum-Enlightenment, see David A. Chappell, "Active Agents versus Passive Victims: Decolonized Historiography or Problematic Paradigm," in *Voyaging through the Contemporary Pacific,* ed. David Hanlon and Geoffrey M. White (Lanham, MD: Rowman & Littlefield, 2000), 209.

71. At the ʻOnipaʻa [Steadfast] protest events, which drew some ten thousand people (including myself) marching in support of Hawaiian sovereignty, Trask (a brilliant poet-scholar and founding director of the Hawaiian Studies Center of the University of Hawaiʻi at Manoa) proclaimed in fiery terms from the stage, "I am not an American. We are not Americans. Say it in your heart. Say it in your sleep." She later polemically urged Hawaiians to abandon the Christian church (even as it was apologizing for its role in the overthrow of Queen Liliuokalani) because it teaches Hawaiians to be *nice:* "Don't make nice. Never make nice. Fight. Fight. Fight." See Stu Glauberman, "Onipaʻa Rites Kindle Warmth—and Bitterness," *Honolulu Advertiser,* Jan. 18, 1993, A1–A6.

72. My usage of "outer-national" reworks the diasporic transoceanic framework of Paul Gilroy, in *Against Race* (Cambridge, MA: Harvard University Press, 2000), 123. Also see Gilroy on the black American converts to born-again Christianity who had been taken from Africa as slaves but survived to be-

come writers, Phillis Wheatley and Olaudah Equiano (115–122). My focus throughout the making of the Pacific into "Oceania" will be on the forces, flows, and shapes of "transpacific" linkages between Hawai'i and New England as between (in Hau'ofa) Tonga and England as well as the Asia-Pacific.

73. Hugh Clark, "Pioneering Hawaiian Finally Coming Home," *Honolulu Star-Bulletin & Advertiser*, Feb. 14, 1993, A1–A2. In the same story, Henry's relatives claimed, innocently enough, that the August 7 observance at the 'Ōpūkaha'ia Memorial Chapel in Punalu'u was "unrelated to the centennial of the overthrow of the Hawaiian monarchy" (A1).

74. On the recalcitrant legacy of Christianity and its spectral returns into the materiality of the New Age multicultural present as forces of that would haunt the "false universalism" and hegemony of capital, see Slavoj Žižek, *The Fragile Absolute: or, Why Is the Christian Legacy Worth Fighting for?* (London: Verso, 2000), 3. We live in a world of globalization that Jacques Derrida has translated (in his Capri dialogue with Vattimo on the "spectral" postmodern return of world religions and civilizational crusades in 1994) into a wholesale enlightenment process of "globalatinization" [French: *mondialatinisation*]. By this defamiliarizing trope of globalization as U.S. Empire, Derrida would de-imperialize and estrange the very neoliberal "worlding" of a post-European life-space taking on the idiom of a market discourse that goes on inscribing the life-world into an empire of capital: a life-world believed in via shock-and-awe spectacles of cinema, cynical reason, cyber-software, and—in the final instance—war. Fetishism of neoliberal market forms often goes hand in hand with the death-of-God as a disappearance into commodity-worship, say, ratified in this Empire by the shopping mall as a displacement of enjoyment under the flux of a "tele-technoscientific capitalism." See Jacques Derrida, "Faith and Knowledge: The Two Sources of 'Religion' at the Limits of Reason Alone," in *Religion* (Stanford, CA: Stanford University Press, 1998), ed. Jacques Derrida and Gianni Vattimo, 11, 13, and 67.

75. "This Morning I Am Born Again," with words by Woody Guthrie, and music by Slaid Cleaves, as used on the latter's album, *Broke Down* (2000). Copyright 2001 Woody Guthrie Publications, Inc. The "You must be born again to see the kingdom of God" mandate from John's gospel on Nicodemus (3:7) inspired many American gospel songs far less original than Woody's, from the raucous version by the do-wop-like Gospel Harmonettes to Charles W. Naylor's didactic version from 1907.

3. "Be Always Converting, and Be Always Converted"

1. James Russell Lowell, *A Fable for Critics*, excerpts reprinted in John Hollander, ed., *American Poetry: The Nineteenth Century* (New York: Library of America, 1996); V. N. Voloshinov/Bakhtin, *Marxism and the Philosophy of Language*, trans. Ladislav Matejka and R. Titunik (Cambridge, MA: Harvard University Press, 1986), 26; Albert Wendt, "Flying Fox in a Freedom Tree," in *Flying Fox in a Freedom Tree and Other Stories* (Auckland, NZ: Penguin, 1988), 140–141.

2. See the introduction by Garrett Caples to the early Beat dual collection of works by Philip Lamantia and John Hoffman, *Tau by Philip Lamantia and Journey to the End by John Hoffman* (San Francisco: City Lights Books, 2008), 2–3. Unlike the mongrel believer Jack Kerouac, post-conversion Lamantia found his brand of Sicilian-American Catholicism incompatible with modes of Buddhism (Caples, 12–13), although by the time of the *Howl* reading at the Gallery Six in 1955, he had another near conversion to Islam after an encounter with the mystical cosmos of the Godhead while reading the *Koran* (Caples, 60–61).

3. 2 Corinthians 5:17, King James Bible.

4. Hawthorne's daughter Rose had also written a memoir of the transcendentalist era and her turn to Roman Catholic Italy in *Memories of Hawthorne* (Boston: Houghton, Mifflin, 1897) and a set of plain poems, *Along the Shore* (Boston: Ticknor, 1888). The Dominican religious order she founded is still active in hospital service and is known as the Dominican Sisters of Hawthorne.

5. "The Parable of the Ten Virgins Unfolded," in *The Works of Thomas Shepard: First Pastor of the First Church, Cambridge, Massachusetts: With a Memoir of His Life and Character* (Boston: Doctrinal Tract and Book Society, 1853), 632.

6. Harold Bloom, *Where Shall Wisdom Be Found?* (New York: Riverhead Books, 2004), 190.

7. Ralph Waldo Emerson," Self-Reliance," in *Ralph Waldo Emerson: Essays and Poems* (New York: Library of America, 1996), 271–272.

8. Ralph Waldo Emerson, "The Fugitive Slave Law," in *Essays and Poems,* 1003.

9. See Sylviane A. Diouf's study, *Servants of Allah: African Muslims Enslaved in the Americas* (New York: New York University Press, 1998), 54: "Numerous Muslims [in the Americas] responded to the forced conversion policy [of Christian slaveholders] by a pseudoconversion" based on miming external signs and keeping to other practices.

10. Gilles Deleuze, *Spinoza: Practical Philosophy,* trans. Robert Hurley (San Francisco: City Lights Books, 1988), 28.

11. Nietzsche would wrest Western culture from priestly "reactive forces which pervert it" and would serve to decompose the self's becoming-active: see Gilles Deleuze, *Nietzsche and Philosophy,* trans. Hugh Tomlinson (New York: Columbia University Press, 1983), 139 and Chapter 4, "From *Ressentiment* to the Bad Conscience."

12. As Dylan asserts in "Thunder on the Mountain," from *Modern Times,* "I've already confessed / No need to confess again," as if freed from Jokerman's "persecutor within."

13. See Gilles Deleuze and Claire Parnet, "On the Superiority of Anglo-American Literature," in *Dialogues,* trans. Hugh Tomlinson and Barbara Habberjam (New York: Columbia University Press, 1987), 62. Activating a version of "geographical becoming," the philosophy of this passage reflects Deleuze's core theory of the American body-soul "encounter" via Spinoza, and the em-

bedded passage cites D. H. Lawrence on Whitman's on-the-road vision from "Song of Myself" and "The Body Electric."

14. Slavoj Žižek, *Organs without Bodies: On Deleuze and Consequences* (London: Routledge, 2004), 14.

15. Ibid., 14.

16. William James, *Talks to Teachers on Psychology and to Students on Some of Life's Ideals* (New York: Dover, 1962), 38–39.

17. Robert D. Richardson, *William James: In the Maelstrom of American Modernism* (Boston: Houghton Mifflin, 2006), 365.

18. As Geneive Abdu notes in her study of American adaptations of Islam, from converted slaves or prairie Muslims to African Americans and post-1965 immigrants, "Some Muslims born into the faith would also describe the transformation of those who are new to the faith as 'reversion,' rather than 'conversion,' because they believe everyone is born a Muslim." See *Mecca and Main Street: Muslim Life in America After 9/11* (New York: Oxford University Press, 2007), 171.

19. Alain Badiou, *Saint Paul: The Foundation of Universalism,* trans. Ray Brassier (Stanford, CA: Stanford University Press, 2003), 17.

20. John R, May, *Nourishing Faith through Fiction: Reflections of the "Apostle's Creed" in Literature and Film* (Franklin, WI: Sheed & Ward, 2001), 62. For a Roman Catholic discussion of "spiritual conversion" renewed by sacramental organization, see also Thomas Dubay, SM, *Deep Conversion/Deep Prayer* (Ft. Collins, CO: Ignatius Press, 2006). "Deep" conversion would be an abiding one, for Roman Catholic subjects, not subject to shifts of sign or moods, although some would not allow for being lastingly "saved," as in born-again dispensations.

21. See "An Interview with Wing Young Huie," in *Rain Taxi*, 13 (2008): 27. For a complex body of photography dealing with these Midwestern ethnic and trans-ethnic complexities of belief, conversion, and mixed American identity, see Wing Young Huie, *Looking for Asian America: An Ethnocentric Tour by Wing Young Huie* (Minneapolis: University of Minnesota Press, 2008).

22. Mitchell Robert Breitwieser, *Cotton Mather and Benjamin Franklin: The Price of Representative Personality* (Cambridge: Cambridge University Press, 1984), 26, 49.

23. Mitchell Robert Breitwieser, *American Puritanism and the Defense of Mourning: Religion, Grief, and Ethnology in Mary White Rowlandson's Captivity Narrative* (Madison: University of Wisconsin Press, 1990), 141.

24. James Macintyre, "The Hitchens Brothers: Anatomy of a Row," *The Independent* accessed online on June 12, 2007, explores the sibling rivalry based partly around Christopher Hitchens's turn from childhood Anglicanism and left-socialism at Oxford to an antiliberal nihilism as trumpeted influentially in his support of the war in Iraq and his screed, *God Is Not Great: How Religion Poisons Everything* (2007).

25. "Richard Rorty's Legacy," *OpenDemocracy* accessed online, June 12, 2007.

26. On counter-conversions into Buddhist and Taoist philosophy, see Jonathan Stalling, *Poetics of Emptiness: Transformations of East Asian Philosophy*

and Poetics in Twentieth-Century American Poetry (forthcoming, Fordham University Press), which tracks Fenollosa's journey from modes of New England transcendentalism into the language and modalities of "New Buddhism" in Japan.

27. Stanley Cavell, *Cities of Words: Pedagogical Letters on a Register of the Moral Life* (Cambridge, MA: Harvard University Press, 2004), 22.

28. See John Freccero, *Dante: The Poetics of Conversion* (Cambridge, MA: Harvard University Press, 1986), 266.

29. Ibid., 266.

30. Denize Lauture, *The Black Warrior and Other Poems* (New York: subpress collective, 2006), 11.

31. On "Missionary Endeavours" in the Pacific, see Rod Edmond, *Representing the South Pacific: Colonial Discourse from Cook to Gauguin* (Cambridge: Cambridge University Press, 1997, 121 and 100 in particular. On the postcolonial dynamics of mimicry, disguise, and trickery, see Vanessa Smith, "Lip Service and Conversion," in *Literary Culture and the Pacific: Nineteenth-Century Textual Encounters* (Cambridge: Cambridge University Press, 1998), chapter 2.

32. A "counter-imperial" reading of Byron's South Pacific romance of liberal dissent is offered in Karen Fang, *Empire of Signs: Periodical Culture and the Post-Napoleonic* (forthcoming). This study tracks the quasi-orientalist fascination of Greece, China, Egypt, Italy, and Tahiti for generating critiques of British Empire in authors like Charles Lamb, James Hogg, and Letitia Landon as well as in Keats and Byron, who felt unconverted to imperial awe by the Elgin Marbles.

33. Owen Chase, *Shipwreck of the Whaleship Essex* (New York: Lyons Press, 1999), quoted by Paul Lyons in his introduction to this reprint of the 1821 text, xxiv.

34. Sacvan Bercovitch, *The Rites of Assent: Transformations in the Symbolic Construction of America* (London: Routledge, 1993), 29, 1.

35. Mary Kawena Pukui, ed., *Ōʻlelo Noʻeau: Hawaiian Proverbs and Poetical Sayings* (Honolulu: Bishop Museum, 1983), no. 1962, 211.

36. Samuel H. Elbert and Mary Kawena Pukui, *Hawaiian Dictionary* (Honolulu: University of Hawaiʻi Press, 1986), 206.

37. Ibid., 211.

38. On the struggle for "self-governance" and recognition of Hawaiians as Native Americans by the U.S. government, see "Affirmative Action in Hawaii: Sun, Surf, and Secession?" *The Economist,* Sept. 3–9, 2005, 32. Stronger forms of Hawaiian nationalism are being defended than this compromised U.S. enframing. See Daviana Pomoaikaʻi McGregor, "Recognizing Native Hawaiians: A Quest for Sovereignty," in *Pacific Diaspora: Island People in the United States and across the Pacific,* ed. Paul Spickard, Joanne L. Rondilla, and Debbie Hippolite Wright (Honolulu: University of Hawaiʻi Press, 2002), 331–354.

39. As discussed by R. A. Knox, *Enthusiasm: A Chapter in the History of Religion* (Oxford: Clarendon Press, 1973), 441.

40. See Susan Ferriss and Julieta Gutierrez, "1st Indian Saint Named—Mexicans Jubilant," *San Francisco Chronicle,* Aug. 1, 2002, A2.

41. In his emphasis via two lectures on what "the value of saintliness" means for a plural cast of subjects, James can said to be following this Protestant line linking grace to acts in *Varieties,* faith to pragmatic consequences.

42. In her ethnographic stress on this reborn language of being "saved," Harding gets at the dialogics of conversion, the very language-basis of Baptist form, what she calls a "poetics of faith" overriding the "hermeneutics of skepticism." See *The Book of Jerry Falwell: Fundamentalist Language and Politics* (Princeton, NJ: Princeton University Press, 2001), 33–60.

43. Joseph Ratzinger or Pope Benedict XVI, *Jesus of Nazareth* (New York: Doubleday, 2007), 46 ff.

44. William James, *Varieties of Religious Experience* (New York: Penguin, 1988), 249 and 256, as evidence in the lecture called "Conversion."

45. Mapping the syncretism of the Pacific Rim in this era of global unevenness and postcolonial emergence, Kenzaburo Ōe links forms of "Black Madonna" worship in Mexico to hedonistic New Age cults of Buddhist-Christian spiritualism in Japan. See *An Echo of Heaven,* trans. Margaret Mitsutani (Tokyo: Kodansha International, 1996), 164–173 and 150.

46. Charles Taylor, *Varieties of Religion Today: William James Revisited* (Cambridge, MA: Harvard University Press, 2002), 15, 63, 43, and 12.

47. James, "Mysticism," in *Varieties of Religious Experience,* 418. Emerson's "I am nothing, I become all" passage from "Nature" was a version of this self-evacuation via the Over-soul.

48. On the contrast between a "sudden" Pauline conversion and the more "gradual" Marcan conversion process as authorizing differing modes and converting-tactics in "rebirth," see Richard V. Peace, *Conversion in the New Testament: Paul and the Twelve* (Grand Rapids, MI: William Eerdmans Publishing, 1999).

49. James, *Varieties of Religious Experience,* 166–258. Cited hereafter parenthetically as *Varieties.* On traits of the "conversion experience" as dispersed across Anglo-American contexts, see also R. A. Knox, *Enthusiasm: A Chapter in the History of Religion.* On James's 1870 conversion experience from modes of nihilism toward stronger forms of willing and affirmation of the self's power in belief and creative power as thinker and writer, which proved a turning point in his whole system of ideas, see Gay Wilson Allen, *William James: A Biography* (New York: Viking, 1967), 163–164.

50. Kuhn's "conversion" is discussed by Lindsay Waters, who offers a critique of the way Kuhn's theorization in *The Structure of Scientific Revolution* (1962), which embraced creative-destructive dynamics of "paradigm building," has led to the embrace of cultural "incommensurability" and the rise of various "tribalisms" in postwar identity politics. See Waters, "Opening the American Mind . . . Towards China" (based on lectures in China, May 2002). See his related essays on professional paradigms of self-formation and betrayal in Lindsay Waters, *Enemies of Promise* (Chicago: Prickly Paradigms, 2004). See Thomas Kuhn, *The Essential Tension* (Chicago: University

of Chicago Press, 1977), xi–xii, on this "conversion" to such a dominant model of science.

51. On the Knight of Faith's willing the eternal via individual leap, see Soren Kierkegaard, *Fear and Trembling* [*Dialectical Lyric by Johannes de silentio*], trans. Alastair Hannay (London: Penguin, 1985), 50; on negative-expectancy whereby "faith" means a state of living with California dreams over tectonic plates, see David Ulin, *The Myth of Solid Ground: Earthquakes, Prediction, and the Fault Line between Reason and Faith* (New York: Viking, 2004).

52. See "Religion beat became a test of faith: A reporter looks at how the stories he covered affected him and his spiritual journey," *Los Angeles Times,* July 21, 2007, accessed online. As Lobdell writes, "Clearly, I saw now that belief in God, no matter how grounded, requires at some point a leap of faith. Either you have the gift of faith or you don't. It's not a choice. It can't be willed into existence. And there's no faking it if you're honest about the state of your soul."

53. James's impact on the conversion tactics of AA is discussed by Richardson, *William James,* 405 and 531 fn. 26, who cites Wilson's avowing "that James, though long in his grave, had been a founder of Alcoholics Anonymous," from *Pass It on: The Story of Bill Wilson* (New York: AA World Services, 1984), 124.

54. See Tanya Erzen, *Straight to Jesus: Sexual and Christian Conversions in the Ex-Gay Movement* (Berkeley: University of California Press, 2006), 163. On the use of *testimony* and confessional language in "queer conversion," she writes, "I call this process of religious and sexual conversion, sexual falls and public redemption through testimony, 'queer conversion' " (14); and she shrewdly goes on to theorize the instability and performative rhetoric of all such "ex-identity" gendered formations.

55. Philip Fisher contends (in effect) that the American conversion experience becomes increasingly centered around a belief less in God than in the creative-destructive dynamics of a mutating American commodity system that frees up objects and immigrants for investment in democratic America. See *Still the New World: American Literature in a Culture of Creative Destruction* (Cambridge, MA: Harvard University Press, 1999): "With constant economic restructuring, every generation must emigrate from and immigrate into a new way of life, of thinking, of training, and earning a living" (183).

56. Ralph Waldo Emerson, "Fate," *The Conduct of Life* (1860), in *Essays and Poems,* 781. On the first-person reactivation of Puritan antinomianism in Emerson, see Amy Schranger Lang, *Prophetic Woman: Anne Hutchinson and the Problem of Dissent in the Literature of New England* (Berkeley: University of California Press, 1987), 116.

57. Ralph Waldo Emerson, "Experience," in *Essays and Poems,* 485.

58. Ralph Waldo Emerson, *Essays and Poems,* 82, 78, 413.

59. Dylan to Robert Hilburn of the *Los Angeles Times,* quoted in Steve Turner, "John Lennon's Born-Again Phase," *Christianity Today,* Sept. 10, 2007, accessed online.

60. See Harold Bloom on the gnosticism of grace suffusing post-Emersonian religiosity, in *The American Religion: The Emergence of the Post-Christian Nation* (New York: Simon & Schuster, 1992), 32.

61. On the deathbed conversion or the odd *double-baptism* of Wallace Stevens to Catholicism in 1955, see the testimony of Reverend Arthur Hanley in *Parts of a World: Wallace Stevens Remembered, an Oral Biography,* ed. Peter Brazeau (San Francisco: North Point Press, 1985), 294–296. The Catholic priest claims that Stevens wanted to "get in the fold" (by converting to Roman Catholicism) before his death, a fact countered by Margaret Powers, whose husband James (who used to visit churches all over New York City with the poet) said "I think Wallace would like to be in a Church but he can't do it" (297). A conversion, while a challenge to the will to mutating fictions and perpetual troping, is consistent with Stevens's claim that "god and the Imagination are one," as in poems like "A Final Soliloquy to the Interior Paramour" or "Puella Parvula," where the imagination resurrects and transfigures reality. Throughout his career, Stevens rendered poetry into a space in which to refigure "conversion" as fluid, through the active *poesis* of meditation: "After one has abandoned a belief in God, poetry is that essence [of language] that takes its place as life's redemption" On these materials, see "Adagia" in Wallace Stevens, *Opus Posthumous: Poems, Plays, Prose* (New York: Vintage, 1990. On quasi-religious dynamics of meditation, metaphor, and belief in the shifting body of his poetry and poetics, see Rob Wilson, "Wallace Stevens, Christian Interiority, and the Symbolic Action of Meditation," *Poetica* 42 (1994): 105–122, published in Japan. Oscar Wilde was a belated Catholic convert: see Joseph Pearce, *Literary Converts: Spiritual Inspiration in an Age of Unbelief* (San Francisco: Ignatius Press, 1999), 3–7: "the Catholic Church is for saints and sinners alone," as Wilde jested (5).

62. Bloom, *The American Religion*, 16.

63. See Fredric Jameson, *The Ideologies of Theory: Essays, 1971–1986* (Minneapolis: University of Minnesota Press, 1988), 54–55, 133–147.

64. Julia Kristeva, *Black Sun: Depression and Melancholia,* trans. Leon S. Roudiez (New York: Columbia University Press, 1989), 9. Hereafter cited parenthetically as *Black Sun*.

65. Ibid., 44, 190. Judith Butler critiques Kristeva's overvaluation of "the semiotic [which] expresses that original libidinal multiplicity [of the maternal body and its substitutes] within the very terms of [patriarchal] culture," released in a "poetic language" that pushes toward semantic nonclosure and transgressive prosody: see *Gender Trouble* (New York: Routledge, 1999), 101–102. In *Gender Trouble,* see also 101–117, on the "subversive body politics"; and on Kristeva's aesthetic glorification of feminine abjection via "the matricidal impulse" and "an internally directed masochism," see 206–207.

66. René Girard, *Deceit, Desire, and the Novel: Self and Other in Literary Structure,* trans. Yvonne Freccero (Baltimore: Johns Hopkins University Press, 1965), 59. Hereafter cited parenthetically as *Deceit*.

67. The importance of Girard's anti-Nietzschean transfiguration of the whole "anthropology of religion" around this mechanism of sacred scapegoating is

discussed in Roger Scruton, "The Sacred and the Human," *Prospect Magazine* 137 (August 2007), accessed online. For Girard, religion, particularly Christianity above all as a mimetic form, is not the cause of social violence but the solution to such deformations of humanity.

68. Jack Kerouac, *Mexico City Blues (242 Choruses)* (New York: Grove Weidenfeld, 1959), 61. On Beat "beatitude," see Jack Kerouac, "*Beatific:* The Origins of the Beat Generation" in *The Portable Jack Kerouac,* ed. Ann Charters (New York: Penguin, 2007), 565–573. See also Rob Wilson, ed., *On the Roads to Beatitude: An Archive of "Beatitudes" for the Postmodern World* (forthcoming), for various origins and broader theo-poetic applications of Beat beatitude.

69. Gerald Nicosia, *Memory Babe: A Critical Biography of Jack Kerouac* (Berkeley: University of California Press, 1994), 76, 187.

70. Paul Giles, *American Catholic Arts and Fictions: Culture, Ideology, Aesthetics* (Cambridge: Cambridge University Press, 1992), 408–416.

71. Jack Kerouac, *Big Sur* (New York: Farrar, Straus, & Cudahy, 1962), 205.

72. Giles, *American Catholic Arts and Fictions,* 422.

73. Letter quoted by David Stanford in foreword to Jack Kerouac, *Some of the Dharma* (New York: Viking, 1997), x.

74. Ibid., xii.

75. William James, "The Energies of Man" (1907), in *The Writings of William James: A Comprehensive Edition,* ed. John J. McDermott (Chicago: University of Chicago Press, 1977), 681.

76. William Dean Howells, *The Rise of Silas Lapham* (New York: Penguin Classics, 1983).

77. Taylor, *Varieties of Religion Today,* 42.

78. See Kenneth Burke, *The Rhetoric of Religion: Studies in Logology* (Berkeley: University of California Press, 1970), 69 and 105.

79. See Giles, *American Catholic Arts and Fiction,* 136.

80. John E, Smith, Harry S. Stout, and Kenneth P. Minkema, eds., *A Jonathan Edwards Reader* (New Haven, CT: Yale University Press, 2003 165. Contemporary tenets of American Calvinist soteriology are staged against "Venusian" mores of New Age popular culture and codes of grace in Richard J. Mouw, *Calvinism in the Las Vegas Airport: Making Connections in Today's World* (Grand Rapids, MI: Zondervan, 2004).

81. William James, "The Gospel of Relaxation," in *Talks to Teachers on Psychology,* 100. Mother Teresa's posthumous work shows her "acting faithfully" as Catholic nun in India even when she was tormented by doubt and felt the absence of Christ's presence fitfully: see *Mother Teresa: Come Be My Light,* ed. Brian Kolodiejchuk (New York: Doubleday, 2007).

82. On semiotic dynamics and "interpretive community" of American pragmatism, see Walter Benn Michaels, "The Interpreter's Self: Peirce on the Cartesian 'Subject,' " *Georgia Review* 31 (1977): 399–401.

83. On this American *gnosis* as solitary conversion, see Harold Bloom, *Omens of Millennium: The Gnosis of Angels, Dreams, and Resurrection* (New York: Riverhead Books, 1996): "Americans truly believe that God loves them, and they frequently interpret this as meaning that they have walked with Jesus, the

Jesus who went about with his disciples in a forty-day interval between his Resurrection and his Ascension" (165).

84. Harold Bloom, *Jesus and Yahweh: The Names Divine* (New York: Riverhead Books, 2005), 11.

85. Werner Sollors, "A Critique of Pure Pluralism," in *Beyond Ethnicity: Consent and Descent in American Culture* (New York: Oxford University Press, 1986), 276, 279. Hereafter cited parenthetically as *Beyond Ethnicity*.

86. Charles Taylor, *A Secular Age* (Cambridge, MA: Harvard University Press, 2007), 524.

87. On *re-ethnicized* modes of identification and multilingual translation across national frames of belonging, see also Werner Sollors, ed., *Multilingual America: Transnationalism, Ethnicity, and the Languages of American Literature* (New York: New York University Press, 1998). On contradictory modes of filiation (descent) and affiliated coalition (cultural consent) as transforming the Asian American literary field, see David Leiwei Li, *Imagining the Nation: Asian American Literature and Cultural Consent* (Stanford, CA: Stanford University Press, 1998).

88. Lisa Lowe, *Immigrant Acts: On Asian American Cultural Politics* (Durham, NC: Duke University Press, 1996), 125.

89. Ibid., 126.

90. See Act V of William Shakespeare's *The Tempest* (1610), which Leo Marx famously recast as "Shakespeare's American Fable" in *The Machine in the Garden: Technology and the Pastoral Ideal* (London: Oxford University Press, 1964), 34–72.

91. Wendt, "Flying Fox in a Freedom Tree," 144.

92. Dietrich Varez, *The Legend of La'ieikawai* (Honolulu: University of Hawai'i Press, 2004).

93. See Cristina Bachillega's timely study of American and Hawaiian modes as reading and using these genres, *Legendary Hawai'i and the Politics of Place: Tradition, Translation, and Tourism* (Philadelphia: University of Pennsylvania Press, 2007); and Rob Wilson's review of the linguistic, cultural-political issues it raises, in the *Journal of Hawaiian History* (forthcoming, spring 2009).

94. This is the psychologized thesis of John Owen King III, *The Iron of Melancholy: Structures of Spiritual Conversion in America from the Puritan Conscience to Victorian Neurosis* (Hanover, NH: University Press of New England, 1987). On "melancholia" leading to states of theo-poetic exaltation as well as semiotic powers, see also Kay Redfield Jamison, *Touched with Fire: Manic-Depressive Illness and the Artistic Temperament* (New York: Free Press, 1994), chapter 4. William James is a case study, as are religious poets in the postevangelical British tradition of William Blake and the Puritan terms (influential in America) of John Bunyan in *Pilgrim's Progress* and *Grace Abounding*.

95. On psychological consequences from states of identity dispersal, melancholic depression, and will to rebirth running in the James family, see Jamison, *Touched with Fire*, 207–216; this study assumes a biographical plot of

identity struggle, death, and "manic" rebirth, which Jamison applies with sweeping empathy to writers as diverse as Eugene O'Neill, Gerard Manley Hopkins, F. Scott Fitzgerald, Virginia Woolf, Robert Lowell, Sylvia Plath, Ernest Hemingway, and John Berryman. These "violent moods of the soul," as Virginia Woolf called fits of depressiveness, are often tinged in a psycho-religious vocabulary of soul-search, as when she writes in her suicide note to her husband Leonard in 1941, "We do not know our own souls, let alone the souls of others" (quoted by Jamison, 226). "Self," in modern therapy, becomes a word for "soul," as in Walt Whitman or James Hillman.

96. Patricia Caldwell, *The Puritan Conversion Narrative: The Beginnings of American Expression* (Cambridge: Cambridge University Press, 1983), 164.

97. Edmund Morgan, *Visible Saints: The History of a Puritan Idea* (Ithaca, NY: Cornell University Press, 1965). See also Norman Pettit, *The Heart Prepared: Grace and Conversion in Puritan Spiritual Life* (New Haven, CT: Yale University Press, 1966).

98. According to Mitchell Breitwiser's illuminating study of subject formation in the early-modern period of the colonies, *Cotton Mather and Benjamin Franklin*, 28.

99. For Sartre's reading of Flaubert in *L'idiot de la Famille*, see Neil Hertz, *The End of the Line: Essays on Psychoanalysis and the Sublime* (New York: Columbia University Press, 1985), chapter 4, "Flaubert's Conversion."

100. Hertz, *The End of the Line*, 72.

101. Sartre's existential break from a religious vocabulary toward a vocation to write literature in *Words* is elaborated as "deconversion" by John D. Barbour, *Versions of Deconversion: Autobiography and the Loss of Faith* (Charlottesville: University of Virginia Press, 1994), chapter 7.

102. Josiah Royce, "The Doctrine of Signs," in *The Problem of Christianity* (1913) (Washington, DC: Catholic University of America Press, 2001): "Paul died at his conversion; but only in order that henceforth the life of the spirit [charity] should live in and through him" via ever-expansive loyalty to this community of grace and belief.

103. Taylor, *Varieties of Religion Today*, 27–29.

104. See Johannes Fabian on conversions into cultural otherness and trans-scientific excess, *Out of Our Minds: Reason and Madness in the Exploration of Central Africa* (Berkeley: University of California Press, 2000), 8, 280, in which "ecstasy" becomes a mode of accessing other modes of counter-Christian knowledge.

105. On the counter-converting potential of a quasi-Christian-socialist *multitude* connecting across the contemporary global dispensation, see Michael Hardt and Antonio Negri, *Empire* (Cambridge, MA: Harvard University Press, 2000).

106. Quoted in James Berger, *After the End: Representations of Post-Apocalypse* (Minneapolis: University of Minnesota Press, 1998), 133.

107. Using himself as case study of a dissatisfied modern subject questing for philosophical renewal via belief, Chesterton discusses the turn of Anglican and

American Puritan offspring et al. back to the Catholic church and his well-argued struggle to find "truth" and sacramental reality therein, in *The Catholic Church and Conversion* (London: Macmillan, 1926; Ft. Collins, CO: Ignatius Press, 2006). See also G. K. Chesterton's "slovenly autobiography," *Orthodoxy: The Romance of Faith* (Ft. Collins, CO: Ignatius Press, 1995).

108. See Dennis Kawaharada, *Storied Landscapes: Hawaiian Literature and Place* (Honolulu: Kalamaku Press, 1999), 34 and 8; see also the review of this re-indigenizing approach used by Kawaharada in his provocative study by Rob Wilson, in *The Contemporary Pacific* 13 (2001): 597–599.

109. See Haunani Kay Trask, *Night Is a Sharkskin Drum* (Honolulu: University of Hawai'i Press, 2002), and Rodney Morales, *When the Shark Bites* (Honolulu: University of Hawai'i Press, 2002), both of which offer countervisions of place in indigenous visions of ocean, shark, land, and community. For Hawaiian beliefs in Pele that would challenge geothermal heating on the Big Island of Hawai'i, see James Houston's novel, *The Last Paradise* (Norman: University of Oklahoma Press, 1998). For a post-Christian account of such contemporary encounters with primitive "mana" as travelogue-quest, see Charles Montgomery, *The Shark God: Encounters with Ghosts and Ancestors in the South Pacific* (New York: HarperCollins, 2006). On the resurgence of cultural-political Hawaiian attitudes in popular music forms, see also James Houston and Eddie Kamae, *Hawaiian Son: The Life and Music of Eddie Kamae* (Honolulu: 'Ai Pōhaku Press, 2004).

110. Taylor, *Varieties of Religion Today*, 38.

111. Mike Davis, "Planet of Slums," *New Left Review* 26 (2004): 15. Davis gives a quasi-socialist context to this "evangelical" version of contemporary conversion: "With roots in early ecstatic Methodism and African-American spirituality, Pentecostalism 'awoke' when the Holy Ghost gave the gift of tongues to participants in an interracial prayer marathon in a poor neighborhood of Los Angeles (Azusa Street) in 1906" (15).

112. Bloom, *Jesus and Yahweh*, 12.

113. Ibid., 13.

114. See Juliana Spahr's place-based work, *Dole Street* (Honolulu: subpress collective, 2000), on colonial history and postcolonial refiguration taking place in contemporary Hawai'i, and her essay on global/local modes of reading peripheral literatures from sites like Hawai'i, Mexico, and Samoa, "Connected Disconnection and Localized Globalism in Pacific Multilingual Literature," *boundary 2* 31 (2004): 75–100.

115. This "portrait of the artist" as a young man is played by Dean Stockwell in the 1962 movie version of *Long Day's Journey into Night* (directed by Sidney Lumet), who confides this moment of oceanic "beatitude" to his father (Ralph Richardson) on that long-day's "journey" into confession and male transformation, while the vision-absorbed mother (Katherine Hepburn) descends into a morphine-induced purgatory as she goes on recalling the innocence she felt as a child believing in Mary. (Earlier in the play, Schopenhauer is acknowledged as one philosophical source for O'Neill's fleeting, self-abnegating sense of *oceanic consciousness*.)

116. Eugene O'Neill, *Long Day's Journey into Night* (New Haven, CT: Yale University Press, 2002), 156.
117. Harold Bloom urges O'Neill's anti-*Emersonianism* as the dramatist's battle of death-force against death-force: see the forward to the Yale University paperback edition of *Long Day's Journey into Night*, vi. Bloom connects this turn from Emersonianism to the dramatist's Irish-American Catholicism and his "heroic resentment of the New England Yankee tradition," a cultural complex of multiethnicity and class tension I will return to in my quasi-autobiographical epilogue.

4. Writing down the Lava Road from Damascus to Kona

1. John Pule, *The Shark That Ate the Sun* (Auckland, NZ: Penguin, 1992), Pule's "silence," loud with historical countermemory, would rebuke Henry Kissinger's insult to Pacific Islanders (amid Micronesian calls for independence) as irrelevant to U.S. global security concerns, at the same time these islands were used as military sites during the Nixon administration. See Paul Lyons, *American Pacificism: Oceania in the U.S. Imagination* (London: Routledge, 2006), 177.
2. "A 'South Pacific' Epiphany" is how the journalist Stephen Holden phrases Brian Stokes Mitchell's "Unplugged" performance of the 1949 Broadway musical *South Pacific*, in quasi-religious terms of *epiphany* (a Greek word recalling the manifestation of Christ or other superhuman beings). See Holden, "A 'South Pacific' Epiphany," *New York Times:* Jan. 14 2006, A19.
3. The Hollywood movie *Big Kahuna* (1999) takes its title from the Hawaiian word for priest *(kahuna)*, which has become slang for commercial operator: it was directed by Roger Rueff and starred the rambunctious Danny Devito.
4. I allude here to ecological cautionary-tales of Jared Diamond, UCLA geographer and physiologist, who contends that Pacific Islander people of Easter Island destroyed their forests, plants, and animals and descended into chaos and cannibalism to support the building of megalithic moai figures of cultural aggrandizement: see his "Easter's End," Discover 9 (1995): 62–69; and *Collapse: How Societies Choose to Fail or Succeed* (New York: Viking, 2005). Terry L. Hunt, a Pacific-based anthropologist and archaeologist from the University of Hawai'i at Mānoa has challenged Jared's paradigm of "collapse" by time-frame (the island was not settled until around 1200 a.d., not four hundred years earlier as Diamond had claimed to establish his fall-from-abundance model of native Pacific abuse) and disruptive impacts of the Polynesian rat, as well as postcontact Western diseases and exploitation patterns (like slavery); see Hunt, "Rethinking the Fall of Easter Island," *American Scientist* (Sept.–Oct. 2006): http://www.americanscientist .org/template/AssetDetail/assetid/53220 (accessed on Aug. 25, 2006). The closest habitable island to Rapa Nui is Pitcairn Island, which, since being settled by the Bounty mutineers in the eighteenth century, has continued to serve as fable for tales of cultural degeneration and fall-from-Eden scenarios (except perhaps for Marlon Brando).

5. On these "cargo cults" that arose in the postwar 1940s and 1950s as vernacular critique of white capitalism by islanders (like those in the Tannu island) waiting for prophets to return with "a white cargo laden with riches," see Lamont Lindstrom, "Cargo Cult at the Third Millennium," in *Cargo, Cult and Cultural Critique,* ed. Holger Jebens (Honolulu: University of Hawai'i Press, 2004), 15–35, who urges that "Cargo cult prophets [like John Frum] drew on Christian millenarianism, sometimes conflating the arrival of cargo with Christ's second coming, often called 'Last Day'" (15). See also Lamont Lindstrom, *Cargo Cult: Strange Stories of Desire from Melanesia and Beyond* (Honolulu: University of Hawai'i Press, 1993).

6. For de-orientalizing "feedback" to this Pacific body-image and writing back to the romanticism of ex-imperial countries like France, England, and the United States, see Teresia Teiawa, "Reading Paul Gauguin's *Noa Noa* with Epeli Hau'ofa's *Kisses in the Nederends*," in *Inside Out: Literature, Cultural Politics, and Identity in the New Pacific,* ed. Vilsoni Hereniko and Rob Wilson (Lanham, MD: Rowman & Littlefield, 1999), 249–263; and, in the same collection, Robert Nicole, "Resisting Orientalism: Pacific Literature in French," 265–290.

7. See "A Sea of Islands: A New Paradigm for the Pacific," *East-West Center Views* 3 (May–June 1993): 1–4. Hau'ofa's gave his talk while a visiting fellow at the East-West Center, which since its founding in 1960 in Honolulu (just after Hawai'i became the fiftieth state in 1959) has sought (in its own terms) "to foster mutual understanding among the governments and peoples of the Asia-Pacific region, including the United States," which had funded and promoted such internationalist views. (Grady Timmons was editor of *East-West Center Views* at the time and may have authored this response, which is paraphrastic and affirmative.) As I know from some twenty years at the University of Hawai'i in Mānoa and participation at events "across the road," the East-West Center held conferences and residencies that proved crucial to making possible the interconnected Pacific of literary authors like Albert Wendt, KenzaburoŌe, Subramani, Epeli Hau'ofa, Patricia Grace, Richard Hamasaki, Michael Ondaatje, Maxine Hong Kingston, Vilsoni Hereniko, and Joseph Puna Balaz.

8. Epeli Hau'ofa, "Our Sea of Islands," in *A New Oceania: Rediscovering Our Sea of Islands,* ed. Eric Waddell, Vijay Naidu, and Epele Hau'ofa (Suva, Fiji: The University of South Pacific, 1993, 5–6, 7. Further references to Hau'ofa's talk will occur parenthetically. This collection also gathers dissenting perspectives from the interior Pacific on Hau'ofa's expansive talk, which I will return to throughout this chapter. Hau'ofa's influential essays have been reprinted in the mixed-genre collection, *We Are the Ocean: Selected Works,* ed. Geoffrey White (Honolulu: University of Hawai'i Press, 2008).

9. Ralph Waldo Emerson, "Worship," from *The Conduct of Life* (1860), in *Emerson: Essays and Poems* (New York: Library of America, 1996), 888.

10. MIRAB societies are what Hau'ofa calls those "pitiful microstates" in the Pacific "condemned forever to depend on migration, remittance, aid, and bureaucracy"; "Our Sea of Islands," 4.

11. David Hanlon and Geoffrey M. White, eds., introduction to *Voyaging through the Contemporary Pacific* (Lanhman, MD: Rowman & Littlefield, 2000), 5–6.

12. The quasi-Hegelian commitment to modes of "oceanic consciousness" in Western hegemonic powers from the eras of Captain Cook, Admiral Mahan, and Sigmund Freud, have been historicized and critiqued by Christopher Leigh Connery, in *The Oceanic Feeling: Aqueous Ideologies and the Geo-Imaginary of Capitalism*. This forthcoming study centers on the figure of the ocean as situated in—and beyond—the brutal dynamics of world-capitalist teleology. This ocean is discussed in multiple contexts in pre- and late modernity from China and Germany, England, France, the Mediterranean, to the United States as it has become tied to propagating forms of "Pacific Rim discourse" across this "last ocean."

13. Epeli Hauʻofa, "The Ocean in Us," reprinted in *Voyaging through the Contemporary Pacific*, 113. This essay was first given as an Oceania Lecture at the University of the South Pacific in Suva, Fiji on March 12, 1997; it later appeared in *Dreadlocks in Oceania* (Suva, Fiji: University of the South Pacific, 1997): 124–148; and in *The Contemporary Pacific* 10 (1998): 391–410. Like this one, each of Hauʻofa's recent talks and essays have become talked about, cited, and circulated as vision-statements in the region, as has his fiction in postcolonial circles from Germany to Taiwan.

14. Albert Leomala, "Kros" [Cross]," a bilingual pidgin/English poem that contains this standard English translation of the quoted stanza, "Cross I hate you / You are killing me / You are destroying /My traditions / I hate you Cross," appeared in the Honolulu journal *Seaweeds and Constructions,* 7 (1984) in a prescient special issue "A Pacific Islands Collection" edited by Richard Hamasaki: 64–65.

15. For an ethnographic analysis of these rooted to routed cultural identity issues, see Cathy A. Small, *Voyages: From Tongan Villages to American Suburbs* (Ithaca, NY: Cornell University Press, 1997), on Tongan migrants to California in successive waves from the 1960s to the 1990s.

16. Sudesh Mishra, "OM," responding to Hauʻofa in *A New Oceania*, 20–22. This is a shrewd response, one in keeping with the poetry and social force of Hauʻofa's vision. At the East-West Center after Hauʻofa had delivered his talk in 1993, the first respondent—a well-known Western researcher on the Pacific and supposed ally—jumped up to ask, white hair flailing, "And who funded you to give this talk here, didn't a western institution fund your visit?," thus repeating the whole MIRAB apparatus of dependency and belittlement. It was embarrassing to say the least, but such cynicism did not carry the day.

17. Alain Badiou, *Saint Paul: The Foundation of Universalism*, trans. Ray Brassier (Stanford, CA: Stanford University Press, 2003), 106.

18. As Amilcar Cabral had urged in postcolonial African contexts of "liberation," "a spiritual reconversion—of mentalities—is thus seen to be vital for their true integration in the liberation movement. Such a reconversion—*re-Africanization* in our case—may take place before the struggle, but is com-

NOTES TO PAGES 125–127   271

pleted only during the course of the struggle, through daily contact with the mass of the people and the communion of sacrifices which the struggle demands"; see *Unity and Struggle* (New York: Monthly Review Press, 1979), 145. I thank poet-scholar David Buuck for this reference.

19. Badiou, *Saint Paul,* 109.

20. For a fine study of Hau'ofa's fictional critiques of late-capitalist developmentalism, global tourism, and "full-blown commodification of indigeneity" by culture-co-opting forms in "the Pacific Way," see Charlene S, Gima, " 'Developing' the Critical Pacific: Epeli Hau'ofa's 'The Glorious Pacific Way,' " *Hitting Critical Mass 5* (1998). For a discussion of competing formations of this Pacific region from within and outside, which draws upon speculations on the Black Atlantic and Caribbean as linked counterformations to the domination schemes of U.S. Empire, see Jolisa Gracewood, "Sometimes a Great Ocean: Thinking the Pacific from Nowhere to Now and Here," *Hitting Critical Mass 5* (1998), in the same issue put together by Pacific scholars at Cornell University. Both of these articles can be accessed online: http:// socrates.berkeley.edu/~critmassv5n1 (accessed Jan. 14, 2001).

21. Douglas A. Borer, "Truth or Dare," in *A New Oceania,* 86.

22. Commentary by Epeli Hau'ofa et al. in response to "Our Sea of Islands," in *A New Oceania,* 73–75.

23. Grant Wacker, *Heaven Below: Early Pentecostals and American Culture* (Cambridge, MA: Harvard University Press, 2001), 178.

24. Hau'ofa, "The Ocean in Us," 114–117. Meditating on the semiotics and politics of "Oceania," Hau'ofa admits to having had "Wansolwara" in mind, by then the name for a newspaper produced by Pacific Islander journalism students at the University of the South Pacific, when he founded the Oceania Centre for Arts and Culture (124).

25. Hau'ofa, "The Ocean in Us," 126. Stressing its allegorical implications as a Pacific bridge (metaphorically passing over) from past to future, Hau'ofa adds, "In a metaphorical sense the ocean has been our waterway to each other [and] should also be our route to the rest of the world" (127). By now given to such affirmative metaphorics of Oceania, Hau'ofa credits (128) as precursor Albert Wendt's polemical and vision-opening essay, "Towards a New Oceania" for reframing Pacific regional identity via such tropological expansion and quasi-literary critique; *Mana Review* 1 (1976): 49–60, reprinted in the "Pacific" special issue of *Seaweeds and Constructions* 7 (1983), edited by Richard Hamasaki, where I first encountered its Pacific-linked vision amid the Bamboo Ridge–centered literatures of emergence in Hawai'i.

26. Wisconsin's Senator Beveridge, notorious U.S. imperialist during this expansionist era when Admiral Mahan and Teddy Roosevelt began to challenge Britain, Germany, Russia, France, and Japan for Pacific hegemony, is quoted in L. E. Freedman, *The United States Enters the Pacific* (Sydney: Angus and Robertson, 1969), and invoked, as context of transnational capital and U.S. led neoglobalization, by Vijay Nai to challenge Hau'ofa's "visionary essay [which] is a timely cri de couer," in "Whose Sea of Islands?," in *A New Oceania,* 54.

27. Isaiah Bowman, "A Department of Geography," *Science* 98 (Dec. 1943): 564, quoted and discussed in Neil Smith, *American Empire: Roosevelt's Geographer and the Prelude to Globalization* (Berkeley: University of California Press, 2004), 258. Bowman, unlike Beveridge, Mahan, Melville, or Charles Olson, was "Atlanticist" in his geography of geopower (351–390).

28. Smith, *American Empire*, 411.

29. R S. Sugirtharajah, *Postcolonial Criticism and Biblical Interpretation* (New York: Oxford University Press, 2002), 41. On "postcolonial" tactics decolonizing the Bible from social margins, see also R. S. Sugirtharajah, *The Bible and Empire: Postcolonial Explorations* (Cambridge: Cambridge University Press, 2005); Fernando F. Segovia, *Decolonizing Biblical Studies: A View from the Margins* (New York: Orbis Books, 2000); and R. S. Sugirtharajah, *The Bible and the Third World: Precolonial, Colonial and Postcolonial Encounters* (Cambridge: Cambridge University Press, 2001).

30. See Albert Wendt, "Afterward: Tatauing the Native Body," in *Inside Out*, 399–412.

31. Rod Edmond, " 'Kiss My Arse!': Epeli Hau'ofa's Politics of Laughter," *Journal of Commonwealth Literature* 25 (1990): 142.

32. For shifting views on his training, see Epeli Hau'ofa, "Anthropology and the Pacific Islanders," *Oceania* 45 (1975): 283–289, which he gave as a talk at a symposium on the future of anthropology as fieldwork in Melanesia, held in Canberra in January 1975. This was later published by the Institute of Papua New Guinea Studies as Discussion Paper Number 8 (Port Moresby, 1975). At this time, Hau'ofa was taken as, or disciplined into knowledge maker as, a "Melanesia" social scientist more than those transregional (and transdisciplinary) terms he would come to use after these borders had been decolonized, challenged, and deconstructed by more Pacific-based knowledge forms.

33. For this generic turn, see Henry Louis Gates Jr., "Zora Neal Hurston: 'A Negro Way of Saying,' " in Zora Neal Hurston, *Their Eyes Were Watching God* (New York: HarperCollins, 1990), 201–202.

34. Epeli Hau'ofa, "The Writer as Outsider," presentation at the Pacific Writer's Conference, East-West Center in Honolulu, Aug. 1984.

35. Epeli Hau'ofa, "Epilogue: Pasts to Remember," in *Remembrance of Pacific Pasts: An Invitation to Remake History*, ed. Robert Borofsky (Honolulu: University of Hawai'i Press, 2000), 455–456. This essay was based upon talks given at the University of South Pacific in October 1994 and, later, at the "Inside Out" conference and Pacific Writers Forum, which I helped (under the leadership of Vilsoni Hereniko and Geoffrey White) to organize at the East-West Center in Honolulu, in August 1994. Uncanny Pacific cultures, erupting into present contestation and struggles over justice in the Fijian island of Rotuman, are evoked in Vilsoni Hereniko's film, *The Land Has Eyes/Pear ta ma'on maf* (Te Maka Productions, 2004).

36. Hau'ofa, "Pasts to Remember," 457.

37. Hau'ofa is troping on, if not trumping, the prior French name for this geographical area of the Pacific, *Oceanía*, which came into broader use around that same time.

38. For a far-reaching approach to studying this counter-Pacific in de-orientalizing as well as coalitional place-based modes of research and art, see Lyons, *American Pacificism;* for "cultural studies" methods as situated in this de-colonizing transpacific approach, see Houston Wood, "Cultural Studies in Oceania," *The Contemporary Pacific* 15 (2003): 340–374. As Wood writes (in a survey of Pacific-based approaches), "Hauʻofa inaugurated his project of building a regional identity by emphasizing that Pacific islanders have a long history of connectedness, trade, exploration, and reciprocity, a history temporarily slowed but not ended by colonialism" (349). Wood invokes the Pacific art historian Margarent Jolly, who countered Hauʻofa's ocean-based vision of "routed" identity with the rooted claim that for many Pacific Is-landers, perhaps the majority, they "have no sense of ancestral connections to the ocean, no knowledge of how to make canoes, and indeed [have] never seen the ocean." See "On the Edge?: Deserts, Oceans, Islands," *The Contem-porary Pacific* 13 (2001): 423.

39. Hauʻofa, "Pasts to Remember," 458–459. A counterformation of Pacific his-tory encodes time in "cycles," circles, and "spirals," whereby "the past is ahead, in front of us" (460). While Hauʻofa invokes the Hawaiian-history model of Lilikala Kameʻeleihiwa in *Native Lands and Foreign Desires* (Hon-olulu: Bishop Museum Press, 1992), which puts the past in front of the pres-ent as culture-shaping model, he also notes that such notions of *circular time* would also recall "Christian calendrical rituals and festivals" more than the capitalist teleology of linear time as money-making resource (459–460) that we know from the American Protestantism of Max Weber theorizing the worldly theology of Ben Franklin as a disciplined form of money making and upward social mobility as driving the business-minded elect. Izaak Walton conveys this "circular" sense of Christianized time in *Life of George Herbert* (1670), the poet-priest of *The Temple* who turned from courtly life to the vo-cation of Anglican minister effacing self in daily rounds of lauds, hymns, homilies, and vespers: "Thus, the Church keeps an historical and circular commemoration of times, as they pass by us; of such times as ought to incline us to occasional praises, for the particular blessings which we do, or might re-ceive, by those holy commemorations"; see *The Lives of John Donne and George Herbert by Izaak Walton,* ed. Charles W. Eliot (Danbury, CT: Grolier, 1988), 404.

40. Hauʻofa, "Pasts to Remember," 466. On the mnemonics and codes of such place-making tactics in traditional Hawaiian chant and story, see Dennis Kawaharada, *Storied Landscapes: Hawaiian Literature and Place* (Hon-olulu: Kalamaku Press, 1999).

41. Epeli Hauʻofa, *Kisses in the Nederends* (Honolulu: University of Hawaiʻi Press, 1995), 101. Further references will occur parenthetically. In an inter-view by Subramani at the end of this novel, "A Promise of Renewal," Hauʻofa explains the autobiographical basis for this comic-grotesque por-trayal of Oilei Bomboki's illness in Fiji (155–175).

42. For a reading of this novel as a satirical challenge to normative abjection via postcolonial mimicry and menace, see Michelle Keown, "Purifying the Abject

Body: Satire and Scatology in Epeil Hau'ofa's *Kisses in the Nederends*," in *Postcolonial Pacific Writing: Representations of the Body* (London: Routledge, 2005), chapter 3.

43. Taking such hyperboles as theoretical transformations in a postcolonial mode, Michelle Keown summarizes the de-sublimating politics of Hau'ofa's satire in the following (quasi-Pauline) terms: "The comic resolution of the novel, like Babu's philosophy, therefore works toward possible solutions to global problems [like nuclear weaponry, male domination, and economic exploitation] through reconciling extremes and collapsing distinctions of race and gender, thereby transcending systems of exclusion or discrimination"; see *Postcolonial Pacific Writing*, 63.

44. The paradox of Christian *beatitude,* by which the highest sublimity incarnates itself into the most humble, fallen, broken-down, and forlorn modes of "Beat" humanity is memorably captured in this Pauline formulation of the *logos* from the New Testament: "Let this mind be in you, which is in Christ Jesus: Who, being in the form of God, thought it no prize to be equal with God: But emptied himself out, taking the form of a servant, becoming in the likeness of men . . . he humbled himself becoming obedient unto death, even the death of the cross. Wherefore God also hath highly exalted him, and given him the name which is above every name." (Philippians 2:6–11). In his populist compassion and capacious humanity, Hau'ofa never strays too far from this self-humbling ethos.

45. For underlying targets of Asia-Pacific satire and a "Bakhtinian" reading of these comic-grotesque figurations, see Rod Edmond, " 'Kiss My Arse!': Epeli Hau'ofa's Politics of Laughter," *Journal of Commonwealth Literature* 25 (1990): 142–155.

46. As Edmond reads the desublimating Swiftean allegory of the upper and lower body at war in *Kisses of the Nederends,* "The Lowertuks inhabit tropical zones of the body and their guerilla war is couched in anti-imperialist terms [against Uppertuk superiority]"; Ibid., 147.

47. For a reading of Hau'ofa that draws on the satirical terms and mimetic tactics of Mikhail Bakhtin's *Rabelais and His World,* trans. Helen Iswolsky (Bloomington: Indiana University Press, 1984), see John Hovell, "More of a Licking than a Spitting: Epeli Hau'ofa's *Kisses in the Nederends," Landfall* 42 (1988): 299–300, and Edmond, " 'Kiss My Arse!,' " 142–155.

48. See the trenchant study of *Kisses in the Nederends* by Teresia K. Teiawa, "Reading Paul Gauguin's *Noa Noa,*" as well as the pan-Pacific vision of antinuclear geopolitics and critique of postwar "militourism" by Teresia K. Teiawa, "bikinis and other s/pacific n/oceans," in *Voyaging through the Contemporary Pacific,* 91–112.

49. This success of Christianization in Tonga was largely due to the early conversion of Taufa'ahau (akin to the convert-figure of Queen Ka'ahamanu in Hawai'i), who valorized and modeled the gospel of rebirth among his people and destroyed the images of the old deities. He became King George Tupou I, ruled from 1845 to 1893, and adopted a modern constitution in 1875. In some ways, his royalty remained tied to the mythic descent from the sky god

Tangaloa and shared kinship with the Tui Tonga, who was both high chief and high priest mediating connections between sacred and human spaces. The *malae* was not so much sacred shire, as in Aeotearoa, as meeting place for secular gatherings and sporting events.

50. See "Tonga's Jester Has Last Laugh," BBC Asia-Pacific News, Oct. 6, 2001 accessed online, which urged that Tonga's King Taufaahau Tupou IV made this Bank of America account investment because the "government would only spend it on building roads."

51. In another sad incident, the eight thousand Tongans living in the Bay Area mourned the death of Prince Tu-ipelehake, hailed as the "People's Prince" for his political reform efforts, when he was killed along with another royal family member in a freeway crash on Highway 101 in Menlo Park in 2006 while visiting Tongan expatriates to gauge public opinion on the homeland political system.

52. See Andrew Quinn, "Laughing All the Way to the Bank," Reuters News Service, San Francisco, June 6, 2002.

53. This is the *only* Pacific work referred to in the global literary system portrayed by Pascale Casanova as a function of securing literary and cultural capitalist recognition and translations into the dominant languages (French, English, German, Spanish), at the center of this system, meaning the key Euro-American global cities of Paris, London, New York, Frankfurt, and (to a lesser extent) Barcelona: see *The World Republic of Letters*, trans. M. B. Debevoise (Cambridge, MA: Harvard University Press, 2004), 120. Keri's Hulme's *bone people* (winner of the New Zealand Book Award for Fiction and the Pegasus Prize in 1984 and the Booker Prize in 1985) was a hybrid novel of "postmodernist heteroglossia" and subaltern abjection, as Louis Menand points out in mapping how Casanova's system of "literary recognition" functions to validate such "world-readable" works: "Now nationality is transcended downward. Recognition comes from having one's work identified with a marginalized or 'endangered' community within the larger national or global polity—with Ibo culture (rather than Nigerian), or Maori (rather than New Zealand)"; "All That Glitters: Literature's Global Economy," *The New Yorker*, Jan. 2, 2006, 138–139. As "a trauma-and-recovery story, with magical realist elements, involving abuse and family dysfunction, that arrives at a resolution by the invocation of spiritual of holistic values," as Menard describes the award-winning *genre* of postcolonial literature Casanova (and its prize system) dominantly honors in the novel, *bone people* fits the generic codes, whereas antimagical works like Alan Duff's *Once Were Warriors* or any comic work by Hau'ofa does not easily fulfill these generic obligations. To date, Hau'ofa's novels have been translated into German but *not* French. (Poetry does not count for anything, nor does essay making, in this global literary system, though translation into world-dominant languages becomes crucial for literary recognition and global survival.)

54. See Terrence Wesley-Smith, *Contemporary Pacific* 12 (2000).

55. Amy Chua, *World on Fire* (New York: Doubleday, 2003).

56. Eric Waddell, "The Power of Positive Thinking," in *A New Oceania*, 29–30.

57. Hauʻofa, "The Ocean in Us," 119.

58. Kuan-Hsing Chen, "Civilizationalism," *Theory Culture & Society* 23 (March–May 2006): 428. Special issue on "Problematizing Global Knowledge."

59. In *Two Years before the Mast* (1840; Danbury, CT: Grolier, 1988), Richard Henry Dana memorably saw these forces of heart *(aloha),* reciprocal generosity *(mana),* and community-building in the Hawaiians who were working along the Pacific coast of America, in the 1830s, on ships and in the tanning industry and fur trade, as in the nonincorporated California site of San Diego. Speaking in pidgin English and some Hawaiian to these diasporic Hawaiians, Dana notes (as he is about to return to "Boston," which the Hawaiians take to be the center of the United States), "The Saturday night before our sailing, I spent an hour in the [tanning] oven, and took leave of my Kanaka friends; and, really, this was the only thing connected with leaving California which was in any way unpleasant. I felt an interest and affection for many of these simple, true-hearted men, such as I never felt before but for a near relation" (271). This kind of *aikāne* relationship of brotherly love and mutual devotion and service recalled what the New Englander Edward Dwight had felt for the Hawaiian convert Henry ʻŌpūkahaʻia (see Chapters 1 and 2), although Dana's seafaring Hawaiians friends "Hope" and the strangely named "Old Mr. Bingham" (who must have been nicknamed after the first-generation missionary head Hiram Bingham) remained unconverted Hawaiian laborers in California. Christian or not, these diasporic Hawaiians did want their beloved friend Dana to know that "Sandwich Island Kanaka—no [eat white man] like "New Zealand Kanaka" do (144); and that, as Old Mr. Bingham insists to Dana about Hawaiian contact history, " 'Me no eat Captain Cook! Me pikinini—small—so high—no more! My father see Captain Cook! Me—no!' " (144).

60. Susan Najita, "Decolonizing Pacific Literatures in English," in *Pacific Rim Cultural Formations,* ed. Christopher Leigh Connery (University of California Press, forthcoming). Najita also offers a splendidly contextualized reading of Hulme's *bone people,* which links it to ongoing Maori struggles for sovereignty, land, and language (something Casanova's metropolitan version of "literary value" cannot account for) more than global status.

61. For an American-Pacific based version of such postcolonial tactics of global/local engagement, see Rob Wilson, *Reimagining the American Pacific: From* South Pacific *to Bamboo Ridge* (Durham, NC: Duke University Press, 2000), chapter 3. Hauʻofa's works are also discussed on pages 89, 109, 112, and 139, especially *Tales of the Tikongs,* which is read as a countergeography of smallness, dialogical multiplicity, and place-based contestation.

62. My use of the geospatial term "Western Asia" for a *region* of strategic space and ethno-nationalist disturbance that encompasses India, Pakistan, and Afghanistan as well as Iran, Israel, Iraq, and the Arab world and opposes regime-changes imposed by the United States draws upon Fred Halliday's usage in *The Middle East in International Relations* (Cambridge: Cambridge University Press, 2005), chapter 5. My sense of "inter-Asia" as a region of

cultural innovation and transnational connection draws upon trans-area assumptions of the journal *Inter-Asia Cultural Studies*, for which I work as advisory editor.

63. Elias Canetti, "The Sea," in *Crowds and Power*, trans. Carol Stewart (New York: Noonday, 1998), 81. While discussing modern nation-forms, Canetti warns that for the island nation of the English, "The sea is there to be ruled" and to be commanded by its ships and tamed as extension of "some British territory" (171). The sea, for the British, becomes the site of mutiny and disaster, as in *Mutiny on the Bounty* and *Lord Jim*.

64. Albert Wendt, "Towards a New Oceania," *Mana Review* 1 (1976): 49–60. The "Pacific Islands Collection" of *Seaweeds and Constructions* (1984) also contained this literary declaration of Pacific independence as "New Oceania" (71–85) and made an impact in Hawai'i.

65. Hau'ofa, "Pasts to Remember," 470.

66. Epeli Hau'ofa, "Blood in the Kava Bowl," in *Lali: A Pacific Anthology*, ed. Albert Wendt (Auckland, NZ: Longman Paul, 1980), 239–240. In another Pacific belief-drenched poem, "Our Fathers Bent the Wind," Hau'ofa proclaims this shift away from Christian to Polynesian gods via this place-based *non serviam:* "Yesterday Tangaloa made men, / but the God of Love breeds children."

5. Regeneration through Violence

1. Galway Kinnell, "The Supper after the Last," in *A New Selected Poems* (Boston: Houghton Mifflin, 2001), 10; Ai, "Charisma," in *Vice: New and Selected Poems* (New York: Norton, 1999), 199; "A Conversation with Ai," *Standards* 7 (Spring–Summer 2001): http://www.colorado.edu/journals/standards/V7N2/ai2.html (accessed on Aug. 17, 2006).

2. See Victoria Nelson, *The Secret Life of Puppets* (Cambridge, MA: Harvard University Press, 2001), chapters 5 and 12, on the "gothic" religiosity of this fantastic mode as materialized in subliterary and film genres as well as the "insouled" machinery of puppets, robots, cyborgs, vampires, and computers.

3. See Ilene Lelchuk, " 'Convert or Die' Game Divides Christians," *San Francisco Chronicle*, Dec. 12, 2006, A1. This dynamic of "convert or die" reflects a postmodern recall of the monotheisms that clashed during the medieval Crusades and haunts our global-civilizational cultures. As Geneive Abdu notes in *Mecca and Main Street: Muslim Life in America after 9/11* (New York: Oxford University Press, 2007), " 'conversion by the sword' was reserved for idol worshippers, not the People of the Book" (171), who presumably shared one and the same God.

4. The romantic consequences of such a computer game is explored in Alexandra Alter, "Virtual Infidelity," *This Week* 7 (Aug. 31, 2007): 36–37, whereby husbands find an "online wife" or, as with some South Korean youths I have met, a whole new online family more to their liking.

5. Henry Adams, *The Education of Henry Adams: An Autobiography* (Boston: Houghton Mifflin, 1961), 476, 479.

6. Walter Benjamin, "This Space for Rent," in *One-Way Street, Reflections: Essays, Aphorisms, Autobiographical Writings,* trans. Edmund Jephcott (New York: Schocken Books, 1986), 86.

7. See Charles Taylor, *A Secular Age* (Cambridge, MA: Harvard University Press, 2007) on the failed "excarnation" of religious forces from the material world via modern regimes of the "buffered self" (613–615). (Ai's poetry overcomes all such "buffering" of self-other.)

8. See Michael Taussig, *Mimesis and Alterity: A Particular History of the Senses* (New York: Routledge, 1993), 35, 65.

9. C. S. Lewis, *Mere Christianity,* in *The Complete C. S. Lewis Signature Classics* (San Francisco: Harper, 2002), 115: "the man [reborn] is being caught up into the higher kinds of life—what I call Zoë or spiritual life: he is being pulled into God, by God, while still remaining himself" (89).

10. *The Gnostic Bible,* ed. Willis Barnstone and Marvin Meyer (Boston: New Seeds, 2006), 259. The "Gospel of Philip," in Coptic translation, was part of the Na Hammadi Codex rediscovered in Egypt in 1945.

11. Ai, "Pentecost," in *Vice,* 40–41. This collection won the National Book Award for American poetry in 1999, which raised the social impact of Ai as American poet: "some guardian angel somewhere was lookin' down on Baby Ai," as she put it in her *Standards* interview in 2001. (Further references to *Vice* will occur parenthetically.)

12. Review of Ai's *Dread* (2003) for *Booklist,* accessed online.

13. Information in this paragraph is taken from author page on *Modern American Poetry* website: http// www.english.uiuc.edu/maps/poets/a_f/ai/ai/htm (accessed Aug. 18, 2006).

14. Kenneth Burke, *Language as Symbolic Action* (Berkeley: University of California Press, 1966), 186–200.

15. See Chapter 2 for more on Burke et al., conversion "turns," and counter-turns.

16. A truncated, differently framed version of this chapter appeared as an essay in *Canadian Review of American Studies* 17 (1986): 437–448. It grew out of an InterArts Hawaii symposium on literature and the arts, where I chaired the panel discussion on "The Masks of the Poet, Ai" in Honolulu, June 18, 1979, which Ai took part in. At one point during audience discussion, when questioned by Leon Edel about sources of the violence and aggression her poetry masked as coming from what he called *autobiographical* obsessions "deep inside your own psyche," the poet laughed, cursed, and stormed out of the session at the Art Institute.

17. Ai, "Blue Suede Shoes," in *Sin* (Boston: Houghton Mifflin 1986), 13.

18. Elias Canetti, "The Survivor," in *Crowds and Power,* trans. Carol Stewart (New York: Noonday Press, 1998), 227–228.

19. Ray McDaniel, review of *Dread* in *The Constant Critic:* http://www.con stantcritic.com/archive/cgi?rev=Ray_McDaniel&name=Dread (accessed Aug. 18, 2006). The "impersonal intimacy" of Ai's dramatic monologues, repeated as a "career" in survivorship (both as poet and as traumatized subject), suggests for McDaniel what "seems a failure of imagination." As if to ward off

this technical repetition as imaginative failure, Ai has mentioned turning to works of memoir and fiction to deal with these subjects in a different genre.

20. David Wojahn, "Monologues in Three Tones," *New York Times*, June 8, 1986, a review of Ai's *Sin*, which he declares a fine collection by a "harrowing and courageous writer, one of the most singular voices of her generation."

21. For a reading of this poem as an interiorized critique of American militant ideology, see John Gery, *Nuclear Annihilation and American Poetry: Ways of Nothingness:* (Gainesville: University of Florida Press, 1996).

22. See Richard Drinnon's jeremiad, *Facing West: The Metaphysics of Indian-Hating and Empire Building* (Minneapolis: University of Minnesota Press, 1980). Richard Slotkin, *Fatal Environment: The Myth of the Frontier in the Age of Industrialization* (New York: HarperCollins, 1994), contains critiques of Custer's exterminationist rhetoric (384–385) and West Point–shaped beliefs in "The Red Man," as doomed (like buffalo) by "the masculine tools of advancing Christian-industrial civilization" (380).

23. Karl Malkoff, *Escape from the Self: A Study in Contemporary American Poetry and Poetics* (New York: Columbia University Press, 1977), 28–33. Other examples of the historical monologue as symbolic mask for the self would be John Berryman's *Homage to Mistress Bradstreet* (1967) and the pseudo-Victorian dramas of Richard Howard in *Untitled Subjects* (1969), with its epigraph from Browning, "I'll tell my state as though 'twere none of mine"; and the at times violent personae of Frank Bidart and Norman Dubie, closer to Ai's mode. David Wojahn, in "Monologues in Three Tones," calls attention to the dramatic monologue form in Edward Hirsch's *Wild Gratitude* (1986) and Nicholas Christopher's *A Short History of the Island of Butterflies* (1986). On the "theatrics" of symbolization in this mode, see Therese Catherine Irwin, "Voices in the Mirror: Sacrifice and the Theater of the Body in Dramatic Monologue of Ai and Frank Bidart," PhD diss., University of Southern California, 2003.

24. Ralph Waldo Emerson, "Nature," in *Emerson: Essays and Poems* (New York: Library of America, 1996), 10.

25. Emerson, "Fate," in *Essays and Poems,* 781.

26. Jackson Lears, "The Thought Experimenter," *The Nation*, Feb. 26, 2007, 29: "[for William James] pluralism in religious matters could be a polite name for polytheism—the paradoxically antimodern impulse animating many forms of Modernist thought."

27. Emerson, "Circles," in *Essays and Poems,* 407.

28. Emerson, "The Divinity School Address" in *Essays and Poems,* 89.

29. Ibid.

30. Emerson, "The Poet," in *Essays and Poems,* 459.

31. Ibid.

32. Harold Bloom, *Jesus and Yahweh: The Names Divine* (New York: Riverhead Books, 2005), 25.

33. On this post-Puritan genre of national-empowerment and self-alteration, see Rob Wilson, *American Sublime: The Genealogy of a Poetic Genre* (Madison: University of Wisconsin Press, 1991).

34. Interview by Michael Cuddihy with Ai, in *Ironwood* 12 (1978), 27.
35. Recall that Christopher Ricks named his study of Bob Dylan's poetry and poetics *Dylan's Visions of Sin* (New York: Ecco Press, 2004). See Chapter 6.
36. Review of *Killing Floor*, *Yale Review* 68 (1979): 568.
37. On the mytho-poetic drive to "world redemption" coming down to the present from poets as diverse as Timothy Dwight, Emerson, and Whitman, which might haunt Ai's dramatic monologues, see Ernest Lee Tuveson, *Redeemer Nation: The Idea of America's Millennial Role* (Chicago: University of Chicago Press, 1974). Woodrow Wilson's mission, which Tuveson critiques, would become literalized as global manifest destiny, from World Wars I and II if not down to wars in the Middle East led by Bush I and II: "America had the infinite privilege of fulfilling her destiny and saving the world." Ai's characters, from common to political, seem driven by such sacralized violence.
38. On the mytho-poetic use of sacrificial victims to displace social aggression, see René Girard, *Violence and the Sacred* (Baltimore: Johns Hopkins University Press, 1977), and the special issue of *Diacritics* devoted to Girard's work (vol. 8, Spring 1978). On Ai's particular mode of religious abjection and dramatic monologues of ego-release, see also Claudia Ingram, "Writing the Crisis: The Deployment of Abjection in Ai's Dramatic Monologues," *Literature Interpretation Theory* 8 (1997): 173–191.
39. Norman O. Brown, *Apocalypse and/or Metamorphosis* (Berkeley: University of California Press, 1991), 158.
40. On the theatrical and semiotic consequences for "representation" embedded in such a transubstantiating commitment to "the mystery of the Eucharist" and the "doctrine of the Real Presence" in the sacrament of the mass, see Stephen Greenblatt, "The Wound in the Wall" and "The Mousetrap" (chapters 3 and 5), in Catherine Gallagher and Stephen Greenblatt, *Practicing New Historicism* (Chicago: University of Chicago Press, 2001). In our postmodern era of deconstructive skepticism and critical wariness before incarnational or messianic modes of writing, Ai's language goes against the contemporary grain and in its uncanny ("unhomely") power—embodying what Norman O. Brown called "love's body"—may be closer to the spectral poetics of a Bob Dylan or Maxine Hong Kingston than to a W. S. Merwin or a Mark Strand.
41. Richard Slotkin, *Regeneration through Violence: The Mythology of the American Frontier, 1600–1860* (Middletown, CT: Wesleyan University Press, 1973), 22; see also his index on violence as a mode of self-transcendence (667). See also Canetti, *Crowds and Power.*
42. Canetti, "Reversal Crowds," in *Crowds and People*, 61.
43. This quotation from Ai and biographical information (most of which is online at sites for W. W. Norton) is taken from liner notes to "Passages into Another Life," distributed at the InterArts Hawaii symposium alluded to above in footnote 16.
44. Nineteenth-century background on the romantic will to transcendence and the modernist urge toward immersion in real particulars are discussed in Robert Onopa, "The End of Art as a Spiritual Project," *TriQuarterly* 26 (Winter 1973): 363–82. See also Michael Taussig, *Mimesis and Alterity* on

"mimetic exchanges" of energy, power, and *mana*, via contact with (metonymy) and imitation of (metaphor) "alterity," what is for Ai her lifetime project in bio-mimesis.

45. Gery, *Nuclear Annihilation and American Poetry.* Gery is speaking of Ai's poetic world up to *Sin*, but *Greed* and *Dread* would continue this "Americanist" ethnoscape of horror and dread, all the more so in post-terrorist terms of global antagonism, religion, and revenge.

46. See the special issue on white-Anglo "new nativism" and the rise of U.S. anti-immigrant sentiment, addressed against Latino workers but connected to a long history of "know-nothing" reaction against Irish, Italians, Chinese, Japanese et al., in *The Nation* 283, Aug. 28/Sept. 4, 2006: Daniel Tichenor, "Same Old Song: For the New Natives, What's Past Is Prologue," 25–28.

47. See Ihaemara's two cannibalism-debunking poems, "Skulls & Cannibals" and "Dinner with the Cannibals," in Witi Ihaemara et al., eds., *Te Ao Marama/The Flowering*, vol. 3 (Auckland, NZ: Reed Books, 1993), 218–221.

6. Becoming Jeremiah inside the U.S. Empire

1. Robert Shelton, *No Direction Home: The Life and Music of Bob Dylan* (New York: Ballantine, 1986), 559.

2. In *This Is Pop: In Search of the Elusive at Experience Music Project,* ed. Eric Weisbard (Cambridge, MA: Harvard University Press, 2004), 17. Firth maps the impact of American popular music in the United Kingdom as "hybrid" force that does not fit a "cultural imperialist" paradigm.

3. Bob Dylan, *Lyrics, 1962–2001* (New York: Simon & Schuster, 2004), 392. Further references to this collection will occur parenthetically as *Lyrics.*

4. Saint Paul, Timothy 1, 1:6, King James translation.

5. Linda Kintz, *Between Jesus and the Market: The Emotions That Matter in Right-Wing America* (Durham, NC: Duke University Press, 1997), reports that in 1976, fifty million Americans claimed to have had a born-again experience, including a key proponent of this fundamentalism of marketplace, nation, and God, Ronald Reagan (23). On George W. Bush's regime, see *Newsweek*, March 10, 2003, cover story "Bush and God": Martin E. Marty, "Why His 'God Talk' Worries Friends & Foes," 32–33. This is the theocratic religiosity against which I write, trying, as Langston Hughes urged, to take back a visionary America of counter-conversion: "Let America be America again. / Let it be the dream it used to be." See Langston Hughes, *Let America Be America Again and Other Poems* (New York: Vintage, 2004).

6. Cited in J. Shawn Landres and Michael Berenbaum, eds., introduction to *After The Passion Is Gone: American Religious Consequence* (Walnut Creek, CA: AltaMira, 2004), 7. Patrick Buchanan, in an essay defending *The Passion* against anti-Semitism and in praise of atonement-theologist director Mel Gibson, urges that "Braveheart has led and won a great victory in the crusade that is the culture war that will determine the fate of the civilization that came out of what happened on Calvary and on that first Easter morning" (32).

7. Trillin's long (for him) thirty-two-line poem surveying presidential eating habits was published in *The Nation,* Sept. 11, 2006, 8. More endearing is his claim that Reagan's wandering mind "could focus on that jar / Of jelly beans and know just where he was."

8. On this theocratic turn, see Kenneth J. Heineman, *God Is a Conservative: Religion, Politics, and Morality in Contemporary America* (New York: New York University Press, 2005).

9. James Baldwin, *Go Tell It on the Mountain* (New York: Laurel, 1981), 215, 189.

10. James Baldwin, "Sonny's Blues," in *Anthology of American Literature,* vol. 2, ed. George McMichael et al. (Upper Saddle River, NJ: Pearson, 2004), 782.

11. Bob Dylan, "Visions of Johanna," in *Lyrics, 1962–2001,* 193–194. On faux-Catholic dimensions of American popular culture, see also Victoria Nelson, "Faux Catholic: The History of a Gothic Subgenre from Monk Lewis to Dan Brown," *boundary 2* (2007): 87–107.

12. The Calvary in Mel Gibson's *The Passion of the Christ* (2004), reversing the resurrection-stress of Pauline scriptures, presents a Passion shorn of spectral elements, life works, and ecumenical tolerance—a mode of death-drive religiosity I would put closer to strands of American fundamentalism or a medieval version of Roman Catholicism. On Gibson's attempt to reverse the "Protestantizing" reforms of the Second Vatican Council and reinstate the divide between Judaism and Christianity via an iconography of "deicide," see Richard L. Rubenstein, "The Exposed Faultline," in *After* The Passion *Is Gone,* 207–218. On Gibson's blood-drenched medievalism, see Karen Jo Torjensen, "The Journey of the Passion Play from Medieval Piety to Contemporary Spirituality," in this same collection, 93–104.

13. I thank Christopher Leigh Connery for sending a bootleg CD of this Dylan concert in Santa Cruz, the first-hand experience of which he compared to hearing a Sermon on the Mount. Dylan followed "Doubting Thomas" with his own "Song to Woody Guthrie" brought back from Dustbowl tombs. On Thomas "becoming a Gnostic saint," see Glenn W. Most's exegesis of doubt and faith as fitfully materialized in word and image, *Doubting Thomas* (Cambridge, MA: Harvard University Press, 2005), 100.

14. Alan Cooperman, "Robertson Apologizes for Remark on Chavez: Call for Assassination Result of 'Frustration,'" *San Francisco Chronicle,* Aug. 24, 2005, A2.

15. Bob Dylan, "Señor (Tales of Yankee Power)," in *Lyrics: 1962–2001,* 390.

16. Stanley Cavell, "The Good of Film," in *Cavell on Film,* ed. William Rothman (Albany, NY: SUNY Press, 2005), 346.

17. Marcus credits San Francisco social-anarchist and Asian-facing poet Kenneth Rexroth with using his title phrase to express "the infinite idealism of American democracy" in figures like Carl Sandburg, Harry Smith, and Abraham Lincoln; *The Old, Weird America: The World of Bob Dylan's Basement Tapes* (New York: Picador, 1997), 88–89.

18. Jim Lewis uses this phrase in his prescient review of Johnson's sixth novel, *Tree of Smoke* (2007), "The Revelator," *New York Times Book Review,* Sept. 2, 2007, 8.

19. Denis Johnson, *Seek: Reports from the Edges of America and Beyond* (New York: HarperCollins, 2001), 118.

20. Denis Johnson, *Already Dead: A California Gothic* (New York: Harper Perennial, 1997), 184.

21. Mike Davis, "Pentecostal Earthquake," in *Dead Cities, and Other Tales* (New York: New Press, 2002), 120.

22. Robert Johnson, "Me and the Devil Blues" (take one), *Robert Johnson: The Complete Recordings,* Columbia Legacy CD C2K 649616, 1990.

23. See the multiauthored cover story, "Does God Want You to Be Rich?," *Time,* Sept. 18, 2006, on "the prosperity gospel" of capitalist spirituality in televangelists whose theology is rooted in positive thinking applied toward real estate deals and everyday life, what William James called the pragmatic psychology of "mind cure" and "self-suggestion." Holy Ghost forms are *messier* and uncanny, it seems to me: Pentecostal vision often breaks out from everyday molds and forms of middle class normality.

24. Greil Marcus, *Invisible Republic: Bob Dylan's Basement Tapes* (New York: Holt, 1997), 86.

25. See Robert Pogue Harrison, *The Dominion of the Dead* (Chicago: University of Chicago Press, 2003), 93–104.

26. On the political demands of this "prophetic" mode which uses Gospel analogue, social denunciation, and Bible-based critique from theo-politicians like John Winthrop through Abraham Lincoln, William Lloyd Garrison, and Martin Luther King down to post-1960s heirs in the arts such as Allen Ginsberg, Philip Roth, Pere Ubu, and David Lynch, see Greil Marcus, *The Shape of Things to Come: Prophecy and the American Voice* (New York: Farrar, Straus, and Giroux, 2006). Winthrop's 1630 speech, "A Modell of Christian Charity," to the Massachusetts Puritans proves paradigmatic of this quasi-Jeremaic mode of nation-making as covenanted project in "city on the hill," what Ernest Tuveson called the "redeemer Nation" in Enlightenment contexts like those of the Connecticut Wits.

27. Robert Duncan, *Roots and Branches* (New York: New Directions, 1964), 172, 174. Duncan's investment in the "historical grammar" of an American Pacific as proposed in Charles Olson's *Call Me Ishmael* is discussed in Nathaniel Mackey, *Discrepant Engagement: Dissonance, Cross-Culturality, and Experimental Writing* (Tuscaloosa: University of Alabama Press, 2000), 75–78.

28. Bob Dylan, "Lay Down Your Weary Tune," in *Lyrics, 1962–1985,* 120. Exorcizing Pacific memories, Dylan has his first wife, Sarah Lownds, recall ex-muse Joan Baez in the collage of "Sad-Eyed Lady of the Lowlands": "With your sheet-metal memory of Cannery Row" (240). The Catholicism of this "saint-like" woman with prayer beads and holy medallions suggests, more likely, that there is a *fusion* of Sarah Lownds/Joan Baez into poetic Muse-figure for Dylan's

"sad-eyed prophet" voice on this love song of beatific romance from *Blonde on Blonde*. For contexts moving between Greenwich Village, Cambridge, Cornell, and up and down the Pacific coast, see also David Hajdu, *Positively 4th Street: The Lives and Times of Joan Baez, Bob Dylan, Mimi Baez Farina, and Richard Farina* (New York: Farrar, Straus, and Giroux, 2001). Hajdu recounts how, in Carmel Highlands above Big Sur, Dylan wrote the song for Baez, not as love song, but "as a lament to hazards of singing the same tired music derived from the gospel song 'I Came to Jesus,' " which at the time was the genre of song Baez was singing. Baez was to give a concert at the Hollywood Bowl to a sold-out crowd (189–190), where Dylan and Baez sang "Lay Down Your Weary Tune" as a duet. They would soon meet the *genius loci* of Big Sur on the way back to Carmel, Henry Miller, who knew nothing of the hip poet Dylan but wanted to put the make on sisters Joan and Mimi (190). (The quasi-beat Brooklyn guru did play ping-pong with Dylan, as Miller and novelist Richard Fariña talked about the U.S. literary scene.) North Beach and Big Sur called to Dylan as sites of left-coast Beat transformation at this point in his multi-trajectory and mercurially masked career as poet-songwriter on the road to his calling.

29. This chapter was based initially on an interview in Honolulu between filmmaker Linda Ching (then working on a "Bob Dylan as Trickster" video) and Rob Wilson, reflecting upon Dylan's poetics of mask, conversion, and trickster-like disavowals. Bernie Richter transcribed it in May 2002. I thank both Linda and Bernie for their help, care, and wit in these matters.

30. Dylan told a *Chicago Daily News* reporter in 1965 that he was named after an uncle named Dillon, not Dylan Thomas: Shelton, *No Direction Home*, 45.

31. Jim Jerome, "Bob Dylan: A Myth Materializes with a New Protest Record and a New Tour," *People Weekly*, Nov. 10, 1975, 26.

32. Dylan's name comes from Welsh legend via Dylan Thomas; his poetry's affiliation to "enigmatic" Judeo-Christian parables of darkness and light are discussed in Jenny Ledeen, *Prophecy in the Christian Era: A Study of Bob Dylan's Work from 1961 to 1967* (St. Louis: Peaceberry Press, 1995), 24. In Ledeen's theological reading, Dylan's tambourine remains God-addressed (12) and Messiah-haunted (61), even in the Civil Rights era; or, more oddly, in the semi-druggy days of vision-quest when Dylan had wanted to get a book of poems published by City Lights Books in San Francisco and was turned down, as was the hippie-era pastoral novel *Trout Fishing in America* by Richard Brautigan which went on to sell two million copies for Dell paperbacks. On Dylan's mixtures of philosophy, theology, and literature, see also Peter Vernezze and Carol J. Potter, eds. *Bob Dylan and Philosophy: It's Alright, Ma (I'm Only Thinking)* (Chicago: Open Court, 2006). In particular, see Frances J. Beckwith, "Busy Being Born Again: Bob Dylan's Christian Philosophy," 145–155, which sees Dylan turning from "the nihilism and historicism" of our time back to foundational "first principles" (155), which does not allow for the play or irony, mask, and allegory that complicate, or show in a glass darkly, those "unchanging truths" in poetry.

33. Joel Selvin, "Bob Dylan's God-Awful Gospel," *San Francisco Chronicle*, Nov. 3, 1979, 34. Like Nietzsche, castigating what he calls Pauline bitterness

toward Christ, Selvin notes of this antirock didacticism, Dylan "displayed no joy in singing the gospel according to Bob."

34. Duncan is speaking of his myth-drenched conversion to Christ as figure of suffering humanity: see Nathaniel Mackey, "The World-Poem in Microcosm: Robert Duncan's 'The Continent,' " in *Discrepant Engagement*, 87.

35. Mitchell Robert Breitwieser uses this phrase to explain the aggression in American Puritan typification patterns, in *American Puritanism and the Defense of Mourning: Religion, Grief, and Ethnology in Mary White Rowlandson's Captivity Narrative* (Madison: University of Wisconsin Press, 1990), 25. *Slow Train Coming, Saved,* and *Infidels* are not unusual in Dylan's applications of this "holy aggression" toward the American polity and its (transnationalizing) downfall, as in the rage of "Union Downfall": "Democracy don't rule the world, / You better get that in your head. / This world is ruled by violence / But I guess that's better left unsaid."

36. Greil Marcus is still struggling with this shift: "I've been listening to the soundtrack of the Todd Haynes [Dylan biopic wherein six actors play phases of his life] *I'm Not There. . . .* [T]here were two things in Dylan's career that I've never been able to understand. One was the reaction of people at the Newport Folk Festival [when Dylan went electric in 1965]. . . . The idea that people would be upset by this, be offended or betrayed, it was incomprehensible to me. But this movie absolutely made it real to me, that people could react that way. The other thing is his conversion to fundamentalist Christianity. The sequence in this movie that depicts that is so beautiful, and so strange. . . . John Doe's version of the Dylan gospel song 'Pressing On' is playing [in the scene]; it reminded me of visiting the Chartres cathedral [in France]. I thought, 'God, I wish I believed in God, because then I could really appreciate this in a way that I probably can't.' I feel the same way when I listen to John Doe sing 'Pressing On.' I realize that there are things that I'll always miss." Marcus interviewed by Frances Reade in *San Francisco Weekly* online, Aug. 15, 2007.

37. On this core theme in Dylan, as expressed in Todd Haynes's biopic of masked multiplicity, *I'm Not There* (2007), see Kent Jones, "Chaos, Clocks, Juxtapositions," *The Nation*, Dec. 24, 2007, accessed online.

38. *Bob Dylan: The Essential Interviews*, ed. Jonathan Cott (New York: Wenner Books, 2006), 276. This interview of May 21, 1980, with Karen Hughes for *The Dominion* (Wellington, NZ) is the most forthright Dylan gave on his "born-again" experience (275–277). See also Joel Gilbert's documentary, *Inside Bob Dylan's Jesus Years* (Highway 61 Entertainment, 2008).

39. Letter to President Lyndon Baines Johnson, quoted in Nancy Gibbs and Michael Duffy, "The Political Confessions of Billy Graham," *Time*, Aug. 20, 2007, 43.

40. Ralph Waldo Emerson, "The Poet," in *Emerson: Essays and Poems* (New York: Library of America, 1996), 465.

41. Courtney Haden, "Jeremiah Gets His Groove Back: Bob Dylan's Latest Disk Offers a Mix of Laughter and Rue," *Birmingham Weekly*, Aug. 31, 2006. In Haden's shrewd overview of Dylan's career as the drive toward *atonement*, after the motorcycle wreck forty years ago, "a deep sense of obligation compels

him to stay on the road playing his songs, endlessly crisscrossing the country in the footsteps of Robert Johnson and Dan Rice and the Rabbit Foot Minstrels and the Hadacol Caravan." Dylan, like some latter-day King David, "[sings] of praise adoration, and vengeance, often all in the same lyric," as in "Nettie Moore," a ghost-haunted refiguring of an 1857 song lyric.

42. Elias Canetti, "The Figure and the Mask," *Crowds and Power*, trans. Carol Stewart (New York: Noonday Press, 1998), 375. Dylan's withdrawal from identification with social-protest movements in the mid-1960s can be read in a poetic sense as allegory of his whole vocation-as-poet, that is, as a withdrawal from identifications with "the crowd" and a return to masks, stories, and figures of self-relying power as spelled out in "Trust Yourself."

43. See Avis's video, which, along with the God-haunted yet polytheistic Columbia artistry of "Jokerman," are the best videos as yet at capturing the visionary reach and intertextual sources of Dylan's middle-period lyrics: they can be accessed at http://video.google.com (I thank Lindsay Waters and Rip Lhamon for emailing links to such multigeneric Dylan sites; accessed on Aug. 30, 2006).

44. Rodney Jones, *Salvation Blues: One Hundred Poems, 1985–2005* (Boston: Houghton Mifflin, 2006).

45. Quoted in Clinton Heylin, *Bob Dylan: Behind the Shades Revisited* (New York: Harper, 2001), 490, and chapter 27, "1978–79: On the Holy Slow Train," concerning the making of *Slow Train Coming* and *Saved* from born-again fundamentals. See also Robert Hilburn's interview with Dylan on born-again matters, "Dylan: 'I Learned That Jesus Is Real and I Wanted That,' " in *Studio A: The Bob Dylan Reader*, ed. Benjamin Hedin (New York: Norton, 2004), 147–154.

46. For the "voice" mode of this Jerusalem-derived culture of "Prophecy and Reform," see John W. O'Malley, *Four Cultures of the West* (Cambridge, MA: Harvard University Press, 2004), 40 and 69. Such a poetic of prophecy is anti-academic and counterhumanist in tactic, if the voice (as in Dylan) is still tied to the theatrics of "performance" culture.

47. See Heylin on all this, *Bob Dylan*, 498–499 and 524–525.

48. Alex Ross, "The Wanderer," in *Studio A: The Bob Dylan Reader*, 309. Ross urges that his "belated conversion to Dylan" (in Berlin circa 1996 listening to *Highway 61 Revisited*) was that of a rock-fan who "undergoes a sudden conversion or 'self-surrender,' often in a state of isolation or in a foreign land" (311), in terms recalling conversion in William James's *Varieties of Religious Experience*. See Chapter 3.

49. Norman O. Brown, epigraph to *Apocalypse and/or Metamorphosis* (Berkeley: University of California Press, 1991), v.

50. Ralph Waldo Emerson, "Fate," *The Conduct of Life* (1860), in *Essays and Poems*, 781.

51. In a study that would turn against the 1960s and align Dylan with (help!) the birth of hard and soft and utterly didactic "Christian rock," Stephen H. Webb reads his born-again work as a neoconservative turn toward "political agnos-

ticism" rooted in "the Christian doctrine of original sin, which describes human freedom as being bound by fault and fallibility"; *Dylan Redeemed: From* Highway 61 *to* Saved (New York: Continuum, 2006), 52, 7. Bypassing Dylan's "invisible republic" of the spirit, Webb's study is, at times, poetically simplistic and theologically reductive. Marcus is more nervously on the mark reading Dylan's evasive shifts of tone, voice, and belief like some con-man "radio evangelist" in his subtle reading of "Sign on the Cross" (*The Old, Weird America*, 83). At this preconversion point in his career we could say, with that Dylan song from the *Basement Tapes*, "I'm Not There" meaning self-present as a fixed identity or dead-certain state of beliefs via conversion.

52. *Bob Dylan: The Essential Interviews*, 298.

53. Johnny Cash, Letter to *Broadside*, March 10, 1964, in *Studio A: The Bob Dylan Reader*, 20.

54. A messianic song that appears—unexpectedly—amid the rabble-rousing carnival of the *Basement Tapes* (1975) would be "Sign on the Cross," in which "it's still that sign on the cross / That worries me" (300) amid all his worldly or romantic triumph. See note 48 to this chapter.

55. Michael Gray, *Song and Dance Man III: The Art of Bob Dylan* (London: Continuum, 2002), 42–49.

56. Paglia is reflecting on "Dylan at 60" for *Rolling Stone* in May 2001, in *Studio A: The Bob Dylan Reader*, 262.

57. Simon Frith, "European Thoughts on American Music," in *This Is Pop*, 18.

58. Dylan interviewed by Karen Hughes, May 21, 1980, in *Bob Dylan: The Essential Interviews*, 276.

59. As Gray summarizes this quest, "Along with an unfailing sense of the need for moral clarity, Dylan's work has also been consistently characterized by a yearning for salvation. In fact the quest for salvation might well be called the central theme of Bob Dylan's entire output"; *Song and Dance Man III*, 208.

60. Marvell's reading, in "On *Paradise Lost*," in modes opposing poetry and belief, whereby poetic meaning overcomes doctrinal formulation, is used as epigraph to Harold Bloom's study of this dilemma between truth and trope, *Ruin the Sacred Truths: Poetry and Belief from the Bible to the Present* (Cambridge, MA: Harvard University Press, 1989), 12ff.

61. "My Life in a Stolen Minute," in *Studio A: The Bob Dylan Reader*, 3–5.

62. The mysterious song called "I'm Not There (I'm Gone)," from the *Basement Tapes* outtakes, captures this directionless romantic abyss, the past trying to overthrow the present self in a battle of specter and emanation for domination: see Marcus, *The Old, Weird America*, 198–204.

63. William Blake, *The Complete Poems*, ed. Alicia Ostriker (London: Penguin, 1977), 494–497. Further references to Blake's poems will occur parenthetically. On this crisis in Blake's marriage and the psycho-political implications as figured in longer poems on the poet's Specter and Emanation, including "Milton" and "Jerusalem," see John Sutherland, "Blake: A Crisis of Love and Jealousy," *PMLA* 87 (1972): 424–431, as well as the entries for Specter

and Emanation in S. Foster Damon, *A Blake Dictionary* (Providence, RI: Brown University Press, 1965).

64. Cohen's *turns* from his Hebraic upbringing in Montreal to a kind of Catholic mysticism-cum-romantic hedonism in the 1960s and 1970s and then his conversion into a Zen Buddhist monk in the 1990s and later *back* to the Jewish faith (which he claims he never left) registers another richly poetic journey of conversionary quest. "Tower of Song" is from his album *I'm Your Man* (1990) that later became the title of a tribute album CD and documentary film (2006).

65. This song embodies the paradox of "fortunate fall" and other paradoxes of New Testament sermons about the sublime in the humble: the poem (via its heroine set for a fall) embodies codes of hipness that Dylan associates with the 1960s. It images the aura of a smug false-knowing he spends decades to repudiate and would instead link himself to a kind of innocence of the 1950s when he grew up, before he became that Village artiste woman. She is Dylan, his emanation and specter at once more than the mocking voice, even as "hipness" now has such a painful ring and has lost its association with the Beat/Beatitudes it once had, like Gap clothing taking on the Kerouac look. See Bob Dylan, *Chronicles,* vol. 1 (New York: Simon & Schuster, 2004), chapter 3, for this renunciation of the 1960s via a turn to a "New Morning" and semi-allegorized masks of faith and middle-class domesticity; see also readings of this poem by Greil Marcus, Lindsay Waters, and Christopher Ricks: "Pride," in *Dylan's Visions of Sins* (New York: Ecco Press, 2004).

66. John D. Barbour, *Versions of Deconversion: Autobiography and the Loss of Faith* (Charlottesville: University of Virginia Press, 1994), 13. "Figurative self-writing" is drawn from Avrom Fleischman, *Figures of Autobiography: The Language of Self-Writing* (Berkeley: University of California Press, 1983), 55.

67. For visionary dimensions of Blakean *poesis* as social critique, see Rob Wilson, " 'Hireling in the Camp, the Court & the University': Some Figurations of U.S. English Departments, Area Studies, and Masao Miyoshi as Blakean Poet," *Comparative American Studies* 2 (2004): 385–396.

68. Dylan, *Chronicles,* 1:34. Subsequent references will occur parenthetically.

69. George M. Marsden, "Fundamentalism since the 1970s: What Fundamentalists Learned from the Counterculture and Secular Doomsday Prophets," *Bookforum* 12 (Dec./Jan. 2006): 39.

70. Joel Rosenberg describes this Hebraic mode in "Jeremiah and Ezekiel," in *The Literary Guide to the Bible,* ed. Robert Alter and Frank Kermode (Cambridge, MA: Harvard University Press, 1987), 192. New Testament refiguration of such images, forms, and the prosodic syntax and dialectics of the "born-again" evangelical patterns that prove crucial to Dylan's conversion works are described by Michael Goulder, "The Pauline Epistles," 479–502, in this same collection.

71. *Saved!: The Gospel Speeches of Bob Dylan* (Madras and New York: Hanuman Books, 1999), 38–42.

72. As James Wolcott in "Idiot Wind: What Did Bob Dylan Ever Do to Deserve Christopher Ricks?" (*New Republic,* Aug. 30, 2004) caustically summarizes

this turn in reviewing Christopher Ricks's study of Dylan as poet, *Dylan's Visions of Sin:* "Shifting his gaze from the wicked parlors of sin to the wooden pews of virtues and heavenly graces, Ricks must overcome the resistance of those who find Dylan's born-again phase an episode best forgotten, like Ethel Merman's foray into disco. Dylan, who was visited by a vision of Jesus in a hotel room in Tucson in 1979, recorded three albums of Christian devotion and previews of Armageddon, *Slow Train Coming, Saved,* and *Shot of Love.* In concert, Dylan laced into nonbelievers who heckled his sermonettes between songs, telling them if all they wanted to do was rock and roll, 'You can go and see KISS and you can rock and roll all the way down into the pit!' "

73. Bloom, *Ruin the Sacred Truths,* 45.
74. Quoted in "With God on His Side," in the British rock magazine *Uncut, Legends,* no. 1, special issue on Bob Dylan, entitled "From Folk Hero to Electric Messiah," 2003, 78.
75. Romans 3:9–10 avows to Jews and Gentiles alike, converted and counter-converted, "As it is written, There is no man righteous, no, not one," in a syntax Dylan comes close to echoing in its string of negations.
76. Harold Bloom, *The Anxiety of Influence: A Theory of Poetry* (New York: Oxford University Press, 1997), 95. Bloom, the Samuel Johnson of our age, seems never to have discussed Dylan as a theo-poetic writer of this revisionary Yeshua/Yahweh agon.
77. "For the Evangelical," as Gerard Defaux describes its early-primitive traits of this mode in France, "the divine Word is the infallible source of salvation of souls and also of the social and political world, the 'republic,' " in *A New History of French Literature,* ed. Denis Hollier (Cambridge, MA: Harvard University Press, 1994), 164.
78. Harold Bloom, *Jesus and Yahweh: The Names Divine* (New York: Riverhead Books, 2005), 225, 170.
79. See the Wikipedia entry "List of Converts to Christianity," as accessed on Sept. 9, 2006. See also the hugely pluralist entry for "Religious Conversion."
80. Ginsberg to interviewer Wes Stace in 1985, quoted in Scott Marshall, "Bob Dylan's Unshakeable Monotheism," Feb. 16, 2004, part 3 (accessed online, Sept. 1, 2007).
81. As well as troping on the Bible and an eclectic array of traditions from the Beats and Rimbaud to Milton, Dante, and Donne, Dylan refigures blues, folk, and American song lyrics from a range of prewar black and white authors. The most detailed study of this lyrical uncanniness from a "Highway 61" U.S. locality linking North to South remains (for me) Michael Gray, *Song and Dance Man, III:* see chapter 9, "Even Post-Structuralists Ought to Have the Pre-War Blues," on Dylan's visionary blues refiguration; as an example of this genre, see chapter 15, "Bob Dylan, Blind Willie McTell, and 'Blind Willie McTell.' "
82. Here the semi-debunking analysis of Dylan's masks and poses of voice by Louis Menand might prove helpful in its myriad subterranean linkages of Dylan songs to folk artists like Van Ronk, Tom Rush, Judy Collins, and the Beatles, in "Bob on Bob," *The New Yorker,* Sept. 29, 2006.

83. See the study by Mark Brend, *American Troubadours: Groundbreaking Singer-Songwriters of the 60s* (San Francisco: Backbeat Books, 2001), 63–67. In addition to Blue's song work, Brend tracks the careers, formed in the Village shadows of Dylan, for crucial figures like Fred Neil, Phil Ochs, Tom Rush, Tim Hardin, and Tim Buckley. Ochs was a talented "topical" songwriter of political authenticity and compassion who rivaled Dylan in certain genres of American leftist social vision, which Dylan abandoned as "just journalism" (103) by 1965 when *Highway 61 Revisited* took over the whole Village folk scene, as it were, with its hipster codes and beatitudes.

84. Brend, *American Troubadours*, 94–95. Brend notes that Fred Neil's *Bleeker and McDougald* (Elektra, 1965) "was an album on the cusp of a new era" (94), after Dylan had broke open the forms and modes and allowed for more possible folk-rock fusions and quasi-literary risks.

85. Menand, "Bob on Bob."

86. On Dylan as a "master of ambiguity" refusing interpretive closure during this era, see Wendy Lesser's reading of "Lily, Rosemary, and the Jack of Hearts," in *The Rose and the Briar: Death, Love and Liberty in the American Ballad*, ed. Sean Wilentz and Greil Marcus (New York: Norton, 2005), 315–325.

87. See Andy Gill, *Don't Think Twice It's Alright: Bob Dylan, the Early Years* (New York: Thunder's Mouth Press, 1998); for more of this "story behind the songs" via a quasi-biographical approach to Dylan's studio session, life, and albums, see Andy Gill and Kevin Odegard, *A Simple Twist of Fate: Bob Dylan and the Making of* Blood on the Tracks (Cambridge, MA: Da Capo Press, 2004).

88. Barry Shank has discussed Dylan's move from folk-persona identifications toward imaginative autonomy in *Highway 61 Revisited*: see "'That Wild Mercury Sound': Bob Dylan and the Illusion of American Culture," *boundary 2* 29 (2002): 97–123. As Elijah Wald put Dylan's postblues creation of "a whole new kind of fusion and revivalism [as a] sideways turn into modern art," "it was no longer going back to Chicago and Mississippi, it was about creating the new sound of the 1960s, and Jimi Hendrix built on that vibe, and after a little while no one was calling it blues anymore"; see *Escaping the Delta: Robert Johnson and the Invention of the Blues* (New York: HarperCollins, 2004), 245–246.

89. See the reading of this six-minute AM song and the studio sessions and U.S. cultural-political contexts that helped to generate it and almost did not allow for its emergence, in Greil Marcus, *Like a Rolling Stone: Bob Dylan at the Crossroads* (New York: Public Affairs, 2005). This is a study worthy of a work that has come to be considered, by *Rolling Stone* et al., as the best rock lyric of all time. I did see it change lives in Waterbury, Connecticut (in 1965, the year I graduated from high school), including in my own life; it helped to generate my "dharma bum" move to the West Coast like a stone rolling toward City Lights Bookstore, the Haight-Ashbury, UC Berkeley, and parts unknown in Asia/Pacific (see the epilogue).

90. On tensions between representation and doctrines of faith and grace, which Dylan (like Shakespeare) lives out in his poetic art and masks in public, see

Stephen Greenblatt, "The Wound in the Wall," in Catherine Gallagher and Stephen Greenblatt, *Practicing New Historicism* (Chicago: University of Chicago Press, 2001), 98–99.

91. On neoplatonic, Christian allegorical, and courtly dimensions of this poetic complex clustered around the beauty and love of woman, see C. S. Lewis, *The Allegory of Love: A Study in Medieval Tradition* (New York: Oxford University Press, 1985).

92. On cross-racial tactics of this "love and theft" from Dylan into depths of minstrelsy white and black and into neo-Village Beat as well, see Eric Lott, *Love and Theft: Blackface Minstrelsy and the American Working Class* (New York: Oxford University Press, 1993).

93. On working-class and racial crossing of identifications in such works and masks, in terms of affiliated comradeship and WASP defiance, see W T. Lhamon Jr., *Raising Cain: Blackface Performances from Jim Crow to Hip Hop* (Cambridge, MA: Harvard University Press, 2005). On the racial and cultural hybridity in the 1950s that proves crucial to Dylan as an artist as he urged in *Chronicles*, see also W. T. Lhamon Jr., *Deliberate Speed: The Origins of a Cultural Style in the American 1950s* (Cambridge, MA: Harvard University Press, 2002).

94. Marcus, *The Shape of Things to Come*, 11–12, 250–251.

95. This is Marcus's "prophetic" reading of Philip Roth in *American Pastoral* (New York: Vintage International, 1997). In this three-generational novel, Roth gets to the subject-forming conversion of "smart Jewish kids" like Meredith Levov from miming Wasp-like codes of the "flawlessly Americanized" life in suburbia (3), into "another America" of the displaced and dispossessed (86) who inherit the earth in ruination as students of Fanon and Angela Davis (at one extreme of activism) and Gandhi and Buddha (at the other extreme of "ahimsa" or nonviolent retreat). The Swede, and his Miss New Jersey wife of Irish Catholic stock, have given birth to "The daughter who transports him out of the longed-for American pastoral, into the fury, the violence, and the desperation of the counter-pastoral—into the indigenous American berserk" (86). She has converted America back into a wilderness of alien Gods, ruination, and condemnation on the death-filled, piss-stained streets of postindustrial Newark.

96. Marcus, *The Shape of Things to Come*, 43.

97. See Menand, "Bob on Bob," for this evocation of Dylan as Terence for the humanism of our time.

98. As quoted in Leah Garchik's gossip column for the *San Francisco Chronicle*, Sept. 21, 2006, E6. This amusing left-coast columnist then retorted to the unbelieving and debunking fan, "Say, Mr. Malcontent: Dylan is Dylan is Dylan. You want audience engagement, go see Chuckles the Clown."

99. One of the best studies of Dylan's ability to perform as a writer over these years remains that by "Crawdaddy" editor and writer Paul Williams, *Bob Dylan, Performing Artist: 1974–1986, The Middle Years* (London: Omnibus Press, 1994). "Crawdaddy" was, for me, the place where rock and Dylan criticism started, more so than *Rolling Stone* magazine.

100. Gilles Deleuze (with Claire Parnet), *Dialogues* (New York: Columbia University Press, 1977), 8.

101. Charley Chaplin wrote, produced, and directed *Modern Times* (1936), in which Charley the tramp played a singing waiter in a cabaret and a worker on the assembly line: this figure of cultural front populism in the workers' movements of the 1930s gets run through gears and gets clobbered by time-saving machines as he eats. Dylan wrote and produced (under the mask of "Jack Frost") his own *Modern Times,* but in his commitment to refunctioned uses of studio technologies, to iPods, and as a deejay for XM radio I do not think that Dylan is satirizing (like Chaplin) "the dehumanizing effects of technology (the machines speak—they whir and pound and screech)," as Pauline Kael describes the movie in *5001 Nights at the Movies* (New York: Holt, 1991), 491. In some sense, "Dylan" gets *born again* through shifting mimetic technologies.

102. Jonathan Lethem, "The Genius of Bob Dylan," *Rolling Stone* Sept. 7, 2006, 128.

103. I owe this insight to Lindsay Waters in an e-mail to me (Aug. 30, 2006). Recalling theo-poetic contexts, "Those who have ears to hear let them hear" is how Jesus explained tactics of poetic parable and story to Saint Matthew (Matthew 11:15), and he used such methods to teach the humble "multitudes" while baffling those too proud or blind to these parables: "Therefore speak I to them in parables: because they seeing see not; and hearing hear not, neither do they understand, "For blessed *are* your eyes, for they see: and your ears for they hear" (Matthew 13:13–16). In *Modern Love,* Dylan makes clear he is not claiming pop Messiah status à la *Blood on the Tracks* and that his suffering and prayers sent up in the darkness are no better than anyone else's: "We all wear the same thorny crown / Soul to soul" ("When the Deal Goes Down").

104. Saint Herman, as far as I can tell, comes from Russian Alaska and his beatitude is associated with being patron saint of the native peoples and "orphans" in the Americas, which Dylan jests he will form into an army to oppose death forces.

105. Joe Levy, review of Bob Dylan's *Modern Times* (Columbia, 2005), *Rolling Stone,* Sept. 7, 2006, 100.

106. Dylan quoted in Scott Marshall, "Bob Dylan's Unshakeable Monotheism," Feb. 16, 2004, part 3 (accessed online, Sept. 1, 2007).

107. Lyrics from *Modern Times* are taken from the informative website on day-by-day Dylan, Expecting Rain: http://expectingrain.com (accessed Aug. 30, 2006).

108. "Nettie Moore" can be found in a nineteenth-century song sheet published by H. D. Marsan in New York (n.d.). For cross-racial vernacular borrowing in popular cultural forms, see Lott, *Love and Theft;* and Cecil Brown, *Stagolee Shot Billy* (Cambridge, MA: Harvard University Press, 2003), on "Bob Dylan's Stagolee" (184–188), wherein "Dylan's identification [in his performance of Frank Hutchinson's ballad set in a St. Louis Negro saloon in *World Gone Wrong*] with an outlaw figure resembles Benjamin's flaneur,

who is looking for hidden truths, the traces of an invisible world," before or after the coming of the Messianic (188–189).

109. Brown, *Stagolee Shot Billy,* 189. Dave Van Ronk, one of Dylan's mentors in the defamiliarization of traditional song forms, black and white, "was said to have over five hundred versions of Stagolee," which Van Ronk denied to Cecil Brown at the Freight and Salvage folk club in Berkeley in 1998 (255). Dylan's command of myriad genres and traditions has been demonstrated weekly on his XM satellite radio show for "Deep Tracks," which organizes eclectic weekly presentations around such themes as "mothers," "baseball," "the weather," "jail," and "the Bible." He has been accused not so much of *borrowing* as *stealing* from others, from Van Ronk himself to Henry Timrod to Muddy Waters et al., a charge that fails to see the refunctioning of sources Dylan *always* brings to bear, as when he ends his version of "Rollin' and Tumblin'" with Blakean pleas for Mutual Forgiveness that go beyond cycles of male rage, narcissism, and grief. This is the complex of cultural borrowing Eric Lott calls "love and theft," and Dylan acknowledges with unassuming quotation marks around *"Love and Theft."*

110. David Yaffe, "Tangled up in Bob," *The Nation,* April 2005 accessed online.

111. "Pope [Benedict XVI] Reveals Unease over John Paul II's Appearance with Bob Dylan," Agence France Presse, May 7, 2007 (accessed online May 7, 2007).

112. See Paul Williams, *Bob Dylan, Performing Artist 1986–1990 & Beyond: Mind Out of Time* (London: Omnibus Press, 2005), ix–xiv, 339.

Epilogue. Conversions through Literature

1. The first epigraph is from Ryan K. Smith's study, *Gothic Arches, Latin Crosses: Anti-Catholicism and American Church Designs in the Nineteenth Century* (Chapel Hill: University of North Carolina Press, 2006), 115; the second is a comment from "A Conversation with Gertrude Stein" (1935), in *The Creative Process: A Symposium,* ed. Brewster Ghiselin (New York: Signet, 1952), 161; and John Yau, *Radiant Silhouette: New and Selected Works, 1974–1988* (Santa Barbara, CA: Black Sparrow Press, 1989), 25.

2. See Stephen Greenblatt, *Shakespearean Negotiations: The Circulation of Social Energy in Renaissance England* (Berkeley: University of California Press, 1988); and *Renaissance Self-Fashioning: From More to Shakespeare* (Chicago: University of Chicago Press, 2005).

3. Ralph Waldo Emerson, "Success" from *Society and Solitude* (1870), http://www.rwe.org (accessed Aug. 13, 2005).

4. Ralph Waldo Emerson, *Essays and Poems* (New York: Library of America, 1996), 1003; the emphasis is mine.

5. Gilles Deleuze and Felix Guattari, *Kafka: Toward a Minor Literature,* trans. Dana Polan (Minneapolis: University of Minnesota Press, 1986), 27. Further references will occur parenthetically.

6. Gilles Deleuze and Claire Parnet, *Dialogues,* trans. Hugh Tomlinson and Barbara Habberjam (New York: Columbia University Press, 1987), 50. Further references will occur parenthetically.

7. Frank Lentricchia, *Luchesi and the Whale* (Durham, NC: Duke University Press, 2001): the death-haunted protagonist, Thomas Luchesi, leaves middle America for an "open-ended cruise in the South Seas, for the purpose of retracing Herman Melville's early career, in hopes of summoning, from places Melville had touched, that writer's robust tutelary ghost" (4).

8. Ibid., 63.

9. See Ralph Nader, *The Seventeen Traditions* (New York: Harper, 2007).

10. "'Connecticut, Connect-I-cut!' cries little Joey" in Gilles Deleuze and Felix Guattari, *Anti-Oedipus: Capitalism and Schizophrenia,* trans. Robert Hurley et al. (Minneapolis: Minnesota University Press, 1983), 37.

11. Wallace Stevens, "Connecticut," in *Opus Posthumous* (New York: Knopf, 1957), 296. This is the script for the "This Is America" radio series for April 1955, one of the last pieces of prose Stevens wrote, done out of gratitude for the people, place, and ethos of the state in which he had composed his greatest poetry and a poetics of suspended belief; the talk is reprinted as "Connecticut Composed" in *Stevens: Collected Poetry and Prose* (New York: Library of America), 894–896.

12. This remark is from a *Tel Quel* special issue on the United States and is quoted in a chapter exploring the "Poetics of Space" in the French and European imagination of America by Jean-Phillippe Mathay, *Extreme-Occident: French Intellectuals and America* (Chicago: University of Chicago Press, 1993), 163.

13. Norman O. Brown, *Apocalypse and/or Metamorphosis* (Berkeley: University of California Press, 1991), iv. Brown's chapter 8, "The Turn to Spinoza," helps unpack what he means by "conversion": "As in Blake, the opposition of Body and Soul [in Spinoza's theology] is overwhelmed in the concept of energy" (138), as drive to enhance "joyous" feelings for self and community, a reading Brown draws via Antonio Negri and Etienne Balibar, using "savage" Spinoza against the Empire of capital.

14. Fredric Jameson, *Brecht and Method* (London: Verso, 2000), 23.

15. On the "deconversion" narratives in ex-communists and socialists that resonate with religious disillusionment, see John D. Barbour, *Versions of Deconversion: Autobiography and the Loss of Faith* (Charlottesville: University of Virginia, 1994), on *The God That Failed* (1949), 48, as well as on socialist- and Marxist-influenced writers like Edwin Muir in his *An Autobiography* (1954) and John Paul Sartre in *Les Mots* (*Words;* 1964).

16. See Angus Fletcher on the open-ended syntax of "the environment-poem" from Whitman and John Clare to John Ashbery et al. in *A New Theory for American Poetry: Democracy, the Environment, and the Future of Imagination* (Cambridge, MA: Harvard University Press, 2004). Charles Olson, while still tied to the geography and New England community of Gloucester, Massachusetts, as linked, early and late, to transnational market flows across the Atlantic and Pacific Oceans, in *The Maximus Poems,* would still be for myself and others (from Garrett Hongo to Robert Creeley, Michael Davidson, and Christopher Leigh Connery), such a hugely "environmental" U.S. poet of democratic world-possibility.

17. Gayatri Chakravorty Spivak, forward to *Other Asias* (Malden, MA: Blackwell, 2008), 13.

18. Nancy M. Malone, *Walking a Literary Labyrinth: A Spirituality of Reading* (New York: Riverhead Books, 2003), 3–4.

19. Ibid., 101.

20. Religion, broadly associated with modes of settlement and sacred dwelling sites ("rooting"), can also be connected to processes of movement, quest, and the crossing of cultural borders ("routing"): see Thomas A. Tweed, *Crossing and Dwelling: A Theory of Religion* (Cambridge, MA: Harvard University Press, 2006), particularly chapter 5, on "The Kinetics of Itinerancy."

21. Thomas Wolfe, "The Story of a Novel," in *The Creative Process*, 199.

22. Jack Kerouac, *On the Road* (New York: Penguin, 1979), 11.

23. In a special issue of *South Atlantic Quarterly* 105 (2006) on "AmBushed: The Costs of Machtpolitik," edited by Dana D. Nelson, see this formulation of "techno-medievalism" applied by Timothy Brennan and Keya Ganguly, "Crude Wars," 29.

24. U.S. right-wing media scourge Ann Coulter, for example, has called for the *forcible* conversion of all Muslims and on a CNBC talk show recently urged that, in her righteous America, Jews could be "perfected" through conversion to Christianity: see Tim Rutten, "Coulter's Anti-Semitic Comment Too Dangerous to Ignore," *Los Angeles Times*, Oct. 13, 2007, accessed online the same day.

25. William Empson, quoted in Stephen Burt, "Adventures in Ambiguity," a review of the *Selected Letters of William Empson* and *William Empson: Among the Mandarins*, in the *New York Times Book Review*, Sept. 10, 2006, 28.

26. On Japanese militarism across Asia and the Pacific that enlisted Zen Buddhism into its self-abolishing imperial project in World War II, see Brian Daizen Victoria, *Zen at War* ((Lanham, MD: Rowman & Littlefield, 2006).

27. Norimitsu Onishi, "Koreans Quietly Introducing Jesus to Muslims in Mideast," *New York Times*, Nov. 1, 2004. Since Americans have had a bad image globally during the eight-year Bush administration of stagnation, if not global and national ruination, Koreans (long tutored by American missionaries from Roman Catholic to various Protestant denominations) nowadays can more commonly assume this conversion work on the postcolonial periphery of our Empire without that "sense of guilt because of their imperialist past" that Western missionaries feel, as Onishi details.

28. Walt Whitman, *Leaves of Grass*, ed. Sculley Bradley and Harold W. Blodgett (New York: Norton, 1973), 245.

29. See Gananath Obeyesekere's study of "rebirth" figures, in *Imagining Karma: Ethical Transformation in Amerindian, Buddhist, and Greek Rebirth* (Berkeley: University of California Press, 2002), chapters 1 and 2. He argues that although "two models—instantaneous rebirth [by which he means 'reincarnation'] and delayed rebirth—are found throughout western Africa and Asia in their various cultural and ethical transformations" (317), "salvation has to be sought outside of" such rebirth eschatologies (355). This

means that "when a Buddhist converts to Christianity," there is a "para-digm abandonment" more than there is just a "paradigm shift" (355) from such a vision of plural rebirth. But such was not the case for Kerouac, who thought of himself as a Catholic beatitude-seeker even as he tried to convert the world to "waking up" to the Buddha in *Some of the Dharma*. See Chapter 3.

30. Waichee Dimock offers a reading of the "vernacularizing" multireligious id-iom in the Dead's "Blues for Allah" and "Deep Elem Blues," sung by the Shelton Brothers in the 1930s, in *Through Other Continents: American Literature across Deep Time* (Princeton, NJ: Princeton University Press, 2007), elaborating these lyrics as "speak[ing] as much to Islam as to Christianity [and carrying on] the work of Hafiz and Emerson both" (50).

31. Bob Dylan, *Lyrics, 1962–2001* (New York: Simon & Schuster, 2004), 594. Subsequent references will occur parenthetically to page numbers for songs.

32. "For Bob Dylan, it is essential that every feeling even those about the coun-try, one could say especially about the country be mediated by love figures, his muse, as you show," is how Lindsay Waters phrased his response to my reading of Bob Dylan as love poet (in an e-mail of Sept. 10, 2006).

33. Ernst Bloch, "Can Hope Be Disappointed?" in *Literary Essays* (Stanford, CA: Stanford University Press, 1998), 340.

34. John Perkins, *Confessions of an Economic Hit Man* (New York: Plume, 2005).

35. David Palumbo-Liu, *Asian/American: Historical Crossings of a Racial Fron-tier* (Stanford, CA: Stanford University Press, 1999), 5.

36. John Steinbeck, *Cannery Row* (New York: Penguin, 1973), 5.

37. Robert Frost, "A Poet's Boyhood," in *Collected Poems, Prose and Plays* (New York: New American Library, 1995), 894–895.

38. Kerwin Lee Klein, *Frontiers of Historical Imagination: Narrating the Europe-an Conquest of America, 1890–1990* (Berkeley: University of California Press, 1999), 220. A Pacific-linked vision of U.S. frontierism was elaborated by one of my mentors, Henry Nash Smith, in *Virgin Land: The American Land as Myth and Symbol* (1950; Cambridge, MA: Harvard University Press, 1986), in its section "A Brief Passage to India," which takes its framing metaphor from Whitman's poem by that name. (I had also worked as research assistant with Masao Miyoshi on linkages of this American polity to Meiji-era Japan, a move beyond U.S. orientalism that proved crucial to my reformation as an "American Scholar" in Hawai'i, Asia-Pacific, and California.)

39. I thank Phoebe Kosman at Harvard University Press for this Frost prose ref-erence to the Pacific. Frost's poem "The Gift Outright" enacts this U.S. providential will to take possession of the continent as Manifest Destiny from Atlantic to Pacific. The poetry of Robinson Jeffers does this, in ironic reversal, via reductions to elemental Big Sur forces like rock, hawk, and tides.

40. On translated-becoming through cultural mobility and "articulated" con-figurations, see James Clifford, interviewed by Robert Borofksy, *On the Edges of Anthropology (Interviews)* (Chicago: Prickly Paradigm Press, 2003), 80.

41. I allude to the belletristic "global system" tracked in Pascale Casanova's *The World Republic of Letters*, trans. M. B. DeBevoise (Cambridge, MA: Harvard University Press, 2004), whose breadth of global literary emergence and turn to postcolonial "minor literatures" (from Western and Eastern Europe and Africa to China, Japan, and Korea) encompasses *one* Pacific literary work, a Booker Prize–winning work by the Maori novelist Keri Hulme, *bone people* (120). For land-based and transoceanic figurations in Hulme's novel, see Susan Najita, *Decolonizing Cultures: Reading History, Trauma, and Fiction in the Contemporary Pacific Islands* (New York and London: Routledge, 2006), chapter 3.

42. On terms of "lived hybridity," see Joel Robbins, *Becoming Sinners: Christianity and Moral Torment in a Papua New Guinea Society* (Berkeley: University of California Press, 2004).

43. Ambivalent fantasies range from fears of cannibal savagery to utopic longings for cross-racial friendship and lotus-eating Edens and comprise what Paul Lyons calls "American Pacificism," in *American Pacificism: Oceania in the U.S. Imagination* (London: Routledge, 2005).

44. Gilles Deleuze, *Spinoza: Practical Philosophy*, trans. Robert Hurley (San Francisco: City Lights Books, 1988): "Spinoza is categorical on this point: all the phenomena that we group under the heading of Evil, illness, and death are of this type: bad encounters, poisoning, intoxication, relational decomposition" (22).

45. Nathaniel Mackey, "Other: From Noun to Verb," in *Discrepant Engagement: Dissonance, Cross-Culturality, and Experimental Writing* (Tuscaloosa: University of Alabama Press, 2000), 272.

46. Replayed on the Larry King Show, CNN, July 2, 2004, after Brando's death in Los Angeles.

47. *Hembemba: Rivers of the Forest* (Suva, Fiji: Institute of Pacific Studies/ University of Papua New Guinea, 2000).

48. Ralph Waldo Emerson, journal entry from 1849, in *Basic Selections from Emerson: Essays, Poems, and Apothegms*, ed. Eduard C. Lindeman (New York: Mentor, 1954), 198.

49. Stanley Cavell, "Thinking of Emerson," in *The Senses of Walden* (San Francisco: North Point Press, 1981), 138. "Dwelling" can be linked to abandoning for Thoreau and Emerson, in quest for a relation to earth-forces of deepened meaning: see Robert Pogue Harrison, *Forests: The Shadow of Civilization* (Chicago: University of Chicago Press, 1992), 265.

50. Dan Chiasson, "The View from Eagle Pond Farm," review of Donald Hall's *White Apples and the Taste of Stone: Selected Poems, 1946–2006* (Boston: Houghton Mifflin, 2006), *New York Times Book Review,* July 9, 2006, 12.

51. See Hayden Carruth, "On Being Marginalized and Other Poems in Measured Resistance," as well as Christian Thompson, "On Hayden Carruth's 'Contra Mortem,' " *American Poetry Review* 33 (July/August 2004): 19–23. The exacting poet Carruth was also the editor of *Poetry Magazine* in Chicago and editor of the capacious anthology *The Voice That Is Great Within One: American Poetry of the Twentieth Century* (New York: Bantam,

1978), which my mentor in the American Sublime poetics and poetry, Josephine Miles, used in her era-crossing UC Berkeley graduate seminars.

52. My hometown newspaper, *The Waterbury Republican,* carried a "Piersall at Bat" column on the sports pages of summer to follow his hitting average in my youth. I rooted more, at that time, for the pennant-winning New York Yankees than those perennial losers to the north. Ted Williams at bat was another matter: *amazement* was the only response. The manically driven Piersall, who led his Leavenworth High School basketball team to state and New England championships in 1947, after his rise and breakdown during his outfield career as a Red Sox, was reborn so to speak as a baseball announcer in Chicago, where he still lives and works. *Fear Strikes Out* foreshortens his career and admirable struggles to move on and transform his life and work.

53. See Frances Chamberlain, "Was There a Saint Born in Waterbury?" *New York Times,* Sept. 13, 1998 (accessed online Nov. 11, 2007). A tender-minded hero of caritas in my mind, Father McGivney has been nominated for the path to beatified sainthood, defying that biblical rebuke that seldom stopped the lowborn apostles of Jesus from signing on to his world conversion mission, "Can anything good come out of Nazareth?" Waterbury, like Lowell, Massachusetts, another milltown full of factories, rivers, churches, and hardworking people, has seen many good things come out of its urban constellation of social forces from shoes, clocks, buttons, and watches to the Beat writer Jack Kerouac and the post-Beat photographer Annie Leibovitz (born in Waterbury in 1949) who shrewdly ("like a rolling stone"?) headed westward in 1970 to art school in San Francisco and her brilliant work with the rock magazine, *Rolling Stone,* as later with Susan Sontag.

54. The movie *Autofocus* tells the narrative of Bob Crane, also Waterbury-born, who falls from small-town grace and familial decency, becoming a charismatic television star on *Hogan's Heroes* and falling into sexual excess and pornography, ruining his life and finally being murdered by a satanic friend and rival in this Hollywood-as-Babylon setting.

55. Grant Wacker, *Heaven Below: Early Pentecostals and American Culture* (Cambridge, MA: Harvard University Press, 2001), 8–11.

56. Emerson's mandate to Young American to "hitch his wagon to a star" (which I first read in a Wilby High School anthology of American literature back in my senior year, where it stuck as life-mandate) is not a call to dreamy idealism or wagon-wheel pioneering but a call to link one's vocation to energies of historical and geographical becoming and to forces of Nature like wind, ocean, gravity, electricity, galvanism, and water-power. For a commentary on this power from Emerson's essay "Civilization" in *Society and Solitude,* see Barry Lopez, *Emerson and Power: Creative Antagonism in the Nineteenth Century* (Dekalb: Northern Illinois University Press, 1996), 102–103.

57. Letter of July 25, 1919, in Valerie Eliot, ed., *The Letters of T S. Eliot,* vol. 1, *1898–1922* (San Diego, CA: Harcourt Brace Jovanovich, 1988), 323

58. See Ralph Waldo Emerson, chapter 1 of "Nature" (1836), in *Essays and Poems,* 10.

59. See William Everson, *Birth of a Poet: The Santa Cruz Meditations,* ed. Lee Bartlett (Santa Barbara, CA: Black Sparrow Press, 1982), 18, and the chapter "Meditation Fourteen, "on the psycho-geographical dynamics of the west as region.

60. Gilles Deleuze, "Spinoza and Us," in *Spinoza: Practical Philosophy,* chapter 6. "Joyful passions" are active passions, affects that lead to expansive states of being (50–51)—for example, states of "blessedness" sought by Beats in off-center spaces and abodes.

61. Izaak Walton, *The Life of Mr. George Herbert* (Danbury, CT: Grolier Books, 1988), 414.

62. Gilles Deleuze, "Literature and Life," in *Essays Critical and Clinical,* trans. Daniel W. Smith and Michael A. Greco (Minneapolis: University of Minnesota Press, 1997), 4.

63. Susan Sontag, *The Volcano Lover* (New York: Farrar, Strauss, and Giroux, 1992), 150. See also Susan Sontag, *Reborn: Journals and Notebooks, 1947–1963,* ed. David Rieff (New York: Farrar, Straus and Giroux, 2008), which urges that Sontag's quest for art, love, and literature was animated by desires to become "reborn."

64. Ed Sanders, *1968: A History in Verse* (Santa Rosa, CA: Black Sparrow Press, 1997), 41.

65. Willis Barnstone and Marvin Meyer, eds., *The Gnostic Bible* (Boston: New Seeds, 2006), 54. Dylan's folk song "Man of Constant Sorrow" is a vernacular version of this messianic drifter, an early mask that took on deeper meanings in his life and poetic calling.

66. "Lord, I Just Can't Keep from Crying," by Blind Willie Johnson, recording of December 1928, Dallas, Texas, from *Complete Recordings of Blind Willie Johnson* (Columbia C2K-52835). "Well you gots to be converted to join this band," as he puts it in "I'm Gonna Run to the City of Refuge."

67. See Sara Schaefer Munoz, "When It Takes a Miracle to Sell Your House," *Wall Street Journal* accessed online, Oct. 30, 2007. Even nonbelievers do such acts, as if following Pascal's paradox that the practice believes for them and can at times create miraculous consequences.

68. Susan Schultz, review of Rob Wilson's *Reimagining the American Pacific,* in *Contemporary Pacific* 15 (2001): 219–221.

69. John Ashbery, *Other Traditions* (Cambridge, MA: Harvard University Press, 2000): "Or is there something inherently stimulating in the poetry called 'minor,' something it can do for us [would-be poets] when major poets can only wrings its hands?" For Ashbery, "minor voices" include John Clare, Thomas Lovell Beddoes, Raymond Roussel, John Wheelwright, Laura Riding, and David Schubert, who empower his meandering tactics of poesis (121–122).

70. *Minority* and *minor* may not be the same thing, for the minority is tied to its minor literature and need not see this as a failure but as a distinctive mode for a career: in this regard, as models of this localized integrity on edges of Empire, I would invoke the "local writer" careers of the pidgin-based novelists and poets from Hawai'i, Milton Murayama and Joseph Puna Balaz, who have new works forthcoming from the University of Hawai'i Press.

71. Jessica Hagedorn, "The Exile within/The Question of Identity," in *The State of Asian America: Activism and Resistance in the 1990s,* ed. Karin Aguilar-San Juan (Boston: South Point Press, 1994), 173–182.

72. See Fredric Jameson, "Culture and Finance Capital," in *The Cultural Turn: Selected Writings on the Postmodern, 1983–1998* (London: Verso, 1998), 152–154.

73. Ibid.

74. See Evelyn Nien-ming Chi'en, *Weird English* (Cambridge, MA: Harvard University Press, 2004), chapter 2, on forms of "Chinky Writing." See also Deleuze and Guattari, *Dialogues,* on "American English" deployed "in the service of minorities," Third World linkages, and counternational becoming (58).

75. Bob Dylan interviewed by Kurt Loder for *Rolling Stone* (June 21, 1984), in *Bob Dylan: The Essential Interviews,* ed. Jonathan Cott (New York: Wenner Books, 2006), 303.

76. F. Scott Fitzgerald, *The Crack-Up, with Other Uncollected Pieces, Note-Books and Uncollected Writings,* ed. Edmund Wilson (New York: New Directions, 1956), 71.

77. John Ashbery, "The Task," in *Selected Poems* (New York; Penguin, 1986), 83.

78. Fanny Howe, "Robeson Street," in *Selected Poems* (Berkeley: University of California Press, 2000), 45–46.

79. For "counter-worlding" configurations of Asia-Pacific, see the essays in Rob Wilson and Christopher Leigh Connery, eds., *The Worlding Project: Doing Cultural Studies in the Era of Globalization* (Santa Cruz, CA: New Pacific Press/North Atlantic Press, 2007).

80. "Airline to Heaven," by Woody Guthrie, as performed on the album *Mermaid Avenue,* volume 2. Wilco and Billy Bragg, debuted this song on April 27, 2000, at the Varsity Theatre, Baton Rouge, amen.

81. Geoffrey Himes, "Woody Guthrie's Music, Alive and Well," *International Herald Tribune,* Sept. 3, 2007, accessed online.

Acknowledgments

Was it Goethe who jested, with Dylanesque self-confidence in the originality of his writings and fieldwork in world literature, "We will burn that bridge when we come to it"? My own creativity and will to world poetics is more pious, indebted, and broken down; it drags along the tangle of obligations from Connecticut to Oceania to South Korea to Taiwan and back, and gladly so. Not so much abandoning every bridge, friend, mentor, or accomplice that might lead to self-empowerment and *poesis* but preserving them in the layering of who I am and what I can do. Here let me limn just a few of these forces of literary, ethical, and vocational mandates that got me to these concerns that there may be "no lasting knowledge without conversion."

From the multicultural streets of Waterbury, Connecticut, I thank the abiding input of Rocco Sileo, Ken Curzi, Judi Becker, Jeffrey Wilson, and our Watertown/ Waterbury families; in Berkeley, California, Masao Miyoshi has been there all along, across decades and contexts. Younger accomplices from Colleen Lye, Carlo Arreglo, and Christine Hong to the poets and students around the *Berkeley Poetry Review* have amplified this impact as has Vicky Nelson in her singular way. Arif Dirlik, in Oregon, Hong Kong, and North Carolina, opened up worlds and obligations of critical theory to me, as did the Pacific Workshop he formed in workaday summers on the West Coast. To Hawai'i, my list of obligations could go on for decades, but here let me thank Bruce Stillians, Bob Onopa, Paul Lyons, Gary Pak, Juliana Spahr, Laura Lyons, Theophil Reuney, John Rieder, Cristina Bacchilega, Craig Howes, Susan Schultz, Milton Murayama, the late Michael McPherson, Masako Ikeda, the Bamboo Ridge co-editors, the Muktananda Ashram, Tino Ramirez, Robin Stephens, the Roy Sakuma basketball team in the over-30 league in Pearl City, and the Hoashi family who are *always* there for me. In Korea, I owe abiding thanks for the inspiration and prodding of Kim U-chang, Kim Chi-gyu, Kim So-young, Peter Lee, John Eperjesi, Drayton Hamilton, Tim O'Grady, and Earl Jackson. In Taiwan, Pinghui Liao created my first linkages and kept these trans-Pacific exchanges going across years and contexts; Steve Bradbury, Amie Perry, Neifi Ding, and Andy Wang kept me honest there. To the journal *Inter-Asia Cultural Studies*, I thank many across this region for making me part of it, but above all Kuan-Hsing Chen and Meaghan Morris for their international-localist visions and pedagogies showing how it all can be done. To the *boundary 2* collective, I owe much of my reformation as a globalizing scholar trying to survive the Reagan and Bush eras: Paul Bovè, Donald Pease, Bruce Robbins, Jonathan Arac et al. figured the metamorphosis of a post-Emersonian "American Scholar" into something more demanding as transnational and counterimperial fieldwork. To the University of California at Santa Cruz where I moved in early 2001, I owe abiding thanks and care for "worlding" prodding to Chris Connery, Karen Tei Yamashita, James Clifford, Susan Gillman, Kirsten Gruesz, Carla Freccero, Donna Haraway, Sharon Kinoshita, Jin Jirn, Pam Kido, David Watson, and the World Literature and Cultural Studies configuration and New Pacific Press. I would also here acknowledge funding support and fellowships from the Humanities Research Institute and the Committee on Research at the University of California at Santa Cruz that allowed me to visit research sites, scholars, and libraries in New England and Hawai'i and helped to secure permissions (see below) from the Cornwall Library to Special Rider Music. Leonard Peters, at the outset, *believed* in me more than most.

On Tuesday, October 3, 2006, in the middle of work on this book, Lindsay Waters emailed one of his caring missives:

> I am getting the hang of your MS. I saw at once that your focus on conversion could give others a much more valuable idea and practice for understanding the world than something like hybridity or border crossing, not that it trashes those ideas. It's just that it is bigger and encompasses them. Then I was reading and thinking a lot about Greil Marcus's *SHAPE [of Things to Come]* and the imperative announced by Melville and focused on by Greil that we must each make ourselves. We cannot shy away from that task. In *American Pastoral*, the "Swede" as Greil analyzes Roth's novel, will not rise to the essential American task of making himself (making myself) despite and even through all my self-doubts despite the impossibility of being certain ever; your first two chapters and I think the whole book are congruent with these ideas; and they are ideas that are not current in American literary academy, so I'm beginning to see your light. (Email used with permission.)

For if we are not *born again,* as Norman O. Brown once prodded in quest of those liberationist energies and metamorphoses from the 1960s, *we are not born at all.* All along the line, Lindsay Waters has cared for, provoked in the strong Emersonian sense, and exemplified this quest to reframe beatitude in more self-relying ways than I can name. Phoebe Kosman has also nurtured and helped with her caring and insightful comments at Harvard University Press as did Meredith Phillips at Westchester Book Services. Paul Giles, amid the learned post-Catholic pastures of Oxford University, gave an earlier draft of this book a keen reading that prodded me to situate the project more broadly in the field imaginary of American poetics and the refigured energies of the American sublime. All these and others unnamed have nurtured and provoked insights all along the Asia/Pacific Americas line of making and remaking this "conversion book" over these past five years. The three anonymous readers for Harvard University Press helped immensely to shape and scale this project: *Pax vobiscum* in all your works and days.

For Mari Therese Hoashi Wilson, she abides tenderly at the core of every sentence I write and every prayer or good gesture I can make. George Herbert once said of his own still-unpublished poetry manuscript, *The Temple* (as he was writing this farewell note on his deathbed and had been long and—shall we say— *deeply converted* from a post-Cambridge career in courtly service into a becoming a poet-priest serving as pastor in a small Layton parish of the high Anglican Church), "For I and it are less than the least of God's mercies"; furthermore, "They be good works [that I do in my church work and poems], if they be sprinkled with the blood of Christ, and not otherwise."

Trailing in the wake of what had come to be called and advocated across the 1960s as *Beat beatitude*, Don McClean crooned at the end of his one mish-mash pop lyric hit, "American Pie," that "the three men I admire most, the father, son and holy ghost/ They caught the last train for the coast." But these forces of beaten-down beatitude, spiritual becoming, and American poetic renewal have not disappeared into coffee houses and bars of North Beach, nor have they gone to the West-Coast beaches of Malibu and Venice; they have kept on rolling and moiling across oceans and ecumenes, raising Cain and troping Henry, making these works and days new. Richard Dawkins admitted that *The God Delusion's* stated aim was to "convert" readers to modes of atheism, but he acknowledges as well that as a proselytizing tool, in public domains of England and the United States, it has largely failed to shake what William James called *the will to believe*. My own set of will-to-believe assumptions remain closer to the humble, scaled back, and broken beatitude-quest of post-Beat Bob Dylan, as he limns it in the recently released "Red River Shore" from *Time Out of Mind*, embodying a kind of Madonna worship and beat Jesus from the North Country enduring like poetic innocence through it all:

> Now, I've heard of a guy who lived a long time ago
> A man full of sorrow and strife
> Whenever someone around him died and was dead
> He knew how to bring 'em on back to life
> Well, I don't know what kind of language he used
> Or if they do that kind of thing anymore
> Sometimes I think nobody ever saw me here at all
>   'Cept the girl from the Red River shore

I also want to thank the following for permission to use their copyrighted materials:

The Collection of the Cornwall Historical Society, Cornwall, Connecticut, for the digitalized reproduction of Henry Obookiah engraved by Asher Durand et al. from the first edition of *The Memoirs of Henry Obookiah*. It is used here as frontispiece to this book.

The University of Hawai'i Press for the poem used here in the front matter by Rob Wilson, "Henry, Torn From the Stomach," from *Automat: Unsettling Anglo-Global American Poetics Along Asia/Pacific Lines of Flight* (forthcoming); and the epigraph for chapter one from Martha Beckwith, *Hawaiian Mythology* (Honolulu: University of Hawai'i Press, 1976).

Penguin Group of New Zealand for permission to use as an epigraph to Chapter 4 a poem by John Pule from his work, *The Shark That Ate the Sun*.

Woody Guthrie Publications Incorporated for permission to cite the words to "This Morning I Am Born Again" (Copyright, 2001) and "Airline to Heaven" (Copyright, 2000). These are recently discovered songs published after Guthrie's death with music by Slaid Cleaves in the case of "This Morning I Am Born Again," and with music by Jay Bennet/Jeff Tweedy in the case of "Airline to Heaven" (as on the album *Mermaid Avenue*, Vol. II by Billy Bragg & Wilco which was used on the soundtrack for the movie, *Jesus' Son*, where I first encountered its "born again" missive).

I also thank John Yau and David R. Godine Publishers for giving me permission to use, as an epigraph to the Epilogue, a poetry passage from his collection, *Radiant Silhouette: New and Selected Works, 1974–1988)* (Santa Barbara, CA: Black Sparrow Press, 1989).

In addition to thanking Bob Dylan for writing an array of life-changing poems and songs over all these years and contexts and his manager Jeff Rosen for caring for him and these works in all ways, I want to acknowledge as well the conscientious care of Callie Gladman in helping me to secure permissions from the Bob Dylan Music Company & Special Rider Music to cite and interpret the following materials from an array of albums and works, listed chronologically as follows:

Bob Dylan (1962):

The Times They Are A-Changin' (1964):

Another Side of Bob Dylan (1964):

Bringing It All Back Home (1965):

Oh Mercy (1989):

"SERIES OF DREAMS"
Copyright ©1991 Special Rider Music

Under the Red Sky (1990):

"BORN IN TIME"
Copyright ©1990 Special Rider Music

Bootleg Series, 1–3 (1991):

"ANGELINA"
Copyright ©1981 Special Rider Music

Time Out of Mind (1997):

"NOT DARK YET"
Copyright ©1997 Special Rider Music

"HIGHLANDS"
Copyright ©1997 Special Rider Music

"THINGS HAVE CHANGED"
Copyright ©1997 Special Rider Music

"Love and Theft" (2001):

"MISSISSIPPI"
Copyright ©1997 Special Rider Music

"BYE AND BYE"
Copyright ©1997 Special Rider Music

Modern Times (2006):

Tell Tale Signs (2008):

Pax vobiscum to you, Bob Dylan, composing poetry on all those roads leading to beat beatitude you are on as comrade, muse, and friend speaking "the Christ who lives in me."

Index

Adams, Henry, 144
Ahlquist, Dale, 116
Ai (Florence Anthony Ogawa), 3, 9, 21, 103, 145–165, 193, 235n22; Catholicism in, 161–162, 280n40; *Cruelty,* 147, 148, 150, 158; "Cuba, 1962," 154–155; *Dread,* 147, 155; *Greed,* 155; *Killing Floor,* 146, 154–155, 156–157, 158, 160, 163; "Nothing but Color," 156–157; *Sin,* 148, 158–159; *Vice,* 149, 150, 158, 163, 164, 278n11
Akana, Kalani, 77–78
Alcoholics Anonymous (AA), 100–101, 262n53
Alcott, Bronson, 6, 234n16
Ali, Muhammad, 10, 237n36
Allah, 23, 89
America: as "invisible republic," 13, 19; as land of sublimity, 5; religion in, 1–2, 5, 8–10, 18–19, 21, 42, 97, 143–145, 234n11, 236n34, 239n53, 283n23, 295n20, 299n67. *See also* American sublime; Bloom, Harold; Dylan, Bob; Emerson, Ralph Waldo; Empire; Frontier history; Great Awakenings; James, William; Marcus, Greil; New England; Postcoloniality; Puritanism; Subject-formation; United States
American Board for the Commission of Foreign Ministers (ABCFM), 30, 37, 39, 43, 45, 48, 51–52, 54–55, 62, 73,

250n81. *See also* Foreign Mission School
American sublime, 153, 157, 161, 235n19, 279n33. *See also* America
America Tract Society, 53
Amherst, Massachusetts, 47, 54
Andover Theological Institute, 40
Angelica, Mother, 116
Apocalypse Now Redux (movie), 219
Apostle, The (film), 77, 81
Aristotle, 100
Ashbery, John, 103, 173, 227, 299n69; "The Task," 229; *Three Poems,* 159
Asia-Pacific, 124–125, 135, 137–139, 212, 217–218, 224, 226, 250n81, 256n69, 274n45. *See also* Oceania; Pacific Rim; Western Asia
Asia Pacific Economic Cooperation (APEC), 139
Auntie Mame (movie), 221
Australia, 32, 66, 74, 121, 130
Avis, Meijert, 174, 286n43
Azusa Street, 14, 126, 70

Bacharach, Burt, 194
Badiou, Alain, 12, 39, 90; *Saint Paul,* 12, 64, 91–92, 125, 238n44, 252n16
Baez, Joan, 171, 283n28
Bakhtin, Mikhail, 87, 134, 274n47
Balaz, Joseph Puna, 32, 219, 228, 299n70
Baldwin, James, 167–168
Balibar, Etienne, 52